EGR 100

Introduction to Engineering Design

Timothy Hinds - Lead Instructor

Michigan State University

A Pearson Custom Publication

Pearson Prentice Hall
Vice President and Editorial Director, ECS: *Marcia J. Horton*
Executive Editor: *Eric Svendsen*
Associate Editor: *Dee Bernhard*
Vice President and Director of Production and Manufacturing, ESM: *David W. Riccardi*
Executive Managing Editor: *Vince O'Brien*
Managing Editor: *David A. George*
Production Editor: *Barbara A. Till*
Director of Creative Services: *Paul Belfanti*
Creative Director: *Carole Anson*
Art Director: *Jayne Conte*
Art Editor: *Greg Dulles*
Manufacturing Manager: *Trudy Pisciotti*
Manufacturing Buyer: *Lisa McDowell*
Marketing Manager: *Holly Stark*

Pearson Custom Publishing
Director of Database Publishing: *Michael Payne*
Executive Marketing Manager: *Nathan L. Wilbur*
Operations Manager: *Eric M. Kenney*
Editorial Assistant: *Victoria L. Ravin*
Development Editor: *Amy Galvin*
Project Specialist: *Zach LaRosa*
Cover Designer: *Renee Sartell*

PEARSON CUSTOM PUBLISHING
501 Boylston Street, Suite 900
Boston, MA 02116

ISBN-13: 9780536109217
ISBN-10: 0536109214

Package ISBN-13: N/A
Package ISBN-10: N/A

Excerpts taken from:
Design Concepts for Engineers, 2/e by Mark N. Horenstein
0-13-093430-5 © 2002 by Prentice-Hall, Inc., a Pearson Education Company

Engineering Design and Problem Solving, 2/e by Steven K. Howell
0-13-093399-6 © 2002 by Prentice-Hall, Inc., a Pearson Education Company

Engineering Ethics by Charles B. Fleddermann
0-13-784224-4 © 1999 by Prentice-Hall, Inc., a Pearson Education Company

Engineering with Excel by Ronald W. Larsen
0-13-017696-6 © 2002 by Prentice-Hall, Inc., a Pearson Education Company

Engineering Success, 2/e by Peter Schiavone
0-13-041827-7 © 2002 by Prentice-Hall, Inc., a Pearson Education Company

Exploring Engineering, 2/e by Joe King
0-13-093442-9 © 2002 by Prentice-Hall, Inc., a Pearson Education Company

Graphics Concepts by Richard M. Lueptow
0-13-030687-8 © 2000 by Prentice-Hall, Inc., a Pearson Education Company

Introduction to AutoCAD® 2000 by Mark Dix and Paul Riley
0-13-016732-0 © 2000 by Prentice-Hall, Inc., a Pearson Education Company

Introduction to Engineering Analysis by Kirk D. Hagen
0-13-016733-9 © 2000 by Prentice-Hall, Inc., a Pearson Education Company

Introduction to Excel 2002 by David C. Kuncicky
0-13-008175-2 © 2003 by Pearson Education, Inc.

Introduction to MathCad® 2000 by Ronald W. Larsen
0-13-020007-7 © 2001 by Prentice-Hall, Inc., a Pearson Education Company

Introduction to MatLab® 6 by Delores M. Etter and David C. Kuncicky with Doug Hull
0-13-032845-6 © 2002 by Prentice-Hall, Inc., a Pearson Education Company

Introduction to PowerPoint 2002 by Jack Leifer
0-13-008179-5 © 2003 by Pearson Education, Inc.

Introduction to Unix® by David I. Schwartz
0-13-095135-8 © 1999 by Prentice-Hall, Inc., a Pearson Education Company

Introduction to Word 2002 by David C. Kuncicky
0-13-008170-1 © 2003 by Pearson Education, Inc.

Power Programming with VBA/Excel by Steven C. Chapra
0-13-047377-4 © 2003 by Pearson Education, Inc.

About ESource

ESource—The Prentice Hall Engineering Source— www.prenhall.com/esource

ESource—The Prentice Hall Engineering Source gives professors the power to harness the full potential of their text and their first-year engineering course. More than just a collection of books, ESource is a unique publishing system revolving around the ESource website—www.prenhall.com/esource. ESource enables you to put your stamp on your book just as you do your course. It lets you:

Control You choose exactly what chapters are in your book and in what order they appear. Of course, you can choose the entire book if you'd like and stay with the authors' original order.

Optimize Get the most from your book and your course. ESource lets you produce the optimal text for your students needs.

Customize You can add your own material anywhere in your text's presentation, and your final product will arrive at your bookstore as a professionally formatted text. Of course, all titles in this series are available as stand-alone texts, or as bundles of two or more books sold at a discount. Contact your PH sales rep for discount information.

ESource ACCESS

Professors who choose to bundle two or more texts from the ESource series for their class, or use an ESource custom book will be providing their students with an on-line library of intro engineering content—ESource Access. We've designed ESource ACCESS to provide students a flexible, searchable, on-line resource. Free access codes come in bundles and custom books are valid for one year after initial log-on. Contact your PH sales rep for more information.

ESource Content

All the content in ESource was written by educators specifically for freshman/first-year students. Authors tried to strike a balanced level of presentation, an approach that was neither formulaic nor trivial, and one that did not focus too heavily on advanced topics that most introductory students do not encounter until later classes. Because many professors do not have extensive time to cover these topics in the classroom, authors prepared each text with the idea that many students would use it for self-instruction and independent study. Students should be able to use this content to learn the software tool or subject on their own.

While authors had the freedom to write texts in a style appropriate to their particular subject, all followed certain guidelines created to promote a consistency that makes students comfortable. Namely, every chapter opens with a clear set of **Objectives**, includes **Practice Boxes** throughout the chapter, and ends with a number of **Problems**, and a list of **Key Terms**. **Applications Boxes** are spread throughout the book with the intent of giving students a real-world perspective of engineering. **Success Boxes** provide the student with advice about college study skills, and help students avoid the common pitfalls of first-year students. In addition, this series contains an entire book titled *Engineering Success* by Peter Schiavone of the University of Alberta intended to expose students quickly to what it takes to be an engineering student.

Creating Your Book

Using ESource is simple. You preview the content either on-line or through examination copies of the books you can request on-line, from your PH sales rep, or by calling 1-800-526-0485. Create an on-line outline of the content you want, in the order you want, using ESource's simple interface. Insert your own material into the text flow. If you are not ready to order, ESource will save your work. You can come back at any time and change, re-arrange, or add more material to your creation. Once you're finished you'll automatically receive an ISBN. Give it to your bookstore and your book will arrive on their shelves four to six weeks after they order. Your custom desk copies with their instructor supplements will arrive at your address at the same time.

To learn more about this new system for creating the perfect textbook, go to www.prenhall.com/esource. You can either go through the on-line walkthrough of how to create a book, or experiment yourself.

Supplements

Adopters of ESource receive an instructor's CD that contains professor and student code from the books in the series, as well as other instruction aides provided by authors. The website also holds approximately **350 PowerPoint transparencies** created by Jack Leifer of University of Kentucky–Paducah. Professors can either follow these transparencies as pre-prepared lectures or use them as the basis for their own custom presentations.

Titles in the ESource Series

About the Authors

No project could ever come to pass without a group of authors who have the vision and the courage to turn a stack of blank paper into a book. The authors in this series, who worked diligently to produce their books, provide the building blocks of the series.

Martin D. Bradshaw was born in Pittsburg, KS in 1936, grew up in Kansas and the surrounding states of Arkansas and Missouri, graduating from Newton High School, Newton, KS in 1954. He received the B.S.E.E. and M.S.E.E. degrees from the University of Wichita in 1958 and 1961, respectively. A Ford Foundation fellowship at Carnegie Institute of Technology followed from 1961 to 1963 and he received the Ph.D. degree in electrical engineering in 1964. He spent his entire academic career with the Department of Electrical and Computer Engineering at the University of New Mexico (1961-1963 and 1991-1996). He served as the Assistant Dean for Special Programs with the UNM College of Engineering from 1974 to 1976 and as the Associate Chairman for the EECE Department from 1993 to 1996. During the period 1987-1991 he was a consultant with his own company, EE Problem Solvers. During 1978 he spent a sabbatical year with the State Electricity Commission of Victoria, Melbourne, Australia. From 1979 to 1981 he served an IPA assignment as a Project Officer at the U.S. Air Force Weapons Laboratory, Kirkland AFB, Albuquerque, NM. He has won numerous local, regional, and national teaching awards, including the George Westinghouse Award from the ASEE in 1973. He was awarded the IEEE Centennial Medal in 2000.

Acknowledgments: Dr. Bradshaw would like to acknowledge his late mother, who gave him a great love of reading and learning, and his father, who taught him to persist until the job is finished. The encouragement of his wife, Jo, and his six children is a never-ending inspiration.

Stephen J. Chapman received a B.S. degree in Electrical Engineering from Louisiana State University (1975), the M.S.E. degree in Electrical Engineering from the University of Central Florida (1979), and pursued further graduate studies at Rice University.

Mr. Chapman is currently Manager of Technical Systems for British Aerospace Australia, in Melbourne, Australia. In this position, he provides technical direction and design authority for the work of younger engineers within the company. He also continues to teach at local universities on a part-time basis.

Mr. Chapman is a Senior Member of the Institute of Electrical and Electronics Engineers (and several of its component societies). He is also a member of the Association for Computing Machinery and the Institution of Engineers (Australia).

Steven C. Chapra presently holds the Louis Berger Chair for Computing and Engineering in the Civil and Environmental Engineering Department at Tufts University. Dr. Chapra received engineering degrees from Manhattan College and the University of Michigan. Before joining the faculty at Tufts, he taught at Texas A&M University, the University of Colorado, and Imperial College, London. His research interests focus on surface water-quality modeling and advanced computer applications in environmental engineering. He has published over 50 refereed journal articles, 20 software packages and 6 books. He has received a number of awards including the 1987 ASEE Merriam/Wiley Distinguished Author Award, the 1993 Rudolph Hering Medal, and teaching awards from Texas A&M, the University of Colorado, and the Association of Environmental Engineering and Science Professors.

Acknowledgments: To the Berger Family for their many contributions to engineering education. I would also like to thank David Clough for his friendship and insights, John Walkenbach for his wonderful books, and my colleague Lee Minardi and my students Kenny William, Robert Viesca and Jennifer Edelmann for their suggestions.

Mark Dix began working with AutoCAD in 1985 as a programmer for CAD Support Associates, Inc. He helped design a system for creating estimates and bills of material directly from AutoCAD drawing databases for use in the automated conveyor industry. This system became the basis for systems still widely in use today. In 1986 he began collaborating with Paul Riley to create AutoCAD training materials, combining Riley's background in industrial design and training with Dix's background in writing, curriculum development, and programming. Mr. Dix received the M.S. degree in education from the University of Massachusetts. He is currently the Director of Dearborn Academy High School in Arlington, Massachusetts.

Delores M. Etter is a Professor of Electrical and Computer Engineering at the University of Colorado. Dr. Etter was a faculty member at the University of New Mexico and also a Visiting Professor at Stanford University. Dr. Etter was responsible for the Freshman Engineering Program at the University of New Mexico and is active in the Integrated Teaching Laboratory at the University of Colorado. She was elected a Fellow of the Institute of Electrical and Electronics Engineers for her contributions to education and for her technical leadership in digital signal processing.

Charles B. Fleddermann is a professor in the Department of Electrical and Computer Engineering at the University of New Mexico in Albuquerque, New Mexico. All of his degrees are in electrical engineering: his Bachelor's degree from the University of Notre Dame, and the Master's and Ph.D. from the University of Illinois at Urbana-Champaign. Prof. Fleddermann developed an engineering ethics course for his department in response to the ABET requirement to incorporate ethics topics into the undergraduate engineering curriculum. *Engineering Ethics* was written as a vehicle for presenting ethical

theory, analysis, and problem solving to engineering undergraduates in a concise and readily accessible way.

Acknowledgments: I would like to thank Profs. Charles Harris and Michael Rabins of Texas A & M University whose NSF sponsored workshops on engineering ethics got me started thinking in this field. Special thanks to my wife Liz, who proofread the manuscript for this book, provided many useful suggestions, and who helped me learn how to teach "soft" topics to engineers.

Kirk D. Hagen is a professor at Weber State University in Ogden, Utah. He has taught introductory-level engineering courses and upper-division thermal science courses at WSU since 1993. He received his B.S. degree in physics from Weber State College and his M.S. degree in mechanical engineering from Utah State University, after which he worked as a thermal designer/analyst in the aerospace and electronics industries. After several years of engineering practice, he resumed his formal education, earning his Ph.D. in mechanical engineering at the University of Utah. Hagen is the author of an undergraduate heat transfer text.

Mark N. Horenstein is a Professor in the Department of Electrical and Computer Engineering at Boston University. He has degrees in Electrical Engineering from M.I.T. and U.C. Berkeley and has been involved in teaching engineering design for the greater part of his academic career. He devised and developed the senior design project class taken by all electrical and computer engineering students at Boston University. In this class, the students work for a virtual engineering company developing products and systems for real-world engineering and social-service clients.

Acknowledgments: I would like to thank Prof. James Bethune, the architect of the Peak Performance event at Boston University, for his permission to highlight the competition in my text. Several of the ideas relating to brainstorming and teamwork were derived from a workshop on engineering design offered by Prof. Charles Lovas of Southern Methodist University. The principles of estimation were derived in part from a freshman engineering problem posed by Prof. Thomas Kincaid of Boston University.

Steven Howell is the Chairman and a Professor of Mechanical Engineering at Lawrence Technological University.  Prior to joining LTU in 2001, Dr. Howell led a knowledge-based engineering project for Visteon Automotive Systems and taught computer-aided design classes for Ford Motor Company engineers. Dr. Howell also has a total of 15 years experience as an engineering faculty member at Northern Arizona University, the University of the Pacific, and the University of Zimbabwe. While at Northern Arizona University, he helped develop and implement an award-winning interdisciplinary series of design courses simulating a corporate engineering-design environment.

Douglas W. Hull is a graduate student in the Department of Mechanical Engineering at Carnegie Mellon University in Pittsburgh, Pennsylvania. He is the  author of *Mastering Mechanics I Using Matlab 5*, and contributed to *Mechanics of Materials* by Bedford and Liechti. His research in the Sensor Based Planning lab involves motion planning for hyper-redundant manipulators, also known as serpentine robots.

Scott D. James is a staff lecturer at Kettering University (formerly GMI Engineering & Management Institute) in Flint, Michigan. He is currently pursuing a Ph.D. in Systems Engineering  with an emphasis on software engineering and computer-integrated manufacturing. He chose teaching as a profession after several years in the computer industry. "I thought that it was really important to know what it was like outside of academia. I wanted to provide students with classes that were up to date and provide the information that is really used and needed."

Acknowledgments: Scott would like to acknowledge his family for the time to work on the text and his students and peers at Kettering who offered helpful critiques of the materials that eventually became the book.

Joe King received the B.S. and M.S. degrees from the University of California at Davis. He is a Professor of Computer Engineering at the University of the  Pacific, Stockton, CA, where he teaches courses in digital design, computer design, artificial intelligence, and computer networking. Since joining the UOP faculty, Professor King has spent yearlong sabbaticals teaching in Zimbabwe, Singapore, and Finland. A licensed engineer in the state of California, King's industrial experience includes major design projects with Lawrence Livermore National Laboratory, as well as independent consulting projects. Prof. King has had a number of books published with titles including MATLAB, MathCAD, Exploring Engineering, and Engineering and Society.

David C. Kuncicky is a native Floridian. He earned his Baccalaureate in psychology, Master's in computer science, and Ph.D. in computer science from Florida State University. He has served as a faculty member in the Department of Electrical Engineering at the FAMU–FSU College of Engineering and the Department of Computer Science at Florida State University. He has taught computer science and computer engineering courses for over 15 years. He has published research in the areas of intelligent hybrid systems and neural networks. He is currently the Director of Engineering at Bioreason, Inc. in Sante Fe, New Mexico.

Acknowledgments: Thanks to Steffie and Helen for putting up with my late nights and long weekends at the computer. Finally, thanks to Susan Bassett for having faith in my abilities, and for providing continued tutelage and support.

Ron Larsen is a Professor of Chemical Engineering at Montana State University, and received his Ph.D. from the Pennsylvania State University. He was initially attracted to engineering by the challenges the profession offers, but also appreciates that engineering is a serving profession. Some of the greatest challenges he has faced while teaching have involved non-traditional teaching methods, including evening courses for practicing engineers and teaching through an interpreter at the Mongolian National University. These experiences have provided tremendous opportunities to learn new ways to communicate technical material. Dr. Larsen views modern software as one of the new tools that will radically alter the way engineers work, and his book *Introduction to Math-CAD* was written to help young engineers prepare to meet the challenges of an ever-changing workplace.

Acknowledgments: To my students at Montana State University who have endured the rough drafts and typos, and who still allow me to experiment with their classes—my sincere thanks.

Sanford Leestma is a Professor of Mathematics and Computer Science at Calvin College, and received his Ph.D. from New Mexico State University. He has been the long-time co-author of successful textbooks on Fortran, Pascal, and data structures in Pascal. His current research interest are in the areas of algorithms and numerical computation.

Jack Leifer is an Assistant Professor in the Department of Mechanical Engineering at the University of Kentucky Extended Campus Program in Paducah, and was previously with the Department of Mathematical Sciences and Engineering at the University of South Carolina–Aiken. He received his Ph.D. in Mechanical Engineering from the University of Texas at Austin in December 1995. His current research interests include the analysis of ultra-light and inflatable (Gossamer) space structures.

Acknowledgments: I'd like to thank my colleagues at USC–Aiken, especially Professors Mike May and Laurene Fausett, for their encouragement and feedback; and my parents, Felice and Morton Leifer, for being there and providing support (as always) as I completed this book.

Richard M. Lueptow is the Charles Deering McCormick Professor of Teaching Excellence and Associate Professor of Mechanical Engineering at Northwestern University. He is a native of Wisconsin and received his doctorate from the Massachusetts Institute of Technology in 1986. He teaches design, fluid mechanics, an spectral analysis techniques. Rich has an active research program on rotating filtration, Taylor Couette flow, granular flow, fire suppression, and acoustics. He has five patents and over 40 refereed journal and proceedings papers along with many other articles, abstracts, and presentations.

Acknowledgments: Thanks to my talented and hardworking co-authors as well as the many colleagues and students who took the tutorial for a "test drive." Special thanks to Mike Minbiole for his major contributions to Graphics Concepts with SolidWorks. Thanks also to Northwestern University for the time to work on a book. Most of all, thanks to my loving wife, Maiya, and my children, Hannah and Kyle, for supporting me in this endeavor. (Photo courtesy of Evanston Photographic Studios, Inc.)

Larry Nyhoff is a Professor of Mathematics and Computer Science at Calvin College. After doing bachelor's work at Calvin, and Master's work at Michigan, he received a Ph.D. from Michigan State and also did graduate work in computer science at Western Michigan. Dr. Nyhoff has taught at Calvin for the past 34 years—mathematics at first and computer science for the past several years.

Acknowledgments: We thank our families—Shar, Jeff, Dawn, Rebecca, Megan, Sara, Greg, Julie, Joshua, Derek, Tom, Joan; Marge, Michelle, Sandy, Lory, Michael—for being patient and understanding. We thank God for allowing us to write this text.

Paul Riley is an author, instructor, and designer specializing in graphics and design for multimedia. He is a founding partner of CAD Support Associates, a contract service and professional training organization for computer-aided design. His 15 years of business experience and 20 years of teaching experience are supported by degrees in education and computer science. Paul has taught AutoCAD at the University of Massachusetts at Lowell and is presently teaching AutoCAD at Mt. Ida College in Newton, Massachusetts. He has developed a program, Computer-aided Design for Professionals that is highly regarded by corporate clients and has been an ongoing success since 1982.

Robert Rizza is an Assistant Professor of Mechanical Engineering at North Dakota State University, where he teaches courses in mechanics and computer-aided design. A native of Chicago, he received the Ph.D. degree from the Illinois Institute of Techno-  logy. He is also the author of *Getting Started with Pro/ ENGINEER*. Dr. Rizza has worked on a diverse range of engineering projects including projects from the railroad, bioengineering, and aerospace industries. His current research interests include the fracture of composite materials, repair of cracked aircraft components, and loosening of prostheses.

Peter Schiavone is a professor and student advisor in the Department of Mechanical Engineering at the University of Alberta, Canada. He received his Ph.D. from the University of Strathclyde, U.K. in 1988. He has authored several books in the area of student aca-  demic success as well as numerous papers in international scientific research journals. Dr. Schiavone has worked in private industry in several different areas of engineering including aerospace and systems engineering. He founded the first Mathematics Resource Center at the University of Alberta, a unit designed specifically to teach new students the necessary survival skills in mathematics and the physical sciences required for success in first-year engineering. This led to the Students' Union Gold Key Award for outstanding contributions to the university. Dr. Schiavone lectures regularly to freshman engineering students and to new engineering professors on engineering success, in particular about maximizing students' academic performance.

Acknowledgements: Thanks to Richard Felder for being such an inspiration; to my wife Linda for sharing my dreams and believing in me; and to Francesca and Antonio for putting up with Dad when working on the text.

David I. Schneider holds an A.B. degree from Oberlin College and a Ph.D. degree in Mathematics from MIT. He has taught for 34 years, primarily at the University of Maryland. Dr. Schneider has authored 28 books, with one-half of them computer programming books. He has developed three customized software packages that are supplied as supplements to over 55 mathematics textbooks. His involvement with computers dates back to 1962, when he programmed a special purpose computer at MIT's Lincoln Laboratory to correct errors in a communications system.

David I. Schwartz is an Assistant Professor in the Computer Science Department at Cornell University and earned his B.S., M.S., and Ph.D. degrees in Civil Engineering from State University of New York at Buffalo. Throughout his  graduate studies, Schwartz combined principles of computer science to applications of civil engineering. He became interested in helping students learn how to apply software tools for solving a variety of engineering problems. He teaches his students to learn incrementally and practice frequently to gain the maturity to tackle other subjects. In his spare time, Schwartz plays drums in a variety of bands.

Acknowledgments: I dedicate my books to my family, friends, and students who all helped in so many ways.

Many thanks go to the schools of Civil Engineering and Engineering & Applied Science at State University of New York at Buffalo where I originally developed and tested my UNIX and Maple books. I greatly appreciate the opportunity to explore my goals and all the help from everyone at the Computer Science Department at Cornell.

John T. Sears received the Ph.D. degree from Princeton University. Currently, he is a Professor and the head of the Department of Chemical Engineering at Montana State University. After leaving Princeton he worked in research at Brookhaven National Laboratory and Esso Research and Engineering, until he took a position at West Virginia University. He came to MSU in 1982, where he has served as the Director of the College of Engineering Minority Program and Interim Director for BioFilm Engineering. Prof. Sears has written a book on air pollution and economic development, and over 45 articles in engineering and engineering education.

Michael T. Snyder is President of Internet startup Appointments123.com. He is a native of Chicago, and he received his Bachelor of Science degree in Mechanical Engineering from the University of Notre Dame. Mike also graduated with honors from Northwestern University's Kellogg Graduate School of Management in 1999 with his Masters of Management degree. Before Appointments123.com, Mike was a mechanical engineer in new product development for Motorola Cellular and Acco Office Products. He has received four patents for his mechanical design work. "Pro/ENGINEER was an invaluable design tool for me,

and I am glad to help students learn the basics of Pro/ENGINEER."

Acknowledgments: Thanks to Rich Lueptow and Jim Steger for inviting me to be a part of this great project. Of course, thanks to my wife Gretchen for her support in my various projects.

Jim Steger is currently Chief Technical Officer and cofounder of an Internet applications company. He graduated with a Bachelor of Science degree in Mechanical Engineering from Northwestern University. His prior work included mechanical engineering assignments at Motorola and Acco Brands. At Motorola, Jim worked on part design for two-way radios and was one of the lead mechanical engineers on a cellular phone product line. At Acco Brands, Jim was the sole engineer on numerous office product designs. His Worx stapler has won design awards in the United States and in Europe. Jim has been a Pro/ENGINEER user for over six years.

Acknowledgments: Many thanks to my co-authors, especially Rich Lueptow for his leadership on this project. I would also like to thank my family for their continuous support.

Royce Wilkinson received his undergraduate degree in chemistry from Rose-Hulman Institute of Technology in 1991 and the Ph.D. degree in chemistry from Montana State University in 1998 with research in natural product isolation from fungi. He currently resides in Bozeman, MT and is involved in HIV drug research. His research interests center on biological molecules and their interactions in the search for pharmaceutical advances.

http://www.prenhall.com/esource

Reviewers

We would like to thank everyone who has reviewed texts in this series.

ESource Reviewers

Christopher Rowe, *Vanderbilt University*
Steve Yurgartis, *Clarkson University*
Heidi A. Diefes-Dux, *Purdue University*
Howard Silver, *Fairleigh Dickenson University*
Jean C. Malzahn Kampe, *Virginia Polytechnic Institute and State University*
Malcolm Heimer, *Florida International University*
Stanley Reeves, *Auburn University*
John Demel, *Ohio State University*
Shahnam Navee, *Georgia Southern University*
Heshem Shaalem, *Georgia Southern University*
Terry L. Kohutek, *Texas A & M University*
Liz Rozell, *Bakersfield College*
Mary C. Lynch, *University of Florida*
Ted Pawlicki, *University of Rochester*
James N. Jensen, *SUNY at Buffalo*
Tom Horton, *University of Virginia*
Eileen Young, *Bristol Community College*
James D. Nelson, *Louisiana Tech University*
Jerry Dunn, *Texas Tech University*
Howard M. Fulmer, *Villanova UniversityBerkeley*
Naeem Abdurrahman *University of Texas, Austin*
Stephen Allan *Utah State University*
Anil Bajaj *Purdue University*
Grant Baker *University of Alaska–Anchorage*
William Beckwith *Clemson University*
Haym Benaroya *Rutgers University*
John Biddle *California State Polytechnic University*
Tom Bledsaw *ITT Technical Institute*
Fred Boadu *Duke University*
Tom Bryson *University of Missouri, Rolla*
Ramzi Bualuan *University of Notre Dame*
Dan Budny *Purdue University*
Betty Burr *University of Houston*
Dale Calkins *University of Washington*
Harish Cherukuri *University of North Carolina –Charlotte*
Arthur Clausing *University of Illinois*

Barry Crittendon *Virginia Polytechnic and State University*
James Devine *University of South Florida*
Ron Eaglin *University of Central Florida*
Dale Elifrits *University of Missouri, Rolla*
Patrick Fitzhorn *Colorado State University*
Susan Freeman *Northeastern University*
Frank Gerlitz *Washtenaw College*
Frank Gerlitz *Washtenaw Community College*
John Glover *University of Houston*
John Graham *University of North Carolina–Charlotte*
Ashish Gupta *SUNY at Buffalo*
Otto Gygax *Oregon State University*
Malcom Heimer *Florida International University*
Donald Herling *Oregon State University*
Thomas Hill *SUNY at Buffalo*
A.S. Hodel *Auburn University*
James N. Jensen *SUNY at Buffalo*
Vern Johnson *University of Arizona*
Autar Kaw *University of South Florida*
Kathleen Kitto *Western Washington University*
Kenneth Klika *University of Akron*
Terry L. Kohutek *Texas A&M University*
Melvin J. Maron *University of Louisville*
Robert Montgomery *Purdue University*
Mark Nagurka *Marquette University*
Romarathnam Narasimhan *University of Miami*
Soronadi Nnaji *Florida A&M University*
Sheila O'Connor *Wichita State University*
Michael Peshkin *Northwestern University*
Dr. John Ray *University of Memphis*
Larry Richards *University of Virginia*
Marc H. Richman *Brown University*
Randy Shih *Oregon Institute of Technology*
Avi Singhal *Arizona State University*
Tim Sykes *Houston Community College*
Neil R. Thompson *University of Waterloo*
Dr. Raman Menon Unnikrishnan *Rochester Institute of Technology*
Michael S. Wells *Tennessee Tech University*
Joseph Wujek *University of California, Berkeley*
Edward Young *University of South Carolina*
Garry Young *Oklahoma State University*
Mandochehr Zoghi *University of Dayton*

Contents

1

Introduction to Discovering Engineering

1 INTRODUCTION

You are beginning an exploration of engineering that will continue throughout your life. This chapter will explore the ways that this journey may begin. In Section 2, you will be asked to examine your own motivation for becoming an engineer. In Section 3, some surprising advice on how to discover engineering is shared. In Section 4, the clock is turned back 175 years to show how history affects your engineering education.

2 WELCOME TO ENGINEERING

In some ways, it is amazing that you found engineering in the first place. Most people select careers and academic programs based on their high school experiences. You probably took math and science classes in high school, perhaps even some technology classes. However, you probably did not take *engineering* classes in high school.

Some of your high school friends may be comfortable with their exposure to chemistry or French or English literature in secondary school. They may be looking forward to majoring in one of those fields in college. Although their college experiences will challenge and extend them, your friends probably have a pretty good idea what to expect in college based on their high school experiences.

You may be a little envious. After all, you took a chance on a field that is a little less familiar to you. Your motivation for doing so is unique to you.

OBJECTIVES

After reading this chapter, you will be able to:

- identify why people choose engineering as a career;
- find engineers to speak with about engineering;
- list what you should expect in your engineering education.

From *A User's Guide to Engineering*, James N. Jensen. Copyright 2006 by Pearson Education, Inc. Published by Prentice Hall, Inc. All rights reserved.

PONDER THIS

What is *your* motivation for becoming an engineer?

Key idea: Engineering is the right place for people who have curiosity, a strong work ethic, a desire to help other people, and a deep respect for math and science.

Many students pursue a degree in engineering because they performed well in math and science classes in high school. Some engineering students have relatives who are engineers. Some pursue engineering because the job opportunities and salaries for recent engineering graduates are pretty good. Whatever your motivation, you are taking a small leap of faith in entering a profession that may seem a mystery to you right now. Have no fear: if you have curiosity, a strong work ethic, a desire to help other people, and a deep respect for math and science, then you have found a home in engineering. For a few stories about why working engineers chose engineering, see *Focus on Choosing Engineering: So Why Did You Become an Engineer?*

FOCUS ON CHOOSING ENGINEERING: SO WHY DID YOU BECOME AN ENGINEER?

Every engineer has a unique answer to the question: Why did you choose engineering? Compare your motivation for becoming an engineer with the following stories from practicing engineers.

Helping People

My long-term goal has been to work for and with people, that's why I became an engineer. I like helping people, and that's why I want to use my talents to better other people's lives. This project is exactly the kind of thing I want to do with the rest of my life.

—*From a Northwestern University senior, commenting on her involvement in a project to build a toy car for disabled children* (http://www.asme.org/mechanicaladvantage/fall98/CHILD'SPLAYCARPAGE.HTM)

Problem Solving

When the tragic Challenger disaster occurred in 1986, I found myself not only touched by the loss, but also driven to understand why, and motivated to ensure such a tragedy did not happen again.

—*From a Lockheed Martin mechanical engineer* (http://www.lmaeronautics.com.about/eweek/why)

Math and Science

I always liked science and math anyway, so the idea of working in a profession where one can apply the laws of nature for the benefit of mankind was very inspiring.

—*From a civil engineer working at the Philadelphia District of the U.S. Army Corps of Engineers* (*District Observer ONLINE*, Jan–Feb 2000)

Curiosity

Growing up on a 200-acre cotton farm in middle Georgia, I became fascinated and elated with the mechanical equipment that was becoming available to do work on the farm.

—*From another Lockheed Martin mechanical engineer* (http://www.lmaeronautics.com/about/eweek/why)

Impact

One of the reasons why I became an engineer is because I believe engineering is a profession that allows you to predict the future. As I tell my students, "...(Y)ou can use (the laws of physics) to predict how something... should work. Then, you can... build that something and test it. If it works the way you thought it should, then you effectively forecast the future."

—*From Dr. James Meindl, electrical engineering professor at the Georgia Institute of Technology* (*Georgia Tech Alumni Magazine Online*, Vol. 72, No. 1, Summer 1995)

3   HOW TO DISCOVER ENGINEERING

Key idea: Discover engineering by talking to engineers.

So how do you learn more about the engineering profession? First, *put down this book.* No words on the page can help you realize the richness and satisfaction of your career. No book can bring alive the dramatic and compelling history of engineering, where two steps forward are invariably followed by one step backward. And no mere textbook can do justice to the triumphs, diversity, and human stories of the engineers themselves.

Textbook authors usually do not tell you to stop reading their text. But engineering is not about textbooks. It is about people: people who learn, people who translate ideas into reality, people who solve problems, people who communicate their ideas to others, and people who behave responsibly. To truly discover engineering, you must talk to engineers. But how do you find them?

PONDER THIS

How can you find engineers to speak with about engineering?

Key idea: Learn more about your future career by finding engineers at a university.

The best place to find engineers is at your university. Almost all engineering faculty are trained engineers,° and many have work experience outside of the university. Find a faculty member to help you understand the profession. Many universities have freshman mentoring programs, where freshmen are assigned faculty mentors or advisors. If your school does not have such a program, read the departmental brochures or Internet information and find a professor in an area that interests you. Call him or her for an appointment. Be persistent: the faculty are as busy as you are.

Engineering societies are another great source of information about this practice. These societies are professional organizations; some societies are general in scope, while others focus on a specific discipline. The major discipline-specific engineering societies are listed in Table 1. Other discipline-specific organizations are listed in Table 2. Table 3 lists the main engineering societies that are not associated with a specific engineering field. In Table 4, engineering societies focused on increasing the diversity of engineers are shown. For more information about any of these organizations, search on the Internet. For a story about historical diversity in engineering, see *Focus on Diversity in Engineering: The Real McCoy.*

TABLE 1 Major Discipline-Specific Engineering Societies

Name	Date Started	Number of Members
American Institute of Chemical Engineers (AIChE)	1908	58,000
American Society of Civil Engineers (ASCE)	1852	120,000
American Society of Mechanical Engineers (ASME)	1880	125,000
Institute of Electrical and Electronics Engineers (IEEE)[a]	1884	330,000
Institute of Industrial Engineers (IIE)	1948	24,000

[a]The American Institute of Electrical Engineers (founded in 1884) and the Institute of Radio Engineers merged in 1962 to form IEEE.

°You must be a registered professional engineer to use the title "professional engineer." Almost all engineering faculty have received training as engineers, but not all faculty are registered professional engineers.

TABLE 2   Other Discipline-Specific Engineering Societies

Name	Discipline[a]
American Academy of Environmental Engineers (AAEE)	civil
American Ceramic Society (ACerS)	several
American Institute for Medical and Biological Engineering (AIMBE)	several
American Institute of Aeronautics and Astronautics (AIAA)	mechanical
American Institute of Mining, Metallurgical, and Petroleum Engineers (AIME)	several
American Nuclear Society (ANS)	several
American Public Works Association (APWA)	civil
American Society for Quality (ASQ)	industrial
American Society of Agricultural Engineers (ASAE)	civil
American Society of Heating, Refrigerating and Air Conditioning Engineers (ASHRAE)	mechanical
American Society of Naval Engineers (ASNE)	several
American Society of Safety Engineers (ASSE)	several
Associated General Contractors of America (AGC)	civil
Association for Facilities Engineering (AFE)	industrial
Biomedical Engineering Society (BMES)	several
Human Factors and Ergonomics Society (HFES)	industrial
National Association of Power Engineers (NAPE)	several
Society of American Military Engineers (SAME)	several
Society of Automotive Engineers (SAE)	mechanical
Society of Fire Protection Engineers (SFPE)	several
Society of Manufacturing Engineers (SME)	several
Society of Petroleum Engineers (SPE)	chemical
Society of Plastics Engineers (SPE)	chemical
SPIE—The International Society for Optical Engineering[b]	several

[a]"Discipline" refers to the major engineering area(s) (chemical, civil, electrical, industrial, and mechanical engineering) targeted by the society.
[b]Originally, this was the Society of Photo-Optical Instrumentation Engineers.

TABLE 3   General Engineering Societies

Name	Date Founded
American Association of Engineering Societies (AAES)	1979
American Consulting Engineers Council (ACEC)	1910
American Society of Engineering Education (ASEE)	1893
Junior Engineering Technical Society (JETS)	1957[a]
National Council of Examiners for Engineering/Surveying (NCEES)	1920
National Society of Professional Engineers (NSPE)	1934
Tau Beta Pi[b] (TBΠ)	1885

[a]JETS was established in 1950 and incorporated in 1957.
[b]Tau Beta Pi is the national engineering honor society. Several disciplines have their own national honor societies (e.g., Sigma Gamma Tau for aerospace engineering and Eta Kappa Nu for electrical engineering).

TABLE 4 Engineering Societies Focused on Diversity in Engineering

Name	Date Founded
American Indian Science and Engineering Societies (AISES)	1977
Mexican American Engineers and Scientists (MAES)	1974
National Action Council for Minorities in Engineering (NACME)	1974
National Society of Black Engineers (NSBE)	1976
National Organization of Gay and Lesbian Scientists and Technical Professionals (NOGLSTP)	1983
Society of Hispanic Professional Engineers (SHPE)	1974
Society of Woman Engineers (SWE)	1950

student chapter: a student-run organization or club associated with a national society.

The easiest way to meet engineers in professional societies is through student chapters. A **student chapter** is a student-run organization affiliated with a national society. Student chapters of engineering societies typically have a faculty advisor and a practicing engineer who serves as a liaison to the parent society. Most of the organizations listed in Tables 1 through 4 have student chapters. The student chapters may invite practicing engineers to share their experiences with students. Look for opportunities to speak with the presenters.

Another way to learn from engineers in professional societies is through participation in National Engineers Week. National Engineers Week was established by the National Society of Professional Engineers in 1951 to increase public awareness of the profession. It is held each year during the week of George Washington's birthday (February 22) to acknowledge Washington's contributions as a surveyor. The local activities during National Engineers Week will provide a great opportunity to learn from professional engineers.

Key idea: To learn more, speak with professionals at engineering firms or engineering departments.

Finally, practicing engineers are a wonderful source of information. Many offices, departments of large companies, and government departments offer office tours and internship programs. Summer jobs and co-op programs provide good opportunities to ask questions. The telephone book and Internet are useful guides to engineering practice in your area. In addition, ask the career planning staff at your university to help locate practicing engineers who have volunteered to act as student mentors.

4   ENGINEERING EDUCATION: WHAT YOU SHOULD EXPECT

For many engineers, the discovery of engineering begins with their college years. To see what is in store for you as you begin your engineering education, it is instructive to look back in time. Engineering education has a long history in the United States. Engineering education, as with engineering itself, began with military applications.

In the United States, the first formal training program for engineers began in 1794, when Congress added the rank of cadet to the Corps of Artillerists and Engineers. The Corps was assigned to the garrison at West Point. A four-year degree program began at West Point in 1817, under the direction of Sylvanus Thayer (1785–1872). Civilian education in engineering began in 1820 at the American Literary, Scientific, and Military Academy (now Norwich University) in Norwich, Vermont, under the guidance of Alden Partridge (1785–1854).

The work of Thayer and Partridge expanded the traditional university curriculum to educate soldiers and citizen-soldiers about the applied sciences. A different approach was developed by Amos Eaton and Stephen Van Rensselaer. In 1824, they founded the Rensselaer School (now called Rensselaer Polytechnic Institute in Troy, New York) to "teach the application of science to the common purposes of life" (Griggs, 1997).

FOCUS ON DIVERSITY IN ENGINEERING: THE REAL MCCOY?

BACKGROUND

Engineering has made great strides in becoming more diverse and increasing the participation of previously underrepresented groups. Few people realize that one of the most productive engineers of the post–Civil War era was African-American. Elijah McCoy was born in Colchester, Ontario, on May 2, 1844. McCoy's parents were former slaves who fled from Kentucky before the outbreak of the Civil War. (In fact, McCoy's wife was born in 1846 at an Underground Railway station.) After receiving training as a mechanical engineer in Scotland, McCoy moved to Detroit and obtained a job as a fireman on the Michigan Central Railroad.

THE PROBLEM AND ITS SOLUTION

In his job, McCoy became aware of a problem that plagued the railroads and other industries that relied on steam engines. Steam engines required lubrication, which, in the mid-19th century, was usually accomplished by hand. Hand lubrication meant that the machinery had to be turned off or idled to be oiled. McCoy realized that a well-designed automatic lubricator would solve the problem and allow equipment to be run continuously.

McCoy's solution was to improve the hydrostatic lubricator based on a drip cup. In a steam engine, steam from the boiler fills the cylinder and pushes the piston back. In the McCoy lubricator, a small portion of the steam was used to pressurize the lubricator body containing the oil. The pressurized oil drips continuously into the cylinder, thus lubricating the cylinder and piston. The steam condenses into water inside the

lubricator body and the oil floats on top. Eventually, the water drains off and the oil is replenished.

The device was patented in 1872. With McCoy's improved lubricator, the continuous operation of steam engines was easier and the transcontinental railroad (completed in 1869) was exploited.

MCCOY'S CONTRIBUTIONS

Elijah McCoy's contributions to lubrication have been exaggerated by some historians and underemphasized by others. While McCoy did not invent the hydrostatic lubricator, he contributed significantly to its optimization and usage. In fact, McCoy's original patent was titled *"Improvement* in Lubricators for Steam-Engines" (emphasis added). Elijah McCoy was a prolific inventor. He was eventually responsible for 57 patents, most involving lubrication equipment. One of his greatest contributions to the field was the graphite lubricator. By suspending graphite in oil, McCoy developed a device to lubricate the then-emerging superheated steam engines.

As with many inventors, McCoy had to assign a number of his patents to investors in his companies. As a result, he did not reap great financial benefits from his inventions. McCoy died at age 85 and was inducted into the National Inventors Hall of Fame in 2001.

IS HE THE "REAL MCCOY"?

The story goes that McCoy's device was prized for its performance, even above the many other automatic lubrication devices that were patented later. Engineers were purported to have asked if their machinery was equipped with "the real McCoy."

Elijah McCoy

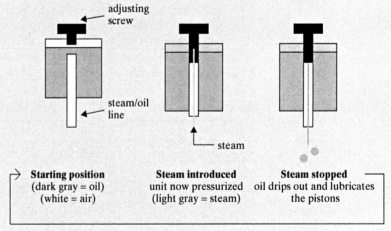

Water from condensed steam drained off, oil refilled, cycle restarts

Charles "Kid" McCoy

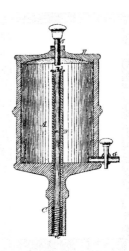

McCoy's lubricator

Did Elijah McCoy's inventions contribute to the popularization of the phrase "the real McCoy"? This question may be impossible to answer. Several people (and objects) from the mid-19th century could be the source of the phrase. Explanations range from Elijah's lubricator to boxer Norman Selby (the Light Heavyweight Champion of the World in 1904, who fought under the name "Kid McCoy") to Mssrs. Mackay's whiskey (made in Edinburgh and marketed as "the real Mackay.")

Regardless of the etymology of "the real McCoy," it is remarkable that a black railroad fireman could have a significant impact on railroad operations within a dozen years of the end of the Civil War. Elijah McCoy stands as a testament to problem solving, perseverance, and intelligence. In these characteristics, he truly was a real McCoy.

Amos Eaton based the program on five rules of education. Eaton's rules are reproduced next, with the original spelling and punctuation (Griggs, 1997). Although the engineering profession and engineering education have changed greatly in almost 200 years,° Eaton's rules are still meaningful today. In this section, Eaton's rules shall be interpreted for the 21st-century engineering curriculum.

4.1 Eaton's First Rule: " . . . make practical applications of all the sciences . . . "

Key idea: Discover engineering through problem solving and hands-on work.

"Let the student make practical applications of all the sciences, with the immediate direction and shewing [showing] of the teacher, before studying any elementary rules. For example, shew him in taking the courses and distances around a field with the compass and chain, before he studies any of the rules of surveying—let him measure a pile of wood and attempt to calculate it before teaching him duo-decimals; let him use optical instruments, under the teacher's shewing, before studying optics, let him give an experimental course on chemistry, before reading any work on chemistry; excepting a textbook of experimental description while in the course of experimenting."

Engineering education must be a marriage of fundamental science and practical applications. *Let the applied problem serve as your introduction to and motivation for theory and analysis.* As Amos Eaton might have put it: engage the hands first and the mind will follow.

°For example, Eaton speaks of students using only the pronouns "he" and "him," since women engineers were rare in the late 19th century. In addition, the original engineering program at the Rensselaer School could be completed in one year!

4.2   Eaton's Second Rule: " . . . take the place of the teacher . . . [in] exercises."

> "Let the student always take the place of the teacher on his exercises. He must make every subject his own and then teach his fellow and the schoolmaster, as though there were not a book in the world which treated on this subject, and he was the very oracle of science. Extemporaneous lectures on Tuesday, Wednesday, Thursday, and Friday, and written lectures on Mondays, is a good exercise for that student, in the acquisition of knowledge. He must not speak without a specimen in hand, or the apparatus before him."

Key idea: Learn by teaching others.

Teaching others is a valuable learning strategy. To master engineering fundamentals, practice explaining your reasoning to faculty and fellow students. Most professors feel that teaching deepens their understanding and appreciation of any material. In the last sentence of the quote, note again Eaton's emphasis on the practical problem.

4.3   Eaton's Third Rule: " . . . attend to but one branch of learning at the same time."

> "Let a student attend to but one branch of learning at the same time. Personal exercise in the afternoon, at surveying, engineering, collecting plants and minerals, inspecting factories, machines, and agricultural operations, may be permitted. For, although reflection is required, such exercises call such different faculties into action, that the mind is not thereby burdened or fatigued."

Unfortunately, engineering curricula usually do not allow the luxury of immersing the students in only one subject at a time. In fact, the modern engineering curriculum ensures that the courses you will take are integrated together and build on one another. However, *you can focus on one topic at a time.* A key to success in engineering is mastering the material from one lecture or set of readings before the next lecture occurs.

Key idea: Take the time to master material before new concepts are presented.

It is absolutely critical that you give yourself time to master the material. As Eaton said, "reflection is required." In high school, you may have been able to master some material by sitting passively in class and listening to your teacher. In your engineering courses, you will need to think and talk about the material *outside* of the classroom. You must give yourself the time to think, to make mistakes, and to explore. In reading this text, use the *Ponder This* questions as a springboard for reflection.

In this rule, Eaton once again urges you to return to practice. Talking to professionals, going on field trips at every opportunity, and searching the Internet are some 21st-century versions of Eaton's "personal exercises" (see also Section 2).

Finally, Eaton's advice about the importance of using "different faculties" of the mind should serve as a guide to your college education. Use liberal arts and social science courses to exercise the different parts of your brain. These courses are every bit as valuable as your technical courses.

4.4   Eaton's Fourth Rule: "Let the amusements and recreation of students be of a scientific character."

> "Let the amusements and recreation of students be of a scientific character. Collecting and preserving minerals and plants, surveying, and engineering, are good amusement."

Eaton's idea of amusement may not jibe with *your* idea of amusement, but the sentiment is important. Eaton's comment focuses on how you spend your time away from the classroom. In modern times, this rule should remind you to get involved with

Key idea: Join student clubs and enter student engineering contests.

student clubs and student engineering contests. In addition, consider getting involved in service-oriented organizations (such as Habitat for Humanity) where your engineering skills can be used to help others immediately. Also, look for engineering in your everyday life—from the automatic teller machine to the roller coaster at your local amusement park to your cell phone.

Eaton also is speaking about commitment. To be a successful engineer, it is **not** necessary to spend every waking moment with your nose in a technical journal. However, *you must make a commitment to getting your degree* or graduation day will never come. Success in engineering is all about using your time wisely to achieve your goals. Start now: make earning an engineering degree a high priority in your life.

4.5   Eaton's Fifth Rule: "Let every student daily criticize those whose exercise he has attended."

"Let every student daily criticize those whose exercise he has attended. Such as to point out all errors in language, gesture, position, and manner of performing experiments, etc. The teacher must always preside during the hour of criticism. No exercise sharpens the faculty of discrimination like this, while it causes each student to be perpetually on his guard."

Key idea: Challenge your instructors and respect the value of good technical communication skills.

Give constructive feedback to your instructors. Challenge them as they challenge you. Learning requires two-way communication, giving you the responsibility to interact with your instructors. Eaton's fifth rule is also a reminder of the importance in the engineering profession of both *technical communications* (i.e, avoiding "errors in language, gesture, position") and *data collection* (i.e., avoiding errors in the "manner of performing experiments").

5   SUMMARY

Your discovery of engineering has begun. It is sincerely hoped that your sense of discovery will be just as keen 40 years from now as it is today. Although you may have some trepidation as you begin your exploration of engineering, know that engineering is the place for you if you are curious, have a strong work ethic, wish to help other people, and respect and enjoy math and science. Discover engineering by talking with engineers, including your professors, members of professional societies (and the student chapters of professional societies), and practicing engineers. Consider the wisdom of Amos Eaton when discovering engineering in your classes.

SUMMARY OF
KEY IDEAS

- Engineering is the right place for people who have curiosity, a strong work ethic, a desire to help other people, and a deep respect for math and science.
- Discover engineering by talking to engineers.
- Learn about your future career by finding engineers at a university.
- To learn more, speak with professionals at engineering firms or engineering departments.
- Discover engineering through problem solving and hands-on work.
- Learn by teaching others.
- Take the time to master material before new concepts are presented.
- Join student clubs and enter student engineering contests.
- Challenge your instructors and respect the value of good technical communication skills.

Problems

1. Find and record the Internet home page of each society listed in Table 1. Organizations often write a mission statement that succinctly states their goals and aspirations. Read the mission statement of each organization.

2. Using Table 1, pick two societies that interest you the most and explain why they interest you.

3. Summarize the purpose and goals of three societies listed in Tables 2 through 4.

4. Using the library and the Internet, write a short essay on the contributions to engineering education from Sylvanus Thayer, Alden Partridge, Amos Eaton, or any other pioneering educator in a technical field.

5. Devise a way to teach a high school student about a technical topic using the approach suggested in Eaton's first rule. Pick a topic that you learned about in high school or are learning about now. Possible topics might be Newton's laws of motion, Boyle's law, or Ohm's law.

6. State an applied problem that interests you. Looking at the curriculum for your field of study, list the courses that you think will help you solve this problem.

7. How can you use the ideas in Eaton's second rule to study engineering?

8. Write a paragraph on the opportunities at your university to teach others.

9. Make a list of the liberal arts and social science courses that you plan to take and explain why they interest you.

10. Ask an engineering professor how teaching deepens his or her understanding and appreciation of engineering.

11. Make a list of "amusements and recreation ... of a scientific character" in your community. Pick an activity to participate in this year.

12. Attend a meeting of a service-oriented organization in your community. Write a short paragraph about how you might use your engineering training to help the organization.

13. Attend a meeting of an engineering student club. Write a short paragraph about the plans of the student club for the year.

14. Make a list of local engineering firms in the discipline of most interest to you. Visit a local office and report on your visit.

2

What Is Engineering?

1 INTRODUCTION

The question posed by the title of this chapter may seem a bit strange. After all, you do not have to ask the meaning of brain surgery, soccer, or veterinary science—and there are many more engineers in the world than brain surgeons, professional soccer players, or veterinarians. Your familiarity with engineered *systems* (highways, buildings, computers, and factories, to name a few) does not tell you much about the *process* that made those systems. The process is engineering. In this chapter, you will explore the characteristics that engineers and engineering disciplines have in common.

2 DEFINING ENGINEERING

What is engineering? This simple question has a very complex answer. Engineering is a diverse collection of professions, academic disciplines, and skills. You can start your exploration of engineering with the dictionary. Your ego may be boosted to learn that the word "engineering" stems from the Latin *ingenium*, meaning skill. (Other words sharing this Latin root include "ingenious" and "ingenuity.") Engineers are skilled at what they do. But what do they do? The dictionary offers you further insight. The Latin root *ingenium* comes from *in* + *gignere*, meaning to produce or beget (also the source of the words "generate" and "kin"). Thus, engineers are skilled producers or creators of things.

This exercise in word origins does not do justice to the field of engineering. Many definitions of "engineering" and "engineer" are possible. Most definitions have some elements in common.

OBJECTIVES

After reading this chapter, you will be able to:

- identify the elements that all engineering disciplines have in common;
- describe how engineers help others.

PONDER THIS   **Based on your experiences, what is your definition of engineering?**

Key idea: Engineers are professionals who apply science and mathematics to useful ends, solve problems creatively, optimize, and make reasoned choices.

Common elements in the definitions include the following:

- Engineers apply science and mathematics to useful ends.
- Engineers solve problems creatively.
- Engineers optimize.
- Engineers make choices.
- Engineers help others.
- Engineering is a profession.

You will examine each of these elements in more detail in this chapter.

3   ENGINEERING AS AN APPLIED DISCIPLINE

3.1   Knowledge Generation versus Knowledge Implementation

Almost everyone would agree that engineering is the application of science and mathematics to practical ends. Indeed, the emphasis on practice and application always is in the mind of the engineer. They care more about *using* basic knowledge than *generating* basic knowledge. They care more about converting basic science into technology and converting technology into useful products than in expanding basic science.

However, the emphasis on application tells only part of the story of engineering. The pure engineer may be concerned only with practice, just as the pure scientist is concerned only with generating new knowledge. In reality, both practicing scientists and engineers contribute to the complicated and rewarding process of converting ideas into reality. The pure scientist and the pure engineer are extremes of a spectrum of skills required to make new things.

3.2   The Role of Engineering

The role of the engineer in turning ideas into usable ideas or objects° is illustrated in Figure 1. Both scientists and engineers use mathematics and natural sciences as their tools. Engineers focus on answering the questions that lie on the more applied side of the spectrum. In your career as an engineer, it is likely that you will help develop and implement technology. You will likely work from the middle to the right side of the spectrum

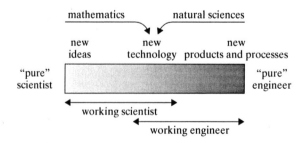

Figure 1.   Spectrum of Skills in Engineering and Science.

°Engineers develop both *products* (e.g., ballpoint pens, toasters, microprocessors, and satellites) and *processes* (e.g., better ways to stock inventory, new approaches to manufacturing compact discs, and innovative ways to treat wastewater).

in Figure 1. As an engineer, you will acquire a pool of skills required to translate new knowledge into usable ideas.

You are urged to return to Figure 1 throughout your career. It may help you remember that knowledge generation and product design are two ends of the same spectrum. Neither skill is useful without the other.

Figure 1 is a good road map for getting the most out of your courses. For example, if you are suffering from motivational problems in your science and mathematics courses, think about how the material can be applied. Speak to your science and mathematics professors about the practical use of the material. Ask engineering mentors how they use basic science and mathematics in their everyday professional lives.

EXAMPLE 1: APPLICATION OF SCIENTIFIC PRINCIPLES

In your high school or freshman chemistry course, you may have learned about the unit of chemical concentration called the *mole*. At first glance, the use of molar units of concentration may seem very theoretical and not applied. Give an example of how each main engineering discipline can use this concept.

SOLUTION

Lithium iodine batteries as small as 4 mm thick have been used in implantable cardiac pacemakers for over 20 years (Photo courtesy of Greatbatch, Inc.)

Engineers use different sets of units to solve different kinds of problems. Molar units express the proportions in which chemicals combine. Therefore, they are very useful for solving problems involving *combining proportions*.

Almost every engineering discipline uses molar units for some applications. For example, a civil engineer (in the environmental engineering specialty) might use molar units for determining doses of chemicals to react with pollutants and solve pollution problems. A chemical engineer may use moles to determine the ratios of chemicals used to synthesize polymers on a commercial scale. An electrical engineer would use molar units to determine the number of electrons per time (also called the current) produced by an electrochemical cell (such as a battery). Molar units could be used by an industrial engineer to design monitoring devices to make the workplace safer. Mechanical engineers use the concept of the mole to optimize material properties. All engineers may work together to use molar units to design sensors capable of detecting chemical or biological agents.

---

4   ENGINEERING AS CREATIVE PROBLEM SOLVING

4.1   Solving Problems

Engineers solve problems. These three simple words have far-reaching ramifications on the life of an engineer. First, since engineers solve problems, engineering work is usually motivated by a concern or roadblock. This idea may conjure up an image of lone warriors furiously performing dense calculations in a cubicle under a green-shaded desk lamp.

No image of engineering could be more incorrect. In reality, engineers often solve other people's problems. Thus, engineers must be able to *listen to a concern* and *map out a solution*. Whether the problem is to make cars that pollute less or to make oil refining more efficient or to reduce the manufacturing cost of a child's toy, engineers must be able to understand problems that their clients face. In this way, engineering is a very people-oriented profession.

4.2   Standard Approaches to Solving Problems

Second, engineers must be skilled in using standard approaches to solve problems. We all respect the brilliant physician who can leap to a diagnosis using intuition and experience. We marvel at the aircraft mechanic who spots the mechanical problem by "feel."

However, we also know that *every* physician must be able to follow standard diagnostic procedures and *every* mechanic must be familiar with the inspection checklist. Similarly, engineers must know the well-established protocols used in solving many problems.

4.3 Creative Approaches to Solving Problems

Key idea: The solution to engineering problems involves both standard and creative approaches.

Third, engineers must be creative in solving problems. Just like the physician and aircraft mechanic, engineers must supplement the standard solution methods with creativity and insight. Engineering is a highly creative profession. As Theodore von Kármán (1881–1963), a well-known Hungarian-born specialist in fluid mechanics and aerodynamics, put it, "The scientist describes what is; the engineer creates what never was" (Mackay, 1991). This quotation should not be interpreted as minimizing the creativity of scientists. Rather, it points out that engineers must have vision to create something that did not previously exist.

5   ENGINEERING AS CONSTRAINED OPTIMIZATION

5.1   Constraints

constrained optimization: determining the best solution to a problem, given limitations on the solution

Key idea: Engineering solutions are often constrained.

Engineering, like life, is about **constrained optimization**. In high school, it was likely that you did not strive to be the *best* student you could be. Rather, you strived to be the best student you could be *given that* you had to work part-time or you had family obligations or you were active in community groups. In other words, your time available for studying was *constrained* by other activities.

Similarly, engineers always face constraints in solving problems. As an example, electrical engineers rarely seek to design the fastest computer chip. To be useful, computer chips must exhibit other characteristics as well.

PONDER THIS

List some constraints on computer chip design.

We could list the various constraints on computer chip design, but a better goal is just to say that we seek to develop the fastest computer chip of sufficiently small size with adequate heat dissipation characteristics that can be mass-produced at a reasonable cost.

Is it *ever* valuable to build the fastest chip? Absolutely! An electrical engineer specializing in the research side of research and development (R&D) may, in fact, seek to design the fastest computer chip. Some major breakthroughs in engineering have been generated by engineers and scientists who ignored constraints. However, most engineers seek to put ideas into practice. This means taking the real world and its constraints into account when designing engineered systems.

Key idea: Engineering solutions must take into account the probability of failure.

One aspect of the constrained nature of engineering is that engineers live in a probabilistic world. In other words, engineers must consider the *chances* of certain events occurring, including the probability of failure. A civil engineer does not design a bridge that will never fall down. Such a bridge would be infinitely expensive. Rather, the civil engineer examines the probabilities that certain loads will occur on the bridge from traffic, earthquakes, and wind. A bridge is designed to perform acceptably for a specified period of time under the anticipated loads and stresses. Similarly, an environmental engineer does not design a drinking water treatment plant to remove *all* pollutants completely. Such a plant is probably not possible (and if it was possible, the drinking water it produced would be unaffordable). Instead, engineers design treatment plants to meet water quality standards and minimize risk at a socially acceptable cost.

Due to constrained optimization in a probabilistic world, engineers must constantly ask: How strong is strong enough? How clean is clean? Have I thought of everything that could go wrong?° An example of extremely constrained optimization is given in the *Focus on Constrained Optimization: A Square Peg in a Round Hole*.

5.2 Feasibility

The ability of an engineering project to meet its constraints is often expressed in terms of feasibility. There are several aspects of feasibility, which will be introduced here. *Technical* (or engineering) *feasibility* measures whether or not a project meets its technical goals. It addresses several questions, such as "Does the new road handle the traffic?" and "Is the upgraded electrical transmission system more efficient?"

Key idea: To be successful, engineering projects must be technically, economically, fiscally, socially, politically, and environmentally feasible.

Most of your undergraduate course work is focused on technical feasibility. However, it is not sufficient for an engineering project to be technically feasible. Engineering projects also must be economically feasible. *Economic feasibility* addresses whether the project benefits outweigh the project costs. In the examples above, economic feasibility addresses whether the road benefits (e.g., tolls collected, elimination of slowdowns, and increased safety) are greater than the road construction and maintenance costs or whether the money saved from the more efficient transmission systems will pay for the upgrade work. Sometimes, the benefits and costs are difficult to quantify. What is the value of a five-minute reduction in commuting time or one less incidence of cancer for every one million people? To answer these questions, engineers may seek the advice of social scientists and economists.

Another factor to consider is *fiscal feasibility*. Fiscal feasibility measures whether sufficient funds can be generated to build the project. Many engineering projects would be profitable (i.e., are economically feasible), but are not built because start-up money cannot be acquired. The difference between economic and fiscal feasibility is important. For large, multimillion-dollar engineering projects, obtaining money through loans or bonds to achieve fiscal feasibility may be the critical step. Engineers who ignore fiscal feasibility will never see their ideas translated into reality.

The last type of feasibility is social, political, and environmental feasibility. Engineers cannot work in a vacuum. Engineering projects must be socially acceptable, have political backing, and result in an acceptable environmental impact. Many engineering projects remain only on paper because societal and political support was lacking. Should you, as an engineer, be upset because some projects die due to nontechnical issues? No. It should remind you that engineers are part of the fabric of society. The public cares about the impact of engineering projects. As a result, you must consider the social consequences of your proposal along with the technical details.

FOCUS ON CONSTRAINED OPTIMIZATION: A SQUARE PEG IN A ROUND HOLE

BACKGROUND

Engineering is about constrained optimization. The need to "make the best with what you have" is demanding when the constraints are the most severe. For example, a space vehicle located 200,000 nautical miles from Earth presents some of the most severe constraints that an engineer will face.

Such was the case with *Apollo 13*, launched April 11, 1970. The crew of the spacecraft—Commander James A. Lovell, Lunar Module Pilot Fred W. Haise, Jr., and Command Module Pilot John L. Swigert, Jr.— was hard at work and enjoying the ride. Suddenly, about 56 hours into the flight, the crew heard a loud noise (which is never a good sign in a spacecraft). The pressure in Cryogenic Oxygen Tank 2 had begun to rise

---

°For an insightful and entertaining discussion of this question as it pertains to civil engineering, see Petroski (1992).

Launch of Apollo 13, Saturday, April 11, 1970

very quickly. Within two minutes, the tank lost pressure. Why did this matter? Electricity on *Apollo 13* was generated by a fuel cell, where oxygen and hydrogen were combined. No oxygen meant no power—and no way to return to Earth.

PROBLEMS AND SOLUTIONS

The ground crew quickly assessed the situation. The three people in space required three things to return to Earth alive: power, water (to drink and to cool the equipment), and oxygen. With the fuel cells virtually inoperable, the only source of power was the batteries in the Lunar Module (LM, the *Aquarius*). It became clear that the LM, with its own ample oxygen supplies, would become the lifeboat for the crew. But the LM had its own problems. Its batteries would need to be recharged to provide enough power for the journey home. However, there was no direct electrical connection between the Command Service Module (CSM, the *Odyssey*) and the LM to recharge the batteries. Engineers on the ground discovered a way to leak current slowly from the CSM to the batteries. By turning off nonessential equipment,

the crew limped home with an amazing 20% of the LM power left.

The problem with water could be addressed only by drinking less. The crew cut its water ration to 200 milliliters per person per day (a little over one-half of a soft drink can). The crew lost a collective 31 pounds on the trip home, arriving in poor health and with 10% of the water supply remaining.

The LM had a sufficient oxygen supply, but the ground crew soon realized that *another* air supply problem would threaten the astronauts: the build-up of carbon dioxide (CO_2) exhaled by the crew. The CO_2 was removed by lithium hydroxide (LiOH) canisters through a chemical reaction. The LM was designed to transport two members of the crew from lunar orbit to the surface of the Moon. It had a sufficient canister capacity to remove the CO_2 produced by two people for about 30 hours, not the CO_2 exhaled by three people for the long trip back to Earth. Even by allowing the CO_2 levels to rise a little, the canisters could operate for only about 187 person-hours, when at least 288 person-hours would be needed. The solution? The CSM had its own LiOH canisters. But as luck would have it, the CSM canisters had *square* connectors that would not fit in the *round* fittings of the LM.

CONSTRAINED OPTIMIZATION

In a brilliant feat of constrained optimization, the ground crew had to develop an interface between the square CSM canisters and the round LM fittings from material available to the astronauts. (The near-impossibility of this task is shown dramatically in a famous scene from the movie *Apollo 13.*) The adapter, called the "mailbox," was designed by ground engineer Ed Smylie. (In NASA-speak, the adapter is known officially as the "supplemental carbon dioxide removal system.") It was made of two CSM canisters, a space suit exhaust hose, cardboard from instructional cue cards in the LM, plastic stowage bags from liquid-cooled undergarments, and one roll of duct tape. (Ironically, much of this material would have been otherwise unused by the astronauts. The cue cards contained instructions for lifting off from the moon and the undergarments were to be worn on moonwalks.)

Timeline for the Apollo 13 Carbon Dioxide Crisis
(all times are Central Standard Time for Houston, TX)

**Deke Slayton displays
the prototype**

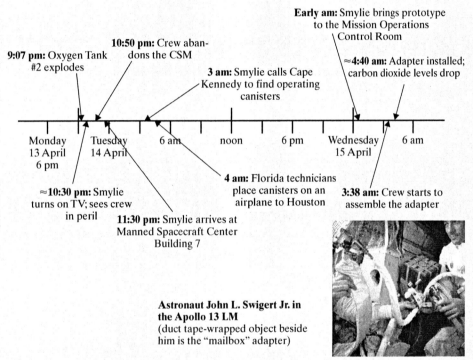

Early am: Smylie brings prototype
to the Mission Operations
Control Room

9:07 pm: Oxygen Tank
#2 explodes

10:50 pm: Crew abandons the CSM

3 am: Smylie calls Cape
Kennedy to find operating
canisters

≈4:40 am: Adapter installed;
carbon dioxide levels drop

Monday
13 April
6 pm

Tuesday
14 April

6 am

noon

6 pm

Wednesday
15 April

6 am

≈10:30 pm: Smylie
turns on TV; sees crew
in peril

11:30 pm: Smylie arrives at
Manned Spacecraft Center
Building 7

4 am: Florida technicians
place canisters on an
airplane to Houston

3:38 am: Crew starts to
assemble the adapter

**Astronaut John L. Swigert Jr. in
the Apollo 13 LM**
(duct tape-wrapped object beside
him is the "mailbox" adapter)

The efforts of engineer Ed Smylie, the other Houston personnel, and the astronauts were truly unbelievable. Only about 30 hours elapsed between the time Smylie turned on his television set to learn of *Apollo 13's* problems and the time that the astronauts finished building the mailbox in space. (See the accompanying timeline.) Smylie and his assistant, Jim Correale, had no operational LiOH canisters to test the interface. Working canisters from Florida (intended for *Apollo 14* or *Apollo 15*) were airlifted to Houston to enable testing of the device. After testing on the ground, the ground crew issued about an hour's worth of instructions by radio so that the astronauts could construct the adapter in space.

The *Apollo 13* flight had a very happy ending, due to the bravery of the astronauts and the ingenuity of the engineers. When faced with an overwhelmingly constrained problem, the engineers created a solution that saved the lives of three American heroes.

6   ENGINEERING AS MAKING CHOICES

Key idea: Engineers make recommendations by selecting from a list of feasible alternatives.

feasibility assessment: evaluation of the feasibility of an engineering project

The discussion thus far has centered on what engineering *is* rather than what engineers *do*. So what *does* an engineer do? Engineers listen carefully to the problem. (See Section 4.1.) Using accepted and creative methods (see Sections 4.2 and 4.3), they develop a list of feasible solutions or alternatives. Here, "feasible" means that each solution is technically, economically, fiscally, and socially/politically/environmentally feasible. (Evaluating whether a project is feasible is called a *feasibility assessment*. See Example 2 for an example.) Finally, engineers select an alternative from among the feasible solutions and recommend it to their client.

In a real sense, engineering is about generating alternatives and selecting feasible solutions. The selection step sets engineers apart from other professionals (e.g., technicians and designers) who may be trained to do the calculations and run the software, but may not be trained to make recommendations. To recommend an alternative, an engineer has to balance the technical, economic, fiscal, and social/political/environmental issues. A person trained only to crunch numbers will fail in this critical decision-making task. A person trained only to crunch numbers is not an engineer.

EXAMPLE 2: FEASIBILITY ASSESSMENT

Conduct a feasibility assessment for buying a used car to commute to a part-time job.

SOLUTION

A feasibility assessment determines the technical, economic, fiscal, and social/political/environmental feasibility of an alternative.

Technical feasibility: Technical feasibility probes whether the alternative will solve the problem. In this case, you need to ask whether buying the car will allow you to commute to work safely and reliably. Perhaps the car you can afford will not be sufficiently reliable. Perhaps other more reliable alternatives exist, such as public transportation.

Economic feasibility: Economic feasibility questions whether the benefits of the alternative exceed its costs. The costs of car ownership include depreciation, financing, insurance, taxes and fees, fuel, maintenance, and repairs. For a used 2000 Honda Accord two-door LX coupe in Buffalo, New York, the purchase and ownership costs average about $7,570 per year for the first five years (as determined by the cost calculator at www.edmunds.com). The benefits include your ability to get to your part-time job and the freedom and convenience that car ownership engenders. Other alternatives (such as a monthly bus pass) may have lower costs, but they do not have the freedom and convenience of car ownership.

Fiscal feasibility: Fiscal feasibility probes whether you can get the start-up funds to finance the project. In this example, purchasing the car is fiscally feasible if you can qualify for a reasonable car loan.

Social/political/environmental feasibility: In this example, social/political/environmental feasibility centers on environmental impact. In spite of the large social, political, and environmental costs of reliance on the internal combustion engine, car ownership remains socially acceptable in North America. You could consider, as an alternative, a car with lower environmental impact. (Buying a new Toyota Prius has about twice the purchase + interest + depreciation costs of the Honda, but about half the fuel + maintenance + repair costs.)

7   ENGINEERS AS HELPING OTHERS

Professions can be characterized in many ways. Some people are attracted to the so-called caring professions.

PONDER THIS   **Make a list of caring professions.**

Caring professions include medicine, nursing, social work, and teaching. Did your list include engineering?

Engineering is also one of the caring professions. Why? Nearly every project that an engineer completes satisfies a need or concern of the public. For example, if you become an electrical engineer, you may develop sensors to make more powerful neonatal incubators. Perhaps as a civil engineer, you may work on earthquake-resistant buildings or develop drinking-water treatment systems for less developed countries. (Water-related diseases, the leading cause of death globally, is responsible for 14,000 deaths *per day* because more than one billion people on the planet lack access to safe drinking water.) Maybe you will become a chemical engineer and work on ways to mass-produce HIV medications, making such drugs affordable to every HIV-positive person in the world. Perhaps you will go into industrial engineering and devise systems to help nonprofit organizations better serve their clients. (Volunteers from several professional and student chapters of the Institute of Industrial Engineers recently helped make a women's shelter in Pittsburgh become more efficient to save resources.) Or maybe you will become a mechanical engineer and develop a robust heart valve for premature infants. Whatever field of engineering interests you, know that you can use your training to make the world a better place and to make people's lives healthier and more fulfilling.

8   ENGINEERING AS A PROFESSION

Finally, engineering is a profession. This means, of course, that engineers get paid for what they do. In addition, it means that to be called an engineer, you must meet certain requirements. Just as the public must be assured that a person called a dentist or lawyer is fully certified, so the public must know that a person using the title "engineer" has been trained properly. The process of meeting the requirements is called *registration*. A registered engineer holds the title *professional engineer*, or PE.

All professions have ethical standards. Engineers, as professionals, must meet high standards of professional ethics.

9   SUMMARY

The dictionary tells us that engineers give birth to things creatively. In particular, the work of engineers is characterized by six elements. First, engineers apply science and mathematics to useful ends. Second, engineers solve problems using both standard and creative approaches. Third, engineers optimize solutions subject to the constraints of the real world. The constraints are often grouped under the headings of technical feasibility (will the system perform the task for which it was designed?), economic feasibility (do benefits outweigh costs?), fiscal feasibility (are start-up funds available?), and social/political/environmental feasibility. Fourth, engineers make reasoned choices. They select and recommend feasible alternatives. Fifth, engineers help others. Without a public to serve, engineering as a profession would not exist. Finally, engineers are professionals. This means that engineers may seek professional registration and must meet ethical standards.

SUMMARY OF KEY IDEAS

- Engineers are professionals who apply science and mathematics to useful ends, solve problems creatively, optimize, and make reasoned choices.
- The solution to engineering problems involves both standard and creative approaches.
- Engineering solutions are often constrained.
- Engineering solutions must take into account the probability of failure.
- To be successful, engineering projects must be technically, economically, fiscally, socially, politically, and environmentally feasible.
- Engineers make recommendations by selecting from a list of feasible alternatives.
- Engineering is a profession and engineers have ethical responsibilities.

Problems

1. What are the six main elements of engineering?

2. Some pharmaceuticals are manufactured by genetically engineered bacteria to produce the drug. Discuss the role of the engineer (if any) in the following steps of the development of a new drug:
    - Synthesis of the drug for animal tests
    - Genetic engineering of the bacteria
    - Mass production through bacterial synthesis
    - Clinical trials
    - Development of the time-release capsules and transdermal patches
    - Efficiency study of the manufacturing process, and
    - Design of the marketing strategy

3. Explain the differences in the contributions to society of scientists and engineers. Which contribution appeals more to you and why?

4. Give an example of constrained optimization in an engineering problem.

5. For Problem 4, what is a possible solution, given the constraints? How would the solution change if the constraints were different?

6. From your local newspaper, find an example of an engineering project that was not implemented because it was not economically or fiscally feasible.

7. Explain the difference between economic feasibility and fiscal feasibility.

8. Give an example of an engineering project that is economically feasible, but not fiscally feasible. Give an example of an engineering project that is fiscally feasible, but not economically feasible.

9.   From your local newspaper, find an example of an engineering project that was not implemented because it was not socially, politically, or environmentally feasible.

10.   For your answer in Problem 9, how would you change the project to make it feasible?

11.   Talk with an engineer in government service (e.g., a town, city, or county engineer) about the difference between economic and fiscal feasibility. Illustrate the difference with an example from your community.

12   Two towns are separated by a river and wish to exchange goods. List several alternative solutions to this problem. Perform a feasibility assessment and rank the alternatives according to their feasibility. (Be sure to include all types of feasibility.) Recommend a solution to the problem.

13.   Make a list of the professions that are licensed by your state. What do the professions have in common? Which licenses are in technical fields?

14.   Which agency in your state licenses engineers? (Try searching the Internet for your state name and the phrase "professional engineer.") How many engineers are licensed in your state?

15.   How do engineers in your area participate in public service?

3

Project Management

This chapter is devoted to the subject of project management. As a student of engineering, you may ask, "Why is this topic so important?" The answer lies in the nature of design problems. Design problems are inherently open ended; the more open ended the task, the greater the need for a management infrastructure to ensure that elements of the project ultimately fit together. Accomplishing this goal requires that all teams and team members work together with a common strategy. Sometimes, managing a project requires only the most basic application of common sense: get things done on time, hold regular meetings to discuss progress, write things down so you don't forget them. At other times, a more formal structure is required; this formal structure often relies on time-tested methods of project management. A good engineer must know how to work within the framework of a team, keep a project on track, maintain good documentation, address legal issues, and work within a well-defined management plan. This chapter introduces several project management skills that are essential elements of engineering design.

SECTIONS

OBJECTIVES

In this chapter, you will learn about:

- The importance of project management in ensuring design success
- Teamwork as an essential element of engineering design
- How engineers determine the tasks that will lead to a finished product
- Scheduling and managing design tasks
- The role of the project manager
- How members of a design team interact
- Documentation and its vital role in the design process
- Legal issues and their relevance to the design engineer

From *Design Concepts for Engineers,* Third Edition, Mark N. Horenstein. Copyright © 2005 by Pearson Education, Inc. Published by Prentice Hall, Inc. All rights reserved.

1   WORKING IN TEAMS

The spirit of rugged individualism is pervasive in society, persisting as a theme in books, movies, and television. The image of a lone hero striving for truth and justice against insurmountable odds appeals to our sense of adventure and daring. Our pioneering spirit dreams of becoming the sole entrepreneur who endures economic hardship to change the face of technology, or perhaps the head of a startup company that single-handedly bests Microsoft or Intel. Yet, in real life, engineers seldom work alone. Most engineering problems are interdisciplinary, and true progress requires cooperative teamwork and the contributions of many individuals. This concept is easy to understand in the context of designing large structures, such as bridges, airports, skyscrapers, or oil refineries. It would be unimaginable to even approach such large tasks without a well-defined hierarchy of managers, job directors, engineers, and craftspeople. Similarly, the great engineering accomplishments in space exploration, such as the Apollo moon landing, the International Space Station, the Hubble space telescope, and the Mars Exploration Rover required hundreds (in some cases thousands) of engineers working with teams of physicists, chemists, astronomers, material scientists, medical specialists, mathematicians, and project managers. Teamwork is also critical to the design of small but complicated devices such as medical prostheses, copy machines, children's mechanical toys, kitchen appliances, and cellular telephones. These devices (not an exhaustive list) cannot be designed by one person alone.

Teamwork is an important skill, and you must master it if you are to be a good engineer. Working in a team, such as the one depicted in Figure 1, requires that you

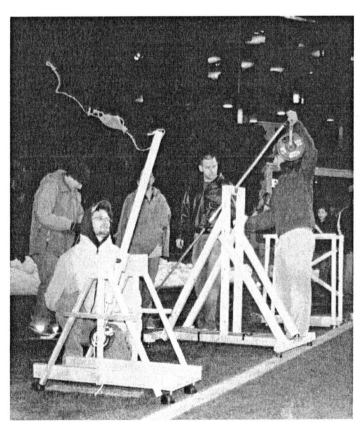

Figure 1.   Design team works on the prototype of a Trebuchet catapult. (Photo courtesy of the Daily Free Press.)

speak clearly, write effectively, and have the ability to assimilate another person's point of view. All members of a team must understand how their tasks relate to the responsibilities of the team as a whole.

When addressing a design problem, dealing with the technical issues is only half the story. Determining how people and their time will be managed is just as important. By properly assigning tasks to the right people and ensuring that they work together cooperatively, the success of the project can be ensured. In the sections that follow, we address some of the major issues related to people management.

1.1   Building an Effective Team

An effective team is one that works well together. It functions at its maximum potential and thrives on a symbiosis of the special capabilities of its individual members. One key characteristic of an effective team is a good supportive attitude among fellow teammates. Team morale and a sense of professionalism can be enhanced if team members agree on some basic rules of behavior. The following set of guidelines illustrates one possible approach to building an effective design team.

1. *Agree Upon Goals.*   The members of your team should agree upon the goals of the project. This consensus is not as easily achieved as you might think. One teammate may want to solve the problem using a traditional, time-tested approach, while another may want to attempt a far-out, esoteric path to success. Define a realistic set of goals at the outset. If the approach you choose brings surprises, you can always redefine your goals midway through the project.

2. *Define Clear Roles.*   Each team member should be assigned a specific function within the team. The responsibilities of each individual should be defined *before* project work begins. Individual roles need not be mutually exclusive, but they should be defined so that all aspects of the design problem fall within the jurisdiction of at least one person. In that way, no task will "fall between the cracks" during the design effort.

3. *Define Procedures.*   You and your teammates should agree on a set of procedures for getting things done. Everything should follow a predetermined procedure, including documentation; the ordering of parts; prototype construction; and communicating with professors, clients, and customers. In that way, misunderstandings about conduct can be greatly reduced.

4. *Develop Good Interpersonal Relationships.*   You must learn to work with everyone on your team, even with those individuals whom you may personally dislike. In the real world, a client will not care about any conflicts that occur behind the scenes. Engineering professionalism demands that you rise above personality clashes and concentrate on the job at hand. Be nice. Be professional. Forbid name calling, accusations, or assigning fault to team members.

5. *Define Leadership Roles.*   Some teams work best when a single person emerges as the chosen leader. Others work better by consensus using distributed leadership or even no leadership at all. Regardless of your team's style, make sure that leadership hierarchy is clearly defined and agreed upon at the start of the project.

It's impossible to get along with all people all the time. When you work closely with other individuals, personal conflicts are inevitable. At times, these disagreements occur because one team member has failed to meet assigned responsibilities. At other times, the conflict arises from fundamental differences in personal outlook or priorities. However complicated your team relationships may become, remember that your customer does not care about them. Your customer is interested in receiving a well-designed product that reflects your best engineering abilities. It's up to you to resolve team conflicts internally. This resolution may mean that some team members will do more work than others, even if they will not be rewarded for their extra efforts. A good leader understands this trade-off and devises a plan to work around an errant teammate. Such situations may seem frustrating and unfair, but they happen in the real world all the time. Learning how to deal with them as a student is part of your engineering education.

PRACTICE!

Define the roles, goals, and procedures that might apply to the following.

1. The design and construction of an eight-lane highway system under a major metropolitan city (*www.bigdig.com*).
2. A team of software engineers developing an auction website (*www.ebay.com*).
3. A team of electrical and mechanical engineers developing a radio-controlled robot (*www.usfirst.org*).
4. A team of biomedical engineers developing an artificial heart for mechanical implantation inside human subjects (*www.abiomed.com*).
5. A software system for scheduling production in a "just in time" textile factory that fulfills customer orders as they arrive (*www.linq.com*).
6. The design and construction of the Mars Exploration Rover (*origin.mars5.jpl.nasa.gov*).
7. An oil pipeline from Prudhoe Bay to Valdez, Alaska (*www.alyeska-pipe.com*).
8. A package tracking system for an air/ground shipping company (*www.fedex.com*).
9. A system for compiling, printing, and distributing a daily national newspaper (*www.usatoday.com*).
10. The design of a mineral extraction plant that produces copper, uranium, gold, and silver (*www.wmc.com*).
11. An oil refinery that must produce a variety of products, including gasoline, diesel, and home heating oil.
12. A machine to selectively apply pesticides to an agricultural area only where parasites have been detected by distributed sensors.
13. A system for monitoring the energy flow and power production in a multi-plant electric power generation system.
14. A system for allowing an expert surgeon to conduct an operation via remote control from a distant location.
15. The design and construction of a portable air conditioning system for roadside tent camping.
16. The design of a command center for communicating with football players wearing individual earpieces.

17. The design of a food court in a shopping mall.
18. The design of a transportation system consisting of autonomous (driver-free) subway trains.
19. The development of an order fulfillment system for a pizza restaurant.
20. The design of an agricultural management system for a large farm collective.

1.2   Organizational Chart

When engineers work on a team-oriented project, they often establish some hierarchy among individuals. It would be nice if an engineering team could always function as a simple group of colleagues, but inevitably some team members will be burdened more than others unless everyone's responsibilities are clearly spelled out. Likewise, it will be easy for some tasks to fall between the cracks if roles and responsibilities are not understood by all. One vehicle for specifying the management structure of a team is called the *organizational chart*. An organizational chart indicates who is responsible for each aspect of an engineering project. It also describes the hierarchy and reporting structure of the team. Figure 2 illustrates a simple organizational chart that might be used by students working on a design project for an engineering class. The objective of this particular project is to design a heart rate monitor for a professor doing research in cardiac defibrillation. Cadence acts as the team leader, and she, in turn, reports to the course teaching assistant for leadership and guidance. In the corporate world, where the structuring of workers and bosses can become complex, organizational charts are essential because each employee must understand the entire responsibility chain beginning with upper management. Note that organizational charts are used by all sorts of organizations, not just engineering firms. Figure 3, for example, provides an abbreviated description of the organization of the National Aeronautics and Space Administration (NASA). The actual NASA organization chart is more complex than the one shown in Figure 3.

1.3   The Job Description

When you work for an engineering company (or any company, for that matter), your responsibilities are spelled out in a document called your *job description*. A job description

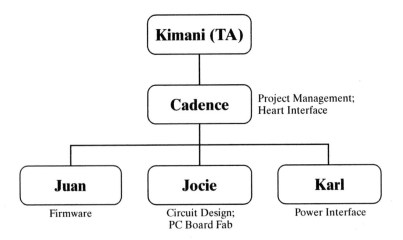

Figure 2.   Team organizational chart for heart defibrilator project.

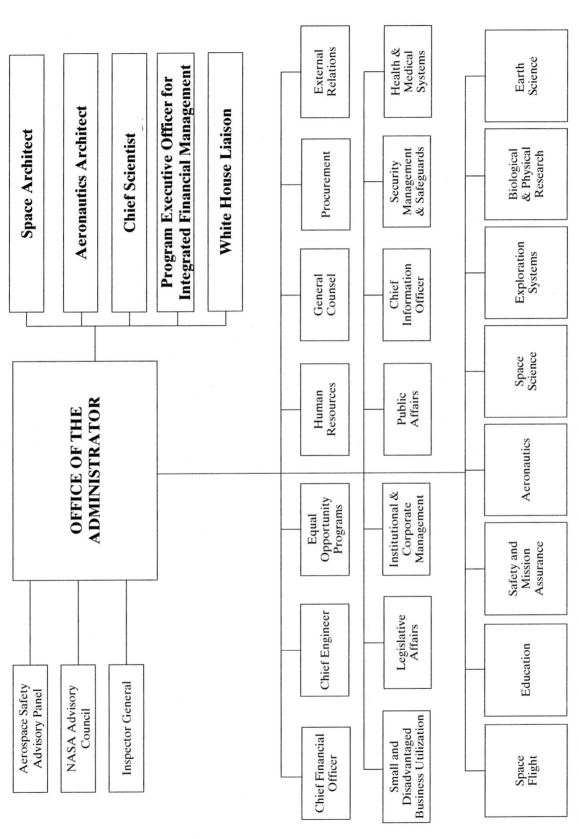

Figure 3. Abbreviated organizational chart for the National Aeronautics and Space Administration (NASA).

can be as informal as a simple letter of employment, or it can be a detailed, multi-page document. In general, the larger the company and the more complex the organizational chart, the more detailed the job description for each person. Smaller companies may have more loosely defined job descriptions because fewer people are available to handle all the tasks required to keep the company running. A job description is tied to the work to be performed and not to any specific individual who may hold the job at any particular time. Job descriptions become most prominent when a job is vacant and is subsequently advertised.

A typical formal job description might contain the following information:

- Job title
- Grade level (defines the salary range of the job)
- Immediate supervisor (specified as another job position, not a named individual)
- List of responsibilities

Note that job descriptions often form the basis of employment postings as well. One example of a specific engineering job description might read as follows:

Photonics Engineer, Photonics Center, SG 74

Tracking Code 1743/G274

Job Description

Develop and manage the Photonics Center's new Integrated Optics Laboratory, consisting of an integration/packaging facility. Coordinate new equipment purchases, installation, and commissioning for the laboratory. Collaborate with Photonics Center staff and partner companies to create processes and manage workflow of the lab. Train interns, Photonics Center staff, and partner companies to use the equipment in the lab, and supervise all equipment use. Recommend future capital equipment investments for the lab. Responsible for the maintenance of the lab: order supplies, establish and enforce policies and procedures, and maintain and calibrate equipment.

Required Skills

Master of science or equivalent in engineering (EE, ME, or Optical) and four to six years of experience with hybrid integration processes and packaging equipment. Excellent interpersonal skills with the ability to work with a variety of individuals.

1.4   Team Contact List

As obvious as it may seem, it's important to maintain a contact list for all personnel working on a particular project. One team member (or a staff person if one exists) should have the responsibility of maintaining the list. It should contain e-mail addresses and telephone numbers for everyone on the team, as well as home or cell phone numbers and instructions for when it's permissible to call outside of working hours. If resources permit, it's a good idea to maintain the list as a web page so that it is easily updated and constrained to a *single*, accurate list. Password protection may be needed in some situations.

1.5   Team Meetings

It's important for an engineering design team to meet regularly to review project status, design issues, and problem resolution. Frequency is entirely up to the team, but it is usually decided by the team leader. Meeting once per week seems to be the norm in many engineering organizations, including college design courses. Others may choose to meet only when deemed necessary (called meeting "on demand"), while other projects may require daily meetings. However often your team meets, it will be important to impose some type of structure so that meetings do not degrade into free-for-all chaos. Although a preset agenda is always helpful, setting the tone for the meeting is the responsibility of the team leader. This task can be particularly difficult in a course situation where the team is composed of otherwise equal peers. Even in company settings, personality differences between employees can get in the way of team cooperation and progress. Learning to deal with these situations in college will help you prepare for the job market. It is an important component of your engineering education.

1.6   Working with Other Teams in the Organization

More often than not, a complex design effort will involve more than one team. Assigning multiple teams to a project is common practice in companies that manufacture products for sale. The classic division of labor, still used in many companies, divides responsibilities into the broad areas of research, development, manufacturing, and marketing. The *research team* conducts fundamental studies that seek to probe new forefronts of knowledge relating to the company's core expertise. The *development team*, often comprised of different individuals, is assigned the task of transforming fundamental discoveries into product concepts that culminate in working prototypes. The *manufacturing team* must take the prototype and develop a method for mass producing the product in a cost effective and profitable way. The *marketing team*, which often contains engineers who understand how the product works, has the job of seeking and securing customers.

Traditional thinking in project management asks these four teams to interact serially, with each one passing its work "over the wall" to the next group down the chain of command. In such a scenario, Research thinks up the ideas, Development reduces them to practice, Manufacturing determines how to make the product in quantity, and Marketing seeks out new customers. Traditionally, the only feedback in the loop might be from Marketing back to Research, wherein the former communicates customers' needs to the latter. For long-term reference, teams typically operate as separate entities, with each holding on to its own set of priorities and rivalries. Often these rivalries bog down the design process and greatly increase the time span from concept to finished product.

More modern project management philosophies recognize the importance of continuous interaction between the various components of a company's organizational chart. The most successful companies are those in which the needs and priorities of each team are considered from the start and given appropriate weight when decisions are made. In such an interactive team environment, for example, Development might not be given sole authority to specify materials and dimensions of a product. Rather, manufacturing will ask that options be limited to pre-existing processes that can be enacted without requiring expensive new tooling. Marketing may insist that the design incorporate ergonomic features that will allow the product to fare well against a competitor's product. Research may seek the assistance of Development and Manufacturing to decide which projects to address, and Development may seek the help of Marketing to assess customer needs. Manufacturing may collaborate with Development to adopt rapid prototyping methods.

In some companies, the classic team divisions described above may not have distinct boundaries at all. Research, Development, and Manufacturing may be the responsibilities of one blended group of individuals. This approach has found success, for example, in the Saturn Corporation, a subsidiary of General Motors. Their team philosophy and work unit structure are summarized in the abridged diagram of Figure 4. The structure of Saturn is based on "work units" and "modules." Work units are responsible for the primary tasks related to automobile production. Modules are groups of work units that perform similar types of labor. Both work units and modules are responsible for all decisions made within the circle; each circle has an elected representative on the next highest order circle. When first introduced, this self-directed, team-integrated ap-

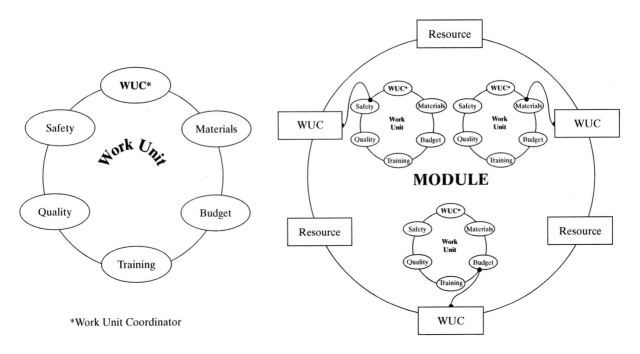

Figure 4.   Work unit and module organizational structure for the Saturn automobile manufacturing company.

proach to project management was unique to the U.S. auto industry and still stands out today as a refreshing way to approach large-scale endeavors.

When confronted with the classic, compartmentalized approach to product design, it's important for engineers to avoid rivalries and "turf wars." Remember that ultimate success requires the symbiotic cooperation of all teams involved in the design process. While the various team structures may occupy distinct branches of the company's organizational chart, as in Figure 5, it's the unseen bridges between them that will keep the company strong and lead to rapid and successful product development.

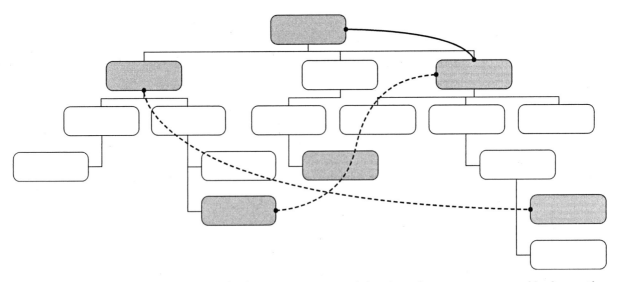

Figure 5.   The unseen bridges between branches of an organizational chart keep the company strong and lead to rapid and successful product development.

PRACTICE!

1. Devise an organizational chart and time line for building a special effects apparatus for a drama production at your college or university.

2. A large, nonprofit organization is planning a walk-a-thon in which 3,000 people will walk 60 miles in 3 days and will sleep in tent camps each night. Develop an organizational chart for all persons involved in planning and implementing this event.

3. A student organization is planning to enter the Mini Baja vehicle competition for students sponsored by the Society of Automotive Engineers (*students.sae.org*). Develop an organizational chart that will guide the team through the design and construction of a competition vehicle.

4. Imagine that you work for a company that makes genetically engineered laboratory mice. Define an organizational chart for such a company.

5. Even sports teams have organizational charts. Choose your favorite professional or college sports team and draw its organizational chart.

6. Your college or university has an administrative organizational structure. Learn about this structure and draw an organizational chart, from the President down to the level of either department heads or deans.

7. Draw the organizational chart for a major civil engineering company of your choice.

8. Write the job description for an engineer assigned to a team designing a plastics processing plant.

9. Write the job description for someone who works for a web-based hardware store.

10. Write the job description for an engineer who has just joined a company that makes underwater hydrophones. The company has a total of ten employees.

11. Write the job description for an engineer who works for a large defense contractor that makes military aircraft.

12. Write the job description for an engineer who works for a company that makes pipeline valves.

13. Write the job description for an engineer who works for a company and helps them optimize factory floor operations for a cosmetics manufacturer.

14. Suppose you want to hire an industrial engineer for a company that makes large kitchen appliances. Write an advertisement that you might put on a nationally circulated job site (e.g., *www.monster.com*).

15. Suppose that you want to hire a petroleum engineer to oversee the operations of a refinery construction project. Write the advertisement that you might submit to a national trade magazine.

2   MANAGING TASKS: KEEPING THE PROJECT ON TRACK

Time management is critical to the success of any engineering project. In a perfect world, engineers would have as much time as needed to work on all aspects of a project; in the real world, however, deadlines have a nasty habit of creating pressure to get the product out the door. Demands for demonstrations of progress, prototype tests, something for "sales and marketing to show," and the pressures of corporate life require that an engineer develop a sense of how much time will be needed for each aspect of product development.

Even the simplest design project requires time management. A systematic approach to design tasks is always preferable to a random, hit-or-miss approach. While the subject of time management can (and does) occupy the contents of entire books, several time management tools form a basic set that should be understood by all engineers.

2.1   Checklist

A simple checklist enables the monitoring of engineering tasks related to a specific design project. It differs very little from the "to-do" list that you might compile for a set of weekend chores. The tasks enumerated on an engineering checklist need not be completed in any particular order. An example of a simple checklist that might apply to the design of an entry for an egg-drop contest is shown in Figure 6.

2.2   Time Line

A *time line* is a valuable tool for keeping a project on schedule. A time line is similar to a checklist, but its various tasks are expected to be completed sequentially by specified milestone dates. The time line is very appropriate when the entire team works in unison, with the differentiation of tasks occurring serially in time. If a given task is in danger of not being completed before its designated milestone date, it's the job of the project manager to allocate more time, and overtime if necessary, so that the task can be completed on schedule. A typical time line (in this case, one prepared by students designing a vehicle for a class design project) is shown in Figure 7.

2.3   Gantt Chart

When a project is complex and involves many people, a simple time line may be inadequate for managing all aspects of the project. Similarly, if the project's various tasks are interdependent, so that the completion of one phase depends on the success of several others, the *Gantt Chart* of Fig. 8 may be a more appropriate time-management tool. The Gantt chart is simply a two-dimensional plot in which the horizontal axis reflects time measured in days, weeks, or months, and the vertical axis represents either the tasks to be completed or the individuals responsible for those tasks. Unlike the checklist, which simply enumerates the tasks to be completed, and the one-dimensional time line, which merely displays sequential time allocations for each phase of the project, the Gantt chart shows how much time is allotted to multiple tasks performed in parallel. It also provides for overlapping time periods that help indicate the interdependency between the various

---

Egg Drop To Do List

- Calculate force in G's
- Design egg-holder sling
- Construct prototype of outer box
- Search for vendor of lightweight foam
- Glue together straw sections
- Buy more eggs

Figure 6.   Checklist for the design of an entry for an egg-drop contest.

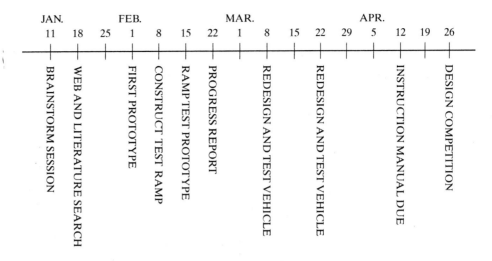

Figure 7. Time line for tasks pertaining to a vehicle design competition.

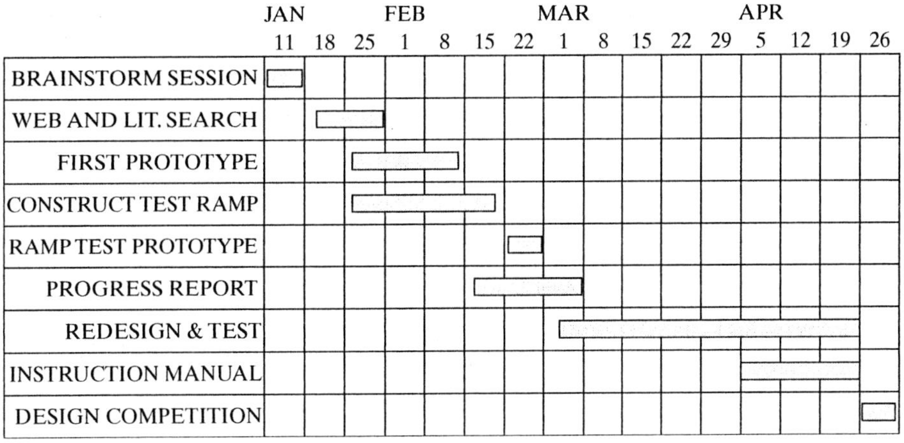

Figure 8. A Gantt chart provides a more comprehensive, two-dimensional method of scheduling the tasks shown in Figure 7.

aspects of the project. When a particular task has been completed, it can be shaded on the Gantt chart, so that the status of the project can be determined at a glance.

2.4   PERT Chart

The Project Evaluation and Review Technique (PERT) was first proposed by the United States Navy and developed by the consulting firm of Booz, Allen, and Hamilton in 1958. Its purpose at the time was to coordinate the activities of over 10,000 separate subcontractors involved in the Polaris missile development program. The PERT method is very similar to the *critical path method* (CPM), and these terms are essentially interchangeable. The PERT technique is fundamentally a method for prioritizing and scheduling complex, interrelated activities. The PERT chart helps to identify the most time-critical events in the design process.

The essence of the technique is embodied in a graphical network called the *PERT chart*, depicted in generic form in Figure 9. The PERT chart consists of numbered mile-

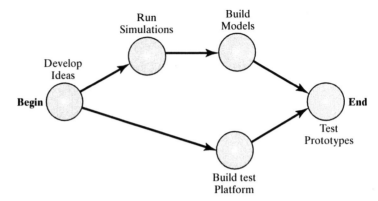

Figure 9. The generic form of a PERT chart. The circles represent milestone points, and each arrow represents a task leading up to a node. Each task is allocated a completion time.

stone circles and pathway branches. Each branch is labeled by a time interval allocated to the completion of the task to which the branch leads. Branches are labeled in appropriate time units (e.g., days, weeks, or months). Like the Gantt chart, the PERT chart summarizes the time allocated for each task and notes task completion milestones. Unlike the Gantt chart, however, the PERT chart also shows the way in which the tasks depend on one another. This interdependency is indicated by the branch lines that connect the task-completion circles of the chart.

A PERT chart must have a starting point, or *node*, and a single ending milestone (the last node to which all pathways must lead). As in the Gantt chart, time progresses from left to right. The time allocated for the pathway between any two milestone nodes will be equal to the sum of the times allocated for each task in the pathway. In Figure 10, for ex-

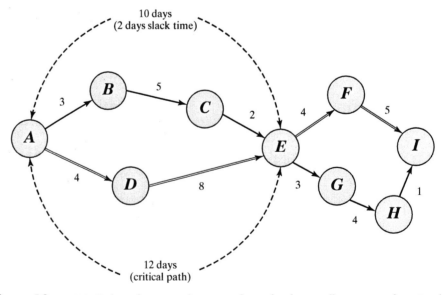

Figure 10. A PERT chart showing milestone nodes and task time allocations in days. On this chart, critical pathways are shown as double lines.

ample, the sequence of tasks leading from milestone A to milestone C is allocated a total of 3 + 5 = 8 days.

As each task depicted on a PERT chart is completed, the project manager checks it off on the chart. The manager can thus monitor the progress of the entire project and be alerted to any possible path delays. Some project managers prefer the PERT chart over the Gantt chart because it clearly illustrates task dependencies. A PERT chart, however, can be much more difficult to interpret, especially on complex projects. Alternatively, some project managers may choose to use both techniques.

When compiling a PERT chart for project management, it's possible (and often preferable) for the sum of branch times over one pathway to be less than the sum of times over a parallel pathway. The excess, called *slack time,* can be used to compensate for the inevitable delays that will accompany the design process. If the delay experienced along the way does not exceed the slack time of the pathway, the entire project will still be on track. Of most interest, therefore, are so-called *critical pathways.* The latter are those branches containing zero slack time. Any delays in a critical pathway can jeopardize the time flow of the entire project and should be monitored carefully. The pathway from node A to node E (via node D) in Figure 10, for example, is a critical pathway.

EXAMPLE 1: MANAGING A BUILDING CONSTRUC- TION PROJECT	The major steps required to erect a framed house (somewhat simplified in this case) are summarized by the PERT chart of Figure 11. Such a chart might typically be used by a general contractor who must hire many different subcontractors to complete various aspects of the project. Node 0 denotes the starting point of construction. Before anything else can transpire, the building site must be excavated so that the foundation can be framed, as well as molded and poured. In Figure 11, the former is allocated 4 days, and the latter 2 days. After the foundation has been poured and cured, the external skeleton or frame of the building can be erected. This frame will form the support structure for all the exterior walls of the building, as well as any interior walls specified by the architect. This task has been allocated a total of 5 days.

After the building frame has been completed, the major tasks continue over parallel pathways. The framing for the roof must be completed, followed by the weather protection (in this case, standard roofing shingles). These tasks have been allocated 2 and 3 days, respectively, leaving considerable slack time compared to the other paths. Similarly, following arrival at node 3, work begins in parallel on the installation of the building's exterior walls. The rough plumbing and electrical tasks, to be described in the next paragraph, require that the interior walls remain open, but not the exterior walls.

In parallel with the finishing of the roof and outside walls, the installation of the rough plumbing is now initiated. Rough plumbing refers to the piping—both supply and waste—that must lie within the walls of the structure. Obviously, this task must be completed before the interior walls themselves can be installed. Yet another parallel pathway begins after node 3, consisting of the rough electrical wiring. The latter must also be completed before the interior walls can go up. The rough plumbing and wiring tasks are allocated 3 and 5 days, respectively.

Following the completion of the rough work, the interior walls can now be installed (2 days). Once the interior walls have been completed, the plumbing and electrical crews can return to install fixtures; afterwards, the interior walls may be painted. Usually, this task is performed after the electrical and plumbing work are finished, because the latter tasks might cause workers to mar the finished paintwork. Some contractors, however,

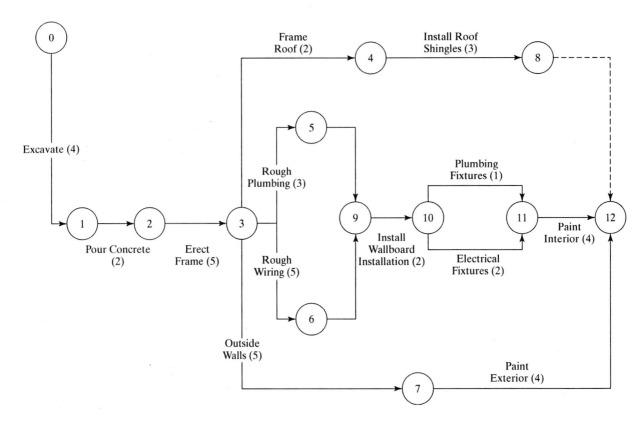

Figure 11. PERT chart that describes the principal steps involved in building a house.

prefer to paint before fixture installation, because the resulting paint job is much cleaner around the edges of the plumbing and electrical fixtures.

The completion of the roof, interior paint, and exterior paint on the PERT chart all arrive at the last node on the diagram (node 12), signifying the completion of the job. The house may now be occupied. The critical pathway in this PERT chart consists of the following tasks, beginning at node 3: rough electrical wiring, wallboard installation, wiring completion, and interior painting. These tasks require a total of $5 + 2 + 2 + 4 = 13$ days. Any delays over this critical pathway will lead to a delay in occupancy of the house.

EXAMPLE 2: MANAGING A SOFTWARE PROJECT

Figure 12 shows a PERT chart used by a development team tasked with the design of a digital hardware device running on firmware (machine-level, binary software). The unit, once manufactured and ready for sale, is to be shipped with help files on a CD ROM. Once the specifications have been set, the PERT chart divides into three distinct pathways—one related to hardware, one to the firmware, and one to the documentation. The critical pathway in this project runs from node 1 to node 2, and then via nodes 3, 5, 6, 8, and 7 to the final node 11, for a total time allocation of $2 + 4 + 2 + 3 + 4 + 1 + 4 = 20$ weeks.

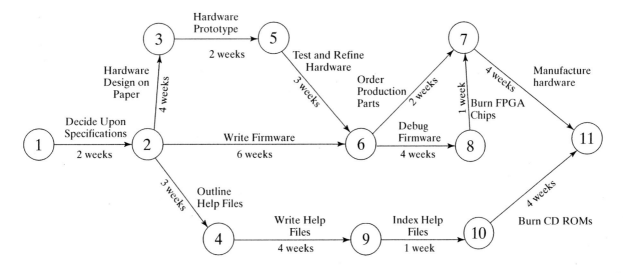

<table>
<tr><td>1</td><td>Start project</td><td>5</td><td>Prototype built</td><td>9</td><td>Help files completed</td></tr>
<tr><td>2</td><td>All specifications finalized</td><td>6</td><td>Hardware functional</td><td>10</td><td>Help files indexed</td></tr>
<tr><td>3</td><td>Hardware design on paper</td><td>7</td><td>Ready for fabrication</td><td>11</td><td>Project complete</td></tr>
<tr><td>4</td><td>Outline of help files completed</td><td>8</td><td>Firmware ready to integrate with hardware</td><td></td><td></td></tr>
</table>

Figure 12. PERT chart that describes the development of a digital hardware device running firmware and shipped with help files on CD ROM.

PROFESSIONAL SUCCESS: THE LAWS OF TIME ESTIMATION

How long will it take to perform a particular design task? How much time should you allocate to each segment of a PERT chart or Gantt chart? The following three Laws of Time Estimation will help you to determine the time required for a given design task:

1. Everything takes longer than expected.

2. If you've done the same task before on a different project, estimate the amount of time required to finish the task. The actual amount of time required will be about twice as long. Something will always be different in the current project.

3. If you've worked on something *similar* before, estimate the amount of time required to finish the task. The actual amount of time required will be about five times as long.

4. If you've *never* worked on something similar before, estimate the amount of time required to finish the task. The actual amount of time required will be the next highest time unit. For example, something estimated to take an hour will really take a day; something estimated to take a day will take a week, etc.

---

3   DOCUMENTATION: THE KEY TO PROJECT SUCCESS

Engineering design is never performed in isolation. Even the simplest of projects involves a designer and an end user. More often, a design effort involves considerably more individuals who worry about many facets of the product. Additionally, the uses of the product may involve an entire segment of the population. The design of an automobile, for example, encompasses the work of mechanical, electrical, industrial, materials, and safety engineers, and the entire driving public constitutes the group of end users. A consumer products company involved in the production of cellular telephones will bring together computer, systems, electrical, mechanical, and manufacturing engineers in a multidisciplinary team that may include people from sales and marketing. A public works management corporation, tasked with designing a waste water treatment facility, might solicit the help of civil, chemical, mechanical, and environmental engineers, along with the city planners and systems engineers. Complex engineering projects are successful only if everyone on the design team communicates with everyone else at all phases of the design effort.

One way in which engineers communicate with each other is through careful recordkeeping. Good documentation is essential when you work as a member of a design team. As a practicing engineer, it will be your responsibility to maintain a comprehensive collection of design concepts, sketches, detailed drawings, test results, redesigns, reports, and schematics—whatever records are pertinent to the project. This *documentation trail* will serve as a tool for passing information on to team members who may need to repeat or verify your work. The documentation trail is critical to those who will manufacture your product from a prototype, apply for patents based on your inventions, or even take over your job if you are promoted or move to another company. Written records are also a good way to communicate with yourself. Many an engineer has been unable to reproduce design accomplishments due to sloppy recordkeeping. Indeed, one of the marks of a professional engineer is the discipline needed to keep organized, neat, up-to-date records. Documentation should never be performed as an afterthought. If a project is dropped by one team member, the state of documentation should always be such that another team member can resume the project without delay. As a student of engineering, you should learn the art of recordkeeping and develop good documentation habits early in your career. Most companies, laboratories, and other technical firms require their employees to keep records that document the results of engineering efforts.

3.1   Paper versus Electronic Documentation

Today, just about every piece of engineering documentation, with the exception of the engineer's logbook (described in the next section), is produced on a computer. Examples of documents destined for preservation include text documents, spreadsheets, computer codes, schematics, drawings, design layouts, and simulated test results. Most engineers prefer to store information electronically so that it can be viewed onscreen and printed only as needed. Others prefer to preserve documentation by printing everything on paper and storing the documents in a physical file cabinet. Whichever method you choose, take heed of the following important guidelines:

- *Organize your information.* It's important to store documentation in an organized and logical manner. If the project is small, its documentation should be stored in a single folder (paper or electronic). Larger projects may require a group of folders, each relating to different aspects of the project. The folders should be labeled and dated with informative titles (such as "Propulsion System for XYZ Project") and kept in a place that will be easy to find in the future.

- *Back up your information.* It's equally important to store a duplicate copy of all documentation. This guideline applies to written as well as electronic information. Fire, flood, theft, misplacement, the all-too-common disk crash, and the unfortunate havoc wreaked by malicious computer viruses can lead to the loss of a project's entire documentation trail. Archival storage of records in a different physical location will help to keep a project on track should one of these catastrophes occur.

3.2   The Engineer's Logbook (Notebook)

One important vehicle for recordkeeping is the *engineer's logbook*, sometimes called the *engineer's notebook*. A well-maintained logbook serves as a permanent record that includes all ideas, calculations, innovations, and test results that emerge from the design effort. When engineers work in a team, each member keeps a separate logbook reflecting that individual's assigned tasks. When the project is brought to completion, the logbooks of all team members are placed in an archive and remain the property of the company. An engineering notebook thus serves as an archival record of new ideas and engineering research achievements *whether or not they lead to commercial use*. A complete logbook serves as evidence of inventorship and establishes the date of conception and "reduction to practice" of a new idea. It shows that the inventor (you!) has used diligence in advancing the invention to completion. In this respect, the engineer's logbook is more than just a simple lab notebook. It serves as a valuable document that has legal implications. When you work as an engineer, you have a professional responsibility to your employer, your colleagues, and to the integrity of your job to keep a good logbook.

The notebook shown in Figure 13 is typical of many used in industry, government labs, and research institutions. It has permanently bound and numbered pages, a cardboard cover, and quadrille lines that form a coarse grid pattern. A label fixed to the front cover uniquely identifies the notebook and its contents. The company, laboratory, or project name is printed at the top, and the notebook is assigned a unique number by the user. In some large institutions, a central office may assign notebook numbers to its employees when the notebook is issued.

Figure 13.   Cover and label of a typical engineer's logbook.

The techniques for logbook use differ from those used in some science and introductory engineering classes where instructors encourage students to write things down first on loose scratch paper and then recopy relevant items into a neat notebook. This procedure is bad practice for the design engineer. Although notebooks prepared in this way are easier for instructors to grade, the finished notebook seldom resembles a running record of what actually occurred in the laboratory; it is not especially useful for engineering design projects. Design is as much a *process* as it is a final product, and the act of recording ideas as they emerge and events as they happen helps engineers to think and be creative. Also, keeping a record of what did *not* work is just as important as recording what did work; this practice ensures that mistakes will not be repeated in the future.

3.3   Logbook Format

An engineering logbook should be used as a design tool. Enter everything into your logbook, no matter how seemingly irrelevant. Write down ideas as you think of them, even if you have no immediate plans to pursue them. Keep an ongoing record of successes and failures. Record the results of every test—mechanical, structural, electrical, system, flight, flow, pressure, performance—even if the results may not be used in the final design. Stop to write things down. This habit will require discipline but will always be worth the effort. Important information, including some you might otherwise have forgotten, will be in your logbook and will be preserved for a time when you may need it.

Any logbook format that meets your needs and those of your team is suitable, as long as it forms a permanent record of your contributions to the design project. Ban loose paper from the laboratory. It is easily lost, misfiled, or damaged. Resist the temptation to reach for loose paper when you need to do a calculation. Instead of grabbing that pad to draw a sketch or discuss an idea, take the time to open your logbook. You'll be glad you did when those numbers and sketches you need are readily available. Unbound paper used for anything other than doodling has no place in an engineering laboratory.

3.4   Using Your Engineer's Logbook

As chief author of your logbook, you have the freedom to set your own objectives for its use. The following guidelines, however, are typical of those used by many engineers and design teams:

1.   Each person working on a project should keep a separate logbook specifically for that project. All relevant data should be entered. When the logbook is full, it should be stored in a safe place specifically designated for logbook storage. In that way, everyone will know where to find the logbook when it's needed.

2.   All ideas, calculations, experiments, tests, mechanical sketches, flowcharts, circuit diagrams, etc., related to the project should be entered into the logbook. Entries should be dated and written in ink. Pencil has a nasty habit of smudging when pages rub against each other. Any computer-generated plots, graphics, schematics, or photos printed on loose paper should be pasted or taped onto bound logbook pages. This procedure will help prevent loss of important data.

3.   Logbook entries should outline the problem addressed, tests performed, calculations made, and so forth, but subjective conclusions about the success of the tests (e.g., "I believe . . . ") should be avoided. The facts should speak for themselves.

4.   The voice of the logbook should speak to a third-party reader. Assume that your logbook will be read by teammates, your boss, or perhaps someone from marketing.

5. In settings where intellectual property is at stake, the concluding page of each session should be dated and, where appropriate, signed. This practice eliminates all ambiguity with regard to dates of invention and disclosure. Important entries that signify key events in the design process should be periodically and routinely witnessed by at least one other person, and preferably two. Witnesses should endorse and date the relevant pages with the words, "witnessed and understood."

6. Logbook pages should not be left blank. If a portion of a page would otherwise be left blank, a vertical or slanted line should be drawn through it. Pages should be numbered consecutively and not be torn out. These measures are necessary should your logbook ever become part of a legal proceeding where the integrity of the information comes into question. Do not make changes using correction fluid. Cross out instead. This precaution will prevent you from creating obscure or questionable entries should your logbook be entered as legal evidence in patent or liability actions. Although this precaution probably won't be relevant to logbooks you keep for college design courses, it's a good idea to begin following it now so that the procedure becomes a career habit.

Witnessed and understood
Marigold White 10/27/05
Eli Whitney 10/27/05

EXAMPLE 3: AN ENGINEER'S LOGBOOK

The following example illustrates proper use of an engineering logbook. Imagine that the logbook pages shown describe your team's design for a telescoping flag for a motorized wheelchair. The intent is to increase visibility when the user operates the wheelchair in city streets. The first page, Figure 14, shows your preliminary sketch of a basic concept based on the use of a commercially available telescoping car radio antenna. The second page, Figure 15, contains some calculations that estimate the battery drain as the flag is raised and lowered. The entries on the third page, Figure 16, show a list of parts and materials that your team decides to purchase. These parts will enable you to build a prototype and test your system's ability to raise and lower the flag on demand.

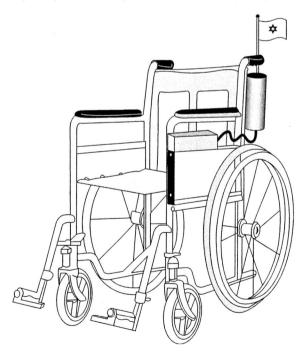

Figure 14.   Preliminary logbook sketch for a telescoping wheelchair flag.

Battery Energy Requirements

Measured motor current: 0.45 A $\approx \frac{1}{2}$ A

Rod Speed: (estimated) abt. 10 cm/sec

$\rightarrow$ *Motor* ON *time* = Dist/Rate = $\dfrac{121 \text{ cm}}{10 \text{ cm/sec}}$ = 12.1 sec

Here 12 seconds = $\dfrac{1}{5}$ *minute* = $\dfrac{1}{300}$ *hour*

...so each extension requires about...

0.45 A $\times$ 1 *hour* $\approx$ 1.5 $\times$ 10^{-3}A-H

A 0.3 amp-hour battery can provide about

0.3 A-H $\approx$ 200 *extensions of flag.*

Note to Mike: Good for a start

Figure 15. Calculations to show estimates of battery drain.

10/2/05

* Wheelchair Flag Project
* Parts List (other than auto car-antenna thingy)

- Nuts and bolts (#8 $\times \frac{1}{2}$" with washers)
- Machine screws (#6 $\times \frac{3}{4}$" long)
- Ubolts (4)
- Flexible pipe clamps—3" (4)
- Epoxy glue (1 tube with hardener)
- Electrical tape (1 roll)
- Solder (Can we borrow a small soldering iron? Don't need to use it much.)
- Switch (from Radio Shack)
- Wire (2 conductor; stranded)

Figure 16. List of parts and materials recorded in logbook.

3.5   Technical Reports and Memoranda

Logbooks represent only one of the methods that a design team uses to keep a good documentation trail. Engineers also communicate by writing technical reports at significant milestones of a design project. A technical report describes a particular accomplishment and perhaps provides some project history or background material as well. The report may contain theory, data, test results, calculations, design parameters, or fabrication dimensions. Technical reports form the backbone of a company's technical database. Reports are typically stored in archival format, each with its own title and catalog number. Information for technical reports is easily gathered from logbooks that are accurate and up to date. When the time comes to write a patent disclosure, journal paper, or product application note, the technical report becomes an indispensable reference tool. A technical report is also an appropriate way to explain why a particular idea did not work or was not attempted. Taking the time to write a technical report about a negative result or design failure can save considerable time should a design concept be revisited by engineers who were not present when the original project was undertaken.

Yet another way in which engineers communicate their ideas to other engineers and scientists is through the writing of formal journal articles. A journal article is appropriate when the work represents new knowledge unknown to those working in the field. While most often used to report experimental and theoretical findings, journal articles are also very frequently used to report design innovations. The structure of a typical journal paper and its relevant components are discussed in more detail in other areas of this book.

Each of the various professional organizations representing engineers worldwide publishes one or more peer-reviewed journals to which anyone can submit a manuscript for consideration. It's also very common for a paper to be authored by multiple authors, especially when the work is the result of a team effort. In addition to the journals published by professional societies, numerous other technical journals are produced by publishing companies.

Peer review is the process by which a paper is evaluated and critiqued, then either accepted or rejected for publication. The editor of the journal will typically send a submitted paper to one or more knowledgeable reviewers who will return a list of comments and questions for the author. It is common for a submitted paper to be returned at least one time to the author for revision. It's most unusual for a paper to be accepted unchanged upon its first submission. Conversely, some papers may be rejected as unsuitable for publication. This peer-review method ensures that papers appearing in the best journals are accurate, relevant, and up to date.

3.6   Schematics and Drawings

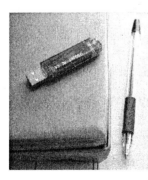

Documentation does not always appear in the form of text. Graphical records, such as drawings, circuit schematics, photographs, and plots, also become part of the documentation trail. These items typically are created with the help of software tools. If the documents are stored electronically, then all files related to a particular project should be organized in a logical hierarchy. Some engineers choose to keep all files for a project in a single file folder on the computer. Others prefer to sort files by the applications that produce them (e.g., CAD drawings in one folder, spreadsheet files in another). Other engineers like to transfer all the computer files related to a given project to a single removable disk or flash memory (USB) drive that can be stored in a physically remote, lockable cabinet. If paper is the storage medium, then graphical output should be printed on paper and kept in a folder along with other written records. Regardless of which storage method is chosen, the information related to a particular project should be carefully preserved in a format that will prevent loss. Backup in a remote physical location provides important insurance for mission-critical projects.

3.7   Software Documentation and the Role of the Engineering Notebook

Of all design endeavors, software writing is the one most prone to poor documentation. The revision loop of a software design cycle can be extremely rapid, because the typical software development tool enables a programmer to make small changes and test their effects immediately. This rapid-fire method of development is good for prototyping but invites poor documentation habits. Seldom does the software engineer find a good time to stop and document the flow of a program, because most pauses are short and change is frequent. As a result, the documentation for many software programs is added after the fact, if at all.

If you find yourself writing software, get into the habit of including documentation in your program as you go along. All software development tools provide a means for embedding comments in the program code. Add them frequently to explain why you've taken a certain approach or written a particular section of the code. Explain the meaning of object names and program variables. Your program documentation should enable other engineers on your team to completely understand and take over your sections of the code simply by reading the comment lines. Good documentation will also be invaluable should you need to modify your code at a later time. It's amazing how quickly a programmer can forget the internal logic of a program after setting it aside for only a short time.

If your program is destined for commercial sale, then good internal documentation and truly helpful "help" files are essential. Documentation included inside the program on a regular basis will easily translate into help files and an online instruction manual when the need arises. One trick used by top-notch software developers is to write the help and instruction files as the program code is developed, rather than as an afterthought. Changes to the help files can be made at the same time that changes are made in the program code. The abundance of commercial software packages with pathetic or poorly written help files or instruction manuals is testimony to generations of software engineers who have perpetuated a tendency toward poor documentation habits. If you master the skill of documenting software, your software products will be better utilized and more successful than those having poor documentation.

Although keeping engineering logbooks is less relevant to software development than to other types of engineering, logbooks can still play a special role. On the pages of your notebook, you can outline the overall structure of the program and the interconnections between its various modules. You can enter sketches of graphical user interfaces without writing actual computer code. You can similarly draw block diagrams of relational databases and make lists of the variables to be used in the software.

PROFESSIONAL SUCCESS: HOW TO KEEP GOOD RECORDS ALL THE TIME

If you want to keep a good documentation trail, get into the habit of carrying your logbook with you wherever you go. In that way, it will be available whenever you have a thought or idea that needs recording. Buy a medium-size notebook that can fit easily into your backpack. Clip a pen right inside the front cover. Be sure to write your name and contact information on the cover in case you misplace your logbook! A tiny, $3'' \times 5''$ bound notebook will do nicely. Although writing space will be limited because of the smaller size, you'll be more likely to carry it if it's not overly large.

PRACTICE!

1. Refer to the logbook calculations in Figure 15. Revise the estimate of the number of extensions if the motor requires 2.1 A.

2. Refer to the logbook calculations in Figure 15. Revise the estimate of the number of extensions if the motor requires 300 mA, and a 200 A-H battery (similar to a lead-acid car battery) is used. Rewrite the logbook page.

3. Do some Internet research and identify sources and vendors for the telescoping antenna shown in Figure 14.

4. For the flag system outlined in Figure 14, what are the advantages and disadvantages of using a separate battery for the flagpole (as opposed to tapping the primary storage battery that powers the wheelchair.) Write a logbook page that records your ideas.

5. On a simulated logbook page, outline some ideas for marketing your telescoping flag invention. Include cost estimates for its manufacture.

6. Imagine that you are one of the Wright brothers developing the first airplane. Sketch a typical logbook page from the project.

7. Research the history of the famous 20th-century American inventor Lee De-Forest. Sketch one page of a logbook that he might have kept during the time of his invention.

8. Sketch a logbook page that might have been recorded by Josephine Cochran, the inventor of the modern dishwasher.

9. Imagine what it was like to be Philo T. Farnsworth, the original inventor of the television. Sketch several logbook pages that summarize how the system works.

10. Keep a brainstorming logbook for one week. Record all ideas that come to mind regarding methods to produce a personalized air transportation device.

3.8   The Importance of Logbooks: A Case Study

This case involves a small, Massachusetts-based biomedical engineering company called Abiomed (pronounced ab-ee-oh-med). Among its other heart-related projects, Abiomed was a leading contender for the development of a self-contained, artificial human heart designed to be a permanent replacement for individuals who could otherwise stay alive only with a human heart transplant. As noted on the company website (*www.abiomed.com*), heart disease is the leading cause of death in developed countries. In the United States alone, hundreds of thousands of people could be saved each year if transplants were available, yet only about 2,000 transplantable hearts become available in any given year. Hence, the need for a permanent artificial heart is real and widespread. Doctors at Jewish Hospital in Louisville, Kentucky, installed the first Abiocor artificial heart in a human patient in July 2001.

Abiomed began its total artificial heart project in earnest in the early 1990s. The major components of the heart system, depicted in Figure 17, include the central implanted pump that connects to the subject's principal blood vessels, and a system for transferring electrical power to run the pump through the skin from a battery pack worn outside the body. One key feature of the power transfer process, the lack of wires piercing the skin, is essential for the long-term efficacy of the artificial heart, because skin perforations are prime entry points for infection and require constant medical supervision in a skilled-care facility. Rather than requiring the patients to be tethered to a console, the fully self-contained Abiomed device is designed to provide the patient some semblance of a normal, mobile, home life. The system for transferring

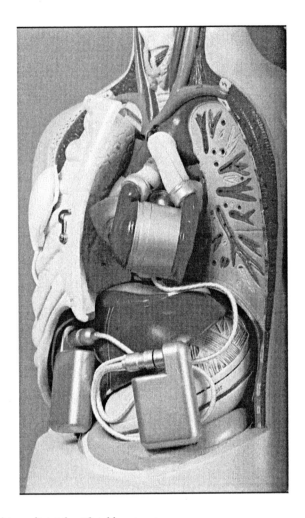

Figure 17. Abiomed's total artificial heart system.

electrical power, called the transcutaneous energy transfer device, or "TET," is essentially a pair of concentric, high-frequency magnetic coils. One is implanted under the skin, and the other is worn outside the skin. (Transcutaneous means "through the skin.") Abiomed wished to have its engineers fully focus on the daunting task of developing the heart pump itself, so it hired another biomedical engineering company, World Heart Corporation of Ottawa, Canada, to design the energy transfer module.

After about four years of effort, World Heart was still unable to produce a TET that met Abiomed's stringent technical specifications. Although World Heart claimed to be converging on a solution, Abiomed was not convinced that a satisfactory TET device was imminent. Faced with an impending critical animal test that would determine future funding of its entire heart project from the National Institutes of Health, Abiomed decided to sever its reliance on the World Heart TET. The Abiomed CEO instructed one of his engineers, Dr. Z, to develop a home-grown TET device as quickly as possible. Dr. Z was a very capable fellow, and after only four months of effort, he succeeded in designing and testing a fully working version of a TET device that met all the requirements of Abiomed's impending heart-pump test.

This development led to a lawsuit by World Heart, who claimed that Abiomed could not have developed its own TET device in the mere time span of four months without having stolen secrets and technology from World Heart. After all, World Heart claimed, its engineers had worked on the project for four years and were only just beginning to converge on a possible solution. How could the Abiomed engineer have designed a superior TET in only four months? Abiomed countered with a claim that its short path to success was due solely to the high competency of its engineer, and that, in fact, it had taken special precautions to ensure that nothing would be stolen from the previous unsuccessful World Heart design effort. The suit went to court and, in the end, Abiomed prevailed. The jury recognized that Abiomed's TET design, while performing the same basic transcutaneous energy-transfer function as the World Heart device, was completely different with regard to all details of implementation. The Abiomed device, the jury concluded, used different circuits, materials, magnetic construction, and semiconductor components.

During the trial, a key component of Abiomed's defense was the logbook kept by the engineer who designed the TET. His logbook was used to prove that Abiomed had designed its own independent version of the TET. Following the company's customary logbook policy, as well as sound engineering practice, Dr. Z had kept careful records of his TET design, having entered every design concept, schematic, circuit layout, and test result that emerged during the design process. He had even noted the various circuit configurations that had gone up in smoke on the test bench before his first working model emerged. Each page of his logbook had been dated, and each lab session involving successful tests had been signed and countersigned by another Abiomed engineer. During trial, entire pages of Dr. Z's logbook were reproduced and projected on a large screen for the jury to see. Dr. Z's logbook played a crucial role in the success of Abiomed's legal defense.

The presentation of Dr. Z's logbook in court, while critical to the outcome of the trial, did not proceed flawlessly, however. Several pages of the logbook involving work done in January 1996 had been incorrectly dated with the year 1995. Following a common mistake that many individuals make when the year changes, Dr. Z had, without thinking, hastily written the year from the previous month of December. The lawyers for World Heart were quick to seize upon this error as prima facie evidence that something was "fishy." They claimed Dr. Z had forged portions of his logbook in an attempt to present a false picture of his accomplishments. In the end, the jury was not convinced and realized that Dr. Z's error was nothing more than a common calendar mistake. Nevertheless, this seemingly small lack of attention to detail in logbook procedure put the case against Abiomed in jeopardy for a time.

PROFESSIONAL SUCCESS: DEVELOPING GOOD LOGBOOK HABITS

Most of us follow routines without thinking. When we wake up in the morning, we brush our teeth. When we eat, we instinctively reach for a clean plate. When we get into a car, we (hopefully) buckle our seatbelts automatically. An as engineer, the urge to write things down in a logbook should become as instinctive as these other common tasks. In contrast to these personal procedures for our own well being, however, we engineers are not trained from childhood to record our experiences in a notebook. Developing this instinct requires practice, but it can become part of your routine over time. When personal computers and the Internet first came into being, most people did not think very much about the novelty of e-mail. Now checking one's mail has become a daily routine for most. You developed this unnatural skill by practicing it over time. It should be the same with your engineer's logbook. Force yourself to get into the habit of using your logbook whenever you practice design. Over time, it will become as natural as brushing your teeth.

4   LEGAL ISSUES: INTELLECTUAL PROPERTY, PATENTS, AND TRADE SECRETS

It would be nice if engineers could focus solely on technical issues. After all, engineering students spend an enormous amount of time learning about fundamentals and applications, plus many technical skills. While most curricula in engineering include elements that address the social impact of engineering, including ethical, economic, and social issues, arguably the most important of these is the role that legal issues play in the design process.

The juxtaposition between legal issues and design practice falls squarely with the domain of project management. Hence, we conclude this chapter with a discussion of patent lore. The worldwide system of patents and licensing, part of the broader world known as *intellectual property,* has as its noble goal the protection of new ideas and inventions. The patent system originated as a means of encouraging innovation by preventing large companies with lots of money from gobbling up the ideas of smaller inventors and dominating the market. While well intentioned in concept, the patent system has evolved into a maze of regulations and practices that can be most perplexing to engineers uninitiated in the world of legal procedures. For this reason, most large companies employ attorneys whose job it is to navigate the company through the often bewildering world of intellectual property.

Another important arena in which legal issues intersect engineering is in the area of product liability. The western world, particularly the United States, has become a litigious society in which companies can be sued for all sorts of real or perceived product defects leading to injury, loss of property, or loss of life. The more dramatic stories, particularly those related to automobile accidents, are revealed to the general public via the media. But countless other cases that have filled civil courtrooms everywhere are not as widely disseminated. Understanding how the management of a design project impacts the issue of product liability is a critical engineering skill.

This section introduces some of the basic legal concepts that underscore the relationship between engineering and the law. While the material presented here merely skims the surface of intellectual property law, it will introduce you to the language of the legal profession and build your awareness of legal issues as they relate to engineering design.

4.1   Patents

A patent can be issued for any invention provided that certain criteria are met. The invention must introduce a new concept or way of doing something. The product must be something that can actually be produced, and it must have been *reduced to practice* (i.e., produced in at least prototype form) prior to the initial patent application. Also, the subject of the patent must not simply be an obvious synthesis of preexisting ideas. The first page of a typical patent document is shown in Figure 18.

A patent is valid for seventeen years (in the United States) during which time the inventor has sole rights to produce or license the invention. A patent *license* is a legal contract binding the inventor, who may not have the resources to actually produce the invention, with a company that has the resources and desires to manufacture and market the invention. In the United States, patents are awarded, or *issued* by the United States Patent and Trademark Office (USPTO, or simply "Patent Office"). This organization maintains a comprehensive public website (*www.uspto.gov*) from which anyone may download patents dating back as far as 1976. Earlier patents may be ordered from the patent archive as hardcopy for a small fee.

4.2   Patent Jargon

Lawyers have their own vocabulary for describing the patent process. The concept of *prior art* refers to the body of knowledge that existed at the time of the patented invention.

(12) **United States Patent**
Bifano et al.

(10) **Patent No.:   US 6,529,311 B1**
(45) **Date of Patent: Mar. 4, 2003**

(54) **MEMS-BASED SPATIAL-LIGHT MODULATOR WITH INTEGRATED ELECTRONICS**

(75) Inventors: **Thomas Bifano,** Mansfield, MA (US); **Mark Horenstein,** West Roxbury, MA (US)

(73) Assignee: **The Trustees of Boston University,** Boston, MA (US)

(*) Notice: Subject to any disclaimer, the term of this patent is extended or adjusted under 35 U.S.C. 154(b) by 0 days.

(21) Appl. No.: **09/702,054**

(22) Filed: **Oct. 30, 2000**

Related U.S. Application Data

(60) Provisional application No. 60/161,939 filed on Oct. 28, 1999.

(51) **Int. Cl.**[7] G02B 26/00

(52) **U.S. Cl.** **359/291;** 359/290; 359/223; 359/224; 359/298

(58) **Field of Search** 359/290, 291, 359/223, 224, 298, 248, 900

(56)   **References Cited**

U.S PATENT DOCUMENTS

4,954,789 A   *   9/1990 Sampsell..................330/4.3

5,312,513 A	*	5/1994	Florence et al. 156/643
5,535,047 A	*	7/1996	Hornbeck 359/295
5,867,302 A		2/1999	Fleming..................... 359/291
6,028,689 A		2/2000	Michalicek et al. 359/224
6,123,985 A		9/2000	Robinson et al. 428/162
6,181,460 B1		1/2001	Tran et al. 359/291
6,329,738 B1	*	12/2001	Hung et al. 310/309
6,396,619 B1		5/2002	Huibers et al. 359/291

* cited by examiner

Primary Examiner—Hung Xuan Dang
Assistant Examiner—Tuyen Tra
(74) *Attorney, Agent, or Firm*—Weingarten, Schurgin, Gagnebin & Lebovici LLP

(57)   **ABSTRACT**

Method and apparatus for forming an array of reflective elements for spatial light modulation. The array includes a substrate supporting electronically addressable actuators, each associated with a corresponding reflective element, a coupling attaching each actuator to the corresponding reflective element to place each reflective element in a substantially planar surface. Each electronically addressable actuator responds to predetermined addressing from a processing circuit to reposition the corresponding reflective element out of the planar surface a predetermined distance identified in the predetermined electronic addressing.

9 Claims, 7 Drawing Sheets

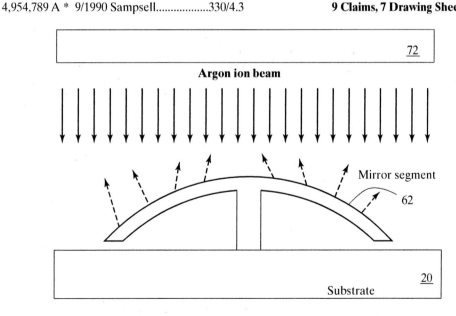

Figure 18.   Top header of a patent issued by the U.S. Patent and Trademark Office.

A device cannot be patented if it is described anywhere in the prior art. The invention must be reproducible, and the language of the patent must be sufficiently clear that it can be understood by an individual *skilled in the art*. The latter phrase is used to describe someone who, at the time of the invention, would have been familiar with the field of endeavor to which the invention applies and would have had the requisite education typical of those working in the general area of technology. To be patentable, a new invention must pass the tests of *obviousness* and *anticipation*. In legal terms, an idea is "obvious" if elements of prior art can be combined to produce the invention, *and* if, at the time of the patent application, the general literature provided suggestions for doing so. An invention is "anticipated" if a single piece of prior art describes the invention in its entirety. These tests are applied as part of the application process, known simply as the patent's *prosecution history*. If an invention is deemed obvious or anticipated in the prior art by the USPTO, then it is not patentable.

4.3   The Process of Obtaining a Patent

When an individual or company seeks to obtain patent protection for an invention, several well-defined steps must be taken to ensure success.[*] The time span from invention to patent issue is typically a year or more and usually requires the assistance of an attorney. At each step in the process, the patent may be rejected by the Patent Office. Conversely, being issued a patent for a particular invention is an exciting event often marked by celebration at the receiving company.

Disclosure—The first step for the inventor is to file a *patent disclosure*. A disclosure stakes claim to the invention and establishes the date of origin of the invention. Compared to a formal patent document, which utilizes a very specific language structure and can be quite lengthy, a disclosure is a much simpler document that describes the invention in plain language. Filing a disclosure does not guarantee that the invention will be patentable, but it contains enough information to uniquely identify both the inventor and the invention, and it firmly establishes the date of invention. An example of a patent disclosure, filed by Boston University on behalf of the author of this text, is shown in Figure 19. This disclosure describes a unique circuit used to control micro-electromechanical (MEMS) devices for optical applications.

Patent Prosecution—Following the filing of a disclosure, the organization seeking the patent has the responsibility of convincing the Patent Office that the invention is unique and worthy of patent protection. This process is formally known as "patent prosecution." Prosecution begins when the inventor, or, more typically, the attorney acting on behalf of the inventor, submits a draft of the formal patent document for review by the Patent Office. Also submitted are all the documents known to describe the prior art at the time of the invention. Patent prosecution is an iterative process during which the Patent Office may question some of the claims made in the patent in light of the prior art, or introduce other pieces of prior art not known to the inventor. An exchange of arguments for and against often transpires between the Patent Office and the inventor's attorney until an agreement is reached as to what exact features of the invention will be covered by the patent. These features are jointly referred to as the patent's *claims*. Patent claims may be *literal*, describing a physical apparatus, or they may be *method claims* that describe a manufacturing technology or way of using the new invention.

---

[*]The steps outlined in this section describe the United States patent process. Procedures in other countries may differ.

BOSTON UNIVERSITY TECHNOLOGY DISCLOSURE

1. Title of Invention:

Method for Linearizing Deflection of a MEMS Device Using Binary Electrodes and Voltage Modulation

2. Inventor(s) Information:

Name(s)	Position Title(s)	School/Department or Collaborating Organization	Telephone Number
Mark N. Horenstein	Professor	Dept. of Elec. and Comp. Eng.	617-353-2800

3. Events:

	Event Description:	Date:	Location:	References & Comments:
A.	First description of complete invention, oral or written (*conception*)	2/27/2003	Precision Engineering Laboratory	Discussions with T. Bifano and P. Bierden
B.	Invention development records, notes, drawings (Evidence of *diligence*)	3/1/2003	Rm. PHO 527 8 Saint Mary's St.	Analysis and Development
C.	First successful demonstration, if any (first actual *reduction to practice*)	3/4/2003	Rm. PHO 527 8 Saint Mary's St.	First Successful Simulation
D.	First publication containing full description of invention			
E.	External disclosures (in the past, or expected in the future, with date): <u>None</u>			

I (We) hereby agree to assign all right, title and interest to this invention to Boston University and agree to execute all documents as requested, assigning to Boston University our right in any patent application filed on this invention, and to cooperate with the Boston University Office of Technology Transfer in the protection of this invention. Boston University will share any royalty income derived from the invention with the inventor(s) according to its standard policies.

Mark N. Horenstein	3/20/2003
Inventor's Signature	Date

44 Cummington St., Boston, MA 02215

Home Address

000-00-0000	United States
Social Security Number (required)	Country of Citizenship

4. Please attach the following (both hard and electronic copies):
   - A detailed description of the invention;
   - A two or three sentence, non-confidential description of its usefulness;
   - A one page non-confidential description of its usefulness;
   - A list of potential licensees.

5. Technology disclosed to and understood by:

Elicia Keyes	*Elicia Keyes*
Name of Non-Inventor Witness	**Signature of Non-Inventor Witness**

Figure 19.   Example of a patent disclosure.

4.4   The Anatomy of a Patent

Much like a technical journal article, a patent has a predefined structure that helps the reader understand the key elements of the described invention as well as the specific claims of the patent. The major elements of a patent are illustrated in block diagram form in Figure 20. Most of these patent components, described in detail below, can be

Bar Code

United States Patent
Inventor Last Name

Patent Number
Date of Patent

Patent Title
Inventor Full Name
Assignee

Prosecution History Information

Abstract

Figures
(Usually several pages)

Background

Detailed
Description

Claims

Figure 20.   Structure of a patent shown in block diagram form.

identified on the top page of the patent shown in Figure 18. The next-to-last page of the patent, showing the last few paragraphs of the detailed description, and the first of the numbered claims, is provided in Figure 21.

Patent Number—Every patent issued by the USPTO is given a unique number assigned according to the order of issue. Currently, this number is well into the six millions.

Patent Title—As part of the application process, the inventor must choose a title that describes the key focus of the patent.

US 6,529,311 B1

3

an oxygen plasma. The polymer photoresist layer **50** is exposed and developed to leave apertures **52** in FIGS. **8A** and B for the deposition of a metalization or metal layer **54** for the anchors and for the diaphragm and its flexures described above. The metal deposition **54** as shown in FIGS. **9A** and B can be sputtered material such as a chromium-aluminum composite, aluminum, gold, or nickel.

The metal layer is patterned and etched in FIGS. **10A** and B to leave the flexure **30** supported diaphragm **20**. A polymer photoresist and reactive ion etch, such as in a chlorine atmosphere, may be used to create and separate the flexures **30** and diaphragm **20**.

At this point, the photoresist may be released by wet solvent procedures as shown in FIGS. **11A** and B or the mirror structure may be begun as shown in FIGS. **12A** and B using a second layer of polymer resist **56**. The resist is patterned to leave upon being developed an aperture **58** for the formation in the steps of FIGS. **13A** and **B** of a metalized or metal layer **60** for the mirror. The procedures are similar to those in forming the metal layer **54** for the diaphragms **20**. The metal layer **60** is patterned and etched as before in FIGS. **14A** and B to separate the mirror structures **62** and their struts or posts **64**. Finally the whole structure is subjected to a wet solvent procedure to remove all polymer. At some point in the procedure, such as at FIGS. **13A** and B, before polymer release, the device may be given a surface polishing to remove surface roughness and improve the quality of reflection.

In some cases and in reference to FIGS. **16–19**, the mirror **62** will exhibit a stress induced curvature resulting from the stresses built into the metal layer **60** during formation and release of supporting polymer at the conclusion of fabrication. These stresses **64**, as shown in FIG. **16**, vary over the depth of the mirror **62**, and in fact change polarity. Thus, the stresses can be balanced giving a planar mirror surface by removal of portions of the mirror element **62** until a point is reached where the stresses combine to keep the mirror surface flat. This point can be reached in the process of removal of surface layers as shown in FIG. **19**. The procedure for removal may utilize an ion beam **70** in an argon atmosphere to cut back the mirror surface. The process can be monitored by an interferometer **72** to detect the point of maximum flatness.

The circuitry **26** shown in FIG. **3** can be of several forms as illustrated in FIGS. **20** and **21**. In FIG. **20** a CPU **80**, off chip, applies instructions including addressing information designating, in a repeating sequence over the whole array **12**, each of mirrors **16** to be moved and data typically in the form of a voltage indicating the amount and polarity of displacement of that mirror. This information is fed to the circuit **26** at each mirror assembly to an address decoder **82** and voltage decoder **84** where the voltage is stored in a capacitive memory **86**. A driver gate **88** is activated when the corresponding mirror is addressed to apply that voltage through it to a capacitive plate **90** which in turn applies an electrostatic force to the actuator diaphragm **20**. Sufficient motion can be achieved with a low voltage of, for example a few volts compatible with CMOS circuitry, to achieve the 360 degree change in light phase on the mirrors.

An alternative CMOS circuit is illustrated in FIG. **21** where an on or off chip processor **100** applies via a data bus **102** to respective decoders **104** addressing and displacement information. In a typical application of eight bit data, a 256×256 mirror array can be addressed and a data byte of eight bits used to achieve a resolution of 256 displacement positions. In this example, the decoder determines from the

4

addressing when its corresponding mirror is being addressed and then uses each of the eight bits to apply a low voltage to corresponding capacitive plates in an array **108**. The plates are sequentially sized, typically each plate being twice the size of its neighbor. Each data bit applies or does not apply a fixed voltage to the corresponding plate based on the bit being of one state or the other, achieving a combined force proportional to the area of activated plates and a resolution of 256 positions.

The invention can be broadly scaled to different size arrays and mirror areas. A total mirror displacement of half a micron can be provided to achieve the desired phase change in the optical spectrum. The spacing of the diaphragms **20** and CMOS circuits **26** is a function of the voltage available and the total desired displacement, response time and other factors within the grasp of those skilled in the art.

The invention is not intended to be limited by any of the above description and is to be interpreted on the scope of the following claims.

What is claimed is:

1. A method for fabrication of an array of individually positioned reflectors for spatial light modulation comprising the steps of:

    providing plural addressable circuits in an array on a substrate;

    forming a flexure supported platform associated with each said circuit, said platform being flexure supported from said substrate; and

    attaching a reflecting element to said platform on a side opposite from said substrate thereby providing a plurality o f reflecting elements of said array aligned in a surface;

    said circuit having electronics operative in response to a signal addressed thereto and operative in association with said platform to apply a force to move said platform and said reflecting element together to a predetermined position out of alignment with the array surface;

    wherein said circuits providing step includes the step of providing a conductive plate on said substrate facing said platform, an addressable gate and a voltage memory, said gate operative to apply a voltage in said memory to said plate in response to said signal;

    said signal having a voltage component corresponding to the predetermined position to which said reflective element is to be moved and an address component for activating said gate of an appropriately addressed circuit.

2. A method for fabrication of an array of individually positioned reflectors for spatial light modulation comprising the steps of:

    providing plural addressable circuits in an array on a substrate;

    forming a flexure supported platform associated with each said circuit, said platform being flexure supported from said substrate; and

    attaching a reflecting element to said platform on a side opposite from said substrate thereby providing a plurality of reflecting elements of said array aligned in a surface;

    said circuit having electronics operative in response to a signal addressed thereto and operative in association with said platform to apply a force to move said platform and said reflecting element togetber to a predetermined position out of alignment with the array surface;

Figure 21. Next-to-last page of the patent of Figure 18. The last paragraphs of the detailed description and the beginning of the numbered claims can be found on this page.

Inventor—The inventor of a patent must always be a person (or persons). The inventor is the individual first responsible for bringing the object of the invention from concept to practice.

Assignee—The assignee of a patent can be an individual, set of individuals, or a company. The assignee has the legal and commercial rights to the patent and also the right to license the patent to others for a privately negotiated fee. When an individual has arrived at an invention while on the payroll of an employer, the assignee is usually the latter.

Abstract—The abstract provides a stand-alone summary of the invention. It allows the casual reader to understand the context and impact of the patent without reading the entire document.

Illustrations—Traditionally, the figures that accompany a patent appear before the written sections. Each element of a figure that will be addressed in the text is labeled with a unique number that is repeated every time that element appears in the patent. This construct may appear cumbersome to the average person, and it can be tedious to read, but it is a time-tested method that reduces ambiguities in the patent document.

Background of the Invention—This section describes the area of technology to which the patent applies and the problem solved by the invention. It also describes the prior art leading up to the time of the invention.

Description of the Invention—Usually the longest portion of the patent document, this section provides a detailed outline of the invention. The goal of this section is to enable an individual "skilled in the art" to completely reconstruct and produce the patented invention.

Claims—In this final section of the patent, the specific elements of the invention claimed by the assignee are outlined in detail. It is the set of claims, not the preceding description of the invention, that forms the legal basis for the patent and defines the specific legal protection granted to the inventor. The first claim listed is called the *primary* claim. Further claims that rely on the primary claim for validity are called *dependent claims*. Lawyers use the phrase *claim limitation* to describe the individual pieces of intellectual property protected by the claims.

Although the description of patents provided above is simplified, it captures the essence of patent structure and format. A more comprehensive look at patents and the patent system can be acquired by perusing the website of the United States Patent and Trademark Office.

KEY TERMS

Documentation	Patent	Teamwork
Gantt chart	PERT chart	Time line
Organizational chart	Project management	

Problems

1.   Develop a simple checklist for your homework assignments over the coming week.

2.   Prepare a checklist of tasks required to tune a bicycle for optimum performance.

3.   Prepare a checklist that will help guide you in the design of a child's safety seat.

4. Imagine that you work for a company that is designing a hybrid gas–electric car for commercial sale. Create an organizational chart for the company and a Gantt chart for designing the vehicle's drive train.

5. Choose an engineering company with which you are familiar or in which you have an interest. Develop an organizational chart for the company. Information about a company's structure and personnel usually can be found on the company's website.

6. Imagine that you wish to start your own company to write software tools for doing business on the Internet. Create an organizational chart that outlines the positions you'll need to fill in order to get the company started.

7. Develop a time line for the completion of the prototype of an automobile powered from fuel cells rather than an internal combustion engine.

8. Develop a time line for completing your course requirements over the time span of 4 academic years.

9. Suppose that you've been given the assignment to develop a human-powered airplane. Develop a time line for completing this ambitious assignment.

10. Create a Gantt chart for an entry into the national solar-powered vehicle design competition, First Solar (*www.firstsolar.com*).

11. Prepare a Gantt chart for the design of a retrofit fire escape for a 10-story city building.

12. Prepare your own version of a Gantt chart that might have been used for the construction of the Golden Gate Bridge in San Francisco, California.

13. Develop a Gantt chart for housing an educational conference on engineering design. Consider all needed arrangements, including food, transportation, lodging, and meeting facilities.

14. Develop a Gantt chart for the design of a cell phone tower.

15. Consider the case of four engineers who are designing an entry into a material handling competition (see *www.mhiq.org*). Develop a Gantt chart for the design of a system based on a complete list of ideas that you develop. The vertical axis of your Gantt chart should reflect members of the design team, not specific project tasks.

16. Construct a "fuzzy" Gantt chart depicting the tasks required to design a software system for tracking inventory at a hardware store. Each time allocation should include an error estimate—an increment of fuzzy time—that allows for possible early or late completion of every task on the chart. Based on your fuzzy estimates, what are the longest and shortest possible time durations of the design effort? The vertical axis of your chart should indicate software developers, not individual design tasks.

17. Consider the fuzzy Gantt chart scenario of the previous problem. Develop one that might apply to the design of a pilotless model surveillance airplane.

18. Can you create a Gantt chart for the creation of the Earth? Your chart can be based on either a religious, evolutionary, or cosmological perspective, as you prefer.

19.   Do some research into the steps required to build a two-story, commercial-grade building. Then construct a PERT chart applicable to the design and construction of a public library.

20.   Construct a PERT chart that you imagine to be applicable to the design of the International Space Station.

21.   Imagine that you lead a team of engineers designing a breakwater for a coastal sea port. Develop a PERT chart for the completion of this project. Consider all elements, from basic research and data analysis to final construction. Identify any critical pathways in your chart.

22.   Consider the case of a car design competition in which the object is to be the first to drop a small beanbag (a "Hacky Sack®") into a 10-cm square hole cut into a 3-m square tabletop. Develop a PERT chart for the competition of a successful design effort. Identify any critical pathways in your chart and then adjust time allocations in the branches so that the project minimizes the former but results in a project that can be completed within one academic semester.

23.   Make a list of conditions under which you might choose a Gantt chart over a PERT chart for time management. Then make a similar list for the opposite case.

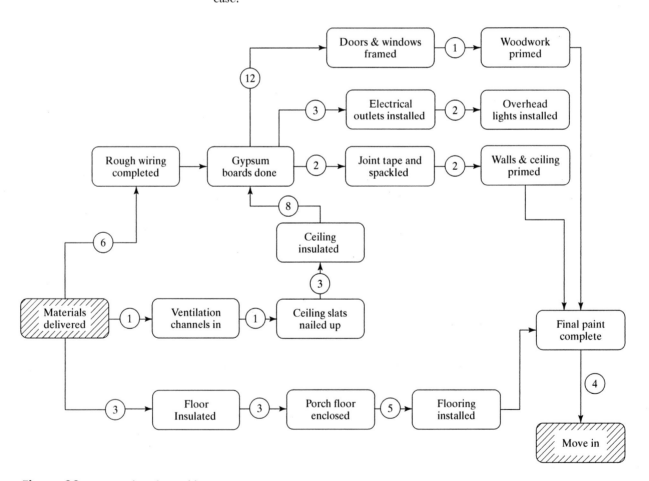

Figure 22. PERT chart for Problems 24–26.

24.   Examine the PERT chart of Figure 22. Make a list of all critical pathways as well as the location and duration of all slack time intervals.

25.   For the PERT chart of Figure 22, what is the total time allocated to the completion of the entire design task?

26.   For the PERT chart of Figure 22, identify all the different pathways and their total allocated path intervals.

27.   Develop a PERT chart for the design of a tunnel linking Beijing to New York City.

28.   Outline a PERT chart for the completion of the first self-sustaining lunar exploration base.

29.   Develop a PERT chart for university commencement exercises.

30.   Begin to keep a logbook of your class activities. Enter sketches and records of design assignments, inventions, and ideas.

31.   Sketch a logbook page that describes a design concept for a recumbent bicycle.

32.   Prepare a logbook page that describes the inner workings of a common DVD player.

33.   Develop a logbook entry describing a machine that shells and stores peanuts.

34.   Develop a logbook page for the design of the cooling system for an indoor ice-hockey rink.

35.   Pretend that you are Alexander Graham Bell, the inventor of the telephone. Prepare several logbook pages that describe your invention.

36.   Pretend that you are Marie Curie, the person who discovered the radioactive element radium. Prepare several logbook pages that describe the activities leading to your discovery.

37.   Pretend that you are Dr. Zephram Cockrane, the inventor of plasma warp drive on the television and movie series *Star Trek*. Prepare several logbook pages that describe your invention.

38.   Imagine that you are Elias Howe, the first inventor to perfect the sewing machine by putting the eye of the needle in its tip. This innovation made possible the bobbin system still in use in sewing machines today. Prepare several logbook pages that describe your invention and its initial tests.

39.   Reconstruct logbook pages as they might have been written by Johan Vaaler, the Norwegian inventor of the common paperclip. (Write your entries in English).

40.   Imagine that you are Dr. Z, the engineer involved in the Abiomed case of Section 3.8. Sketch the logbook pages that outline the basic operating concept of your transcutaneous energy transfer device.

41.   The invention of the incandescent light bulb is largely attributed to the famous American inventor, Thomas Edison. Reconstruct the logbook pages that Edison may have kept describing his classic design efforts.

42.   The cotton gin was developed by an American inventor, Eli Whitney, around 1800. This invention had a profound effect on the economic history of the early United States. Reconstruct logbook pages in which Whitney outlines the basic features and development of his invention. Note that patent law in America was in its infancy around the time that Whitney did his work on the cotton gin.

43.   Samuel F.B. Morse, inventor of the telegraph in the 1830s and the pioneer who launched the world's first "information age," was actually an artist by profession when he developed his classic invention. During a long voyage home from study in France, he passed his time thinking about conversations he had heard concerning ongoing experiments in Europe on electricity and magnetism. He developed his ideas for the telegraph while returning to the United States. Sketch the logbook pages that Morse may have kept during his long sea voyage.

44.   The first pocket calculator was designed by Jack Kilby, an engineer for Texas Instruments. Look up the history of this inventor, and see if you can reconstruct the probable appearance of one or more pages from his logbook.

4

Engineering Tools

If you were to hire a carpenter to install new kitchen cabinets, you would not expect that person to arrive on the job empty-handed. As a professional tradesperson, the carpenter would bring along an array of power and hand tools, saws, hammers, drills, and screwdrivers. A good carpenter probably would also bring some common fasteners and raw materials as needed to finish the job. Likewise, you would not expect to visit a doctor's office without confronting an array of medical diagnostics, including a stethoscope, tongue depressors, blood pressure cuff, reflex hammer, and an examining table. Like these other professionals, engineers also rely on numerous tools to aid in all facets of the design process. While some of an engineer's tools can literally be carried around in a toolkit—such as a calculator, mechanical pencils, and laptop computer, for example—many fall into the category of knowledge tools. A knowledge tool is defined as a practice or methodology that the engineer has learned on the job or in school. Other tools exist in the form of software programs developed to help engineers address specific classes of problems. The purpose of this chapter is to highlight some of the more important knowledge and software tools that are found in an engineer's toolkit.

SECTIONS

OBJECTIVES

In this chapter, you will:

- Learn the importance of estimation in engineering design.
- Examine the important role of the engineering prototype.
- Read about the role of reverse engineering in the design process.
- Examine the role of the computer in engineering design.
- Learn about the Internet and several software programs that are central to the engineering profession.
- Learn when and when not to use the computer.
- Discuss several examples of computer use for analysis, data collection, simulation, and computer-aided design.

From *Design Concepts for Engineers*, Third Edition, Mark N. Horenstein. Copyright © 2005 by Pearson Education, Inc. Published by Prentice Hall, Inc. All rights reserved.

1   ESTIMATION

Engineering and estimation go hand in hand. When considering a new design strategy, it's a good idea to test it for feasibility by doing some rough calculations of important quantities and parameters. A paper-and-pencil or simple hand calculator analysis of a proposed strategy may eliminate gross inconsistencies before the detailed design process even begins. These calculations need not be elaborate or precise. In the age of programmable calculators and computers, students sometimes feel that answers with lots of digits imply better or more accurate answers. In many cases, however, "back of the envelope" calculations done by hand (and recorded in your engineer's logbook) are all that are required to determine the soundness of a design strategy.

EXAMPLE 1: ESTIMATING POWER FLOW FROM A BATTERY

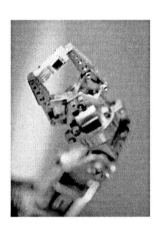

The following example illustrates the usefulness of estimation as a design tool. Suppose that you have been assigned the task of designing the power delivery system for a radio-controlled robot to be entered into the FIRST ROBOTICS design competition (*www.usfirst.org*). The object of this contest is to create a radio-controlled vehicle that can perform a variety of tasks. One task asks the robot to hook onto a 2.2-kg (one pound) weight, then lift the weight and place it into a receptacle located 0.5 meter above the floor. Keeping your robot moving is of prime importance, because other vehicles in the contest will attempt to engage and disable it. Suppose that your team has decided to use separate batteries to power the drive train (the motor and gear system that moves the robot) and the lifting mechanism. In this way, neither system will be affected if the other runs low on battery power. This feature is most important to the drive train system, because a robot without motion becomes useless.

In an effort to conserve weight, your team would like to use the smallest battery possible. For a given battery technology—e.g., alkaline, nickel-metal-hydride (NiMH), and so forth—the total energy stored in the battery is proportional to its physical volume. Hence, one important task requires that you estimate the total energy requirements associated with lifting the 2.2-kg weight to a height of 0.5 meter. The energy required for each lift, multiplied by the number of times the lifting operation must be performed, will help define the size of the battery.

Calculate the Energy Per Lift Required from the Battery

The weight to be lifted has a mass of 2.2 kg. Assuming a gravitational constant of about 10 N/kg (newtons per kilogram), the force of gravity to be overcome is easily calculated:

$$F = mg = (2.2 \text{ kg})(10 \text{ N/kg}) = 22 \text{ N} \tag{1}$$

Another simple calculation will reveal the mechanical energy W, or "work" (measured in joules), required to lift the weight to a height of 0.5 meters:

$$W = Fy = (22 \text{ N})(0.5 \text{ m}) = 11 \text{ J} \tag{2}$$

As this latter calculation shows, a total of 11 joules of potential energy must be imparted to the weight in order to lift it from the ground into the receptacle. Ultimately, this mechanical energy must come from the battery in electrical form. The motor's job is to convert electrical energy into mechanical energy. Thus, the total electrical energy entering the motor will have to equal the total mechanical energy transmitted to the weight plus any electrical and mechanical losses in the system. This energy-flow relationship is summarized in Figure 1,

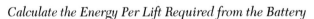

power equals energy flow per unit time.

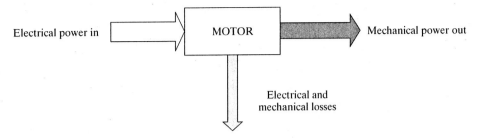

Figure 1. Power-flow diagram.

Estimate the Required Electrical Power

Power flow may be equated to the energy flowing per unit time (measured in joules per second). For estimation purposes, let's assume that lifting the weight requires about 10 seconds. The needed power flow can then be estimated by dividing the total energy added to the weight by the appropriate time interval:

$$P = W \div \Delta T = 11 \text{ J} \div 10 \text{ s} = 1.1 \text{ watts.} \tag{3}$$

This type of calculation should always be examined to make sure that the answer is reasonable. As a basis for comparison, consider a small bathroom nightlight that draws about 4 watts. Your experience shows that such a lamp does not get very hot, even when it is left on all the time. Expecting the car to draw about one quarter that amount for 10 seconds without getting excessively hot indeed seems reasonable. The answer is believable.

Estimate the Battery Current

Another important parameter of the system will be the current drawn from the battery as the robot lifts the weight. By estimating the current, you can appropriately size the electrical components, such as switches and transistors, needed to control the lifting mechanism. The electrical power supplied by the battery to the motor must at *least* be equal to the mechanical power required to lift the weight, plus any losses that may occur in the motor and drive train (e.g., the gears, belts, pulleys, bearings, etc.). Neglecting these losses, you can arrive at the simple conclusion that $P_{mech} = P_{elec}$. The electrical power supplied by the battery will be equal to the battery voltage multiplied by the current drawn out of the battery:

$$P_{elec} = VI \tag{4}$$

Suppose that you try to operate your lifting mechanism from a standard 9-Volt battery (the type used, for example, in transistor radios and smoke detectors.) At a power drain of 1.1 watts, the battery will need to supply a current of

$$I = \frac{P}{V} = \frac{1.1 \text{ W}}{9 \text{ V}} = 0.12 \text{ A} = 120 \text{ mA} \tag{5}$$

At this point, you look up the properties of standard 9-V batteries on the Internet to determine whether 120 mA exceeds the recommended current drain for this type of battery. You find that the typical 9-V battery can supply about 100 mA of current for short periods of time (about 1 hour or less). This level of battery performance places your design specification just below the border of feasibility.

On Second Thought ...

After reviewing your calculations and assumptions, you realize that you've neglected all losses in the system. In reality, the conversion efficiency from electrical to mechanical power will be far from perfect. According to your professor, you could expect a power conversion efficiency of up to 90% from a well-designed electromechanical system, but you've decided to use inexpensive motors and parts that you can buy cheaply over the Internet. Similarly, no more than about 60% of the converted mechanical power supplied by the motor shaft will be usable because of frictional losses in the gears and drive belts, leaving only about 50% of the power taken from the battery to actually lift the 2.2-kg weight. Your robot will thus require about 240 mA, rather than 120 mA, to lift the weight.

A single battery will simply be incapable of sustaining its 9-Volt output while supplying 240 mA of current. As an alternative, suppose that you were to use two 9-Volt batteries in series, for a total of 18 V. This change would reduce the current estimate computed in Equation (5) to 60 mA, so the actual current required, taking losses into account, will now indeed be about 120 mA. This value is again within the range of capability of each battery. The two-battery approach seems to be the more reasonable choice after taking losses into account. This sort of re-evaluation is common in the engineering design process. Using two batteries doubles the net battery volume, and thus the net energy stored in the batteries. Another alternative would be to use two 1.5-V type D batteries (the kind used in flashlights) connected in series. In this latter case, your current estimate would change to the value

$$I = P/V = (1.1\ \text{W})/(3\ \text{V}) \approx 300\ \text{mA} \tag{6}$$

While this current is almost three times the value calculated for a single 9-Volt battery (the voltage is only one-third as large, and the *V-I* product must remain the same), it is well within the capabilities of type-D batteries. Standard alkaline versions of the latter can sustain currents up to about 500 mA (0.5 A) with little degradation in voltage.

PROFESSIONAL SUCCESS: BE WILLING TO MODIFY YOUR CONCLUSIONS WHEN NECESSARY

Despite the time and effort that go into making design decisions, a good engineer knows when it's time to admit an oversight and change a basic design decision. One example of this principle can be found in the standard automobile battery. Its voltage value was set at 12 V around 1940. Prior to that time, automotive engineers had agreed upon a battery voltage of 6 V, equal to the series combination of three lead-acid wet cells. The increasing electrical demands inside vehicles—to power things such as headlights and radios—led to increased power requirements. Keeping the standard voltage at 6 V would have meant large currents (and impractical, thicker wires) running throughout the vehicle. Engineers from all major car makers agreed to increase the standard battery voltage to 12 V, thereby halving the needed current flows for the same amounts of electrical power.

Now, in the first decade of the 21st century, the automotive industry is undergoing another change in design strategy. The electrical loads on modern cars have increased dramatically over the past several years as consumers have demanded more and more accessories. Many of a modern car's safety and fuel-economy systems—antilock brakes, fuel injection, traction steering, and zoned air conditioning, for example—run on electrical power rather than on mechanical power derived from the engine. A move is underway to increase the standard battery voltage to 48 V so that, when compared to 12-V systems, current flow requirements will be reduced by a factor of about four throughout the vehicle.

EXAMPLE 2: ESTIMATING THE VOLUME OF PAINT NEEDED TO COAT A LARGE OBJECT

$ $ $ $

This example, which comes from the real world of automobile manufacturing, illustrates the usefulness of estimation as an engineering design tool. Imagine that you work for a company that makes automobiles. The head of manufacturing thinks that the company could save a lot of money by abandoning conventional painting techniques and instead adopting a finishing process that impregnates color right into the body material during manufacturing using an electrostatic powder coating and baking technique. The comparison is a tough call. Labor and equipment depreciation, not materials, are the main costs involved in most manufacturing processes. The overhead at a typical fabrication facility, including benefits, insurance, the physical plant (the cost of keeping the factory open so that workers can do their jobs), and depreciation can run anywhere from 60% to 200% of wages, salaries, and other direct costs. Adopting the labor-saving powder-coating method, therefore, seems like the better choice. On the other hand, in a large factory that can justify the initial capital cost, cars and other large consumer items can be painted by robots, thereby also eliminating labor costs. A comparison between powder and paint coating methods thus reverts to a cost-of-materials comparison only.

The head of manufacturing has asked you to estimate the total cost of conventional paint needed to cover each vehicle. How can you arrive at such an estimate? The steps are outlined in the following discussion.

Draw a Rough Sketch of the Surfaces to Be Painted

As a first step, you should draw a rough sketch of the car body on paper. One such sketch that depicts the various car surfaces is shown in Figure 2. The largest areas to be painted include the hood, trunk, roof, and two side fenders. The quantity of paint required to cover the posts of the window frames is negligible.

Estimate the Area of Each Section

Next, you must estimate the area of each separate section of the car. The hood forms an approximate 1.2 m × 1.2 m square for a total area of about 1.4 square meters. The trunk is also nearly rectangular, measuring about 1.2 × 1.5 m, for an additional 1.8 square meters. The doors are about 1 m long by 0.8 m tall, for a total area of 0.8 square meter each. The dimensions of the roof are about 1.4 m long by 1.2 m wide, for total of 1.7 square meters. For estimation purposes, each of the fenders can be modeled by one of the shapes shown in Figure 3. The surface area of the windows need not be counted, because they are not painted. The area of each fender can be calculated from the area formula:

$$A = bc + \frac{c(a - b)}{2}. \tag{7}$$

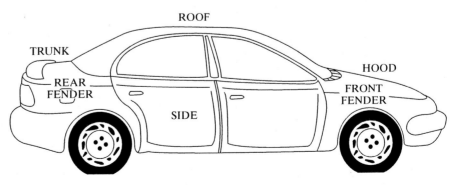

Figure 2. Rough sketch of car body.

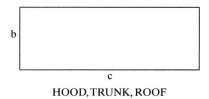

HOOD, TRUNK, ROOF

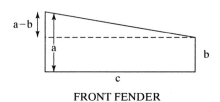

FRONT FENDER

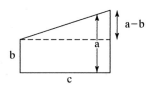

REAR FENDER

Figure 3. Estimated shape of side fenders.

If you assume reasonable numbers for the dimensions of the fenders—for example, $a \approx 0.8$ m, $b \approx 0.4$ m, and $c \approx 1.5$ m for the front of the car, and $a \approx 0.8$ m, $b \approx 0.4$ m, and $c \approx 1$ m for the rear, then you can compute the individual area estimates and add them to obtain an estimate for the total surface area of the car:

Hood: 1.2 m $\times$ 1.2 m $= 1.4$ m^2 (8)

Trunk: 1.2 m $\times$ 1.5 m $= 1.8$ m^2

Doors: 4×1 m $\times$ 0.8 m $= 3.2$ m^2

Roof: 1.4 m $\times$ 1.2 m $= 1.7$ m^2

Front fenders: $2 \times (0.4$ m$)(1.5$ m$) + (1.5$ m$)(0.8$ m $- 0.4$ m$) = 1.8$ m^2

Rear fenders: $2 \times (0.4$ m$)(1$ m$) + (1$ m$)(0.8$ m $- 0.4$ m$) = 1.2$ m^2

Total area: 1.4 m^2 $+ 1.8$ m^2 $+ 3.2$ m^2 $+ 1.7$ m^2 $+ 1.8$ m^2 $+ 1.2$ m^2 $= 11.1$ m^2

The result is equal to about 11 square meters. (Round numbers are appropriate because only a rough estimate is required.)

Multiply by the Thickness of the Paint

Next, you can estimate the volume of paint required to cover the car by multiplying its surface area by the paint thickness. The latter usually is measured in mils (1 mil $\equiv 0.001$ *inch* ≈ 0.025 *mm* $= 25 \times 10^{-6}$ m). A very light coating of paint is typically about 0.5 to 1 mil thick, while a very heavy coating might be as thick as 7 or 8 mils. The choice of thickness for estimation purposes will depend on the paint application and whether you want your estimate to be on the high side or the low side of the actual value. Suppose that you choose an average value of 4 mils. For this thickness, the volume of paint required to coat the car can easily be calculated:

$$\text{Volume} = \text{area} \times \text{thickness} = (11 \text{ m}^2) \times (4 \text{ mils})$$

$$\times (25 \times 10^{-6} \text{ m/mil}) = 0.001 \text{ m}^3 \qquad (9)$$

or about 1 liter.

PRACTICE!

1. Determine the power required of the battery in Example 1 if the weight can be lifted in 25 seconds instead of 10. Will the total energy requirement change?

2. Determine the power required of the battery in the first estimate of Example 1 if a set of four 1.5-V AAA cells is used instead of a single 9-V battery.

3. How much mechanical power can be derived from a 6-V electric motor that is 85% efficient if its maximum allowed current is 1 A?

4. How much internal heat in watts will be generated by an electric motor that is 60% efficient if it provides 20 W of mechanical power to an external load?

5. Estimate the amount of paint required to cover a single wooden pencil.

6. Estimate the physical length of a 90-minute audio cassette tape.

7. Estimate the number of platforms needed to build a scaffolding shell that encircles the Statue of Liberty.

8. Estimate the volume of water contained within the supply pipes of a one-story, single family house. How much energy is required to heat this water from 20°C (room temperature) to 80°C (shower temperature)? What is the significance of this energy quantity?

9. Estimate the number of staples in the loading clip of a standard office stapler.

10. How many gallons of paint (primer and finish coat) should you buy to paint the exterior of a garage that measures 20 ft × 30 ft × 10 ft tall?

11. Estimate the volume of paint required to cover a Boeing 747.

12. Estimate the volume of ink required to print an 8.5 × 11 inch paper document in Arial 10-point font, single-spaced type, with 1-inch margins. How many such pages do you think you could print from a typical black inkjet cartridge?

13. Estimate the cost of the energy required to heat the water needed to take your morning shower.

14. Look up the volume of take-out coffee consumed by the national population each day, then work backwards to estimate the total weight of paper needed to make the required coffee cups.

15. A compact disk (CD) stores its information as pits in the plastic substrate. The presence of a pit signifies a digital *1*, while the absence of a pit signifies a digital *0*. Estimate the number of pits on a standard audio CD if the sampling rate is 44 kilobits/sec.

16. Estimate the number of fiber tufts in a square yard of carpeting.

17. Estimate the number of baseballs lost per season in the stands of a professional league ball park of your choosing.

18. Estimate the time required for a bowling ball to fall to the bottom of an ocean that is 2 km deep.

19. Estimate the number of plastic bags used per year in the supermarkets of the United States.

20. Estimate the total track length of a DVD comprising a two-hour movie.

2   WORKING WITH NUMBERS

2.1   International System of Units (SI)

While much of the corporate manufacturing base in the United States still uses the English system of units (feet, pounds, etc.) the predominant unit system throughout the world (including England!) is the metric International System of units. Originally used only in the sciences, the set of "SI" units (from the French *Le Système International d'Unités*) has become the predominant measurement language in worldwide commerce and trade. The SI units and their associated usage rules were established in 1960 by the European 11th General Conference on Weights and Measures.

Under the SI system, length is measured in *meters*, weight in *kilograms*, and time in *seconds*. Other fundamental SI units include the *ampere* (electric current), *Kelvin* (temperature), *mole* (quantity of atoms or molecules), and *candela* (intensity of light). Other quantities, such as area, volume, velocity, pressure, and density, are described in terms of these seven fundamental SI units. A complete description of the SI system and its rules can be found on the website of the U.S. National Institute of Standards and Technology at *physics.nist.gov/cuu/units*.

The SI system embodies a convention with regard to symbols, punctuation, and capitalization. Every SI unit has a standard abbreviation; some of the more commonly used abbreviations appear in Table 1. Unit abbreviations are always printed in lower case *unless* the unit is derived from the name of a person (e.g., Volta, Pascal, Hertz). In this latter case, the first letter of the unit's abbreviation is capitalized (e.g. V, Pa, Hz). However, when the unit is spelled out as a complete word, it appears entirely in

TABLE 1   Abbreviations for Some Common SI Units*

Unit	Abbreviation	Quantity	Person honored by the unit
meter	m	length	
kilogram	kg	mass	
second	s	time	
volt	V	voltage	Alessandro Volta (1745–1827)
ampere	A	current	Andre-Marie Ampere (1775–1836)
ohm	Ω	resistance	Georg Ohm (1789–1854)
newton	N	force	Sir Isaac Newton (1642–1727)
pascal	Pa	pressure	Blaise Pascal (1623–1662)
hertz	Hz	frequency	Heinrich Hertz (1857–1894)
joule	J	energy	James Joule (1818–1889)
watt	W	power	James Watt (1736–1819)
degrees celsius	°C	temperature	Anders Celsius (1701–1744)
lumen	lm	light intensity	

*The abbreviation of a unit named after a person begins with a capital letter. The word for such a unit always appears in lower case.

TABLE 2 Power-of-Ten Prefixes for the International System of Units

Factor	10^{12}	10^9	10^6	10^3	10^{-2}	10^{-3}	10^{-6}	10^{-9}	10^{-12}
Name	tera	giga	mega	kilo	centi	milli	micro	nano	pico
Prefix	T	G	M	k	C	m	μ	n	p

lower case, even if it's derived from the name of a person (e.g., volt, pascal, hertz). An SI unit abbreviation is never followed by a period except when it appears at the end of a sentence.

When a quantity is much smaller or larger than its corresponding SI unit, it can be expressed using one of the power-of-ten prefixes shown in Table 2. (This table lists the prefixes most often used by engineers; prefixes spanning the entire range from 10^{24} to 10^{-24} exist within the SI system.) Note that the kilogram is the only fundamental SI unit that contains its own prefix. When describing very large or small masses, a power-of-ten prefix is not used with kg. Rather, the mass is converted to grams and then preceded by a prefix. For example, 10^{-6} kg is expressed as 1 mg (one milligram), not 1 μkg (one microkilogram).

2.2   Reconciling Units

When working with equations and numbers, one good way to check the results of a calculation is to make sure that the result has the proper units. If it does not, then an error in calculation has probably been made. This test is sometimes called *unit reconciliation*. The check is easily performed, provided that numbers which have been written are accompanied by their individual SI units. For example, suppose that we wish to compute the volume of a cylindrical tank. The volume of a cylinder is given by the formula $V = \pi r^2 h$. Suppose that $r = 20$ cm and $h = 40$ cm. The calculation would result in the following:

$$\text{Volume} = \pi(0.2 \text{ m})^2(0.4 \text{ m}) = 0.05 \text{ m}^3 \tag{10}$$

The right-hand side of Equation (10) yields m × m × m, or cubic meters, which we know to be the SI unit for volume. Similarly, suppose that we wish to compute the distance that an object has fallen within a fixed amount of time. The vertical distance traveled by an object under the force of gravity is given by the formula $y = -\frac{1}{2}gt^2 + v_o t$, where $g = 9.8$ m/s^2 is the gravitational constant, v_o is the initial velocity in meters per second, and t is the time in seconds. Applying this formula to a projectile shot from a Lyle gun (a tether-carrying cannon used by shoreline rescue brigades at the turn of the 20th century) for the case $v_o = 10$ m/s and $t = 20$ s yields

$$y = -(9.8 \text{ m/s}^2)(20 \text{ s})^2 + (10 \text{ m/s})(20 \text{ s})$$
$$= -196 \text{ m} + 200 \text{ m} = 4 \text{ m} \tag{11}$$

In this case, each of the computations on the right-hand side of the equation yields a net unit of length: m/s^2 × s^2 equals meters, and m/s × s equals meters. Hence the units in Equation (11) match over both sides of the formula. The units are properly reconciled.

2.3   Significant Figures

When a number is used in estimations, prototype fabrication, specification sheets, or other technical calculations, you should be concerned with the number of significant figures that it contains. A significant figure is any nonzero digit, or any zero other than a leading zero. A number cannot be interpreted as being any more precise than its least significant digit, nor should a quantity be specified with any more digits than are justifiable by its measured precision. The numbers 128.1, 0.50, and 5.4, for example, imply quantities that have a known precision of ±0.1, ±0.01, and ±0.1, respectively, but the first is specified to four significant figures, while the second and third are specified to only two. Note that if *trailing* zeros are placed on the right side of the decimal point, they carry the weight of significant figures. Thus, the number 0.50 means 0.5 ± 0.01.

The precision of any calculation will be determined by the least precise number entering into the computation. For example, the product 128.1 × 0.50 × 5.4 entered into a calculator produces the digits 345.87. But because 0.50 and 5.4 are specified to only two significant figures, the rounded-off result of the multiplication should be recorded as 350, also with only two significant figures. Note that a digit is rounded up if the digit to its right is 5 or more. If the digit to its right is less than 5, the digit is rounded down.

PROFESSIONAL SUCCESS: THE RIGHT WAY TO USE YOUR CALCULATOR

The typical calculator allows for 8 or more significant figures in its calculations. The appearance of digits on a calculator display does *not* mean that those digits are significant. As an engineer, you must be mindful of the number of significant figures to which you are entitled in any given calculation, and summarily discard the extra digits produced by your calculator.

Remember that the extra digits *have no meaning* if they do not represent significant figures. Develop the habit of trimming extraneous, trailing digits. Providing answers with the proper number of digits will show your peers and supervisors that you are a professional who understands the importance of significant figures.

2.4   Dimensioning and Tolerance

When numbers find their way into technical drawings, the number of significant figures takes on a special meaning. No physical part can ever be fabricated to exact dimensions, because machine tools do not cut perfectly. A cutting tool, for example, wanders about its intended position during the machining process. Changes in temperature, humidity, or vibration during the cutting process can also cause the tool to follow a less-than-perfect path. Other fabrication methods, such as casting and injection molding, introduce similar uncertainties in a part's dimensions. The tolerance of each dimension shown in a drawing specifies the degree of error that will be acceptable for the finished part. As a rule, creating parts with tight tolerances involves the use of more expensive machining equipment and more time, because material cuts or fabrication steps must proceed more slowly. These features add considerable expense to the finished part. As the designer, you must decide which dimensions are truly critical and worthy of the extra cost.

Suppose that you wish to make the support plate shown in Figure 4. The plate, to be made from 0.4-mm-thick aluminum, contains several holes to which brackets are to be secured. This fabrication job is a bit complicated for simple hand tools, so you've decided to have a professional machinist make it. The job requires specialized machining tools, including a milling machine, drill press, and a reamer to make holes of an accurate diameter. One issue that you might think about concerns the precision with which the part would need to be built. For a rough prototype, you might be content with an approximate

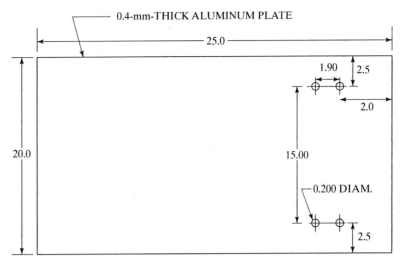

Figure 4. Support plate with dimensions and tolerance table.

version of the plate that can be produced quickly. For the finished product, however, you might want the machinist to take the extra time to adhere more closely to the specified dimensions. One way that engineers and machinists communicate on issues of this nature is through the numerical notations on parts drawings.

Carefully note the labeled dimensions shown in Figure 4. These numbers communicate to the machinist the acceptable deviation, or *tolerance*, for each of the plate's various dimensions. The numbers on the drawing have meaning for any machinist who reads the tolerance table. For this particular machining job, the numbers reveal that only the hole diameters, which are specified with the most significant figures, are especially critical dimensions. The length of the support plate, for example, is 25 cm. The numbers 25.0, 25.00, and 25.000, though all mathematically equivalent, would mean different things to the machinist. According to the tolerance table, the number 25.0, with one digit after the decimal point, should be interpreted by the machinist to mean 25 ± 0.1 cm. A support plate with a finished width diameter anywhere between 24.9 and 25.1 cm would be deemed acceptable. Similarly, the holes are specified as lying 15.00 cm apart, implying a machined tolerance of 15 ± 0.05 cm. The minimum and maximum tolerance limits for the hole centers as machined would be between 14.95 cm and 15.05 cm.

The tolerance table in Figure 4 indicates the most stringent dimensions to be those of the hole diameters. The holes in this particular part are intended to hold pins inserted by friction fit, hence their diameters are specified to three decimal points, implying a strict machining tolerance of 0.200 ± 0.001 cm.

PRACTICE!

1. Refer to the tolerance table shown in Figure 4. Compute the difference between the maximum and minimum permissible physical values for dimensions specified by the following numbers: 21.0 cm, 8.75 cm, 10 cm, 2.375 cm, and 0.003 cm.

2. Write down the result of the following computation, using only the number of significant figures to which you are entitled: $(45 + 8.2) \times 91.0 \div 12.1$.

3. What is the value of the sum $3.00 + 54.0 + 174 + 250$?

4. What is the sum of the integers $3 + 54 + 174 + 250$? How does the issue of significant figures manifest itself in this case?

5. Using the tolerance table in Figure 4, write down the following dimensions specified to ± 1 mm: 5.1 cm; 954 cm; 573 cm; and 15 mm.

6. If all dimensions on a part are specified to be within ± 1 mil (± 0.001 inch), what is the minimum possible angle between the sides of a 1-inch square?

7. The 5-cm sides of a nominally equilateral triangle are specified to have a tolerance of ± 0.2 cm. What are the tolerance limits in degrees for any given angle?

8. The sides of a 3 cm $\times$ 4 cm $\times$ 5 cm triangle are specified to have tolerances of ± 1 mm.

    a. If the sides are perfect, what are the values of the triangle's three angles?
    b. What are the $\pm$ tolerance limits in degrees of each of these angles?

9. To what tolerance can you measure objects using a common tape measure of the type found in most hardware stores?

10. Suppose that you are building a 10 ft $\times$ 12 ft wooden frame in which you will pour a 3-in thick concrete foundation for an outdoor patio. You wish to locate a hole in the geometrical center for the placement of a birdfeeder pole. You plan to locate the exact center by stretching strings across the corners of the box, so as to make an X. By how much will the hole be off center if the cross strings differ in length by 0.5 inch?

11. The typical four function calculator allows for 8 significant figures in its calculations. Think of at least three applications in which such precision is either required or is justified. (One might be computing your income taxes if you are very wealthy.)

12. Compute the percent error if $\sin \theta$ is approximated by θ when $\theta = 10^n$ radians for integer values of n over the range $-4 < n < 0$.

3   TYPES OF GRAPHS

Most engineering students are familiar with the x–y graphs used in algebra and calculus. Graphs depicted in x–y format can convey all sorts of information in compact form. The plot of Figure 5(a), for example, shows the stretching, or *strain*, of a sample of structural steel as a function of the loading force, or *stress*, applied to it. Similarly, Figure 5(b) depicts the percentage of central processor usage of a computation facility as a function of the time of day. These figures are both examples of simple x–y plots having linear scales. By definition, a linear scale has equidistant "tic" marks.

There are times when simple x–y graphs cannot do an adequate job of depicting numerical information. For these situations, engineers resort to other types of graphs,

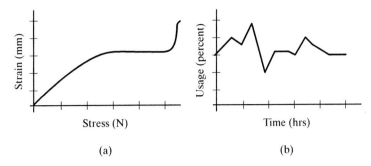

(a)   (b)

Figure 5. Examples of *x-y* plots having simple, linear scales.

including *semilog* plots, *log-log* plots, *polar* plots, *three-dimensional* plots, and *histograms*. We provide brief descriptions of each of these types of graphs in the following sections.

3.1   Semilog Plots

A semilog plot (short for semi-logarithmic) is used if one range of numbers extends over several orders of magnitude. An example can be found in an electronic component called the *pn junction diode*. This device, found in countless electronic circuits, obeys a current versus applied voltage equation of the approximate form

$$i = I_o e^{v/V_T} \tag{12}$$

Here, v is the applied voltage in volts (V), i is the current in milliamperes (mA) that flows in response to the voltage, and I_o and V_T are constants. Suppose that you wish to plot the current flow versus voltage over the range $0 < v < 1$ V for the case $I_o = 10^{-12}$ mA and $V_T = 0.025$ V. Table 3 provides the values of v and i obtained from Eq. (10). A simple *x-y* plot of Equation (12) is shown in Figure 6. As you can see, the exponential dependency of the equation causes the current to rise off the chart for voltages above about 0.8 volts. Although the *x–y* plot depicts the general nature of the device's behavior, it is difficult for the user to obtain useful quantitative information over the full range of data represented.

Note that for equal half-volt increments of v, the current i changes by more that seventeen orders of magnitude. (Increasing a quantity by an order of magnitude means multiplying its value by a factor of 10.)

TABLE 3 Values of Diode Voltage and Current from Equation 12

v (volts)	i (amperes)	v (volts)	i (amperes)
0.00	1.00E–12	0.50	4.85E–04
0.05	7.39E–12	0.55	3.58E–03
0.10	5.46E–11	0.60	2.65E–02
0.15	4.03E–10	0.65	1.96E–01
0.20	2.98E–09	0.70	1.45E+00
0.25	2.20E–08	0.75	1.07E+01
0.30	1.63E–07	0.80	7.90E+01
0.35	1.20E–06	0.85	5.83E+02
0.40	8.89E–06	0.90	4.31E+03
0.45	6.57E–05	1.00	2.35E+05

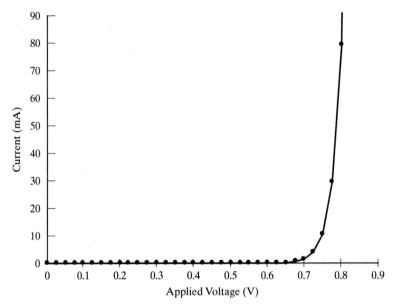

Figure 6. Plot of the diode *i-v* curve from Equation (12) on a linear *x-y* graph. The *v* and *i* data points are obtained from Table 3.

For comparison, the same equation is plotted in Figure 7 with the current represented on a logarithmic scale. Each interval on the vertical axis (e.g., each "tic" mark) represents a factor of 10 increase in the current. The complete range of current values from Table 3 can now be plotted, and the graph allows the user to determine the diode current value for any value of voltage over the range $0 < v < 1$ V.

The vertical scale is called "logarithmic" because the measured span of the axis in physical units (centimeters, for example) will be equal to the logarithm of the number being represented. The plot is called "semilogarithmic" because only one of the axes is

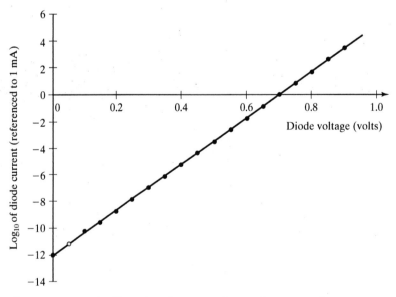

Figure 7. Data points of Table 1 plotted on a semilog graph. Because the current increases exponentially with voltage for positive *v*, using a logarithmic vertical axis allows more points to be included in the range of the graph.

represented on a log scale, and the other is represented by a simple linear scale. Note that a logarithmic scale is a relative scale in which the current value must be normalized to a reference value. In the case of Figure 7, the reference value is 1 mA, and the scale is represented as a base-10 logarithm. Hence, when the actual current i is 1 mA, its logarithmic value becomes zero. Similarly, when $i = 10$ mA, its log value is 1.0; when $i = 100$ mA, its log value is 10.

A semilog plot can also be used when the data to be represented on the horizontal axis extends over many orders of magnitude. One example might be the need to depict the velocity of a high-speed aircraft as a function of engine thrust. Because aerodynamic drag increases as the cube of the velocity, more and more engine power is required to achieve higher speeds, hence a plot of the velocity versus the log of the thrust might be appropriate.

3.2   Log–Log Plots

Sometimes engineers wish to convey data in which both variables extend over many orders of magnitude. In such a case, the *log-log* plot becomes a useful tool. In a log-log plot, both horizontal and vertical axes are represented using logarithmic scales. Log-log plots are often used to represent the physical response of something versus the frequency of the stimulating variable. (The term "frequency" in this case refers to the number of times a periodic stimulus acts per second.) The graph of Figure 8, for example, shows the vibration magnitude of a car's suspension system, measured in centimeters, as a function of the frequency of a sinusoidal force applied to the undercarriage. For this plot, it is understood that the peak magnitude of the applied sinusoidal force is always equal to the same number of newtons regardless of its excitation frequency. The designer might use such a log-log plot to graph a wide range of vibration magnitudes versus a similarly large range of applied frequencies.

3.3   Polar Plots

Sometimes an engineer needs to represent the measured value of a quantity as a function of angle. Examples might include the sensitivity of a directional antenna, the hearing capability of the human ear, or the intensity of a light source. In such cases, the *polar* plot becomes a valuable engineering tool. The coordinate variables of a polar plot are

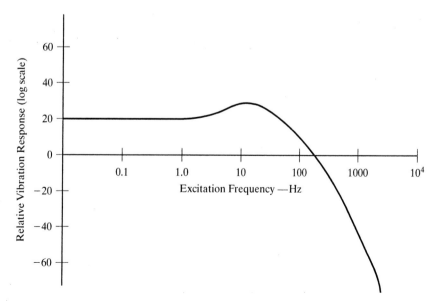

Figure 8.   Response of a car suspension system to a constant magnitude stimulus of varying frequency. In this case, both scales are best represented logarithmically.

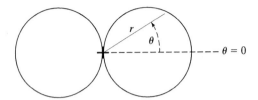

Figure 9.   Polar plot of antenna pattern. The length *r* from the origin represents the strength of the reception as a function of angle *θ*.

the radial value *r* and the angle *θ*, rather than the usual variables *x* and *y*. In a polar plot, the radial distance from the center represents the plotted value for a given angle.

One example of a polar plot is shown in Figure 9. This graph shows the sensitivity of a receiving antenna, called a *dipole*, to radio waves arriving from different angles. The incoming radio waves are assumed have constant magnitude regardless of angle. The signal from the antenna will be fed to a receiving circuit that will convert the coded radio waves into sound or digital data. The maximum sensitivity angles for this antenna (longest values of radial distance *r*) occur at 0° and 180°. Conversely, two *nulls*, or angles of zero reception, occur at 90° and 270°. At these latter angles, the radial distance from the origin to the plot wither to zero.

Sometimes the range of data to be represented on the *r*-axis extends over several orders of magnitude. In such cases, a log-radial plot may be used to adequately depict the data. In a log-radial plot, the linear distance from the center to a point on the graph represents the logarithm of the data value. An example of a log-radial plot is shown in Figure 10. This graph represents the response of a "popcorn" (highly directional) type of

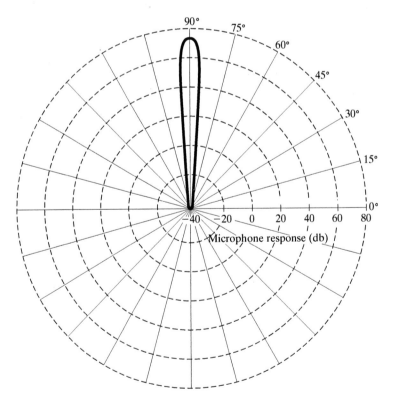

Figure 10.   Response of a highly directional "popcorn" microphone is best plotted on a polar plot in which the radial scale is logarithmic. In this case, the decibel (dB) scale has been chosen. An increase in 20 dB is equivalent to multiplication by 10.

microphone as a function of angle. The radial coordinate in this case is the *decibel* (dB), defined by the formula

$$dB = 20 \log_{10} M \qquad (13)$$

where M is the magnitude of the voltage produced by the microphone for a constant incoming sound pressure level.

3.4   Three-Dimensional Graphs

Sometimes a two-dimensional graph cannot adequately represent engineering data. When a given output variable is a function of *two* input variables, a three-dimensional (x-y-z) plot may be used. Unfortunately, paper and computer screens are two-dimensional, hence special techniques are required to plot functions of two variables. In many cases, an *isometric* plot of the type shown in Figure 11 can be a good choice. This graph represents the surface depth of a semiconductor sample as a function of x and y coordinates. The thickness of the sample, measured relative to a defined zero, or "flat" level, is represented by the height of the mountainlike contour above the x-y ground plane. The plot of Figure 11 was obtained using an interferometric optical scanner; the vertical units are in micrometers, or "microns."

If the z variable varies significantly as a function of the x and y coordinates, sometimes a flat *contour* plot is a better choice. In a contour plot, loci of constant z value are represented by lines (sometimes called *isobars*), and the steepness of the plot is proportional to the distance between adjacent isobars. Figure 12, for example, shows the isometric plot of Figure 11 represented as a contour plot. One common use of contour plots may be found in cartography, where the height of land over the area of a map is represented by lines of constant altitude.

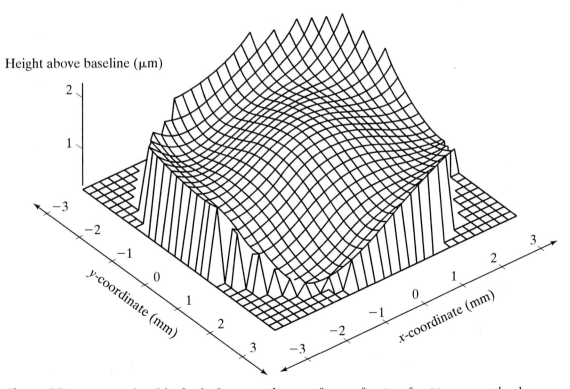

Figure 11.   Isometric plot of the depth of a semiconductor surface as a function of position x-y over the plane.

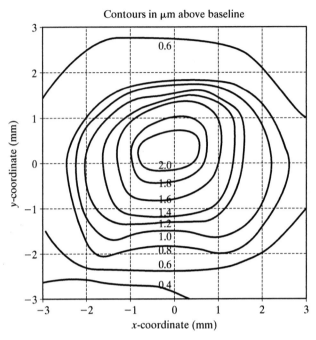

Figure 12. Contour plot of the data from Figure 11.

PRACTICE!

1. Plot the area of a circle as a function of radius over the range $0 < r < 1$ m. Which is more appropriate, a linear x-y plot or a semilog plot?

2. Plot the function $y = \sqrt[3]{x} + 12$ on both linear and semilog axes. For the latter case, should the logarithmic axis be horizontal or vertical?

3. Suppose that you wish to plot the population of the 50 U.S. states as a function of alphabetical order. What type of graph might you use?

4. The growth of bacteria as a function of time can be represented by the equation

$$n = n_0 e^{t/a} \tag{14}$$

Plot this equation for the values $n_0 = 10$, $\alpha = 0.5$ hrs.

5. Under certain conditions, the frequency response of the human ear can be represented by the equation

$$H = \frac{f/f_0}{1 + (f/f_0)^2} \tag{15}$$

where f is the frequency in hertz, or "cycles per second." Plot this equation over the range 1 Hz $< f <$ 100 kHz for the case $f_0 = 15$ kHz. Which type of graph should you choose?

6. Imagine that you are centered in Omaha, Nebraska. Plot the populations of the following cities as a function of compass angle:

Brownsville	Des Moines	Olympia
Butte	Detroit	Orlando
Chicago	Mesa	Providence
Cleveland	Minneapolis	San Diego
Dayton	Mobile	San Francisco

7. The power output of a particular antenna can be expressed as

$$P = 2P_0 \sin(2\pi \cos \theta)$$

where P_0 is the power output that would exist if the antenna output were not a function of angle. Make a polar plot of P as a function of θ.

8. Make a plot of the diameter of each of the planets in the solar system as a function of their respective radii from the sun.

9. Use the appropriate semilog plot to graph the equation $y = K(1 - e^{-x/x_o})$ where $K = 12.2$ and $x_o = 0.01$.

10. Plot the per capita consumption of oil as a function of national population. You can find these data by doing an appropriate Web search.

4   PROTOTYPING

Designing anything for the first time requires careful planning. From the brainstorming phase through the subsequent iterations around the design cycle, foresight is always more valuable than hindsight. In the earlier phases of a project, an engineer often relies on estimation, sketching, approximation, and other noncommittal tools to test ideas for feasibility. Later phases may involve computer simulations, if appropriate. At some point in the design cycle, however, it will be time to construct a first working prototype. A prototype is a mock-up of the finished product that embodies all its salient features but omits nonessential elements, such as a refined appearance or features not critical to fundamental operation. Prototypes are used in nearly every engineering industry. Figure 13, for example, shows the prototype mock-up of one of two Mars Rover vehicles that landed successfully on January 4, 2004 (Spirit) and January 25, 2004 (Opportunity). The Rover prototype is on permanent display in the Smithsonian National Air and Space Museum in Washington, DC.

The prototype of a product can take many forms. If the product is electronic, its prototype is often built on a temporary breadboard. A breadboard allows an engineer to

Figure 13.   Prototype of the Mars Pathfinder Rover developed by NASA. (*Image Courtesy of NASA.*)

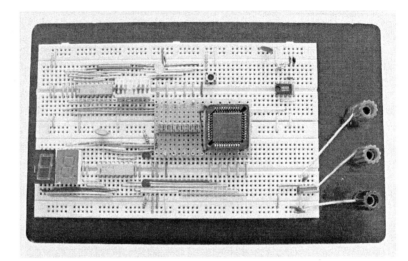

Figure 14.   A well-laid-out circuit on an electronic breadboard.

wire together the various electrical devices, such as resistors, capacitors, transistors, and integrated circuits, to make working circuits. A breadboard readily permits changes and alterations to a circuit—a feature essential to the testing and retesting inherent to the design cycle. An example of a well-laid-out electronic breadboard is shown in Figure 14.

Producing a mechanical product likewise requires the use of easy-to-modify prototypes. The latter may be fabricated from easily machined materials to produce a version that will enable testing and evaluation but may not be as durable or visually attractive as the finished product. A robotic arm, while ultimately destined for fabrication from stainless steel, might be made in prototype form from wood and aluminum for initial tests of part compatibility and overall performance. Wood and aluminum are easily drilled and formed, and they are readily available, but they are much less durable than stainless steel or titanium for demanding applications. Mechanical prototypes also can be fabricated from various forms of bars, straps, angle iron, and similar construction materials. An example of mechanical prototyping is shown in Figure 15. The bars used for this prototype

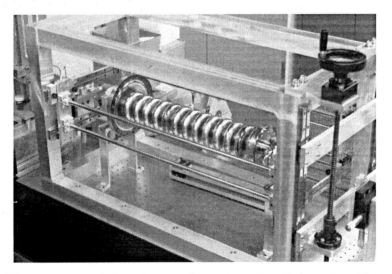

Figure 15.   Structure made from aluminum bars and an adjustable base plate. (*Photo courtesy of Fermi National Accelerator Laboratory.*)

have holes in numerous places to allow for rapid construction and adaptation in revision stages of the design cycle. The base plate consists of a regular array of tapped holes that can accept a standard size screw. This benefit is very useful for a nearly infinite combination of locations for the placement of the mechanical components of the apparatus.

Another example of physical prototyping can be found in the ball-and-socket human hip replacement joint shown in Figure 16. During development, this device might be fabricated from aluminum and polyethylene—again both easily machined materials—for testing its range of motion or for developing the tooling needed to mass produce the device. The finished product ready for implantation would be made from surgical-grade titanium and high-strength polymers at ten times the cost.

Engineers and architects who design large structures, such as buildings, bridges, and dams, face a handicap not encountered by other engineers. It's simply not practical to build a full-size prototype of these structures for testing purposes. It would be cost prohibitive, for example, to test the frame of a tall building, perhaps in some remote desert location, to determine its maximum sustainable wind speed before collapse. Engineers who build large structures rely on scale modeling to guide them through the prototyping phase. Scale modeling uses dimensional similarity to extrapolate to full scale the observations made on a model of reduced size. Effects such as structural stability, wind loading, and large-scale motion are readily scaled, tested, then extrapolated to the full-sized structure. Wind tunnels are widely used to test scale models for aerodynamic effects. Vibration, combustion, and wave phenomena do not scale well because these effects are governed by physical parameters that are fixed regardless of size scale. (That's one reason why movie scenes filmed using scale models of ships at sea or burning buildings often look unrealistic.)

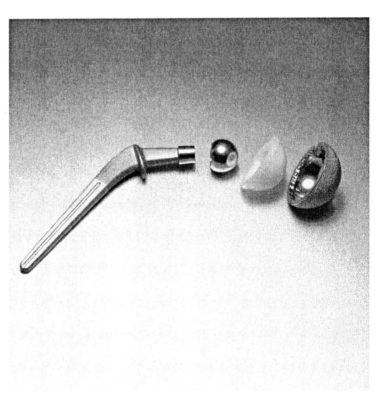

Figure 16. Ball-and-socket human hip joint replacement. The finished product is made from expensive titanium. During development, initial prototypes might be made from aluminum or stainless steel.

Software modules also undergo a prototype phase. The typical software kernel (the part of a software program that does the actual thinking) is surrounded by a graphical user interface (GUI) that provides access to the user. A software designer will sometimes write and test the kernel portions of a program long before writing the graphical user interface.

EXAMPLE 3: ELECTRICAL PROTOTYPING

As discussed in the previous section, the prototype phase helps engineers reveal design flaws and problems that may have escaped the initial planning and estimation phases. The following scenario illustrates the importance of careful prototyping in engineering design. In this scenario, three students, Tina, Tim, and Tally, test the prototype of a heart rate monitor that they have been designing for a multidisciplinary project course. The goal is to design a device that can measure a runner's heart rate and then transfer the data over a wireless interface to the track coach. The device will also be useful as a medical diagnostic tool for monitoring ambulatory heart patients. Tina, an electrical engineering major, has been primarily responsible for the heart-monitoring sensor; Tim, a mechanical engineer, has designed the case and the harness that will hold the sensor over the runner's heart. Tally, a computer engineer, must design the microprocessor system to measure the heart rate and design the wireless link that will transmit the data to a trackside base station. A sketch of their overall system is shown in Figure 17.

The students are currently testing the microphone sensor that will be worn by the jogger. They plan to perfect this particular section, including Tina's circuitry and Tim's harness, before adding Tally's timing circuit, wireless link, and base station. Tina's portion of the system consists of a microphone, amplifier, and signal conditioning circuit. The microphone and amplifier re-create the human heartbeat as an analog signal, while the conditioning circuit transforms each heartbeat signature into a single digital pulse that can be fed to Tally's measuring system. Tina has built her monitoring circuit on a temporary breadboard that sits on a nearby table. In the prototype's final version, the circuit will be hardwired on a compact printed board and placed in Tim's soft plastic case to be worn by the jogger.

Using Tim's harness, the students have mounted a microphone onto Tally, who has volunteered to be the jogger. Tally stands in place while Tina looks at the output of her amplifier on an oscilloscope. The signal looks like the trace shown in Figure 18. The students recognize the waveform as the standard signature of a human heartbeat. Tina connects the oscilloscope to the output of the signal conditioning circuit. The pulses produced by the latter have the form shown in Figure 19. By measuring the number of horizontal graticule divisions between these pulses and noting the time-per-division setting of the "scope," the students estimate Tally's heart rate to be about 60 beats per minute.

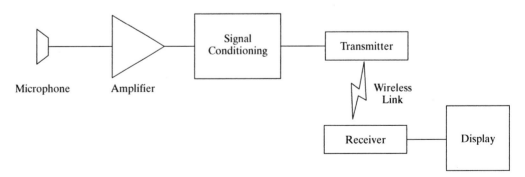

Figure 17. Block diagram of a heart monitor that transmits data about a runner to a trackside base station.

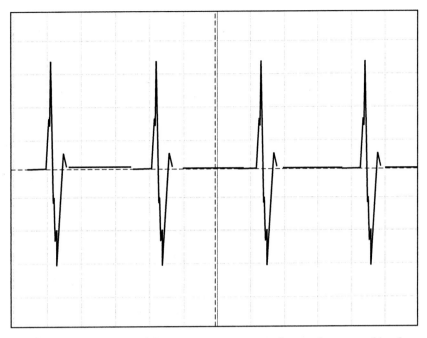

Figure 18. Output of the amplifier section in Figure 17. The waveform resembles the sound signature of the human heartbeat.

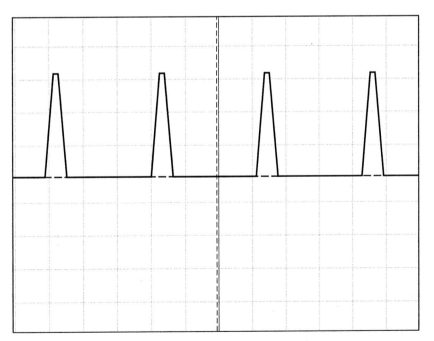

Figure 19. Output of the signal conditioning circuit of Figure 17 in response to the signal shown in Figure 18. The number of pulses per minute is determined by the heart rate.

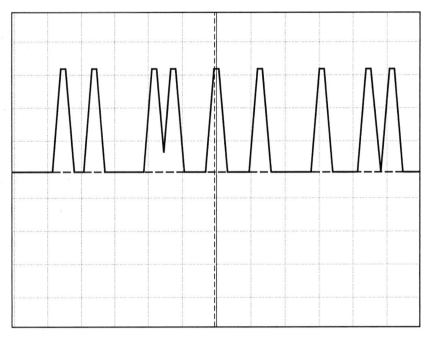

Figure 20. Output of the signal conditioning circuit with runner jogging in place. The signal appears erratic, a sign that something is wrong with the system.

Next, Tina asks Tally to jog in place. The pulses appearing on the oscilloscope now appear as in Figure 20. The pulses are no longer evenly spaced, suggesting that Tally's heart rate has become dangerously erratic. Tally feels fine, of course, and when asked to stop jogging, the pulses return to their evenly spaced, regular timing pattern. The students wisely rule out any health problems that might cause an erratic heartbeat. *What could possibly be wrong?* Tina asks herself. She asks Tally to resume jogging in place, and the same thing happens: the pulse train becomes erratic and unevenly spaced.

After some brief thought, the students suspect a bad microphone connection that manifests itself when Tally begins to jog. They manipulate the microphone wire by jiggling it back and forth but observe no change in the pulse pattern. Tally begins to jog in place again, and the pulses again become erratic.

Tim examines the output of the prototype amplifier at the point where it feeds into Tina's signal conditioning circuit. With Tally at rest, the microphone signal appears normal, as in Figure 18, and the conditioned signal takes the form shown in Figure 19.

"Jog with an irregular step," suggests Tom. "I want to check something." Tally begins a "hip-hop" jog, and the trace takes the form of Figure 21.

"I see what you're after," says Tina. "It looks like our microphone is also picking up the sound of Tally's feet hitting the floor." Mystery solved.

"Can you alter your amplifier circuit somehow?" asks Tally.

Tina replies, "The problem, I think, can be solved by redesigning Tim's microphone harness. Adding some soft padding where it contacts Tally's chest and encasing it in sound-deadening foam might help." The students agree to try this inexpensive solution before embarking on a circuit redesign.

They find some packing foam in the lab and cut it up to test their idea. Adding the foam greatly reduces the unwanted signals on the oscilloscope. They will have to work on perfecting this solution via some design iterations, but they seem to have solved this particular problem.

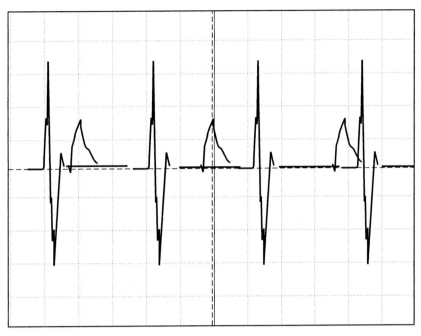

Figure 21. Amplified microphone signal with runner jogging in place. The students discover that the additional portions of the trace correspond to the sound of the runner's feet hitting the floor.

PROFESSIONAL SUCCESS: WHERE TO FIND PROTOTYPING MATERIALS

The materials needed to create prototypes can be found in many places. For building mechanical structures, your local hardware store is a great start. A well-stocked hardware store sells all sorts of nuts, bolts, rods, dowels, fasteners, springs, hinges, and brackets. Many common electrical parts, such as wires, terminal connectors, tape, sockets, and switches, can also be found at the local hardware store. A home center—a large hardware store, lumber yard, plumbing supply, electrical supply, and garden shop all rolled into one—

is an excellent source of structural prototyping materials such as plywood, strapping, angle iron, pipe, and brackets. (See, for example, *www.homedepot.com.*) A selection of very basic electronic parts and breadboards can be found at local consumer stores such as Radio Shack™. More complete selections with lower prices can be found on the Internet. Examples include *www.digikey.com, www.jameco.com, www.mpja.com,* and *www.newark.com.*

EXAMPLE 4: CONSTRUCTING A PHYSICAL PROTOTYPE FOR A MECHANICAL DRIVE

Prism Corporation is a Boston-based company that is developing a process for producing inexpensive, environmentally friendly stampers for making digital video disks (DVDs). A DVD stamper is the master disk placed into an injection molding machine so that common plastic versions of the DVD can be mass-produced. (While many computers now come with DVD-write drives, the latter are not suitable for mass production of DVDs. Disks that must be reproduced in large quantities are made using DVD stamper disks and injection-molding machines.) The present method for making DVD stamper disks involves a time-consuming and expensive process in which a ceramic disk is coated with a thin film of nickel metal. This coating is engraved with pits by a high-intensity laser beam, then peeled off and mounted on the stamper disk plate. The pits in the nickel coating represent the binary 1s and 0s of the digital information stored on the DVD. The chemical substances used in processing the nickel eventually turn into hazardous waste that must be properly disposed of, again at significant cost. Prism has developed a process by which the DVD imprint can be made directly on the stamper disk using a process known as ion machining. A nickel stamper disk is first covered with a light-sensitive photoresist, then exposed to a finely focused laser beam as the disk spins. The laser is pulsed on and off in the binary sequence of information to be stored on the DVD, thereby exposing the photoresist when the beam is on. When the photoresist is developed, it exposes the underlying stamper disk wherever a "pit" is to be etched. The disk is then put in a vacuum chamber and exposed to high-energy argon ions that etch the pits wherever the photoresist has exposed the underlying stamper disk. After etching, the rest of the photoresist layer is removed from the support disk, leaving the finished stamper.

One problem encountered by Prism is the need to hold and release the spinning stamper disk during the laser-writing operation without physically touching the top surface of the disk. The disk must be held firmly on a rotating chuck that is supported by high-speed, high-tolerance, noncontacting air bearings. The latter are similar to ball bearings, but then uses a thin layer of high velocity air. This air is forced between the rotating and stationary bearing surfaces of the chuck, thereby supporting the weight of the chuck. The thin air layer reduces vibrations significantly—a necessary feature if the pits are to be produced accurately on the DVD stamper. Because the chuck is supported by air bearings, however, conventional vacuum techniques for holding objects without top-surface contact will not work; there is no way to bring vacuum lines to the rotating chuck through the air bearings.

Prism has approached a company called K-Volt to develop an electrostatic method for holding the stamper disk on the rotating chuck. In this method, depicted in Figure 22, a sharp needle is held near the edge of the stamper disk and energized to a large positive voltage (several kilovolts). The applied voltage produces an intense electric field at the needle tip, causing the needle to produce positive ions of air via a process known as corona discharge. These ions flow to the stamper disk which becomes positively charged by the ions and sticks to the rotating chuck plate via electrostatic attraction (i.e., "static electricity" or "static cling"). After the laser-writing process, the stamper is released from the chuck plate by applying a large negative voltage to the needle, thereby causing it to produce negative ions that neutralize the stamper disk and eliminate the static cling.

In order to design and test this electrostatic chuck concept, K-Volt has constructed the prototype shown in Figure 23. This prototype in no way resembles the actual electrostatic chuck that will become part of Prism's disk-stamper production system. Its sole purpose is to test the feasibility of using electrostatic forces in this application. Key

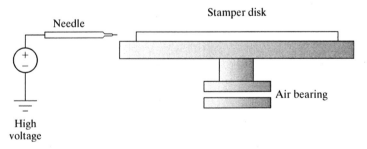

Figure 22.   Electrostatic method for holding a DVD stamper plate on a rotating air chuck.

Figure 23. Prototype of the electrostatic chuck developed for Prism Corporation.

structural details that have found their way into the prototype include a simulated chuck-bearing plate made from aluminum, corona electrodes made from common sewing needles, high-voltage power supplies, and a method for tilting and spinning the mock-up of the bearing plate. The prototype is ugly, but functional. It has allowed K-Volt to test the salient features of the electrostatic chuck and to cycle through several design revisions as it develops its final component parts for Prism.

5   REVERSE ENGINEERING

Reverse engineering refers to the process by which an engineer dissects someone else's product to learn how it works. This design tool is particularly useful if the goal is to create your own version of a competitor's product using your own technology. Reverse engineering is practiced on a regular basis by companies worldwide. Although it may appear to be an unfair practice, it can be a good way to avoid patent infringement and other legal problems by specifically avoiding an approach taken by a competitor. Reverse engineering one of your own company's products can be a good way to understand its operation if its documentation trail has been lost or is inadequate.

One obvious way to reverse engineer a product is to take it apart. Completely disassembling a device will reveal the details of its components and how they interact to allow the device to function properly. Figure 24, for example, shows the disassembled parts of a satellite-based infrared detector module. The dotted lines indicate how the various pieces of the module are to be assembled.

Reverse engineering in the software realm is encouraged when writing webpages on the Internet. All of the major Web browsers provide a means to view and decipher the hypertext mark-up language (HTML) code, the instructions used to encode the webpage that has been downloaded into the computer. This practice fosters an environment of open information exchange that has been the hallmark of the Internet since its inception. In contrast, software that has been written in a high-level programming language such as C, C++, Java, MATLAB, Mathematica, MathCAD, or Fortran, can be especially difficult to reverse engineer, particularly if the software has been

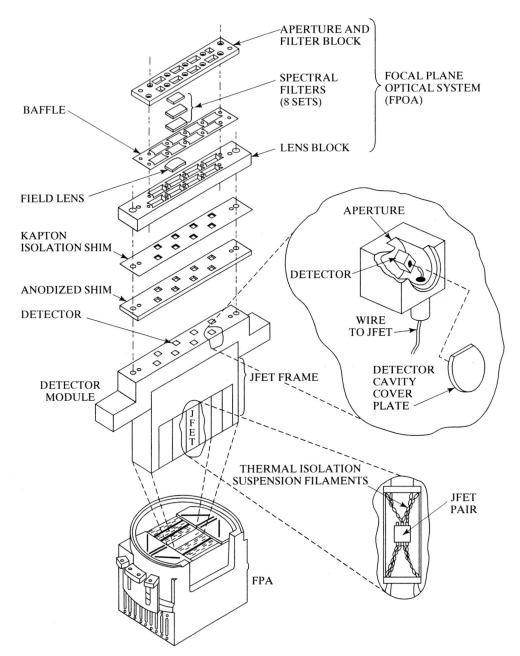

Figure 24. Exploded assembly view of a satellite-based infrared detector module. (*Image courtesy of NASA.*)

poorly documented. A multitude of flow paths and logical junctions in software programs can lead to confusion on the part of the reader and make it hard to understand how a program operates.

6   COMPUTER ANALYSIS

When engineers design something for the first time, they often build simplified prototypes to test the basic operating principles of the device. In many cases, simple hand calculations are all that are needed as a prelude to building a working prototype. At other times, however, more complex calculations are required to verify the feasibility of a design concept. Computers can be an important part of this verification process. Simulation is one major task that computers perform extremely well, and numerous software programs exist that help engineers simulate everything from bridges to electronic circuits. Examples of popular simulation programs include PSpice (electrical and electronic circuits), Pro-Engineer™ and Solidworks™ (solid modeling), Simulink™ (engineering system analysis), and FEMLAB™ (structural and field analysis). General mathematical programs, such as MATLAB™, Mathcad™, and Mathematica™ are also extremely useful in the analysis of engineering problems. In the following example, a simulation is used to aid the design of a kinetic sculpture. The analysis steps are illustrated using the MATLAB programming language. Although this specific software environment has been chosen for the example, the methodology illustrated is universal and could be used with any computer language or software program capable of performing numerical calculations.

EXAMPLE 5: CALCULATING THE TRAJECTORY OF A MOVING OBJECT

This example describes the calculations used to design a kinetic sculpture of the type found in science museums and airports. An example of such a machine is shown in Figure 25. A feeder loads balls into a ball elevator which sets them loose down one of several pathways determined by the travel history of previous balls. Along their way to the bottom of the machine, individual balls ring bells, flip levers, clip-clop down staircases, and perform numerous sorts of acrobatics. One common component of a kinetic sculpture is a downward sloping track that has an upward lip at the bottom. A ball released from the top will accelerate down the track, enter an adjustable launch tube, then be launched upward toward some distant target point. As suggested by the drawing of Figure 26, designing a track and launching tube so that the ball precisely hits its target requires some analysis based on Newtonian physics.

The typical kinetic sculpture may have several such ball launching tracks. The following example explores the calculations needed to ensure that every ball launched from one particular track will hit a wooden "rose box" (a type of wooden musical instrument that makes a hollow sound when struck). The distance between the end of the launch track and its target is one of the parameters set by the designer of the sculpture. After

Figure 25. An example of a kinetic sculpture.

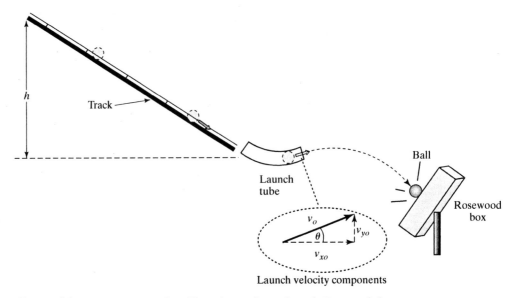

Figure 26. Designing a track and launching tube so that a ball precisely hits its target requires some analysis.

choosing a position for the rose box, the designer must then determine the correct track angle, track length, and launch angle so that the ball hits its target. The chosen track parameters must then be tested on a track prototype before the finished sculpture is built.

The test system, shown in Figure 27, consists of a launching track of fixed length, a flexible launch tube section at the end, and a holding bracket that allows the incline of the track to be set to various angles. Various track lengths are simulated by simply changing the release point of the ball.

For one particular section of the sculpture, the rose box is to be positioned 40 cm beyond, and 20 cm above, the end of a launch tube. The ball has a diameter of 5 cm and weight of 135 gm. If aerodynamic forces are negligible, the ball, once released, will be acted upon only by gravity and will follow a parabolic trajectory. The choices of

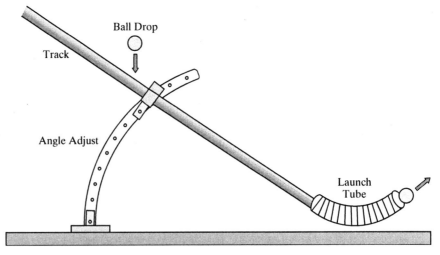

Figure 27. Launch track of fixed length and a flexible tube section at the end. A holding bracket allows the incline of the track to be set to various angles.

track length, angle of inclination, and launch tube angle thus become part of the overall design.

A computer can easily solve for the ball's trajectory. Assuming that the track will impart an initial velocity v_o to the ball, the ball's equation of motion after release will be determined by Newton's law of motion:

$$\mathbf{F} = m\mathbf{a} \tag{16}$$

Here, $\mathbf{F}$ is the total force acting on the ball, and $\mathbf{a}$ is the ball's acceleration. To the extent that aerodynamic forces can be ignored, $\mathbf{F}$ is due solely to gravity and acts in the y-direction only.

The x- and y-components of Newton's law can be integrated using calculus, yielding

$$x = x_o + v_{xo}t \tag{17}$$

and

$$y = y_o + v_{yo}t - \frac{gt^2}{2} \tag{18}$$

Here, x_o and y_o define the position of the ball at $t = 0$, and v_{ox} and v_{oy} describe the initial x- and y-components, respectively, of the ball's initial velocity. The quantity $g = 9.8$ m/s^2 is the gravitational constant, and the quantity $gt^2/2$ describes the fall of the ball due to gravity—a result of integrating the y-component of Equation (16). Note that gravity does not affect the value of x; once free of the launch tube, the ball's horizontal velocity will be constant in time. Only the height of the ball will be affected by gravity.

The ball's exit velocity at $t = 0$ will be determined by the potential energy W stored in the ball at its starting point at the top of the track:

$$W = mgh \tag{19}$$

Here, m is the mass of the ball in kilograms, mg is the gravitational force on the ball, and h is its vertical height in meters relative to the launch point. Equation (19), of course, can be derived using calculus by integrating the vertical force equation $F_y = -mg$ as a function of the vertical direction y to yield the total potential energy, or work, required to lift the ball to a height h:

$$W = -\int F_y \, dy = mgh \tag{20}$$

As the ball rolls down, this potential energy is converted to kinetic energy in the form of forward motion and rotation. Only the former is of interest in determining the ball's trajectory. The rotational energy represents the portion of potential energy that is not converted into the kinetic energy of forward motion.

Although the most accurate analysis would account for the rotational energy stored in the ball, we assume for the sake of this discussion that both frictional losses and the rotational energy of the ball are negligible.

The kinetic energy K of the ball at the moment of launch can be expressed in terms of the energy of forward motion:

$$K = \frac{mv_o^2}{2} \tag{21}$$

where v_o is the ball's initial velocity. Equating K to W (i.e., by assuming that all of the potential energy is converted to kinetic) results in an expression for v_o as a function of initial height h:

$$v_o = \sqrt{2gh} \tag{22}$$

Note that v_o is independent of the ball's mass m. We expect this result from our knowledge that all objects fall at the same velocity regardless of mass.

Using simple trigonometry, the horizontal and vertical components of the launch velocity can be expressed in terms of the launch angle as

$$v_{xo} = \sqrt{2gh}\,\cos\theta \tag{23}$$

and

$$v_{yo} = \sqrt{2gh}\,\sin\theta \tag{24}$$

where θ is the launch angle imparted by the launch tube. Using Equations (17), (18), (23), and (24), one can calculate the evolution of the trajectory in closed algebraic form to find the exact trajectory of the ball as it heads toward the rosewood box. An alternative method is to plot the ball's trajectory using a computer and observe whether or not it hits the box for various choices of track parameters. Although this second method will not provide as accurate an answer as a direct calculation, it has visual appeal and is well suited for implementation on a computer.

**EXAMPLE 6:
PLOTTING
TRAJECTORIES
USING MATLAB**

MATLAB is a versatile and comprehensive programming environment particularly suited for engineering problems. MATLAB is similar in syntax to the programming language C, but it also provides simple commands that enable programmers to plot and organize data, manipulate matrices, observe variables, solve systems of linear equations, and solve differential equations. The strength of MATLAB lies in its ability to manipulate, plot, and graph large amounts of data. Tips on getting started in MATLAB can be found in any of several references.[*]

One possible version of the code in MATLAB is shown below. The program first prompts the user for values of launch tube length, launch tube angle, and the position of the rosewood box relative to the exit of the launch tube. It next computes the starting height of the ball and the x- and y-components of the exit velocity, then plots the trajectory of the ball. This last task is accomplished by incrementing t by a small time dt for each pass through the *while* loop. The looping continues as long as x and y remain within the boundaries of the solution space which is arbitrarily defined as -0.5 m $< x < 0.5$ m and -0.5 m $< y < 0.5$ m. At the end of each loop, the program extends the trajectory plot from the most recently calculated (x,y) position to the newly calculated position. Visual inspection of the plot reveals whether the trajectory hits the rosewood box at the desired location.

The best values for the launch angle θ, track length L, and inclination angle α may be found by trial and error. Figure 28 illustrates the trajectory resulting from the launch parameters $L = 0.51$ m, $h = 0.33$ m, $\alpha = 40°$, and $\theta = 61°$. The target is placed at $x = 0.4$ m and $y = 0.2$ m relative to the point of launch. This solution was found by trial-and-error entry of the various parameter values.

---

[*]Etter, D., Kuncicky, D., and Moore, H. *Introduction to Matlab 7.* Upper Saddle River, NJ: Prentice Hall, 2005. Hanselman, D.C. and Littlefield, B. L. *Mastering Matlab 7.* Upper Saddle River, NJ: Prentice Hall, 2005.

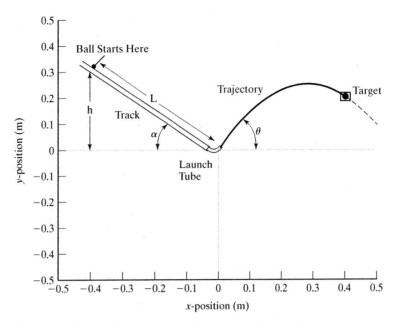

Figure 28. Desired parabolic trajectory and landing site for the ball. The parameters for this particular simulation are $L = 0.51$ m, $h = 0.33$ m, $\alpha = 40°$, $\theta = 61°$. The target is placed at $x = 0.4$ m and $y = 0.2$ m relative to the point of launch.

```
%%%%%         MATLAB PROGRAM CODE    %%%%%%%%
%%%%% Computes trajectory of ball traveling down track
%%%%% and exiting flexible launch tube at specific launch angle
%%%%% Assumes that launch point is at x=0 and y=0
%%%%% SET PARAMETERS:
xT=input('ENTER Target x-position in meters: ');
yT=input('ENTER Target y-position in meters: ');
L=input ('ENTER length of ball travel distance down track, in
meters: ');
alpha=input('ENTER ANGLE OF TRACK INCLINATION in DEGREES: ');
alpha=alpha*pi/180;      %convert angle to radians
theta=input('ENTER ANGLE OF LAUNCH in DEGREES: ');
theta=theta*pi/180;      %convert angle to radians
h=L*sin(alpha);          %Compute height of starting point
                         %relative to y=0
vo=sqrt(2*g*h);          %Compute total ball velocity at moment
                         %of launch
vox=vo*cos(theta);       %Compute x-component of launch velocity
voy=vo*sin(theta);       %Compute y-component of launch velocity
g=9.8;                   %gravitational acceleration in m/s^2

%PREPARE TO CALCULATE AND PLOT
%Set axes for making plot on screen
close                    %close any previously opened figures
S=0.5;                   %Arbitrary axis width
axis([-S S -S S]); hold on
plot(xT,yT,'ob')         %draw target point on screen
line([-L*cos(alpha) 0], [h 0])              %draw the track
line([-L*cos(alpha)+0.01 0.01], [h+0.01 0.01])   %draw the track
xo=0.001; x=xo           %set initial value of x
```

```
yo=0.001; y=yo            %set initial value of y
t=0;                      %set initial time to zero
dt=0.1*L/vo;              %set a time increment
%-------------------------------------------------------------
while (x<S & y>0)         %calculate until trajectory goes out of
                          %bounds
t=t+dt;                   % increment time
xnew=vox*t;               %compute new x-position
ynew=voy*t-0.5*g*(t^2);   %compute new y-position
%plot latest segment of trajectory:
plot ( [x xnew] , [y ynew],'-r' ); hold on
drawnow;                  %put segment on the screen
x=xnew; y=ynew            %update values of x and y
end
%------------------------
```

PRACTICE!

1. Use analytical calculations to compute the trajectory of Figure 28 for a launch angle of 40°, a track length of 1 m, and a track inclination angle of 40°. Determine the x-coordinate at which the rosewood box must be placed if its y-coordinate is at the same height as the launch tube exit.

2. Use analytical calculations to compute the trajectory of Figure 28 for a launch angle of 75°, a track length of 0.5 m, and a track inclination angle of 40°. Determine the y-coordinate at which the rosewood box must be placed if its x-coordinate relative to the launch tube exit is 25 cm.

3. Enter the program from Example 6 into a computer that can run MATLAB. (This code may be found at *http://people.bu.edu/mnh/design.*) Situate the rosewood box target at $x = 25$ cm and $y = -10$ cm. For a track length of 65 cm and track inclination angle of 30°, determine the launch angle required if the ball is to hit its target.

4. What launch angle will result in a ball that travels the farthest horizontal distance in Example 6? Assume that only the portion of the trajectory for $y > 0$ is of interest.

5. What launch angle will result in a ball that travels the farthest horizontal distance in Example 6 if the target point is located 20 cm in height below the end of the launch tube?

6. Draw the flowchart of a program designed to compute the path of a tennis ball after it leaves a player's racquet.

7. Draw the flowchart of a program designed to compute the height of a helium-filled balloon after it has been released from sea level.

8. Draw the flowchart of a program designed to compute the trajectory of a pinball as it makes its way from the top if its launch arc through a maze of obstacle posts.

   The following questions relate to an elastic device that obeys the force-elongation equation $F = -kx$.

9. What is the potential energy stored in a spring that has a restoring force of 1 kN/m and has been stretched by 1 cm?

10. Compute the initial velocity of a 100-gm projectile that is launched by stretching a rubber band by 10 cm. Assume the rubber band has an elastic constant of 50 N/m and obeys a $F = -kx$ law.

11. What is the potential energy stored in a spring that has a restoring force of 500 N/cm and has been compressed by 10 cm? What will be the initial velocity of a 250-gm pinball propelled by the compressed spring after release?

12. A spring has an elastic constant of 100 N/m. (a) How much force will be required to elongate the spring by 5 cm? (b) What will be the landing point of a 100-gm marble propelled from the ground by the spring at a launch angle of 30°?

PROFESSIONAL SUCCESS: THE ROLE OF COMPUTERS IN SOCIETY

Computers have become so enmeshed in our lives that it's hard to imagine society without them. Computers are used in everything—science, engineering, business, commerce, government, education, finance, medicine, avionics, social service—you name it. Computers have even become a form of recreation. One can debate the merit of computers and their effect on human relationships. (Is an AOL chat better than a phone conversation? Is it better to buy online or from a real store?) But in the world of engineering, computers are indispensable. Like most people, engineers use computers for communication, information retrieval, data processing, word processing, electronic mail, and Web browsing. But the special value of the computer to the engineer lies in its ability to perform calculations extremely rapidly. A computer can be programmed to perform all sorts of numerical calculations. Commercial programs for simulation, spreadsheets, and graphing enable engineers to determine everything from the stresses on mechanical parts and the operation of complicated electronic circuits to the force loads on building frames and theoretical predictions of rocket launches. The availability of the computer and the abundance of software tools greatly enhance the productivity of engineers in all disciplines.

EXAMPLE 7: METHOD OF NUMERICAL ITERATION BY COMPUTER

The field of micro-electromechanical systems, or MEMS, has become increasingly important over the past decade. MEMS devices are tiny microscale machines made from silicon, metals, and other materials. They are fabricated using tools borrowed from integrated-circuit manufacturing: photolithography, pattern masking, deposition, and etching. MEMS devices have found their way into mainstream engineering design solutions. The sensors used to deploy safety airbags in automobiles, for example, are built around tiny MEMS accelerometers that are about 1 square millimeter in size, and the nozzles of inkjet printing cartridges are microscale MEMS devices.

One technique for fabricating MEMS devices is called surface micromachining. The basic steps involved in surface micromachining are shown in Figure 29. A silicon

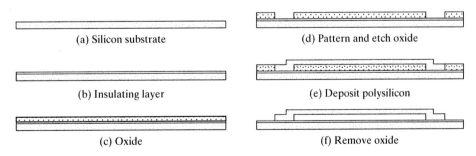

(a) Silicon substrate

(b) Insulating layer

(c) Oxide

(d) Pattern and etch oxide

(e) Deposit polysilicon

(f) Remove oxide

Figure 29. Fabrication sequence for a simple MEMS actuator. (a) Begin with a silicon wafer substrate; (b) deposit an insulating layer of silicon nitride; (c) deposit a thick layer of silicon dioxide ("oxide"); (d) pattern and etch the oxide using photolithography and masking techniques; (e) deposit a layer of polysilicon that will become the actuator bridge; (f) remove the oxide, leaving an air gap between the actuator and the substrate.

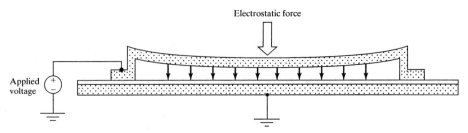

Figure 30 Applying a voltage between the actuator and the substrate causes deflection of the actuator bridge. This mechanical motion can be used to move other devices, change the direction of reflected light, pump liquids and gases, or perform other operations on a microscopic scale.

substrate is patterned with alternating layers of polysilicon and oxide films that build up a desired mechanical structure. The oxide films serve as sacrificial layers that support the polysilicon layers during fabrication but are removed in the final steps of fabrication. This construction technique is analogous to the way that arches of stone buildings were made in ancient times. Sand was used to support stone pieces and was removed when the building could support itself, leaving the finished structure.

One simple MEMS device used in numerous applications is shown in Figure 30. This double-cantilevered actuator consists of a bridge supported on two ends and situated over an underlying, fixed activation electrode. A side view is shown in Figure 30. The bridge has a rectangular shape when viewed from the top. The bridge sits atop an insulating layer and silicon substrate. When a voltage is applied between the bridge and the substrate, the electrostatic force of attraction causes the bridge to bulge toward the substrate. This motion can be used to perform useful functions. For example, the deflecting bridge can open and close tiny valves, change the direction of reflected light, pump fluids, or mix chemicals in small micromixing chambers. A MEMS designer must know the relationship between the voltage applied to the bridge and its deflection. For a given applied voltage V, the electrostatic force F_e will be given approximately by the following equation:

$$F_e = \frac{\varepsilon_0 A V^2}{2(g - y)^2} \tag{25}$$

Here, y is the bridge deflection, A is the area of the bridge as seen from the top, and g is the gap spacing between the bridge and the electrode at zero deflection. The permittivity constant ε_0 is equal to 8.85×10^{-12} F/m (farads per meter) for air. Note that the electrostatic force increases with increasing deflection and becomes infinite for $y = g$ (i.e., when the net gap spacing becomes zero). This increase in force with deflection would cause the bridge to collapse completely when any voltage was applied were it not for the counteracting mechanical restoring force of the elastic material used to make the bridge. To first order, the restoring force F_m will be proportional to the bridge deflection and can be expressed by the simple equation

$$F_m = -ky \tag{26}$$

This force is exactly analogous to that of a rubber band or spring: Its magnitude increases in proportion to the deflection. In the case of the MEMS device of Figure 30, the mechanical restoring force prevents the bridge from collapsing completely when a voltage is applied. As the deflection increases, the restoring force also increases. At some value of deflection, the mechanical force becomes equal to the electrostatic force, allowing no further deflection. A MEMS designer is extremely interested in this equilibrium point, because it determines the bridge deflection for a given applied voltage.

The equilibrium deflection point can be found, in principle, by equating the magnitudes of the electrostatic and mechanical forces given by Equations (25) and (26), yielding the following cubic equation:

$$ky = \frac{\varepsilon_0 AV^2}{2(g-y)^2} \tag{27}$$

Solving this force balance equation by hand is difficult. (Try it!) The calculation is well suited, however, for solution on a computer using the method of numerical iteration. In this latter method, the computer tries many different values of y until it finds one for which both sides of Equation (27) match. One can instruct the computer, for example, to begin with some very small value of y and then increase it by small amounts until the solution point is found. This iterative method is ideal for implementation on a computer, because it typically involves many repetitive calculations that would be time consuming if performed by hand.

The flowchart of Figure 31 illustrates the steps needed to find the equilibrium point by the method of iteration. The program begins with a small value of y, then

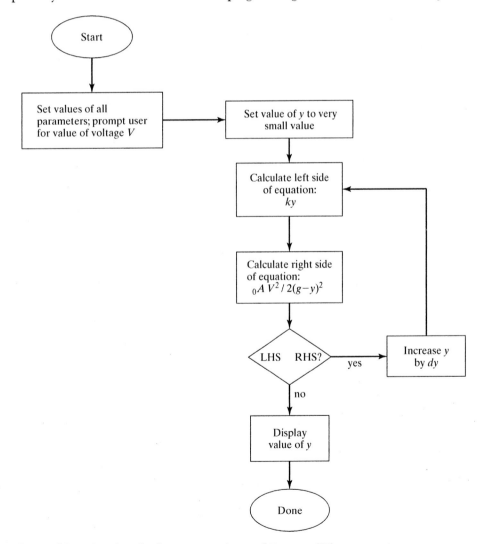

Figure 31. Flowchart for the iterative solution of Equation (23).

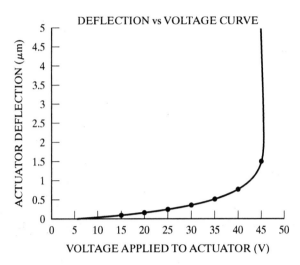

Figure 32. Deflection versus voltage curve resulting from the simulation of Figure 31.

TABLE 4   Parameters for the MEMS Simulation of Example 7

Symbol	Parameter	Value
k	Restoring force	30 N/m
s	Side of square actuator	250 μm
g	Zero-voltage gap spacing	5 μm
y	Bridge deflection	$0 < y < 5\,\mu$m
dy	Deflection increment for iteration	0.05 μm

successively increases y by dy until the left-hand and right-hand sides of Equation (27) agree within some residually small value set by the programmer.

The circles in Figure 32 show the results of the computation for several values of applied voltage and the parameters listed in Table 4. The dotted curve shows the complete analytical solution for comparison. The latter was plotted by solving Equation (27) for numerous values of y and v, storing the data points, and then plotting them.

Above about 45 volts, the restoring force is no longer capable of holding back the electrostatic force, and the deflection becomes "infinite" (i.e., the bridge collapses all the way to its underlying electrode). This phenomenon is called *snap-through* in the world of MEMS. Snap-through commonly occurs at a deflection of about one-third of the zero-voltage gap spacing.

The iteration leading to Figure 32 can be performed using any number of available software programs. Sample program code listings written in MATLAB and C that produce the desired results are provided below. The C program can be turned into a C++ program by simply changing the header files and the functions used for reading and writing variables. The programs prompt the user for an applied value of voltage, calculate the corresponding deflection y, and display the result.

```
%%% ----------------- %%%
%%% MATLAB PROGRAM CODE LISTING %%
% Lines preceded by a percent sign (%) are comment lines
% This program finds the deflection of a MEMS bridge actuator
% for a given applied voltage.
k = 30;   %elastic restoring force in N/m
eo = 8.85e-12;   dielectric permittivity of air
```

```
side = 250e-6;    %dimension of each side of actuator
Area = side^2;    %compute area of actuator
gap = 5e-6;       %spacing between actuator and activation electrode
dy = gap/100;     %incremental deflection to be used in iteration
%Prompt user for value of voltage:
V=input('Enter value of voltage applied to actuator: ')
y=0;                          %initialize deflection to zero
Fm = k*y;                     %Compute magnitude of mechanical force
Fe = eo*Area*V^2/2*(gap-y)^2; %Compute magnitude of
                              %electrostatic force


%-----------------------------------------------------------------
while Fm < Fe;
y = y + dy;  %Try a slightly larger deflection
Fm = k*y;    %Recompute magnitude of mechanical force
Fe = eo*Area*V^2/2*(gap-y)^2;  %Recompute magnitude of
                              %electrostatic force
end
% Display result:
disp('Deflection in microns when Fe = Fm:'), y*1e6
/*-----------------------------------------------------------*/
/* C PROGRAM CODE LISTING */
/* Program to simulate MEMS actuator position versus voltage
curve */
#include<stdio.h>
#include<math.h>
int main() {
int k = 30;
float eo = 8.85e-12,
side = 250e-6,
area,
gap = 5e-6,
dy;
float v,
y,
Fm,
Fe;
/*Square "side" to get area (raise side to the power 2) */
area = pow(side,2);
dy = gap/100;
/* Prompt user for value of voltage */
cout << "Enter value of voltage applied to actuator: ";
cin >> v;
y = 0;
Fm = k * y;
Fe = (eo * area * pow(v,2)) / pow(gap y,2);
while(Fm < Fe) {
y = y + dy;
Fm = k * y;
Fe = (eo * area * pow(v, 2)) / pow(gap y, 2);
}
cout << "Deflection in microns when Fe=Fm: " << y*1e6 << endl;
return 0;
}
/*-----------------------------------------------------------*/
```

PROFESSIONAL SUCCESS: GARBAGE IN, GARBAGE OUT

The computer has become an indispensable tool for engineers because it can perform calculations much more rapidly than can a human. It's superb for storing and retrieving data and producing graphical images. But the computer is no substitute for thinking. A computer should be used to *enhance* the capabilities of an engineer, not replace them. A computer will faithfully follow its program code but is unable to pass judgment on the worth of the results. It's up to the engineer to provide the computer with information that is meaningful and relevant. If you program a computer to calculate the weight of structural steel for a bridge, it can do so flawlessly. But it can never tell you whether such a bridge is feasible, whether the stress–strain equations in its program are correct, or whether the bridge should

be built at all. Only an engineer with experience and good judgment can make those determinations.

When a computer crunches numbers that have little meaning due to programmer error, or when it operates with faulty data that was erroneously entered, the computer operates in a "garbage in, garbage out" (GIGO) mode. GIGO refers to a situation in which bad input data or bad program code leads to a computationally correct but meaningless output. A GIGO condition can be prevented by testing a program on simple, well-known examples for which the solution can be easily computed by hand. If the computer can provide correct answers to numerous simple problems, then it's probably programmed correctly and is ready to be used on more complex problems.

7   SPECIFICATION SHEETS

As a design effort progresses from the initial brainstorming stage, through the various iterations of the design cycle, to finally converging on a likely prototype, a point is reached where the designer has some level of confidence in the details of the product. At this latter stage of evolution, these details may be summarized in a one-page product specification sheet. The contents of this document will vary widely, depending on the discipline, but a representative

Marine Receiver Specifications

Dimensions...................1.49 in. x 5.42 in. x 8.47 in.

Power Requirements................10-30 VDC

System Connectors................D25, RS232 data and power

Antenna Connectors................TNCF

Marine Antenna Specifications

Dimensions..................3 in. diameter, 3.5 in. high

Mounting............... Standard marine 1-14 pole mount

Gain & Impedance................36db, 50ohm

Antenna Connectors................SMAF

Marine Software Requirements

Operating System................Microsoft Windows 98, 2000, NT, XP

Processor................300 MHz or greater

Memory................128MB RAM

Storage................60MB Free Hard Drive Space

Figure 33. A typical specification sheet. This particular set of specifications describes marine-grade radio receiver.

version is shown in Figure 33. This particular set of specifications describes a marine-grade radio receiver for use on ships and boats. The salient information includes the dimensions of the unit, as well as its power connection, software requirements, and operating frequency. A specification sheet for an entirely different class of product—in this case, a protein purification device for chromatography applications—is shown in Figure 34. Note how very different is the information contained in this second example. In general, the format and content of a specification sheet is left up to the designer. The sheet will be ample as long as its purpose is fulfilled: It must convey all the information a user may need to determine the suitability of the product for use in a given application.

8   THE INTERNET

When the first edition of this book was written in 2000, the Internet was described as "an up-and-coming engineering design tool" that was "rapidly gaining popularity." Today, it's virtually impossible to imagine engineering (or any aspect of life, for that matter) without the Internet. Indeed, linking millions of Internet host sites has become vital

BD TALON™ Product Specifications

	BD TALON Superflow	BD TALON CellThru	BD TALON Spin Columns	
Batch/Gravity Flow	Yes	Yes	Yes	No
FPLC	No	Yes	Yes	No
Scale	Analytical Preparative	Analytical Preparative Production	Preparitive	Analytical
Capacity (mg protein /ml absorbent)	5-10	5-14	5-10	2-4
Type of matrix	6% Cross-linked agarose	6% Cross-linked agarose	4% Cross-linked agarose	6% agarose
Bead size, μm	45-165	60-160	300-500	45-165
Maximum linear flow rate (cm/h)	75-150	3000	800	NA
Maximum volumetric flow rate (ml/min)	0.5	50	13	NA
Recommended volumetric flow rate* (ml/min)	0.3	1.0-5.0	1.0-5.0	0.3
Maximum pressure	2.8 psi 0.2 bar 0.02 MPa	140 psi 10 bar 0.97 MPa	9 psi 0.62 bar 0.06 MPa	NA
pH Stability	2−14 (< 2h) 3−14 (< 24h)	2−14 (< 2h) 3−14 (< 24h)	2−14 (< 2h) 3−14 (< 24h)	2−8.5 (< 2h) 2−7.5 (< 24 h)
Protein exclusion limit, D	$\gg 4 \quad 10^7$	$4 \quad 10^6$	$2 \quad 10^7$	NA
Supplied as	50% suspension in 20% ethanol, precharged with Co^{2+} ions	50% suspension in 20% ethanol, precharged with Co^{2+} ions	50% suspension in 20% ethanol, precharged with Co^{2+} ions	50% suspension in 20% ethanol, precharged with Co^{2+} ions, packed in columns
Storage Conditions	RT or 4°C Do Not Freeze	RT or 4°C Do Not Freeze	RT or 4°C Do Not Freeze	RT or 4°C Do Not Freeze

* Determined on 5   1 cm HD (height & diameter) column

Superflow™ and CellThru™ are trademarks of Sterogene Bioseparations, Inc.

Figure 34. Specification sheet for a protein purification product for chromatography.

not only for engineers, but also for individuals involved in business, government, the media, commerce, science, politics, the arts, education, and recreation. The widespread use of data sheets in PDF (portable document format) has made the printed technical data book practically obsolete. Parts and supplies are now more easily purchased from online stores than they are from "brick-and-mortar" vendors. Searching for obscure parts now takes minutes instead of days, and a plethora of information on any engineering topic can be found from a simple "Google" search. The first stop for any engineer seeking information about a particular type of product is likely to be the Internet.

While a comprehensive introduction to the Internet is beyond the mission of this text (and probably unnecessary for most students), a discussion of *when* to use the Internet as part of engineering design is most appropriate. When you access information from the Internet for an engineering project, be sure that it comes from a reliable source. Information is not necessarily accurate just because it has been posted on the Web. Information that comes from the websites of reputable companies and institutions is most likely reliable. Information from personal webpages, student project sites, the amateur press, lone information providers, "bloggers," and other sources outside the mainstream should be viewed with more skepticism. Before the Internet, it took a great deal of time for rumors and misinformation to propagate around the technical community. Now this process takes minutes. Information from one website can be copied to another, leading to the multiple propagation of errors. Although the Internet has provided instant access to limitless information, it has also eliminated an important filter provided by print media: webpages are inexpensive; hence, almost anyone can produce them. Before the Web, only serious companies could afford to disseminate information to the general public. In the print age, technical information seemed more grounded in legitimacy. Now, it's hard to distinguish worthless information from valued information obtained from serious providers. Choose your Internet sources with care.

One other word of caution: The World Wide Web has been around only since the early 1990s. Its growth has been explosive, but the information it can provide on a particular subject is only as complete as the time someone has taken to archive it. The vast majority of engineering data and knowledge existed long before the Internet came into being. As a source of information, the Web can only augment the hundreds of millions of books, reports, and periodicals available in the world's libraries. Although the Internet and its searching tools are important sources of information for your design projects, they should not be the only sources.

PRACTICE!

1. Use the search feature of your Internet browser to perform a search on the term "oil platform." Record the number of listings. Now, narrow the search by adding, in succession, the following additional keywords: "photo," "north," "sea," and "terminal." Determine how many fewer listings are obtained each time the search is narrowed by an additional keyword.

2. Use the search feature of your browser to perform a search on the term "Lyle gun." Record the number of listings. Now, narrow the search by adding, in succession, the following additional keywords: "photo," "history," "rescue," and "reenactment." Determine how many fewer listings are obtained each time the search is narrowed by an additional keyword.

3. Use the search feature of your browser to perform a search on the term "space station." Record the number of listings. Now, narrow the search by adding, in succession, the following additional keywords: "photo," "NASA," "Russian," and "shuttle." Determine how many fewer listings are obtained each time the search is narrowed by an additional keyword.

4. Use the Internet to find a replacement hubcap for a 1994 Toyota Camry. How many different vendors stock this hard-to-find part?

5. The Internet can be a valuable source of technical news. Find everything you can on the subject of the "total artificial heart." What salient feature makes this invention superior to all previous attempts to design a similar device?

6. Use the Internet to find information on the proper design of a "red coachman" fishing lure. Specifically, what type of hackles are recommended for optimum fabrication?

7. The Internet can be the source of misinformation as well as information. Do a search on any of the following topics and find at least two references that contradict each other.

   a. Is there a link between artificial sweeteners and mental health?

   b. Should electrostatic charge decay be measured using the triboelectrification or corona method?

   c. What is the best defense against the winter moth?

   d. Can flexible intermediate bulk containers (FIBCs) be safely used without ground wires?

   e. What is the maximum permissible tolerance on the spacing between the wheels of a light-rail train vehicle?

   f. What is the recommended tread-to-riser ratio for a staircase?

   g. Should bottled water containers be refilled with water for later drinking?

   h. Is there a link between electric power lines and human health?

   i. Will tapping the side of a soda can prevent its contents from foaming over when you open it?

   j. How many spiders does the average person swallow each year?

   k. Can a penny placed on railroad tracks cause a train to derail?

9   SPREADSHEETS IN ENGINEERING DESIGN

A spreadsheet is a programmable table in which each cell consists of text, fixed numerical data, or a formula that relies on other numbers in the spreadsheet for its value. The most popular spreadsheet program continues to be Microsoft Excel. Other types include Lotus 1-2-3, Open Office (a Linux program), Appleworks, Clarisworks, and Corel Quatro Pro. Engineers may use spreadsheets in all phases of the design process for tasks such as performing calculations, analyzing results, planning budgets, tracking parts lists, and performing simulations. A spreadsheet becomes particularly useful when a problem is complex and has many interrelated variables. By programming a spreadsheet to model a complex problem, an engineer can see the effect that changing a single variable has on the entire system. The next two examples illustrate the usefulness of spreadsheets in engineering design. The spreadsheet tables are meant to be generic in form but typical of most commercial spreadsheet software.

EXAMPLE 8: CALCULATING THE CENTER OF MASS

This example describes one phase in the design activities of students Freeda and Froda who have entered the annual "MicroMouse" competition sponsored by the Institute of Electrical and Electronic Engineers (IEEE). The objective of the competition is to design a self-contained, battery-powered mini-vehicle that can learn a maze on its own and then traverse it as rapidly as possible. (See *www.ieee.org*, and enter "micromouse" into the search field.) Because the mouse must make numerous high-speed turns as it negotiates the maze, one concern is the placement of components and the effect of their physical locations on the balance of the vehicle. The students determine that their mouse will perform best if its center of mass is located midway between its front and rear axles. Their simulations have shown that if the center of mass is too far forward, the rear wheels will not maintain enough traction to

drive the mouse at high speed. Conversely, if the center of mass is too far toward the rear, the high torque of the motor and gears may cause the front of the mouse to lift up and temporarily lose its steering capability. The students must now determine where to mount the various components on the chassis of the mouse. The physical location of these components will determine the location of the vehicle's center of mass.

Freeda has weighed each component and recorded the values in her logbook, shown here as Figure 35. She's also entered the sketch of Figure 36 which outlines one possible layout for the components. She's calculated the center of mass of the bare frame (with none of the components yet installed) from basic principles and has found that it lies about 7 cm behind the midpoint between the two axles.

Froda's next step is to decide for certain where to place each of the components on the vehicle chassis. She's prepared a spreadsheet, shown in Table 5, to calculate the center of mass of the entire vehicle, including all its components. (Note that Table 4-5 shows the contents of each cell in the spreadsheet, not what appears on Froda's computer screen.) The discussion that follows focuses on the center of mass in the x-direction. A similar analysis must also be performed for the y-direction.

The location x of each part represents the position of its own individual center of mass relative to the center of mass of the frame. The latter is located at the midpoint between the two axles. The moment M_n of the nth part is equal to its position times its mass:

$$M_n = x_n \times m_n \qquad (28)$$

2/14/99		
Measurements of vehicle parts		
ITEM	APPROX* WEIGHT [gm]	PROPOSED LOCATION
chassis	1000	[defines center line]
wedge fr.	400	−7 cm
battery	120	+8
switch	10	+5
motor	200	−7
gearbox	50	−10
launch tube	15	−12
	*measured on pan balance	

Figure 35. Logbook page showing weights of key vehicle components.

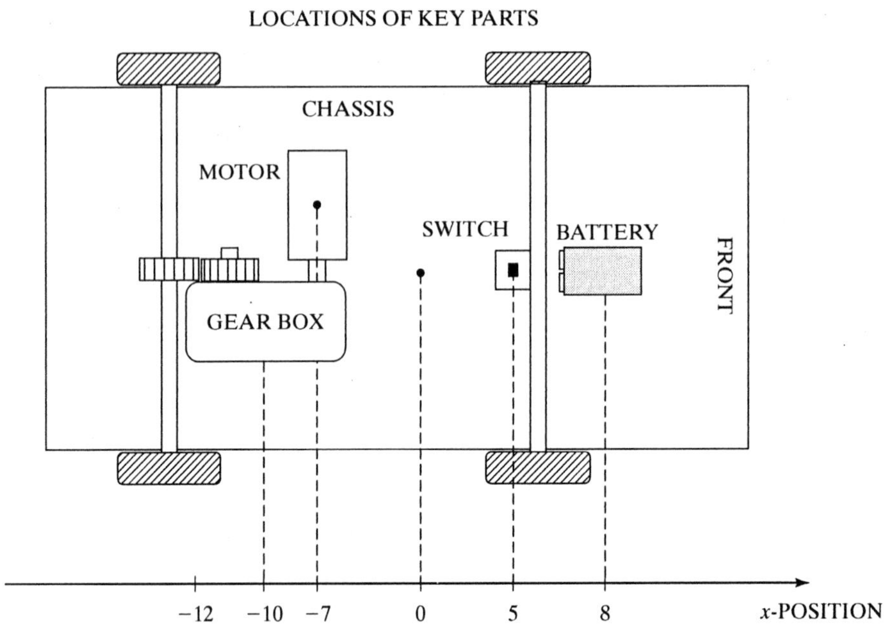

LOCATIONS OF KEY PARTS

Figure 36. Possible layout of vehicle components.

TABLE 5 Cell Entries in Spreadsheet that Calculates Center of Mass

	A	B	C	D
1	Part Name	Mass m (gm)	Location x (cm)	Moment m (gm–cm)
2	Chassis	1000	0	=B2*C2
3	Wedge Frame	400	−7	=B3*C3
4	Battery	120	8	=B4*C4
5	Switch	10	5	=B5*C5
6	Motor	200	−7	=B6*C6
7	Gear Box	50	−10	=B7*C7
8	Launch Tube	15	−12	=B8*C8
9	Total Weight	=SUM(B2:B8)		
10	Total Moment			=SUM(D2:D8)
11	Net C.O.M.		=D10/B9	

The x-directed center of mass x_{CM} of the entire ensemble of parts is given by the sum of the moments divided by the sum of the masses:

$$x_{CM} = \frac{\Sigma M_n}{\Sigma m_n} \tag{29}$$

The output of Froda's spreadsheet, as it appears on her computer screen, is shown in Table 6. The calculations show that the center of mass of the vehicle (Net C.O.M. in the spreadsheet table) lies at $x \approx -2.16$, or about 2 cm behind the geometrical center of the axle mounts. The force calculations that the students have previously performed indicate that the center of mass needs to lie within 1 cm of the vehicle's midpoint.

The students discuss possible alternative arrangements for the vehicle components. Freeda tries to simulate moving the battery forward by changing the entry for

TABLE 6 Screen Output of the Spreadsheet of Table 5

	A	B	C	D
	Part Name	Mass m (gm)	Location x (cm)	Moment m (gm–cm)
1				
2	Chassis	1000	0	0
3	Wedge Frame	400	−7	−2800
4	Battery	120	8	960
5	Switch	10	5	50
6	Motor	200	−7	−1400
7	Gear Box	50	−10	−500
8	Launch Tube	15	−12	−180
9	Total Weight	1795		
10	Total Moment			3870
11	Net C.O.M.		2.16	

battery position on the spreadsheet. Because the battery is connected to the motor by wires of arbitrary length, this change is easy to implement. The change, however, shows that moving the battery all the way to the 15-cm forward position merely shifts the center of mass forward to the −1.7 cm position.

Froda suggests adding a counterweight somewhere between the midpoint of the vehicle and its front axle. She inserts a new row into the spreadsheet and enters data for the counterweight into the cells, as shown in Table 7. The students experiment with different values for the location and mass of the counterweight. The spreadsheet allows them to track changes in the center of mass as they go along. Competition rules specify a 2-kg mouse weight limit, including batteries. The spreadsheet allows the students to see how close they come to this limit as the mass of the counterweight is increased. The cells in Table 7 show the results of placing a 200-gm counterweight 10 cm forward of the vehicle midpoint. The center of mass has been shifted to −0.96 cm behind the midpoint, which lies just on the edge of the targeted range of ±1 cm. The total weight has increased to 1,995 gm, which is five grams below the maximum 2-kg limit. Freeda and Froda decide to stay with these parameters so that they will have a small safety margin with respect to weight; this margin will allow for adding small nuts, bolts, glue, or tape during the competition.

TABLE 7 Screen Output of Modified Spreadsheet

	A	B	C	D
	Part Name	Mass m (gm)	Location x (cm)	Moment m (gm–cm)
1				
2	Chassis	1000	0	0
3	Wedge Frame	400	−7	−2840
4	Battery	120	8	960
5	Switch	10	5	50
6	Motor	200	−7	−1400
7	Gear Box	50	−10	−500
8	Launch Tube	15	−12	−180
9	**Counterweight**	**200**	**10**	**2000**
10	Total Weight	1995		
11	Total Moment		—	1870
12	Net C.O.M.		−0.94	

EXAMPLE 9: KEEPING TRACK OF COST WITH A SPREADSHEET

A spreadsheet also helps Freeda and Froda track the total cost of their mouse vehicle. The funds they have obtained to support their entry set the total cost limit at $100, including batteries. An accounting of the costs must be submitted to the Student Activities Office if they are to be reimbursed for their purchases. Froda has set up a spreadsheet to track these costs. The output screen of the spreadsheet is shown in Table 8.

The Unit Cost column indicates the cost per item, while the Quantity column indicates the number of parts of that type that have gone into the vehicle. The Extended column, equal to the product Quantity × Unit Cost, shows the total cost for each part type. The Total entry at the bottom provides the sum of all the extended prices. As each part is added to the vehicle, the students update their spreadsheet. If the total cost exceeds $100, they can experiment by eliminating various parts, such as extra nuts and bolts, if the design allows it, until the total cost is in compliance. At first, they allot 16 batteries for use on competition day, but this quantity causes the total cost to exceed $100. By using the spreadsheet, they are able to determine by trial and error that reducing the battery allotment to 12 results in a total cost less than $100.

TABLE 8   Cost-Tracking Spreadsheet. The Unit Cost Column Indicates the Cost per Item, and the Extended Column is Equal to Quantity × Unit Cost

	A	B	C	D	E
1	Item	Quantity	Unit Cost $		Extended $
2	Chassis	1	12.50		12.50
3	Wedge frame	1	15.00		15.00
4	Battery	12	2.19		26.28
5	Switch	3	2.29		6.87
6	Motor	1	3.49		3.49
7	Gearbox	1	5.99		5.99
8	Launch tube	1	0.67		0.67
9	Counterweight	1	0.85		0.85
10	Rubber bands	12	0.04		0.48
11	6-32 Screws	24	0.06		1.44
12	6-32 Nuts	24	0.05		1.20
13	6-32 Washers	24	0.02		0.48
14	Two-part epoxy	1	2.29		2.29
15	Wheels	4	1.59		6.36
16	Spool of wire	1	2.49		2.49
17	Tape	1	2.59		2.59
18	Metal brackets	6	1.19		7.14
19	Screw thread	1	0.99		0.99
20	Wing nut	2	0.25		0.50
21	TOTAL				$97.61

PRACTICE!

1. Verify the calculated cells in the spreadsheet of Table 7.
2. Find the center of mass in the x-y plane of a set of objects positioned as follows: The numbers in parentheses indicate each object's x-y coordinates: Object 1: 1.2 kg (0.2 m, 0.4 m); object 2: 3.3 kg (1.3 m, 2.3 m); object 3: 0.9 kg (0.8 m, 0.4 m); object 4: 0.2 kg (0 m, 1.7 m).

3. Using published population data of the twenty most populous cities, find the approximate geographical "center-of-mass" of the country.

4. Using published results from the most recent national election, determine the political "center of mass" of the country; that is, find the geopolitical center that represents a balance between liberal and conservative views.

5. Use a spreadsheet to track your expenditures for one week. Then experiment with possible changes in your cash outflow to enable a budget reduction of 5%.

6. Write a spreadsheet to accurately compute your own grade point average (GPA). Does your result agree with your official transcript? Use your data to project your final graduation GPA. What grades must you get in future courses if you are to meet your GPA goal?

7. Write a spreadsheet to compute the estimated electrical energy use of an average household of four occupants over the course of one week. Include a range of typical electrical loads and their *duty cycles* (percentage of time each one is turned on.)

8. Use a spreadsheet to calculate the cost of the entire wardrobe, including accessories, that you happen to have in your closet at this moment.

9. Use a spreadsheet to calculate the approximate center of mass, relative to home plate, of a nine-person baseball team with each player in position prior to a pitched ball.

10. Use a spreadsheet to estimate the surface area of a 747 airplane. From this information, estimate the volume of paint required to apply one coat of primer.

EXAMPLE 10: MEMS ACTUATOR REVISITED

The method of solution by computer iteration was illustrated in Example 7 using programs written in MATLAB and C. In Table 9, this same problem is solved using an Excel™ spreadsheet formulation for the case V = 35 V. Each cell in column 1 represents a "test" value of y and is greater than the value above it by the incremental *dy* entered into cell B6. When this variable is entered into cell formulas elsewhere in the spreadsheet, the Excel "dollar-sign" notation $B$6 is used, rather than the simple

TABLE 9   Solution to the MEMS Actuator Problem of Example 10

	A	B	C	D	E	F	G
			val. No.	Column 1	Column 2	Column 3	Column 4
1	voltage:	35					
2	k	30		y	F_m	F_e	Difference
3	gap	=5°10^(−6)	1	0	=$B$2°D3	=$B$7°$B$5°$B$1^2/($B$3 − D3)^2	=E3 − F3
4	side	=250°10^(−6)	=C3 + 1	=D3 + $B$6	=$B$2°D4	=$B$7°$B$5°$B$1^2/($B$3 − D4)^2	=E4 − F4
5	area	=(A4)^2	=C4 + 1	=D4 + $B$6	=$B$2°D5	=$B$7°$B$5°$B$1^2/($B$3 − D5)^2	=E5 − F5
6	dy	=B3/20	=C5 + 1	=D5 + $B$6	=$B$2°D6	=$B$7°$B$5°$B$1^2/($B$3 − D6)^2	=E6 − F6
7	ε_0	=8.85°10^(−12)	=C6 + 1	=D6 + $B$6	=$B$2°D7	=$B$7°$B$5°$B$1^2/($B$3 − D7)^2	=E7 − F7
8			=C7 + 1	=D7 + $B$6	=$B$2°D8	=$B$7°$B$5°$B$1^2/($B$3 − D8)^2	=E8 − F8
9			=C8 + 1	=D8 + $B$6	=$B$2°D9	=$B$7°$B$5°$B$1^2/($B$3 − D9)^2	=E9 − F9
10			=C9 + 1	=D9 + $B$6	=$B$2°D10	=$B$7°$B$5°$B$1^2/($B$3 − D10)^2	=E10 − F10
11			=C10 + 1	=D10 + $B$6	=$B$2°D11	=$B$7°$B$5°$B$1^2/($B$3 − D11)^2	=E11 − F11
12			=C11 + 1	=D11 + $B$6	=$B$2°D12	=$B$7°$B$5°$B$1^2/($B$3 − D12)^2	=E12 − F12
13			=C12 + 1	=D12 + $B$6	=$B$2°D13	=$B$7°$B$5°$B$1^2/($B$3 − D13)^2	=E13 − F13
14			=C13 + 1	=D13 + $B$6	=$B$2°D14	=$B$7°$B$5°$B$1^2/($B$3 − D14)^2	=E14 − F14

row–column notation B6. This ensures that any references to B6 will be preserved when cell contents are copied from one cell to another. Without the dollar sign notation, the cell coordinates B and 6 would be automatically incremented during copy operations. The dollar sign notation is similarly used to refer to each of the fixed quantities under the B column of the spreadsheet.

Columns 2 and 3 in Table 9 contain the computed values of the left-hand and right-hand sides of Equation 22, respectively. The entries in column 4, called the residual values, represent the difference between the column 2 and 3 entries. We seek the row for which the residual is zero, i.e., the value of y at which the mechanical force F_m balances the electrostatic force F_e. The actual output of this spreadsheet is shown in Table 10. No single value of y shown in the table yields a precise residual of zero, but the values $y \approx 0.5 \ \mu$m and $y \approx 0.75 \ \mu$m bracket the correct answer, because the residual in column 4 changes from a negative to a positive value between these two rows.

Table 11 shows a second spreadsheet, identical to the first, except that the upper and lower bounds of y values tested are chosen as 0.55 μm and 0.61 μm, and the incre-

TABLE 10 Output of the Spreadsheet of Table 9. Solution lies between y-values (5) and (6)

	A	B	C	D	E	F	G	H
1	voltage	35	Val.No.	Column 1	Column 2	Column 3	Column 4	
2	k	60		y	F_m	F_e	Difference	
3	gap	5.00E-06	1	0	0.00E01	2.71E-05	−2.71E-05	
4	side	2.50E-04	2	2.50E-07	1.50E-05	3.00E-05	−1.50E-05	
5	area	6.25E-08	3	5.00E-07	3.00E-05	3.35E-05	−3.46E-06	← SOLUTION
6	dy	2.50E-07	4	7.50E-07	4.50E-05	3.75E-05	7.49E-06	← RANGE
7	ε_o	8.85E-12	5	1.00E-06	6.00E-05	4.23E-05	1.77E-05	
8			6	1.25E-06	7.50E-05	4.82E-05	2.68E-05	
9			7	1.50E-06	9.00E-05	5.53E-05	3.47E-05	
10			8	1.75E-06	1.05E-04	6.41E-05	4.09E-05	
11			9	2.00E-06	1.20E-04	7.53E-05	4.47E-05	
12			10	2.25E-06	1.35E-04	8.96E-05	4.54E-05	
13			11	2.50E-06	1.50E-04	1.08E-04	4.16E-05	
14			12	2.75E-06	1.65E-04	1.34E-04	3.12E-05	

TABLE 11 Expansion of Spreadsheet of Table 10 Starting with Value (3) from Table 10 and Smaller *dy*

	A	B	C	D	E	F	G	H
1	voltage:	35	Val. No.	Column 1	Column 2	Column 3	Column 4	
2	k	30		y	F_m	F_e	Difference	
3	gap	5.00E-06	1	5.00E-07	3.00E-05	3.35E-05	−3.46E-06	
4	side	2.50E-04	2	5.10E-07	3.06E-05	3.36E-05	−3.01E-06	
5	area	6.25E-08	3	5.20E-07	3.12E-05	3.38E-05	−2.56E-06	
6	dy	1.00E-08	4	5.30E-07	3.18E-05	3.39E-05	−2.11E-06	
7	ε_o	8.85E-12	5	5.40E-07	3.24E-05	3.41E-05	−1.66E-06	
8			6	5.50E-07	3.30E-05	3.42E-05	−1.22E-06	
9			7	5.60E-07	3.36E-05	3.44E-05	−7.71E-07	
10			8	5.70E-07	3.42E-05	3.45E-05	−3.26E-07	← SOLUTION
11			9	5.80E-07	3.48E-05	3.47E-05	1.17E-07	← RANGE
12			10	5.90E-07	3.54E-05	3.48E-05	5.60E-07	
13			11	6.00E-07	3.60E-05	3.50E-05	1.00E-06	
14			12	6.10E-07	3.66E-05	3.52E-05	1.44E-06	

ment dy is reduced to 0.01 μm, or about a tenth as large as the dy used in Table 8. The results of this second spreadsheet show that the actual equilibrium point lies somewhere between $y \approx 0.57 \mu$m and $y \approx 0.58 \mu$m. If an even more precise answer is desired, then these y values could be set as new upper and lower bounds and dy could be reduced to an even smaller value.

10   SOLID MODELING AND COMPUTER-AIDED DRAFTING

When the ultimate goal of a design effort is a real, physical product, formal drawings of the object must augment estimations and rough sketches. Formal drawings form a key link between design engineers and technicians, fabricators, marketing specialists, customers, and other individuals. Pictorial documentation may appear in one of several forms at various stages of the design process. These forms include isometric views, orthographic projections, exploded views, and solid models. Each of these graphic formats serves a particular design need.

Various methods for generating engineering drawings have evolved over the years. Before computers, the skill of manual drafting (sometimes called "technical drawing") was taught to engineers and technicians in all disciplines. Courses on drafting were common in high school and college curricula, and all self-respecting engineering students owned a complete set of drafting tools. A typical engineer's drafting kit included T-squares, triangular rules, mechanical pencils, erasers, inking pens, and drawing templates. Drafting skills learned in school carried over to the workplace, as the practice of manual drafting was a mainstream activity in most engineering companies. In any given engineering firm, entire rooms would be filled with drafting tables and engineers at work.

Nowadays, computers have virtually eliminated the need for manual drafting skills. Much as the typewriter replaced manual penmanship, and the word processor replaced the manual typewriter, so have numerous computer-aided design (CAD) software tools replaced the need for engineers with manual drafting skills. Popular CAD software packages, including ProEngineer™ and SolidWorks™, are used by engineering companies everywhere. This section reviews the key steps involved in using these types of CAD tools for generating engineering drawings.

10.1   Why an Engineering Drawing?

Consider the engineering drawing of the chassis plate shown in Figure 37. For the purpose of this discussion, its end use does not matter. This object might be used, for example, as part of a vehicle for the MicroMouse competition mentioned in Example 7. Contrast the detailed engineering drawing of the figure with the following written fabrication instructions:

The plate should be made from 0.4-mm-thick aluminum stock and should be a rectangle 25-mm long by 20-mm wide. It should be drilled with four holes. The first should be located 2.0 mm from the right-hand, 20-mm edge of the plate, and 2.5 mm from the upper 25-mm edge. The second hole should be located 1.9 mm to the left of the first. These dimensions should be held to a tolerance of 0.1 mm. Both holes should be drilled to a diameter of 0.2 mm with a tolerance of 0.001 mm. These holes should be duplicated using the same dimensions at the other corner of the plate, but located 2.8 mm from the right-hand, 15-mm edge of the plate, and 2.5 mm from the lower 25-mm edge.

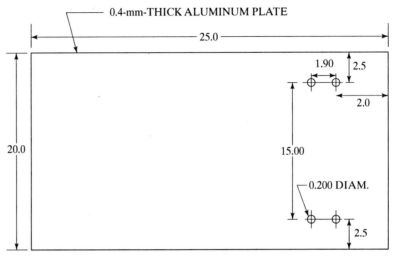

0.4-mm-THICK ALUMINUM PLATE

MAIN CHASSIS PLATE

TOLERANCE TABLE	
All dimensions in cm	
X	±0.5
X.X	±0.1
X.XX	±0.05
X.XXX	±0.001

Figure 37. Drawing of a chassis plate to be sent to a machinist for fabrication.

For most people, the diagram conveys the information much more succinctly than does the written version. The human brain is an extremely efficient image processor, and drawings will almost always surpass written prose as a means for conveying information. The superiority of human imaging power motivates the well-known saying, "A picture is worth a thousand words."

10.2   Types of Drawings

As noted previously, engineering drawings come in several widely accepted forms. Categories include hand sketches, isometric projections, orthographic projections, exploded views, and solid models. Each type of drawing has its own particular use in the engineering design process. During the idea-generation phase, hand sketches can be extremely useful. By quickly drawing things on paper, an engineer can rapidly convey a design concept to other team members. The very act of producing a hand sketch can serve as a catalyst for ideas. Hand sketches also are the medium of choice for entering ideas into engineering logbooks.

When a commitment has been made to pursue a particular design concept, more formal types of drawings are in order. The drawing of Figure 38 shows the isometric view of a simple part. An isometric view is a three-dimensional rendition in which the parallel sides of the actual object are drawn as parallel lines on the page. Isometric views differ from perspective drawings as taught in art and advertising graphics, in which parallel lines point to a distant "vanishing point." An isometric projection becomes a slightly distorted rendition of the object, but if the part is small and distances are short, the differences will be minor. The isometric view of Figure 38, for example,

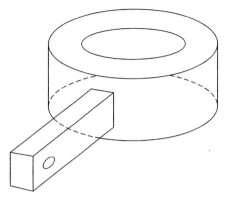

Figure 38.   Isometric view of cylindrical collar with rectangular tab and pin hole.

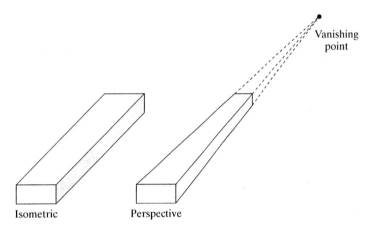

Figure 39.   Isometric and perspective views of a long narrow box. In the isometric view, all parallel lines on the physical object are drawn parallel to each other on the page. In the perspective view, parallel lines on the physical object are drawn so that their extensions intersect at some distant vanishing point.

differs little from its equivalent perspective drawing, whereas the isometric and perspective views of a long narrow box, shown in Figure 39, differ significantly. The principal advantage of the isometric view is that it is much easier to draw than a perspective drawing. Also, compared with its related counterpart, the orthographic projection, the isometric drawing provides a "birds-eye view" of the object that conveys many of its features at a single glance.

The two-dimensional orthographic projections of an object shows its front, side, and end views. In some cases, a fourth view may be necessary. Figure 40 shows an orthographic projection of the same part described by the isometric view of Figure 38. Orthographic projections are principally used by machinists for whom such drawings provide all the information needed to fabricate the actual part. Dimensions, tolerances, and machining details are very easy to convey on an orthographic projection. Compared with other types of drawings, orthographic projections are exceptionally easy to draw but require more interpretation on the part of the person trying to read the drawing.

An exploded view, or assembly drawing, is used to describe how multiple parts are to be assembled to form the working whole. Dotted lines convey paths to connection or attachment. The diagram in Figure 41, for example, shows how the part of Figure 40 is to be assembled with other related parts. Although exploded views some-

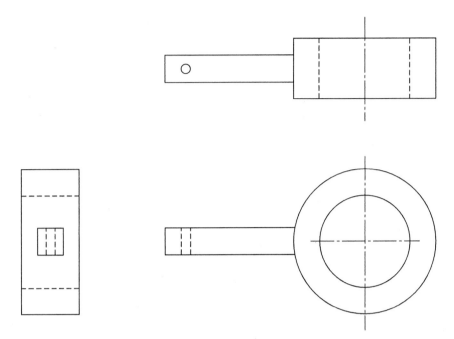

Figure 40. Orthographic projection of the part of Figure 38.

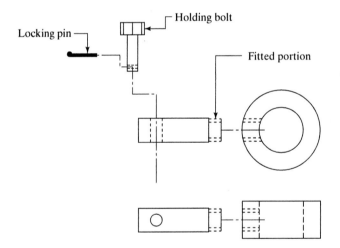

Figure 41. Exploded view of several parts shows the way in which they are to be assembled.

times can be difficult to draw, they are very useful for conveying information about complex structures.

The most computationally sophisticated type of drawing produced by a CAD system is called a *solid model*. Unlike isometric and orthographic projections, which depict just the surfaces of an object, a solid model rendition includes information about the surfaces and the interior details of the object. A solid model is much more than a simple visualization. It contains a complete mathematical description of the object's material properties as well as its interior and exterior dimensions. This additional information makes the solid model useful for many applications besides viewing. For example, the solid model can be used to predict the object's deformation under applied stress, its reaction to temperature changes, and its interaction with other parts in the system. A solid model of a part is invaluable for rendering the sort of animations associated with computer graphics. A solid model allows the user to view an object's hidden features, as well as view the object as its rotation is simulated.

At the core of solid modeling lies a computational method known as finite element analysis (FEA), in which an object is represented by a large number of interconnected cells, or "elements." A finite element analysis keeps track of the mutual interaction between each cell and its neighbors and computes the behavior of each cell in response to internal and external stimuli. The popular CAD tools ProEngineer and SolidWorks, for example, incorporate finite-element analyses into the solid models of parts and objects.

When an object has been rendered in CAD software as a solid model, the latter becomes invaluable when the part is ready for manufacturing. Sophisticated software linked to computer-guided machining tools—lathes and milling machines, for example—can be instructed to fabricate the part directly from its solid model representation. The language used by this class of machines is called *computer numeric control*, or CNC. The CNC system enables an engineer to design a part on the computer screen, then send its CNC code directly to a computer-controlled machine for fabrication from metal, plastic, or other machinable materials. Another method for fabricating things directly from solid models is called rapid prototyping. In this technique, a rendition of the part suitable for prototype needs is produced using a laser beam that shapes the part from very thin cross sections of plastic resins or paper. The prototype part is assembled, literally layer by layer, by stacking its cross sections.

EXAMPLE 11: PRODUCING A SIMPLE PART

This example illustrates the steps involved in producing the solid model of the part shown in Figures 38 and 40. The steps for producing the solid model drawing are summarized here in a generic way, but they are similar to those one would follow when using specific CAD tools such as ProEngineer and SolidWorks.

Step 1. Open a new drawing screen. Open a new part screen in the CAD software by choosing NEW from the software's FILE pull-down menu. A blank screen appears on which the part description will be drawn.

Step 2. Sketch the principal cross section (Figure 42). Using the mouse and keyboard cursors, sketch the part's basic cross section on the screen. Even though the part may have features in all three dimensions, only its principal cross section (e.g., its top view) need be drawn at this stage. The other views of the part will be generated automatically in a later step. This initial cross section of the part can include some of its machined features. For example, the part in Figure 40 includes a drilled hole in its center whose location and dimensions are specified in the initial cross section. The radii of corners and bends in the cross section also can be specified at this stage. This step is sometimes desirable because no machining process can produce perfect angles from solid materials.

Step 3. Dimension the sketch (Figure 43). Major features of the part—lines, circles, and arcs, for example—are selected on the screen and their dimensions are specified in the units chosen for the drawing (e.g., mm, cm, or in.). This step also provides a reference scale for all the other lines and curves that will make up the finished drawing.

Step 4. Extrude the cross section (Figure 44). The defined and dimensioned cross section from the previous step is extruded, or "stretched," in the direction perpendicular to the drawing plane to form a three-dimensional version of the part. The extrusion of a circle produces a cylinder, while the extrusion of a rectangle produces a rectangular solid. The extrusion operation leading to Figure 44 thus

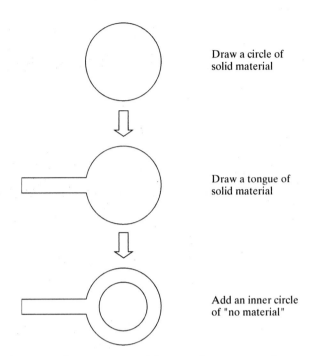

Draw a circle of
solid material

Draw a tongue of
solid material

Add an inner circle
of "no material"

Figure 42. The principal cross section of the part of Figure 40 is drawn on the computer screen.

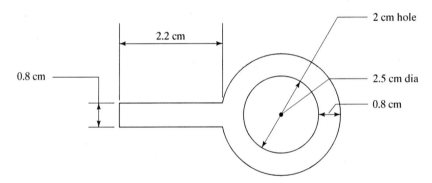

2.2 cm

0.8 cm

2 cm hole

2.5 cm dia

0.8 cm

Figure 43. Dimensions are added to the cross-sectional sketch.

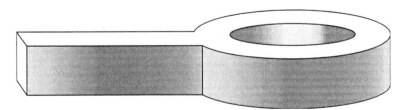

Figure 44. The cross section is extruded to form a solid model.

results in a cylindrical solid with a hole in its center; it also has a rectangular appendage called a tab.

Step 5. Add features to the extruded part (Figure 45). Once the cross section has been extruded to form a three-dimensional solid model, the three orthographic

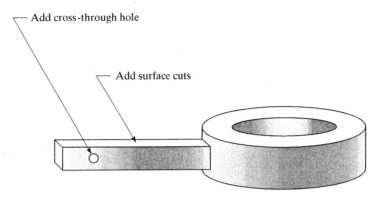

Add cross-through hole

Add surface cuts

Figure 45.   Other features are added to the extruded model that were not created during the first extrusion. In this case, a hole whose axis is parallel to the cross-sectional plane is drawn through the rectangular tab, and the top and bottom faces of the tab are trimmed.

projections of the part will be available to the designer. Features that are not part of the principal cross section, including perpendicular holes, material cuts, and rounded corners, are added to the object at this stage using the appropriate orthographic view. In this case, a hole whose axis is parallel to the cross-sectional plane is drawn through the rectangular tab, and the top and bottom faces of the tab are trimmed.

Step 6. Save the file. The file is saved for future use, printing, and so forth. The solid model rendition of the part is now complete and can be sent as a drawing to other engineers for review in either hard copy or electronic form. Additionally, it can be sent to a CNC-equipped machine tool or to a rapid prototyping machine for computer-controlled fabrication.

11   SYSTEM SIMULATION

Sometimes, engineers must model the dynamic behavior of a system, that is, the way in which the various parts of the system interact over time. A dynamic analysis differs from the finite element analyses provided by simulation tools such as ProEngineer and Solid-Works in that the various parts of the system are represented mathematically in block diagram form, rather than as dimensioned objects having physical properties such as density and elasticity. System simulation is useful for analyzing physical objects such as machinery, but it also is invaluable for analyzing intangible entities such as transportation systems, manufacturing processes, or even financial systems. Dynamic simulation tools are useful whenever the system can be mathematically described by *differential equations* in which the value of a variable depends on its own derivative or that of other variables. A simple pendulum or a guitar string, for example, can each be described by a differential equation.

One popular dynamic system simulation tool that runs as an appendage to MAT-LAB is called Simulink®. The programmer uses Simulink to draw a block diagram that represents the dynamic system to be simulated. The program then determines the relevant differential equations and sends them to MATLAB for solution and display. This layering of software shells, wherein one program produces code that can be solved by another, is common in software engineering.

EXAMPLE 12:
THERMOSTAT
CONTROL

The concept for the following example is derived from an example found in the instruction manual that comes with the student version of Simulink. These block diagrams are more generic than those actually used within Simulink, but they illustrate the concepts involved. Suppose that you were given the task of designing a temperature control system for a small building heated by a furnace. Because the building has thermal memory, that is, it retains heat for some time when the furnace goes off and requires time to heat up when the furnace is turned on, the furnace-building combination constitutes a dynamic system. The variables of the system include the desired temperature (the setting of the thermostat) and the actual indoor temperature. The program determines the difference between the two temperatures and turns on the switch if $T_{actual} < T_{thermostat}$. Turning on the switch causes the furnace to produce heat that increases indoor temperature, but with a time delay τ_1 (sometimes called a time constant). In the meantime, regardless of the status of the furnace, heat continually flows out of the building in proportion to the difference between the indoor and outdoor temperatures. The time constant governing this outward heat flow is τ_2.

A block diagram description of the system is shown in Figure 46. The output of the system, produced by Simulink for the parameters $T_{thermostat} \approx 68°F$, $T_{outdoor} \approx 32°F$, $\tau_1 \approx 4$ min, and $\tau_2 \approx 12$ min, is shown in Figure 47. This plot indicates that the temperature falls slowly until T_{actual} falls below $T_{thermostat}$. At that point in time, the furnace turns on and raises the temperature until $T_{actual} \approx T_{thermostat}$. Note that the building temperature continues to rise for some time after the furnace is turned off. This phenomenon occurs because of the non-zero time delays in the system. Although the thermostat recognizes that T_{actual} has reached $T_{thermostat}$, the time delay governing the transfer of heat from the furnace and the building causes additional heat to flow from the former to the latter.

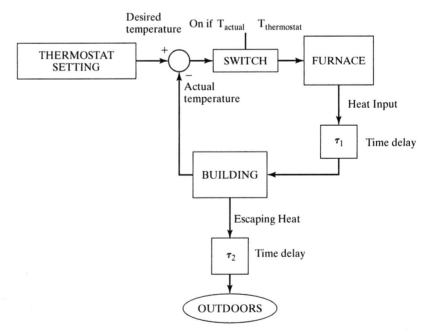

Figure 46. Block diagram description of the dynamic system of a building and its heating furnace.

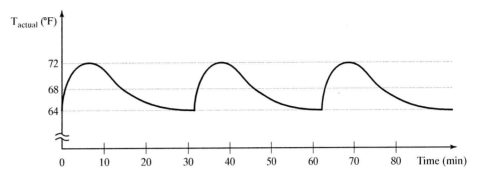

Figure 47.   Results of the simulation with $T_{thermostat} = 68°F$, $T_{outdoor} = 32°F$, $\tau_1 = 4$ min, and $\tau_2 = 12$ min.

12   ELECTRONIC CIRCUIT SIMULATION

Circuits involving electricity can take many forms. A circuit that delivers energy from batteries, generators, or fuel cells is commonly called an *electrical* circuit. Examples of electrical circuits include flashlights, motor drives for electric subway cars, power lines that deliver electricity to homes, and wiring systems inside automobiles and trucks. These systems typically involve only a few basic component types that might include batteries, generators, wires and switches, plus loads that can be modeled as simple resistors. A device such as a resistor is linear and obeys Ohm's law: $v = iR$, where v is the voltage applied to the resistor, i is current that flows in response, and R is the resistance value.

In contrast to resistors, semiconductor devices are usually nonlinear. Their voltage-current equations are not simple linear equations; rather, they take on more complex forms. For example, the current–voltage equation for a simple diode is given by the exponential equation

$$i = I_S(e^{v/nV_T} - 1) \tag{30}$$

where n, I_S, and V_T are constants.[*]

The transistor, a three-terminal device, has an even more complicated set of governing equations. Other nonlinear devices include the light-emitting diode (LED), and the integrated circuit. When a circuit contains nonlinear devices, it is usually called an *electronic* circuit, rather than an "electrical" circuit.

Calculating the voltages and currents in electronic circuits, particularly those with multiple semiconductor devices, can be a daunting task. Even the simple circuit shown in Figure 48 cannot be solved by simple algebra. Circuits that contain multiple diodes, transistors, or integrated circuits are readily solved using a circuit simulation tool called SPICE. Several derivatives of this program, including PSPICE and ORCAD, all use the original core SPICE calculation program, developed for large mainframe computers in the 1970s at the University of California at Berkeley.

---

[*]For $v > V_T$, the equation is sometimes approximated as $i = I_S e^{v/nV_T}$.

SPICE can model voltage sources (e.g., batteries, the output of *dc* power cubes, and ac transformers); resistors; other linear circuit elements called capacitors and inductors; and all sorts of semiconductors, including diodes, transistors, and operational amplifiers. It also enables the entry of devices with user-specified characteristics. SPICE can perform steady-state analyses, simulate circuit behavior over time, and model the effects of temperature, thermal noise, and random component variations. Output is provided in several forms, including text-based listings of the circuit's various voltage, current, and power dissipation values, as well as plots versus time of selected circuit variables. The internal core program within SPICE relies on text-based entry of the circuit description. This entry mode stems from the origins of SPICE, which was developed as public-domain software for implementation on mainframe computers with punched cards and line printer output. More modern versions of SPICE, such as PSPICE-A/D and ORCAD, provide a graphical interface and a list of predefined commercial parts from which to build the circuit. Ultimately, however, these higher end programs translate circuit information entered graphically into traditional text-based SPICE code. Student evaluation versions of SPICE are available for download on the Internet. (See, for example, *www.orcad.com*).

In text-based SPICE code, the circuit is described by a set of program statements stored in a file named FILENAME.CIR, where FILENAME is chosen by the user. This data file is retrieved by SPICE during program execution. Each line of the input file contains one program statement that either describes a single part or instructs SPICE with a command. Comment lines are preceded by an asterisk (°) or a semicolon (;).

The typical input file consists of a required title line, a set of element statements that describe the circuit, and a set of control statements that instruct SPICE during program execution. Control statements always begin with a period. The entire file is terminated by the control statement .END. In order to simulate a circuit in SPICE, its various nodes must be assigned numbers. One node (usually the most common node, or "ground") must be assigned the number zero.

EXAMPLE 13: NONLINEAR CIRCUIT SIMU-LATION

The circuit of Figure 48 is easily solved using SPICE. Following is a program listing that instructs SPICE to calculate the voltage across, current through, and power dissipated in each circuit component. Each node has been numbered, and the bottom, common node has been assigned the number 0:

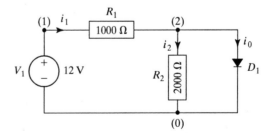

Figure 48. Circuit to be simulated using PSPICE. Each node of the circuit has been assigned a unique number. The common "ground" node at the bottom is assigned the number 0.

```
SPICE SIMULATION OF CIRCUIT OF Figure 48
*Specify the elements in the circuit.
V1 1 0 dc 12V              ;12-V dc voltage source between nodes 1
                           ;and 0 (+ side of source at node 1)
R1 1 2 10000               ; A 10-k   resistor between nodes 1 and 2
R2 2 0 10000               ; A 10-k   resistor between nodes 2 and 0
D1 2 0 diode               ; A diode pointing from node 2 to node 0
.MODEL diode D(Is=1e-5m n=2)   ;A statement that identifies the
                                ;parameters of the diode
.OP                        ;Calculate the operating point (voltage
                           ;and current) of every device
.END
```

Here is a portion of the text output that results from running this simulation:

```
********SMALL SIGNAL BIAS SOLUTION TEMPERATURE = 27.000 DEG C
  NODE VOLTAGE        NODE       VOLTAGE
  (         1)     12.0000      (    2)     0.5995
VOLTAGE SOURCE CURRENTS
       NAME CURRENT
       V1-1.140     E-03
TOTAL POWER DISSIPATION 1.37E-02 WATTS
JOB CONCLUDED
TOTAL JOB TIME .65
****************************************************************
```

This output indicates that the diode voltage will be equal to about 0.6 V, and the source current will be equal to about 1.1 mA. The entire circuit will dissipate 13.7 mW (i.e., it will convert 13.7 milliwatts of electrical power to heat).

13   GRAPHICAL PROGRAMMING

One category of software tool that is extremely useful for certain design tasks is called graphical programming. Marketed under commercial software packages that include LabVIEW™, HP-VEE, and Softwire, graphical programming languages enable engineers to create programs simply by connecting together visual objects on the computer screen. An object can be a formula, a data source, a display, or a logical function. Objects are tied together much like the boxes of a flowchart that describe a computer program. Some graphical programming languages enable the user to interface directly with benchtop instruments, such as multimeters, function generators, and oscilloscopes. Interconnections are made using digital control links, such as the IEEE-488 bus or GPIB (general purpose instrument bus). Data can be sent to and from the instruments via graphical program objects. Connections can also be made to analog-to-digital (A/D) and digital-to-analog (D/A) plug-in cards directly from the computer bus. This environment is ideal for creating automated industrial systems consisting of analog-to-digital and digital-to-analog conversion boards plus a graphical programming interface run from a desktop PC.

An example of a typical graphical program is shown in Figure 49. This program is designed to measure the voltage across and current through a motor being tested under load. The mechanical load, expressed in terms of the number of weights applied to a frictional brake, is entered into the program by the user.

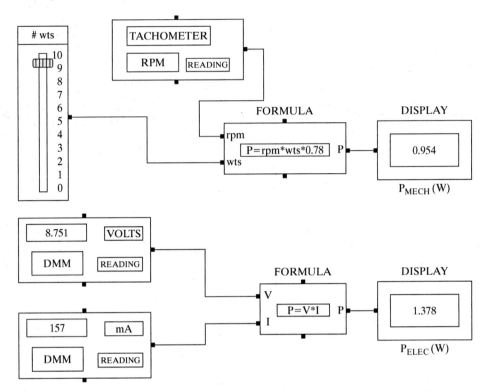

Figure 49. Graphical interface program designed to measure the voltage across and current through a motor under test. The mechanical load, expressed in terms of the number of weights, is entered into the program by the user.

Computers play an important role in solving engineering problems. Their use in virtually all technical disciplines has come to be expected, and the use of computers has become a mandatory part of educational programs in engineering. Despite the highly beneficial symbiosis between design and the computer, a danger exists when use of the computer supersedes human creativity and judgment in the design process. This phenomenon is sometimes called the "can-do" trap. All too often, we spend time doing things on a computer simply because we *can* do them. We simulate mechanical structures or circuits and blindly accept the results without verifying the fundamental principles behind the simulations. We assume a commercial software package will produce genuine results without comparing its output with real physical tests. We create documents that lack real substance but are visually perfect composites of embedded graphics, color printing, and fancy fonts. We create laptop slide presentations with moving arrows, sound, and video, but do an inferior job of conveying any real information. A good engineer learns to harness the power of the computer without falling into the can-do trap. The computer is a precision tool that should be used like a fine instrument, and not as a heavy hammer. In engineering design, computers should become an adjunct to our own creative process, not our preoccupation. The examples of this chapter illustrate several ways in which the computer can rightfully be used as a meaningful part of the design process.

14   MICROPROCESSORS: THE "OTHER" COMPUTER

We usually associate the term "computer" with the desktop PC or networked workstation. In truth, these integrated computational machines represent but a small fraction of all the computers in use today. The most prolific computer, the microprocessor, far exceeds in numbers the desktop PC. A microprocessor is a single-chip computer that performs digital functions at the fundamental logic level. Microprocessors are excellent choices for solving many design problems, especially those involving real-time control by computer. These applications are sometimes referred to as *embedded computing*.

In its most basic form, a microprocessor is a computer with no disk drive, keyboard, monitor, or external memory chips. It simply consists of a silicon microcircuit housed in a plastic or ceramic package. A microprocessor lies at the heart of just about every appliance or piece of equipment that requires intelligent control. Microprocessors can be found inside automobiles, microwave ovens, washing machines, children's toys, cellular telephones, fax machines, printers, and, of course, personal computers. The Pentium® chip made by Intel and the Athlon™ chip made by AMD are examples of high-performance microprocessors that are connected to peripheral devices to create desktop PCs. The more numerous microprocessors found inside appliances and machines are usually much simpler devices than Pentium or Athlon chips, but their operating principles are the same. Microprocessors operate in a base–2 arithmetic system of logic rules known as *Boolean algebra*. The rules of Boolean algebra allow a microprocessor to make decisions based on the status of stored or incoming digital data.

EXAMPLE 14: MICROPROCESSOR SPEED CONTROL

This example illustrates the use of a microprocessor for a timing and speed control operation. The application involves the design of a crane that must lift an object for a predetermined distance. The crane works by winding a flexible steel cable around a rotating drum. A sensor, depicted in Figure 50, provides information about the net distance that the crane has lifted the object. A transparent disk with opaque radial lines passes between the arms of an optical detector. The disk is connected to the drum of the crane. After each increment rotation of the transparent disk, a line passes between the arms of the optical sensor and causes it to send a pulse to the microprocessor. Because the circumference of the drum and the number of pulses per complete rotation is known, the total retraction of the cable, and hence the change in height of the object, can be found. By simply counting pulses, the microprocessor can compute the total cable intake and issue a "stop" command when the desired lift height has been reached. A block diagram of the complete system consisting of the optical encoder, microprocessor, crane motor, and cable drum, is shown in Figure 51.

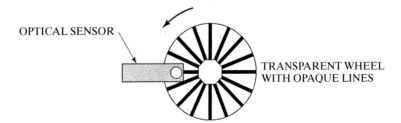

OPTICAL SENSOR

TRANSPARENT WHEEL WITH OPAQUE LINES

Figure 50.   Optical encoder wheel produces a digital pulse every 22.5° of rotation.

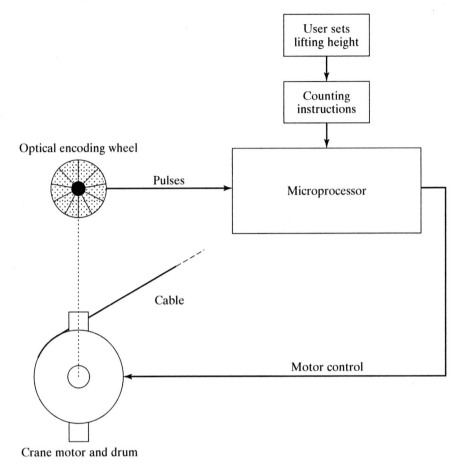

Figure 51. Block diagram of system consisting of optical encoding wheel, microprocessor, crane motor, and cable drum.

PRACTICE!

1. Discuss the way in which a microprocessor might be used to automatically produce timing pulses for a traffic light sequencer.

2. Discuss the way in which a microprocessor might be used to build a digital alarm clock.

3. Identify ten appliances or machines that utilize a microprocessor.

4. A cellular telephone contains a microprocessor that provides its operational functions. If you have a cell phone, make a map or flow chart of all functions performed by its microprocessor.

5. A microprocessor uses internal binary code (a digital system of ones and zeros) to perform its various functions. People who program microprocessors sometimes use *hex code* to represent binary numbers. What is the relationship between binary code and hex code?

6. Do some research and determine the various ways in which microprocessors are used in automobiles.

7. Draw a flowchart and block diagram of the way in which a microprocessor might be used in a vending machine.

8. Your computer printer contains its own internal microprocessor. Discuss why it needs one and the functions that it must perform.

9. Draw the flowchart for a microprocessor program that might be used to make a four-function calculator.

10. What is the difference between a microprocessor and an embedded microcontroller?

KEY TERMS

Dimensioning	SI Units	Specification Sheet
Estimation	Significant Figures	Spreadsheet
Microprocessor	Simulation	Tolerance
Prototype	Solid Model	Unit Reconciliation
Reverse Engineering		

Problems

Estimation:

1. This problem relates to a design competition in which a 1-kg battery-powered vehicle must be propelled up a 0.9-m tall ramp within a 15-second time interval.

   a. For a run time of 9 seconds, how much power must the battery supply to the vehicle? What would be a reasonable estimate of the average power flow over a 15-second run time?

   b. Suppose that batteries are chosen that can supply only 50 mA of peak current. Such a decision might be made to reduce battery weight and produce a lighter vehicle. If vehicle weight is reduced to 0.5 kg, what power flow can be expected? What will be the peak battery current?

   c. If motors are chosen that have 95% efficiency and mechanical losses are 60%, what will be the required battery current?

The following four problems involve vector addition. Vector manipulation is an important skill for estimating forces in mechanical systems. When adding forces or other quantities represented as vectors, the principles of vector addition must be followed. Vectors to be added are first decomposed into their respective x, y, and z components. These components are added together separately, then recombined to form the total resultant vector. Sometimes, it's convenient to decompose vectors into components lying on axes other than rectilinear x-, y-, and z-axes.

4. Two guy wires securing a radio antenna are connected to an eye bolt. One exerts a force of magnitude 3000 N at an angle of 10° to the vertical. The other exerts a force of 2000 N at an angle of 75° to the vertical. Find the magnitude and direction of the total force acting on the eye bolt.

5. A guy wire exerts a force on an eye bolt that is screwed into a wooden roof angled at 30° to the horizontal. The guy wire is inclined at 40° to the horizontal. If the eye bolt is rated at a maximum force of 1000 N perpendicular to the roof, how much tension can safely be applied to the guy wire?

6. A large helium-filled caricature balloon featured in a local parade is steadied by two ropes tied to its midpoint. One rope extending on one side of the balloon is

inclined at 20° to the vertical. A second rope located on the other side of the balloon is inclined at 30° to the vertical. If the balloon has a buoyancy of 200 kN, what will be the tension in each of the ropes?

7.   An eye bolt is fixed to a roof that is inclined at 45° relative to the x-axis. The eye bolt holds three guy wires inclined at 45°, 150°, and 195°, respectively, measured clockwise from the x-axis. These wires carry forces of 300 N, 400 N, and 225 N, respectively. What is the magnitude and direction of the total resultant force? What are the components of force measured perpendicular and parallel to the roof line?

Problems 8 through 25 can help you develop your design-estimation skills. Discuss them with your friends, and see if you arrive at the same approximate answers.

8.   Estimate by hand the amount of paint required to paint a Boeing 767 airplane.

9.   Estimate the cost of allowing a gasoline-powered car to idle for 10 minutes.

10.   Estimate the daily consumption of electrical energy by your dormitory, residence, apartment building, or home. (Check your estimate against real electric bills if any are available.)

11.   Estimate the cost of leaving your computer running 24 hours per day.

12.   Estimate the cost savings of installing storm windows on an average-sized four-unit apartment building.

13.   Estimate the gross weight of a fully loaded 18-wheel tractor trailer.

14.   Estimate the number of single-family houses in your home state.

15.   Estimate the number of bolts required to assemble the Golden Gate Bridge.

16.   Estimate the number of bricks in an average-sized house chimney.

17.   Compute the surface area of all the windows in your dorm, apartment building, or house where you live.

18.   Estimate the amount of carpet that it would take to cover the playing field at Chicago's Wrigley Field.

19.   Estimate the total mass of air that passes through your lungs each day.

20.   Estimate the time required for a stone to fall from sea level to the bottom of Marianas Trench, the lowest point in the Earth's oceans.

21.   Estimate the cost of running a medium-sized refrigerator for a year.

22.   a.   Estimate the weight of a layer of shingles needed to cover a single-family, ranch-style house that has a flat roof.

     b.   Now revise your calculations for a pitched roof.

23.   Estimate the physical length of a standard 120-minute VHS videocassette tape.

24.   Estimate the number of microscopic pits on 2-hour-long digital video disk (DVD).

25.   Estimate the number of books checked out of your school library each week.

Significant Figures:

26.   When calculations are performed, the answer will only be as accurate as the weakest link in the chain. An answer should be expressed with the same number of significant figures as the least accurate factor in the computation.

     a.   Express the result of each of the following computations with an appropriate number of significant figures.

b.   Express the result in the appropriate SI unit.

$$V = (12.9 \text{ mA})(1500 \ \Omega)$$
$$F = 2.69 \text{ kg} \times 9.8 \text{ m/s}^2$$
$$F = -3.41 \text{ N/mm} \times 6.34 \text{ mm}$$
$$i = \frac{(1.29 \text{ mA})}{(100)}$$
$$Q = (6.891 \times 10^{-12} \text{ F})(2.34 \times 10^3 \text{ V})$$

27.   a.   Evaluate each of the following numerical computations, expressing the result with an appropriate number of significant figures.

b.   Express the result in the appropriate SI unit.

$$F = 1221 \text{ kg} \times 0.098 \text{ m/s}^2$$
$$V = 56 \text{ A} \times 1200 \text{ ohms } (\Omega)$$
$$x = 76.8 \text{ m/s} \times 1.000 \text{ s}$$
$$m = 56.1 \text{ lb} + 45 \text{ lb} + 98.2 \text{ lb}$$
$$i = \frac{91.4 \text{ V}}{1.0 \ \Omega}$$
$$P = \frac{(5.1 \text{ V})^2}{1.0 \ \Omega}$$

Dimensioning:

28.   Measure the dimensions of an ordinary coat button. Prepare a dimensioned sketch of the button, complete with a tolerance table.

29.   Prepare a dimensioned sketch of a common coffee cup.

30.   Measure the dimensions of a bicycle and prepare a dimensioned sketch of it.

31.   Make a dimensioned sketch of this textbook.

Prototyping:

32.   Suppose that 100 mA of steady current flows from a 9-V battery via a timer circuit to a motor. If the controller circuit is 92% efficient and the motor is 95% efficient, how much mechanical power is transferred to the motor wheels (neglecting bearing friction)?

33.   Ohm's law states that the voltage across a resistor is equal to the current flowing through it times the resistor value ($V = IR$). Calculate the current flowing through the following resistors if each has a measured voltage of 24 V across it: $1 \ \Omega, 330 \ \Omega, 1 \text{ k}\Omega, 560 \text{ k}\Omega, 1.2 \text{ M}\Omega$ (Note: $1 \text{ k}\Omega \equiv 10^3 \ \Omega; 1 \text{ M}\Omega \equiv 10^6 \ \Omega$).

34.   Ohm's law states that the current flowing through a resistor is equal to the voltage across it divided by the resistor value ($I = V/R$). Calculate the voltage across each of the following resistors if each has a measured current of 10 mA: $1.2 \text{ k}\Omega, 4.7 \text{ k}\Omega, 9.1 \text{ k}\Omega, 560 \text{ k}\Omega, 1.2 \text{ M}\Omega$. (Note: $1 \text{ k}\Omega \equiv 10^3 \ \Omega; 1 \text{ M}\Omega \equiv 10^6 \ \Omega$).

35.   Kirchhoff's current law states that the algebraic sum of currents flowing into a common connection, or node, must sum to zero. Suppose that currents of 1.2 A, -5.4 A, and 3.0 A flow on wires that enter a four-wire node. What current must flow into the fourth node?

36.   Kirchhoff's voltage law states that the sum of voltages around a closed path must sum to zero. Three resistors are connected in series with a 9-V battery. The measured voltages across two of the resistors are 5 V and 2.5 V, respectively.

   a.   What is the voltage across the third resistor?

   b.   The first two resistors have values of 100 Ω and 50 Ω, respectively. What is the current flowing through the third resistor?

37.   A heat sink enhances the thermal contact between a hot surface and the surrounding air, leading to a cooler device and a larger power-dissipation capability. Heat removal is important, because excess heat can cause failure in many types of devices. A heat sink is characterized by a heat-transfer coefficient, or thermal resistance, θ (capital Greek theta), which describes the flow of heat from the hotter sink to the cooler ambient air. The ambient air is assumed to remain at a constant temperature. This thermal flow can be described by the equation $P_{therm} = (T_{sink} - T_{air})/\theta$, where P_{therm} is the thermal power flow out of the device, T_{sink} is the temperature of the heat sink, and T_{air} is the temperature of the air.

   a.   A power device is mounted on a heat sink for which $\theta = 4.5$ °C/W. A total of 10 W is dissipated in the device. What is the device temperature if the ambient air temperature is 25°C?

   b.   A device rated at 200°C maximum operating temperature is mounted on a heat sink. If the ambient air is 25°C and 25 W of power must be dissipated in the device, what is the largest thermal coefficient θ that the heat sink can have?

38.   A switch is a mechanical device that allows the user to convert its two electrical terminals from an open circuit (no connection) to a short circuit (perfect connection) by moving a lever or sliding arm. A switch pole refers to a set of contacts that can be closed or opened by the mechanical action of the switch. A single-pole, double-throw (SPDT) switch has three terminals: a center terminal that functions as the common connection point, and two outer terminals that are alternately connected to the center terminal as the position of the switch lever is changed. When one of the outer terminals is connected to the center terminal, the remaining outer terminal is disconnected from the center terminal.

   a.   Imagine that you must wire the light in the stairway of a two-story house. Ideally, the occupants should be able to turn the light on or off using one of two switches. One switch is located at the top of the stairs, and the other is located at the bottom. Toggling either switch lever should make the light change state. Draw the diagram of a circuit that illustrates the stairway lighting system.

   b.   Now imagine a three-story house in which the lights in the stairwell are to be turned on or off by moving the lever of any one of three switches (one located on each floor). Design an appropriate switching network using two single-pole switches and one double-pole switch. (A DPDT switch has six terminals and can be thought of as two SPDT switches in tandem, with both levers engaged simultaneously.)

39.   A dc motor consists of a multipole electromagnet coil, called the *armature*, or sometimes the rotor, that spins inside a constant magnetic field called the *stator field*. In the small dc motors typically found in model electric cars and toys,

permanent magnets are used to create the stator magnetic field. In larger, industrial-type motors, such as an automobile starter or windshield-wiper motors, the stator field is produced by a second coil winding.

Current is sent through the rotating armature coil via a set of contact pads and stationary brushes called the *commutator*. Each set of commutator pads on the rotor connects to a different portion of the armature coil winding. As the rotor rotates, brush contact is made to different pairs of commutator pads so that the portion of the armature coil receiving current from the brushes is constantly changed. In this way, the magnetic field produced by the rotating armature coil remains stationary and is always at right angles to the stationary stator field. The north and south poles of these fields constantly seek each other; because they are always kept at right angles by the action of the commutator, the armature experiences a perpetual torque (rotational force). The strength of the force is proportional to the value of armature current; hence, the speed of the motor under constant mechanical load is also proportional to armature current.

a. Obtain a small dc motor from a hobby or electronic parts store. Connect two D-cell batteries in series with the motor without regard to polarity. Observe the direction of rotation, and then reverse the polarity of the battery connections. Observe the results.

b. Using a double-pole, double-throw switch like the one described in the previous problem, design a circuit that can reverse the direction of the motor using a single switch.

Reverse Engineering:

40. Take apart a retractable ballpoint pen (the kind that has a push button on top to extend and retract the writing tip). Draw a sketch of its internal mechanism, and write a short description of how the pen mechanism operates.

41. Take apart a common plastic CD case. Make a sketch of its inner construction, and write a short summary of its various components.

42. Take apart a standard desktop telephone. Use your investigative methods to develop a block diagram of how the phone works and connects to the outside world.

43. Suppose that you have been given the assignment to design a desktop stapler. Dissect an existing model from a competitor, draw a sketch of its mechanical construction, and create a parts list for the stapler.

44. Take apart a common flashlight, draw a sketch of its mechanical construction, and create a parts list from which you could reproduce another.

45. Imagine that you have discovered an errant, unoccupied space vehicle in a remote field. Write a report in which you reverse engineer the spacecraft to discover elements of its technology. Examine the vehicle's propulsion system, telemetry, and sensor systems.

The Computer as an Analysis Tool:

46. Write a computer program in the language of your choice to calculate the trajectory of a pebble that falls from an airplane traveling at 200 kph. Include the effects of air resistance.

47. Consider a snapping mousetrap bale. Write a computer program in the language of your choice to plot its angle θ as a function of time from $t = 0$ and $\theta = \pi$ until the time when the bale makes contact with the base at $\theta = 0$.

Assume that the bale has a moment of inertia 0.01 kg-m and that the spring exerts a torque of value 0.5 θ/π N-m, where θ is in radians.

48. A capacitor is a device that stores electrical energy. The degree to which a capacitor is charged at any given moment is indicated by how much voltage appears across its terminals. If a resistor is connected across a charged capacitor, then the current i flowing out of the capacitor and into the resistor will be given by the equation $i = v/R$, where v is the capacitor's voltage and R the value of the resistor. The capacitor will respond to the flow of current by reducing its voltage according the equation, $dv/dt = i/C$. Write a computer program in the language of your choice to plot $v(t)$ for the case $v(t = 0) = 10$ V, $R = 10$ kΩ, and $C = 100$ μF.

    (Note: 10 k$\Omega \equiv$ 10,000 ohms, 100 μF $\equiv 10^{-4}$ farads.)

49. Draw a flowchart for a computer program that could be used to control the traffic at a busy intersection where two streets cross. Traffic should be allowed to flow over the east–west route, unless a car stops at the north- or south-bound streets entering the intersection. Write this program in the language of your choice. Include an input mechanism for indicating the number of cars at each sector of the intersection.

50. Draw a flowchart for a computer program that could be used to control the traffic at a busy intersection where two streets cross. Traffic should be allowed to flow over the east–west route until three cars are stopped at the north street entering the intersection, but only if no car is stopped at the south entrance. If more than three cars become stopped along the east–west route, it should be open to traffic flow, regardless of the number of cars stopped at the north–south streets. Write this program in the language of your choice. Include an input mechanism for indicating the number of cars at each sector of the intersection.

51. Draw the flowchart for a computer program that can serve as a three-digit password decoder for an alarm system. Each of the digits (0–9) entered into the alarm should be represented in binary form. Choose the last three digits of your birthday year as the password. Write this program in the language of your choice. Include an input mechanism for each of the entered digits.

52. Draw the flowchart for a computer program that can tally the voting of a 10-person city council. The output should indicate the majority of "aye" or "nay" votes with a logic high (1) or logic low (0) output. Include a provision for a tie vote. Write this program in the language of your choice. Include an input mechanism for each of the 10 city-council votes.

53. Draw the flowchart and block diagram of a sensor system that can turn on a garden watering system if the temperature rises above 30°C, the sun is not shining on the plants, and the time is not before noon of the same day.

54. Draw the flowchart for a computer program that can be used by a scientific investigator to assess the probability of various events. The system should accept five input signals and provide an output that corresponds to the status of the majority of inputs.

55. Draw the flowchart of a microprocessor program that can be used to sound an alarm in a four-passenger automobile if the ignition is energized but the driver has not put on a safety belt. The alarm also should sound if a passenger is seated but has not put on a safety belt.

56. This problem illustrates the concept of amplitude modulation. Suppose that the function $c(t)$ is equal to a triangular waveform that has peak values of 1 and -1

and frequency f_1. Similarly, $m(t)$ is a square wave function that varies between $+1$ and -1 and has frequency f_2. Write a computer program that plots the amplitude-modulated waveform described by the equation

$$v(t) = c(t)[1 + am(t)]$$

for the case $f_1 = 10$ Hz, $f_2 = 1$ Hz, and $a = 0.4$. The factor a is called the *modulation index*, and hertz (Hz) has the units of cycles per second.

57. Draw a flowchart that will implement the system described in the following memo:

To: Xebec Design Team

From: Harry Vigil, Project Manager

Subject: ATM Simulator

Our client for this project has requested that we develop a machine that can simulate the functions of an automatic teller machine (ATM) such as one might find at any local bank. Your task is to design and build such a simulator using the components and materials of your choice. Here is a list of specifications that you can use as a guide in preparing your initial project proposal and technical plan:

- The simulator should be self-contained with no actual contact with the outside world.
- It should realistically simulate such features as user inquiry, prompting for password, type of transaction, and dollar amounts.
- The simulator should include its own set of entry keys or buttons, display device, printer, and dispenser for (simulated) money.
- The simulator should be triggered into operation by the insertion of an ATM-type bank card. The decoding and interpretation of information stored on the inserted cards is not a necessary feature of the system. An acceptable solution could instead involve storing passwords (possibly as an updatable list) inside the simulator; this list would be activated by the insertion of any card of the appropriate size.

Spreadsheets:

58. Write a spreadsheet program that computes the trajectory of a rubber-band-launched projectile. Your spreadsheet calculations should have cells in which you can enter key parameters of the problem such as dimensions, launch angle, and amount of rubber band stretch. Use an array of cells to indicate the position of the projectile at various points along its trajectory. Choose any appropriate values for the projectile mass m and spring constant k.

59. Suppose that you are trying to come up with a budget for an engineering design project. Your salary is about $6,000 per month, and the technician with whom you work earns about $3,500 per month. You need $5,000 for materials and supplies, $1,200 for traveling to a sales meeting, and you have to contribute 8% of the direct dollars you spend to support clerical staff. In addition, you have to pay 80% of the entire contract cost, including the 8% clerical charges, to overhead that supports the general operation of the company. Write a spreadsheet program that can help determine the maximum number of person-months that you'll be able to charge to the project if the total budget must not exceed $100,000. You'd like your technician to work at least half time on the project.

60.   Write a spreadsheet program that will help you determine the center of gravity of all the passengers on a small commuter airplane. The airplane has ten rows of four seats each, with two seats on either side of the aisle, for a total of forty seats. The centers of the aisle seats are located 0.5 m from the aircraft center-line, and the centers of the window seats are located 1.2 m from the aircraft centerline. The rows are spaced 1 m apart. Your program should compute the center of gravity measured relative to the first row of seats (y-coordinate). Assume that you know the weight of each passenger. Feel free to do your analysis in either kilograms or pounds.

61.   A film-manufacturing plant produces standard 35-mm photographic film for cameras. The film is produced on large rolls between 500 m and 2,000 m long. Each large roll might have a width between 0.5 m and 2.0 m in steps of 0.5 m. That is, there are four possible values for the width. The large rolls are sliced into 35-mm strips and packaged into consumer-sized canisters for 12, 24, or 36 pictures per strip. Assume that each picture requires 35 mm of strip length, and that the 35-mm wide strip inside each canister must allocate 10% of its length to a trailer and leader (i.e., unexposed film at the start and end of each roll). Write a spreadsheet program that will allow you to compute the total number of film canisters of each size obtainable from a large roll for various percentage allocations of the three values of shots per canister. Your spreadsheet should have the following user entries: width of large roll, length of large roll, percent each of 12-, 24-, and 36-shot canisters desired from the entire roll. Assume that the slicing process generates no wasted film.

62.   Suppose that the owner of a ferryboat has asked you to design a system to help load cars and freight in the most balanced way. Write a spreadsheet program that will help you determine the moment of inertia about the center of gravity of the ferry due to all the passengers and freight on the ferry. The ferry is to have 40 parking spaces, each 2.7 m × 4 m, and it should accommodate as many 2.7 m × 8 m shipping containers as possible. The total cargo area for the ferry is 50 m × 100 m. Assume a weight of 1,000 kg per vehicle, 6,000 kg per shipping container, and 60 kg per person.

Microprocessors

63.   Write the flowchart of a microprocessor program needed to run a desktop telephone with the following features: tone dial, redial button, flash button, memory (8 registers), and hold.

64.   Microprocessors communicate with computers and peripherals using either serial or parallel data links. When a parallel link is used, the connection consists of one wire for each of the bits in the digital word, a common return ground wire, plus additional wires for sending synchronizing signals. The latter are needed so that the receiving device will know when to read each digital word sent by the transmitting device.

When a serial link is used, data bits are sent one at a time. In a synchronous link system, one wire is used by the transmitting device to send the data bits in sequence, one wire is used for return ground, and a third wire is used to send a synchronizing signal. The latter is used by the receiving device to determine the timing between each data bit. In an asynchronous link system, typical of the type used to communicate over telephone modems, wireless networks, and the Internet, only one wire pair is available for signal transmission. Data-bit synchronization requires that the sending device and receiving device both be set to the same BAUD (for bits audio), or bit timing rate. Such timing is never perfect, however; if left uncorrected, the BAUD timing of the receiving device will drift apart from the BAUD timing of the sending device. To ensure that the bit-timing sequences will match, the receiving device resets its timer after each digital word. It knows when the received word ends, because the transmitting word appends a stop-bit sequence to each one. After the stop bits are sent, the transmitting device sets the data line to the value 1 as a prelude to sending its next word. It also adds a start bit of value 0 to the beginning of each word so that its arrival will be unambiguous.

- A particular microprocessor sends data in eight-bit packets, or bytes. Determine the content of the two bytes represented by the data sequence shown in Figure 52. The start bit, from which you can determine the time interval per bit, precedes a second 1 bit. The stop-bit sequence consists of two data bits held high.
- Draw the serial data stream for the byte sequence (1001 1100) (0001 1111) (1010 1010).

65. A pulse-width modulation motor drive system applies voltage to a motor while adjusting the duty cycle, or time interval, over which full voltage is applied. The current that flows when voltage is applied will be determined by the motor speed and internal resistance. The average power consumed by the motor will be equal to the time average of the voltage–current product. The pulse-width modulated waveform is produced in response to a digital data signal from a computer module. Draw the microprocessor flowchart for a program that can produce the required voltage waveform. Your program should accept a binary or decimal number between 0 and 255 and then produce an output that is high (logic 1) for an amount of time proportional to the input value.

66. Analog-to-digital interfacing is an important part of many microprocessor-controlled engineering systems. Although most physical measurement and control involves analog variables, most data collection, information transmission, and data analyses are performed digitally. A/D and D/A circuits provide the interfaces between analog and digital worlds. A D/A converter produces a single analog output signal, usually a voltage, from a multibit digital input. One common conversion algorithm produces an analog output proportional to a fixed reference voltage as determined by the equation

$$v_{\mathrm{OUT}} = \frac{n V_{\mathrm{REF}}}{(2^N - 1)}$$

where N is the number of bits in the digital input word, n is the decimal value of the binary number represented by all the input bits that are set to **1** in the digital input word, and V_{REF} is a reference voltage. When n is equal to $(2^N - 1)$, v_{OUT} is equal to V_{REF}.

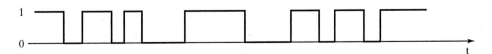

Figure 52. Asynchronous serial data stream.

- Suppose that the input to an 8-bit D/A converter is **0010 1111** with $V_{REF} = 5$ V. Find the resulting value of v_{OUT}.
- A 10-bit D/A converter is fed the input word **00 1001 0001** and is given a reference voltage of 5 V. What is the output of the converter?
- What is the smallest increment of analog output voltage that can be produced by a 12-bit D/A converter with a reference voltage of 10 V if the algorithm previously shown is used?
- What is the largest analog output that can be produced by an 8-bit D/A converter if $V_{REF} = 12$ V?

67.   An A/D converter compares its analog input voltage to a fixed reference voltage and then provides a digital output word B given by

$$B = \frac{int \; v_{IN}(2^N - 1)}{V_{REF}}$$

where the operator *int* means "round to the nearest integer." This encoding operation is called *binary-weighted* encoding. A full-scale binary output (all bits set to **1**) occurs when $v_{IN} = V_{REF}$.

- An 8-bit binary-weighted A/D converter has a reference voltage of 5 V. Find the analog input corresponding to the binary outputs **1111 1110** and **0001 0000**.
- Find the binary output if $v_{IN} = 1.1$ V.
- Find the resolution of the converter.
- Find the additional voltage that must be added to a 1-V analog input if the digital output is to be incremented by one bit.

68.   Boolean algebra is a system of logic used by many computers. In Boolean algebra, variables take on one of two values only: TRUE (logic 1) or FALSE (logic 0). Boolean operators include AND, OR, and NOT. The AND operator is represented by a dot between variables, (e.g., $Y = A \cdot B \cdot C$ means that Y is true if A, B, and C are all true). The OR operator is represented by plus signs (e.g., $Y = A + B + C$ means that Y is true if one or more of A, B, or C is true). The NOT operator, represented by an overbar, simply reverses the state of the variable (e.g., $\overline{A} = 0$ if $A = 1$).

- Verify the following equations in Boolean algebra:

$$A \cdot B + A \cdot \overline{B} = A$$

$$(A + B) \cdot (B + C) = B + A \cdot C$$

$$(A + B) \cdot (\overline{A} + C) = \overline{A} + \overline{C + B}$$

- DeMorgan's theorem states that the Boolean expression $\overline{A \cdot B \cdot C}$ is equivalent to $\overline{A} + \overline{B} + \overline{C}$. Similarly, $\overline{A + B + C}$ is equivalent to $\overline{A} \cdot \overline{B} \cdot \overline{C}$. Verify both forms of DeMorgan's laws.

Use of Computers:

69.   Discuss the way in which a computer or microprocessor (single-chip computer) might improve your approach to designing the following products:

- an all-electronic telephone answering machine
- a tachometer and an odometer for a bicycle

- an energy-saving light switch
- a smart clothes iron that shuts off after 1 hour without use
- a data logger for measuring part weight in a quality-control system
- a voice-synthesized device for a speech-impaired person
- a digital alarm clock
- a system for producing Gantt charts for homework assignments

70. Identify a system or entity in your school, home, or place of work that would benefit greatly from the introduction of a computer system. Write a short summary explaining why.

71. Identify a system or entity in your school, home, or place of work that suffers because one or more computers were introduced inappropriately. Write a short summary explaining why.

72. Take a survey of a select group of people who use computers. (The people you choose could be those who live on your dorm floor, attend one of your classes, or are in your extended family, for example.) Make a list of how many hours per day each person uses a computer and the approximate percentage of time spent at various tasks on the computer. Examples of tasks include word processing, spreadsheet use, CAD drafting, computation, e-mail, etc.

73. Make a list of at least 10 appliances or machines that you encounter on a regular basis, exclusive of desktop computers, that utilize the power of a microprocessor. Now make a list of at least five appliances or machines that you encounter on a regular basis whose function could be greatly improved by the use of a microprocessor.

5

Engineering Careers

1   INTRODUCTION

You have learned about the activities and approaches common to many engineers. This chapter explores the kinds of careers for which an engineering education prepares you. Engineering jobs will be discussed in general terms in this chapter. Jobs specific to each engineering discipline will be presented elsewhere.

2   ENGINEERING JOBS

2.1   Availability of Jobs

What do engineering students do when they graduate? Fortunately, they have the opportunity to work in their field if they wish. In a recent study, a sample of the 109,200 people receiving baccalaureate degrees in engineering in 1999 and 2000 were surveyed to find out what they were doing in 2001. Ninety-three percent of the recent graduates were working. Of those employed, 84% found jobs in engineering and science (NSF, 2003; see Figure 1). Most of the employed engineers (68%) found jobs in the same discipline as their degree. The bottom line? Trained engineers can usually find jobs as engineers.

2.2   Introduction to Engineering Jobs

Where are engineers employed? The range of jobs performed by engineers is truly amazing. They have optimized devices as simple as the pencil and developed systems as complex as the Space Shuttle.° For example, some engineers work on systems as small as very large scale integration (VLSI)

OBJECTIVES

After reading this chapter, you will be able to:

- list the types of jobs available to engineers;
- explain why job satisfaction is high in engineering;
- describe the future of engineering employment.

°The Space Shuttle *Endeavour*, built to replace the Space Shuttle *Challenger*, was first flown in May 1992. This Space Shuttle has several hundreds of thousands of parts, and it was constructed with the assistance of over 250 subcontractors at a cost of approximately $1.7 billion.

Key idea: People trained as engineers generally can find jobs as engineers.

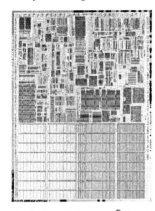

Intel Corp.'s Itanium® 2 microprocessor contains 221 million transistors in an area less than a square inch (421 mm²).

Arecibo observatory (photo courtesy of the NAIC-Arecibo Observatory, a faculty of the NSF)

Key idea: About half of all engineers work in manufacturing, producing motor vehicles, aircraft, electrical and electronic equipment, and industrial or computing equipment.

Key idea: About 28% of engineers work in the service sector, primarily as consulting engineers.

Key idea: Many engineers are small business owners.

consulting engineer: an engineer providing professional advice to clients

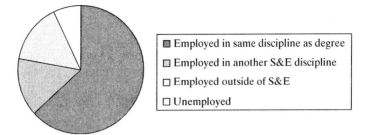

Figure 1. Employment Statistics for Baccalaureate Engineers (S&E = science and engineering)

chips, with millions of transistors and other circuits on each 0.25-inch square speck of silicon. Engineers are helping to develop *nanomachines:* futuristic mechanical devices consisting of only a few thousand atoms. Others work on systems as large as the 305-meter (1,000-foot) radio telescope near Arecibo, Puerto Rico.

Engineers have done work as helpful as creating assistive devices for the disabled and inventing innovative approaches to clean polluted air. In fact, engineers work on systems as controversial as nuclear weapons and nerve gases.

With such a range of experiences, how can you make sense of engineering jobs? It is instructive to examine the distribution of engineering jobs in various economic sectors. In 2002, about 1,769,000 engineers were employed in the United States (BLS, 2004), including about 611,000 computer software engineers. About half of these jobs were in manufacturing industries. A little more than one-quarter of the jobs were in service industries. Government agencies at all levels (federal, state, and local governments) employed about 12% of all engineers in 2000.

2.3   Engineers in Industry

Engineers in industry are involved mainly with the manufacture of products. In 2001, there were 1,000 engineers making toys and sporting goods and 57,000 engineers involved in manufacturing electronic components and accessories. Manufacturing accounts for about half of engineering jobs. Most of these jobs are in transportation equipment (mainly motor vehicles and aircraft), electrical and electronic equipment, and industrial equipment (including computing equipment). Other engineers in industry work in nonmanufacturing areas such as construction and mining.

2.4   Engineers in Service

Engineers in service act as consultants, contribute to product marketing and sales, or conduct research. The service sector accounts for about 28% of engineering jobs, mostly in engineering and architecture, business services (mainly computer/data processing and personnel supply services), and research and testing services.

Most engineering companies are small. In 2001, 59% of engineering firms had fewer than 5 employees, and 35% of the firms employed 5 to 50 people (Rosenbaum, 2002). It is not uncommon to find very small "mom-and-pop" engineering consulting firms.

Consulting engineers may own their own business. About 43,000 engineers in 2000 were self-employed. Most of these engineers worked as consultants.

2.5   Engineers in Government

Government engineers may be employed by federal, state, or local agencies. The military also employs both civilian and active-duty engineers. Government engineers work

Key idea: About 12% of engineers work for government agencies.

for a wide range of agencies, from city engineering offices to the U.S. Army Corps of Engineers to the Peace Corps.

As stated in Section 2.2, about one out of every eight engineering jobs is in government. Over half of these jobs are in the federal government, primarily in such agencies as the Departments of Defense, Transportation, Agriculture, Interior, and Energy and in the National Aeronautics and Space Administration (NASA) (BLS, 2004). Engineers employed by state and local governments typically work in highway and public works departments.

2.6   Other Engineering Jobs

Transportation and public utilities account for another 5% of engineering jobs. Most of these jobs are with electric and telephone utilities. The remaining engineering jobs are mainly in wholesale/retail trade and construction.

2.7   Engineering Education as a Route to Other Fields

Key idea: An engineering education is excellent preparation for many non-engineering professions.

An engineering education provides a strong background in quantitative skills and problem solving. Such tools are highly valued in many fields. Thus, an engineering education is a good start for many nonengineering professions. Trained engineers are well suited to pursue professional degrees in other fields, including law, medicine, business, and education. For example, an engineering background is very desirable for patent and environmental law. Engineers can go on to medical school and contribute to such fields as biomechanics and neurobiology. Many business schools encourage potential students to pursue technical degrees at the undergraduate level. An engineering degree is a fine route to a teaching career in secondary or higher education.

The tools and approaches learned in engineering classes have led to successful careers in other fields. U.S. Presidents Herbert Hoover (mining) and Jimmy Carter (nuclear) were trained as engineers. Other engineers that became politicians include John Sununu (mechanical), Yasser Arafat (civil), Leonid Brezhnev (metallurgical), and Boris Yeltsin (civil).

Several famous entertainers started out as engineers. For example, both *Star Trek* creator Gene Roddenberry (aeronautical) and Academy Award-winning director Frank Capra (chemical) had engineering degrees. Other engineers who landed in entertainment-oriented careers include film directors and Roger Corman (industrial) and Alfred Hitchcock (studied at the School of Engineering and Navigation in London), jazz musician Herbie Hancock (electrical), talk show host Montel Williams (general), and television star Bill Nye, "The Science Guy" (mechanical). For another interesting story of an engineering entertainer, see the *Focus on Nonengineers*.

Herbert Hoover

Engineering careers are not limited to Earth. Nearly all the early astronauts in the Mercury, Gemini, and Apollo programs were engineers. All but four of the 39 U.S. astronaut pilots in the Space Shuttle program in 2004 had engineering degrees.

3   JOB SATISFACTION IN ENGINEERING

3.1   What Does "Job Satisfaction" Mean to You?

As discussed in Section 2.1, people trained as engineers can generally obtain jobs as engineers. Thus, you are not just pursuing a *degree* in engineering, but you are also traveling the road towards a *career* in engineering. One measure of a successful career is a love for the jobs you will have as you progress in your chosen field.

Fans of Mel Brooks's notoriously crude movie *Blazing Saddles* (1974) will recognize the title of this section. The crooked attorney general Hedley Lamarr (played outrageously by Harvey Korman) repeatedly has to remind everyone how to pronounce his name: "It's not Hedy, it's Hedley."

Hedy Lamarr (photo courtesy of Anthony Loder).

So who was Hedy Lamarr, the source of the attorney general's confusion? And what does she have to do with engineering? Hedy Lamarr was born as Hedwig Eva Maria Kiesler in Vienna in 1913. She made dozens of movies, including the 1933 Austrian–Czech film *Ecstasy*, which featured one of the first nude scenes in a movie. Lamarr married arms manufacturer Fritz Mandl in 1933. To escape the Nazi regime and her domineering husband, Lamarr escaped to London in 1938. There, she met movie mogul Louis B. Mayer. Mayer gave her the stage name we know now and took her to Hollywood. She became a famous actress and pin-up girl in World War II, and she was active in the sale of millions of dollars in war bonds.

But Hedy Lamarr was not just a glamorous film star of Hollywood's Golden Age. In fact, Lamarr had the temperament, if not the education, of an engineer. At a dinner party shortly after the onset of World War II, Lamarr was talking with her friend, composer George Antheil. Using the analogy of a player piano, Lamarr and Antheil reasoned that communication between a submarine and a torpedo could be made secret if the information was scrambled by hopping it between frequencies. The pair eventually patented the idea. It became U.S. Patent Number 2,292,387, filed June 10, 1941, and issued August 11, 1942, to Hedy Kiesler Markey (her legal name at the time) and George Antheil for a "Secret Communications System."

The U.S. military decided that the idea of "frequency hopping" was impractical. In fact, given the technology of the time, frequency hopping probably was nearly impossible to implement. The idea, however, would revolutionize communication. The patent expired in 1959 and the concept was generalized as "spread spectrum technology."* Soon, the technology caught up with the idea. Spread spectrum technology has been used in military applications from the Cuban Missile Crisis to the 1991 Gulf War. It was released to the public domain in the 1980s and is now used in applications as diverse as pagers and traffic signals.

Spread spectrum communication is the basis for the operation of garage door openers, cell phones, and wireless Internet communication. Why? In addition to the security of the signal, spread spectrum technology has a number of advantages. By spreading the signal across a number of frequencies, this communication tool makes efficient use of the clogged radio frequency band. In addition, because the devices transmit only for a short time at any one frequency, the signals appear as background noise rather than interfering with existing transmissions at that frequency. This property allows spread spectrum devices (for example, digital spread spectrum [DSS] cordless telephones) to operate at a higher power (and hence, have a longer range) and with less interference.

It is not an exaggeration to say that Lamarr and Antheil's idea for defeating Nazism is the cornerstone of modern digital communication. Not bad for a glamorous actress and avant-garde composer. Hedy Lamarr and George Antheil were honored with an International Pioneer Award in 1997 from the Electronic Frontier Foundation. Hedy Lamarr died in 2000, remembered as an actress and inventor.

---

*The term "spread spectrum technology" refers to any technology where information is distributed over a wide signal bandwidth according to a pattern independent of the data transmitted. One way to accomplish this is to use the frequency-hopping approach of Hedy Lamarr and George Antheil.

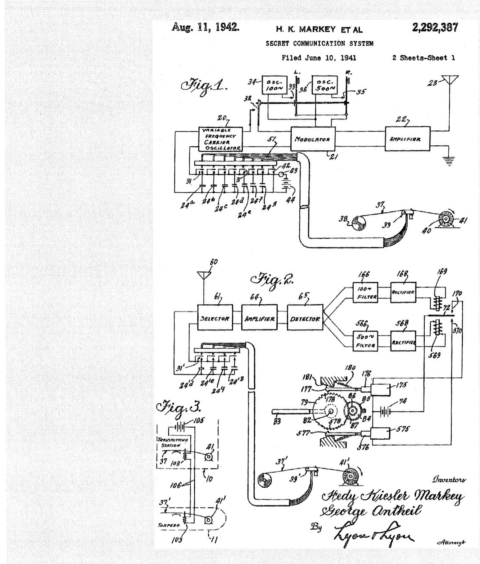

Hedy Lamarr/George Antheil patent

PONDER THIS

When you get your first engineering job, how are you going to measure your own job satisfaction?

Most people measure their job satisfaction in three categories:

- Accomplishments: what they have contributed to society
- Work environment: independence, responsibility, the degree to which they are challenged by their work, and where they work
- Monetary issues: salary, benefits, and opportunities for promotion

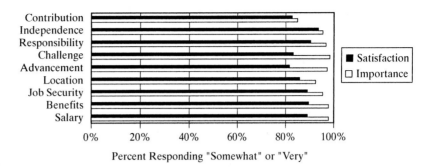

Figure 2. Importance in Job Selection and Level of Satisfaction of Recent Engineering Graduates

Key idea: Job satisfaction includes contributions to society, degree of independence, level of responsibility, intellectual challenge, opportunities for promotion, benefits, and salary.

Key idea: Job satisfaction among engineers is very high.

Key idea: Engineers are well compensated, with salaries varying by discipline, educational level, and experience.

Key idea: Employers expect to receive more value from you than you are paid.

It is not uncommon for people to have very high expectations of their future careers, only to have their visions squashed by reality. Entry-level engineers also have high expectations. In 2001, the National Science Foundation (NSF) surveyed 1999 and 2000 engineering graduates about their job satisfaction (NSF, 2003). The elements of job satisfaction included contribution to society, degree of independence, level of responsibility, intellectual challenge, opportunities for advancement, location, job security, benefits, and salary. As shown in the gray bars in Figure 2, most factors were very important to the recent engineering graduates. (Figure 2 shows the percentage of respondents that said the factor was "very important" or "somewhat important" to them.)

The good news is that their level of job satisfaction was high. The average job satisfaction rating for the nine factors was 88%. (For scientists in the same survey, the average job satisfaction was 82%.) The entry-level engineers were particularly satisfied with the degree of independence and level of responsibility provided in their jobs.

3.2   Engineering Salaries

Compared with other fields, engineers are paid well. Salaries vary by discipline, educational level, and experience. So how much do engineers make? It would be misleading to list detailed salary data here. Information about salaries can become outdated very quickly and should be interpreted with caution. It is almost impossible to know the true average salary of any group as large as the engineering community. Salary surveys invariably cover different populations and may or may not include some benefits. In general, engineers have and continue to be valued in our society. Compensation is expected to remain good for the foreseeable future.

While the higher salaries of engineers are an attraction, avoid choosing a profession (or engineering discipline) strictly on the basis of salary. Your job satisfaction will be low (and your life miserable) if you go for the bucks without listening to your heart.

One final note on salaries: The higher salaries of engineers come with some expectations.

PONDER THIS

What do employers expect of you when they offer you, say, $45,000 as a starting salary?

It means that they expect to receive more than $45,000 worth of value from you. For a company to make money, it must receive more value (in sales or client fees) from you than you are being paid. Remember this fact when you interview for jobs: salaries create an obligation to work responsibly, diligently, and ethically.

4   FUTURE OF ENGINEERING EMPLOYMENT

Key idea: Engineering jobs are expected to grow over 7% from 2002 to 2012, with over about 5% growth in the major engineering disciplines.

The future is good for the employment of engineers. In total, 109,000 engineering job openings are expected from 2002 to 2012. Most of the major engineering disciplines are predicted to show over about 5% growth in that period, with engineering as a whole having a 7.3% job growth. According to the best estimates of the economists, engineers trained today should have reasonable expectations of a job tomorrow.

5   SUMMARY

The present and future states of engineering employment are strong, and students should expect to find jobs in their fields. Engineering jobs may be found in manufacturing (e.g., mainly motor vehicles, aircraft, electrical and electronic equipment, and industrial equipment and computing equipment), services (e.g., consulting services, marketing and sales, and research), government, and other areas (e.g., transportation, public utilities, wholesale/retail trade, and construction).

Engineers are paid well, with salaries varying by discipline and increasing with educational level and experience. While engineering salaries are good, never forget that employers expect you to contribute in value to the company more than they pay you. Job availability and salaries are expected to increase in the future. Finally, an engineering education can lead to rich and rewarding careers in nonengineering fields.

SUMMARY OF KEY IDEAS

- People trained as engineers generally can find jobs as engineers.
- About half of all engineers work in manufacturing, producing motor vehicles, aircraft, electrical and electronic equipment, and industrial or computing equipment.
- About 28% of engineers work in the service sector, primarily as consulting engineers.
- Many engineers are small business owners.
- About 12% of engineers work for government agencies.
- An engineering education is excellent preparation for many nonengineering professions.
- Job satisfaction includes contributions to society, degree of independence, level of responsibility, intellectual challenge, opportunities for promotion, benefits, and salary.
- Job satisfaction among engineers is very high.
- Engineers are well compensated, with salaries varying by discipline, educational level, and experience.
- Employers expect to receive more value from you than you are paid.
- Engineering jobs are expected to grow over 7% from 2002 to 2012, with over about 5% growth in the major engineering disciplines.

Problems

1. For an engineering discipline of your choice (chemical, civil, electrical, industrial, or mechanical engineering), list two jobs from each job sector in Section 2. Which job sector appeals to you and why?

2. Interview practicing engineers from two job sectors listed in Section 2. Write a paragraph explaining how the engineers you interviewed got from their baccalaureate degree to their current job.

3. Which of the job satisfaction criteria discussed in Section 3.1 is most important to you?

4. Describe your ideal engineering job. As a guideline, use the job satisfaction criteria discussed in Section 3.1.

5. Using the Internet, research jobs in the discipline of most interest to you. How closely do the jobs align with the ideal engineering job you described in Problem 4?

6. You have received two job offers: one from Technolico, Inc., at $44,000 per year and one from Engionics at $46,000 per year. What criteria should you use in deciding which job to take?

7. List four questions you would like to ask during an engineering job interview.

8. A small consulting firm wishes to expand. If they hire an entry-level engineer, they can increase their revenue by $4,750 per month. The annual salary for an entry-level engineer in their community is $47,000. Benefits (e.g., health insurance and contributions to retirement accounts) cost 25% of the employee's salary. Can the firm afford to hire an entry-level engineer at the going rate?

9. How much would revenues have to grow for a small consulting firm to justify hiring an entry-level engineer? Assume that the typical annual salary for an entry-level engineer is $48,500 and benefits amount to 30% of the employee's salary.

10. Ask a practicing engineer whether a master's degree in engineering is desirable for engineers in your area.

11. Ask a practicing engineer whether an MBA (master of business administration) is desirable for engineers in your area.

6

Dimensions, Units, and Error

1 INTRODUCTION

The engineering sciences depend on the quantification of physical phenomena. That is, in order for an engineer to make use of a physical quantity, it must have a numerical value. This numerical value is often obtained through measurement. A unit of measurement is associated with the parameter.

Because measurement instruments are imperfect, there will be some error in the experimentally obtained value. It is important for an engineer to have some indication of the size of this error.

In this chapter, we will examine the systems of measurements commonly used by mechanical engineers. Furthermore, we discuss the types of error that occur whenever a measurement is made.

2 DIMENSIONS AND UNITS

In engineering practice, physical quantities are quantified by giving a magnitude and a unit of measurement. For example, the playing surface of a football field is one hundred yards long. In this case, the magnitude is the value one hundred, and the yard is the unit of measurement. A *unit* refers to the arbitrary system of measurement.

Units of measurement are standardized quantities. In the United States, the National Institute of Standards and Technology (NIST) standardizes units of measurement. Standardization of a unit means that within the region where the standardizing organization has jurisdiction, the unit has the same meaning for everyone. For example, the yard in the previous example would imply the same physical quantity of length to a person living in California as it would

OBJECTIVES

After reading this chapter, you should be able to do the following:

- Understand the difference between a unit and a dimension.
- Convert between the different systems of measurement.
- Understand the types of error in a measurement.
- Express large numbers in scientific notation.

to a person living in New York. Furthermore, a standard yard would have the same length for both individuals, because the length of a yard is standardized.

Some units are combinations of others. For instance, the unit of force is a combination of the units for mass and acceleration.

A *dimension* is a measurable quantity of a physical parameter. The yard is a unit of length in a particular system of measurement whose dimension is length. *Fundamental dimensions* are independent of one another. For example, a set of fundamental dimensions may be mass, length, time, and temperature.

Let us define the dimension of an engineering quantity by placing a bracket around the quantity. Thus, if a is acceleration, then $[a]$ would imply the dimensions of acceleration. Furthermore, let M, L, T and θ represent the fundamental dimensions of mass, length, time, and temperature, respectively. Then, the dimensions of acceleration would be

$$[a] = \frac{[L]}{[T^2]} = \frac{L}{T^2}.$$

Therefore, the dimensions of acceleration are length per time squared. The dimension of mass is mass. What are the dimensions of force, F?

The law of *Dimensional Homogeneity* requires that all terms in an equation have the same dimensions. Newton's second law says that the force on a system is equal to the mass of the system times the acceleration. This may be written as $F = ma$, where F is the force, m is the mass, and a is the acceleration. Therefore, the dimensions of force must be the same as those of mass times the acceleration in order for Newton's second law to be valid. Then, the dimensions of force are

$$[F] = [ma] = [m][a] = m\frac{L}{T^2}.$$

A nondimensional quantity is a quantity that has dimensions of one. For example, what are the dimensions of $F(ma)$? The answer is

$$\left[\frac{F}{ma}\right] = \frac{\left[\frac{mL}{T^2}\right]}{\left[m\frac{L}{T^2}\right]} = 1.$$

Nondimensional quantities play an important role in fluid mechanics.

PRACTICE!

You may have noticed that when you pull on a spring, there is a force tending to restore the spring to it's unstretched position. If F is this force and x is the amount that the spring was displaced, engineers write the relationship between the force and spring as

$F = kx,$

where k is a constant called the spring stiffness. What must the dimensions of k be for this equation to obey the law of dimensional homogeneity?

2.1   The British Gravitational System

The units of a quantity depend on the arbitrary system of measurement. One of these systems of measurement is the British Gravitational System (BGS). This particular system uses force, as a fundamental dimension, instead of mass. Because of Newton's second law (i.e., $F = ma$), the dimensions of mass become

$$[m] = \frac{[F]}{[a]} = \frac{FT^2}{L}.$$

In BGS, the unit of force is the pound (lb). Therefore, the unit of mass is related to the unit pound. This unit is called the *slug* and is defined by

$$1 \text{ slug} = 1 \text{ lb} \cdot \text{sec}^2/\text{ft},$$

where ft (foot) is the unit of length.

The weight of an object, W, is the mass times the gravitational acceleration constant, g. This may be written as $W = mg$. In this case, the unit is the pound, as it is a force. Because, on earth, $g = 32.174 \text{ ft/sec}^2$, a slug weighs

$$\text{Weight of slug} = W = 1 \quad \text{slug} \cdot 32.174 \text{ ft/sec}^2 = 32.174 \text{ lb}. \tag{1}$$

Therefore, in BGS, one slug has a weight of 32.174 pounds.

Additional units for BGS are listed in Table 1.

TABLE 1   Listed in the Table are Some Common Units for Engineering Parameters. The Parameter in Parentheses is the Symbol for That Unit

QUANTITY	BGS	EE	SI
Mass	slug	lbm	kilogram
Length	ft	ft	meter (m)
Time	sec (s)	sec (s)	sec (s)
Area	ft^2	ft^2	m^2
Volume	ft^3	ft^3	m^3
Velocity	Ft/s	Ft/s	M/s
Acceleration	Ft/s^2	Ft/s^2	M/s^2
Density	Slug/ft^3	Lbm/ft^3	Kg/m^3
Force	Lbf	Lbf	newton (N) $=$ kg·m/s^2
Pressure (or Stress)	Lbf/ft^2	Lbf/ft^2	pascal (Pa) $=$ N/m^2
Energy (or Work)	ft·Lbf	ft·Lbf	joule (J) $=$ N·m
Power	ft·Lbf/s	ft·Lbf/s	watt (W) $=$ J/s

2.2   The English Engineering System

The English Engineering (EE) system is defined so that 1 unit of mass has a weight of one pound (Lbf) in a standard gravity. The unit of mass in the EE system is the pound-mass (Lbm), and the unit of force is called the pound-force (Lbf). From Newton's second law, we have that 1 Lbf $=$ 1 Lbm·32.174 ft/sec^2. This relation does not have the same units on the right-hand side as the left-hand side of the equation. In order not to violate the law of dimensional homogeneity, the pound-force must be related to the unit of pound mass through the relation:

$$1 \text{ Lbf} = \frac{1 \text{ Lbm} \cdot 32.174 \text{ ft/sec}^2}{32.174 \text{ ft} \cdot \text{Lbm/Lbf} \cdot \text{sec}^2}. \tag{2}$$

Thus, in the EE system, when converting between units of mass or force, one must divide or multiply by a conversion factor, g_c, equal to 32.174 ft·Lbm/Lbf·sec². Then, in order to have dimensional homogeneity, Newton's second law is properly written as

$$F = \frac{ma}{g_c}.$$ (3)

EXAMPLE 1:   What is the force (in Lbf) on a 0.1-Lbm body accelerating at 2 ft/ sec²?

SOLUTION

The force is given by Equation 3. Therefore, we have

$$F = \frac{0.1\ \text{Lbm} \cdot 32.174\ \text{ft/sec}^2}{32.174\ \text{ft} \cdot \text{Lbm/Lbf} \cdot \text{sec}^2} = 0.1\ \text{Lbf}$$

Additional units for the EE system are listed in Table 1.

2.3   The SI System

The Système International (SI), or metric system, was first established in France in about 1800 and has become the worldwide standard. In the United States, voluntary conversion to the metric system began in 1975, even though the system has been recognized by Congress as early as 1866. In time, it is expected that all units will be in SI form.

The unit of mass in SI is the kilogram (kg). The unit of length is the meter (m) and for volume, the liter (L). The system is set up so that one liter of water has a mass of one kilogram. The unit of weight in the SI system is the newton (N). From newton's second law, one newton is defined as

$$1\ \text{N} = 1\ \text{kg} \cdot \text{m/sec}^2.$$

The weight is given by the expression $W = mg$, where g is 9.81 m/sec².

A clear advantage of SI over other systems of measurement is that SI is based on the powers of 10. For example, 1/100th of a meter is a centimeter (cm). To convert from meter to centimeter, all one need do is multiply by 100. This is easily memorized, because "centi" means 1/100th. Therefore, centimeter means 1/100th of a meter. Table 2 lists the prefixes defined in the SI system.

TABLE 2 Prefixes for the SI System

MULTIPLICATION FACTOR	PREFIX	SI SYMBOL
10^{12}	tera	T
10^{9}	giga	G
10^{6}	mega	M
10^{3}	kilo	k
10^{2}	hecto	h
10^{1}	deka	da
10^{-1}	deci	d
10^{-2}	centi	c
10^{-3}	milli	m

TABLE 2   Prefixes for the SI System

MULTIPLICATION FACTOR	PREFIX	SI SYMBOL
10^{-6}	micro	μ
10^{-9}	nano	n
10^{-12}	pico	p
10^{-15}	femto	f
10^{-18}	atto	a

Handling small quantities is very easy in SI. Consider a measurement of 0.03 m. Rather than writing this number in decimal form, multiply it by 100 to get the same measurement in centimeters (i.e., 3 cm). Conversion between SI and the BGS and EE systems is discussed in Section 3.

3   CONVERSION BETWEEN DIFFERENT UNITS

Table 3 contains a table with conversion factors. It is not an exhaustive table, but may be used for the exercises in this book.

TABLE 3   The table lists conversion factors that may be used to solve engineering problems. Some values are approximate

DIMENSION	CONVERSION FACTOR
length	0.3048 m = 1 ft
area	1 m^2 = 10.764 ft^2 = 1550 in^2
Mass	1 kg = 2.2046 lbm
Volume	1 m^3 = 264.2 gal = 35.32 ft^3
velocity	1 m/s = 3.2802 ft/s = 2.237 mi/h
Acceleration	1 m/s^2 = 3.2808 ft/s^2
Force	1 N = 0.22481 lbf
Pressure	1 kPa = 0.14504 lbf/in^2
Temperature	$^{\circ}\text{C} = \dfrac{5}{9}(^{\circ}\text{F} - 32^{\circ})$

Except for the definition of mass, the BGS and the EE system have identical units. Conversion between these two units of measurement is straightforward. Because 1 Lbf accelerates 1 Lbm at 32.174 ft/sec^2, 32.174 Lbm would be accelerated at 1 ft/sec^2. Therefore,

$$1 \text{ slug} = 32.174 \text{ Lbm}. \tag{4}$$

Expression (4) may be used to convert between units of Lbm and slug.

In general, a conversion factor exists between equivalent units. For example, 1 ft = 0.3048 m. When using conversion factors, keep track of the units. In your result, all but the desired unit should drop out from the expression.

EXAMPLE 2:   A structural component has a length of 2 ft 3 inches. What is the corresponding length in centimeters?

SOLUTION

The conversion between feet and meters is given in Table 3 (in particular, 1 ft = 0.3048 m). First, we use the fact that there are 12 inches per foot. Thus, 2 ft 3 inches is equivalent to

$$L = 2 \text{ ft} + 3 \text{ inch} \frac{1 \text{ ft}}{12 \text{ inch}} = 2.25 \text{ ft},$$

which allows us to convert to meters. Thus,

$$L = 2.25 \text{ ft} \times \frac{0.3048 \text{ m}}{1 \text{ ft}} \times \frac{100 \text{ cm}}{1 \text{ m}} = 68.58 \text{ cm}.$$

Notice how all but the units of centimeter drop out in the expression.

PROFESSIONAL SUCCESS

As we have seen, there are three commonly used systems of measurement in engineering. Although the metric system is gaining in popularity, BGS and EE system are still used. Be very careful when performing calculations with values associated with different systems of measurement.

4   ERRORS AND ACCURACY

The engineering sciences are based on measurements of fundamental parameters, such as temperature, velocity, and so on. These measurements are performed for three basic reasons.

The first reason is to obtain information about an unknown process. A classic example is Robert Hooke, who, in the 17th century, measured the extension of wires due to a weight. Hooke was motivated by a desire to understand the deformation of a solid material. In the course of his experiments, he uncovered the relationship between forces acting on a body and the deformation of the body. Today, Hooke's discoveries are contained within a relation known as Hooke's law, which relates stress and strain.

The second reason is to obtain parameters that cannot be obtained by theoretical methods. An example is the forces acting on an aircraft wing. Because it is expensive to numerically obtain these forces, models of the wing or aircraft are placed in a wind tunnel and experimentally measured.

The third reason is to validate theory. A theory is valid only if it explains experimentally obtained observations. A theory is invalid if it contradicts such experimental observations.

Accuracy is defined as the difference between the true value and the measured value of a given parameter. For example, a beaker of water may be measured with a thermometer, and a value of 10.5 °C may be obtained. Suppose the true value of the temperature is 10 °C. There is obviously a difference between the two values, for reasons that will be discussed shortly. The difference between the two values is 0.5 °C. Thus, we would say that the measured temperature is accurate to within 0.5 °C.

For the reasons outlined previously, quantities in engineering depend on one or more measurements. However, all measurements contain error. Obviously, if the error in the measurement is large compared with the measured quantity, then the result is not very useful. Thus, of great importance in the measurement of fundamental engineering parameters is not whether there is error, but is in obtaining an estimate of the error.

The error in a measurement may be divided into two parts. The first part, *bias error*, occurs whenever a particular measurement instrument is used. It is inherent, due to the design and nature of the measurement instrument.

For example, suppose you wanted to cut an 8-foot 2 × 4 piece of lumber to, say, 92 inches. Because the smallest graduation on the tape measure is 1/16 of an inch, the measurement can never be better than half that value. Thus, every time the tape measure is used, the cut will be at least off by 1/32 of an inch.

The second part of the error is called the *precision error* and occurs in a random manner, having a different value whenever the measurement is performed. Precision error is often the result of mistakes made by the technician or external disturbances, such as temperature variations or vibration in a system.

Repeating a measurement several times using different equipment and technicians will randomize the bias error, provided that enough tests are performed. This effectively transforms the bias error into a type of precision error. Statistical analysis of the results of tests will give a mean value for the desired quantity and a level of confidence in the result.

PRACTICE!

In completing the construction of a house, a finish carpenter uses a table saw to rip five pieces from a 4-foot × 8-foot sheet of oak plywood. The desired width of each piece is four inches. After cutting the five pieces, the carpenter accurately measures each piece and obtains the values in Table 4. If the bias error is 1/32 of an inch, what is the precision error for each piece?

TABLE 4 Width of the Five Pieces

NUMBER	WIDTH (INCHES)
1	4.010
2	3.995
3	4.120
4	3.998
5	4.005

5   SIGNIFICANT DIGITS

Engineering calculations are only accurate to a certain number of significant digits, because the calculations are usually based on one or more measurements. The numbers 4.454 and 0.004454 are both given accurate to four significant figures. The absolute error is less than 0.001 for 4.454 and 0.000001 for 0.004454.

For the value 4.454, the true value lies in the range between 4.4535 and 4.4540. However, for the value 0.004454, the true value lies in the range between 0.0044535 and 0.0044540.

Another way to express a number is by the use of scientific notation. Scientific notation is based on the powers of 10. For example, $10^1 = 10$, $10^2 = 100$, $10^3 = 1,000$, and so on.

Scientific notation is useful in expressing very large or very small numbers. Consider the average distance between the earth and the moon, which is 240,000 miles. In scientific notation, this may be expressed as $240 \times 1,000 = 240 \times 10^3$.

In a number such as 240,000, it is hard to see exactly how many of the digits are significant. Scientific notation may be used to remedy this situation. For example, if five significant figures are required, then 240,000 may be written as 2.40000×10^5. Or, if, say, only three figures are significant, then the number may be written as 240×10^3.

With the advent of calculators, there is a tendency to provide too many figures in a response. Many scientific calculators are available with a nine-digit display. This does not mean that all the figures in the display are significant.

When performing a calculation, remember that the number in the calculation with the least number of significant figures determines the number of significant figures in your answer. For example, consider the calculation:

$$D = 4.25 \text{ ft} \times \frac{0.3048 \text{ m}}{1 \text{ ft}} = 1.30 \text{ m.}$$

In this expression, the number 4.25 has fewer significant figures than 0.3048. Thus, the number of significant figures in 4.25 dictates the number of significant figures in the answer.

The answer has been rounded off. Whenever you round off a number, use the following rule: If the first number discarded is 5 or greater, then increase the preceding number by one.

In the previous example, the result to nine digits was 1.29540000. Because of the number of significant figures in the calculation, this number is rounded off to two decimal places. Because the first number to be discarded is 5, the preceding number (9) is incremented by one. This gives the result 1.30.

PROFESSIONAL SUCCESS

When using scientific notation, be aware of the difference between a number raised to the power of 10 and a number times 10 raised to the power of 10.

For example, note that $1.34^{10} \neq 1.34 \times 10^{10}$, because $1.34^{10} = 18.66$ and $1.34 \times 10^{10} = 13,400,000,000$.

KEY TERMS

accuracy	English Engineering (EE) system	scientific notation
British Gravitational System (BGS)	error	units
dimension	metric system	

6   SUMMARY

As we have seen, fundamental quantities in the engineering sciences depend on experimental measurement. These measurements contain error, which is the combination of two types: bias error and precision error. The error in a measurement may be quantified by performing several measurements of the desired quantity. Once the value of the error is quantified, the usefulness of the measurement is known.

Engineering parameters are given in terms of units, which depend on standards codified by governing bodies. A dimension is a measurable quantity of a physical parameter. Dimensions do not depend on the arbitrary system of measurement.

The most widely used system of measurement in the world is SI, or the metric system, although other systems of measurement exist. Once a value of an engineering parameter in known in a particular system of measurement, it may be obtained in another system by using a conversion factor.

7   EXERCISES

E1. What is the mass in slugs of an eight-pound bowling ball?

E2. Which has a greater mass, a block of steel weighing 5 pounds or a block of aluminum weighing 10 N?

E3. The speed of light is 299,792,458 m/s. What is the speed of light in km/hr?

E4. Suppose that the steel and aluminum blocks from Problem 2 were each accelerated by a 1-N force. What is the acceleration of the steel block in ft/s²? What is the acceleration of the aluminum block in m/s²?

E5. The gravitational acceleration constant on the moon is 1/6 the value on earth. What will be the weight of a man on the moon if the same man weighs 210 pounds on the Earth?

E6. Suppose that the viscosity of an oil is 0.0003 Lbf·s/ft². What is the viscosity in N·s/m²?

E7. What are the dimensions of the unit of pressure Pa (pascal)? (*Hint:* Consider Table 1).

E8. The hydrostatic pressure in a fluid is given by

$$p = p_0 + \rho g y,$$

where p_0 is the pressure at the free surface, ρ is the density of the fluid, y is the depth of the fluid, and g is the acceleration due to gravity. Show that this equation obeys the law of dimensional homogeneity.

E9. A Newtonian fluid is governed by the expression

$$\tau = \mu \frac{\partial u}{\partial y},$$

where τ is the shear stress, having dimensions $m/(LT^2)$ and μ is the viscosity of the fluid, with dimensions $m/(LT)$. What must the units of $\partial u/\partial y$ be in order for this equation to obey the law of dimensional homogeneity?

E10. In conduction, heat is transferred in a body between two different temperatures. The amount of heat transferred per unit area, q'', has units of W/m² (1W = 1J/s = 1N·m/s) in SI. For steady, one dimensional heat transfer along direction x, q'' is given by the expression

$$q'' = k \frac{\Delta T}{\Delta x}$$

where $\Delta T = T_2 - T_1$ in kelvin, Δx is the change in the dimension x in meters, and k is a constant called the thermal conductivity. Using this relationship and the given information determine the units of the conductivity in SI.

E11. For the equation in Problem E8, what must the units of $\partial u/\partial y$ be if SI is used?

E12. The average distance between the Earth and the Sun is 98 million miles. Write this value in scientific notation with two digits of accuracy.

E13. If the speed of light is 299,792,458 m/s and the distance between the Earth and the Sun is 98 million miles, how long (in minutes) does it take for light to travel from the sun to the Earth?

7

What Is Design?

design: to create, fashion, execute, or construct according to plan.[1]

Engineers have made tremendous contributions to the quality of life in the 20th and 21st centuries. Automobiles, bicycles, airplanes, space exploration, digital communication, Internet, lifesaving medical devices, all forms of entertainment, global shipping networks, international transportation systems, the national power grid, cellular-telephone networks, fax machines, and the global positioning system all began with one common thread: engineering *design*. Design can be defined as any activity whose objective is to meet a need. The object of design might be a physical device, such as a machine, appliance, or building. Alternatively, the object of design might be something less tangible, such as a software program, operating system, manufacturing method, or process control. In an engineering context, the word "design" simply answers the question, "What do engineers do?"

SECTIONS

OBJECTIVES

In this chapter, you will learn about:

- The engineering design process
- The difference between design, analysis, and replication
- The difference between good and bad design
- The elements of the design cycle
- How to generate ideas through brainstorming

---

[1]Merriam–Webster Online (www.m-w.com)

1   THE USE OF THE WORD "DESIGN"

In this book, the word "design" will be used in many ways. It may be used as a verb (*Design a widget that can slice a pizza into five even pieces*), or it might be used as a noun that defines the creation process itself. (*Learning design is an important part of engineering education.*) Alternatively, the word "design" may be used as a noun that describes the end product of an engineer's efforts. (*The design was a success and met the customer's specifications.*) The word also may be used as an adjective. (*This book will help you learn the design process.*)

Sometimes, another word will be needed to describe the end goal of a particular design process. For this purpose, the word "product" may be used in its generic sense, even if the item being designed is not a product for sale. Similarly, the word "device" may be used to describe the results of a design effort, even if the entity is not a physical apparatus. Thus, the words *product* and *device* refer not only to tangible objects, but also to systems, procedures, processes, and software.

2   THE DIFFERENCE BETWEEN ANALYSIS, DESIGN, AND REPLICATION

Students of engineering are often confused by the distinction between analysis, design, and replication. In science classes, such as chemistry and physics, students are asked to take and evaluate data, and then report the results. This process is known as *analysis*. The word "analysis" can also be applied whenever mathematics is used to predict or confirm the results of an experiment. In contrast, students of engineering are often asked to engage in *design*. Design is an open-ended process where more than one feasible solution may exist. The goal of design is to meet a set of predetermined specifications, rather than to uncover the secrets behind some physical phenomenon. The difference between analysis and design might be defined in the following way: If only one answer to the problem exists, and the answer can be found by putting together the pieces of a puzzle, then the activity is probably analysis. For example, processing data and using it to test a theory is analysis. On the other hand, if more than one solution exists, and if deciding upon a suitable path demands creativity, choice, testing, iterating, and evaluating, then the activity is most certainly design. Design may include analysis as one of its component steps, but it always involves creativity as a key ingredient.

One example of the difference between analysis and design can be found in the weather station shown in Figure 1. This remote-controlled buoy, similar to those located off the coast in many locations around the United States, is maintained by the U.S. National Oceanic and Atmospheric Administration (NOAA). It provides 24-hour data to mariners, the Coast Guard, and weather forecasters. Processing the data stream from this buoy and using it to forecast the weather are examples of analysis. Deciding how to *build* the buoy so that it meets NOAA specifications is an example of design.

Another example that illustrates the difference between analysis and design can be found in the apparatus of Figure 2. Designed in the days of sailing ships, this device was used to launch rescue lines to vessels that ran aground along the rocky coasts of the Atlantic. A crude cannon of sorts, this so-called *Lyle gun* saved numerous lives at a time when ships sailed without the benefit of modern navigational aids. The Lyle gun worked by launching a tethered rescue buoy toward the stricken ship. The tether was then used to string a strong rescue cable from ship to shore. Stricken sailors were pulled ashore in a basket hanging from the breeching cable. Of paramount importance was ensuring that the launched buoy projectile successfully reached its target.

The Lyle gun was invented at the behest of the U.S. government by an engineer named David A. Lyle in the late 1800s. While its development no doubt involved much

Figure 1.   Building a NOAA weather buoy requires engineering design. Interpreting the data involves analysis. (*Photo courtesy of the University of New Hampshire Open Ocean Aquaculture Project.*)

Figure 2.   The Lyle gun was used to launch rescue lines to vessels that ran aground along the rocky coasts of the Atlantic.

engineering design, determining the x–y trajectory of the launched, tethered projectile—a critical part of the effort—was an analysis problem that involved computing the x and y components of Newton's law of motion:

$$\mathbf{F} = m\mathbf{a} \tag{1}$$

The variable $\mathbf{F}$ in Equation (1) is the force in newtons, m is the mass in kilograms, and $\mathbf{a}$ is the buoy's acceleration measured in meters per second squared (m/s^2). Let's go through the steps that define this analysis problem.

The Lyle gun exerts a force on the buoy only at the moment of launch, imparting to the buoy initial x and y velocity components v_x and v_y. Thereafter, the buoy follows a free trajectory, subject only to the forces of gravity, air resistance, and drag of the trailing tether. To help get a feeling for the problem, let's simplify it by ignoring air resistance and tether drag in the analysis to follow. (In a real engineering project, one would never ignore secondary forces of this type without firmly establishing their effects to be negligible.) With these secondary forces ignored, it's a fact of physics that after initial launch, the buoy will feel no x-directed forces; hence, the x-component of its velocity will remain unchanged. Conversely, the y-component of its velocity will be affected by gravity.

If the initial velocity components of the projectile are designated V_{x0} and V_{y0}, the situation for $t > 0$, after the launch at $t = 0$, can be described by the equations

$$v_x = V_{x0} \tag{2}$$

and

$$v_y = V_{y0} - gt \tag{3}$$

Equation (3) is easily derived using integral calculus—a subject you may already have studied in your engineering curriculum.

Here, g is the gravitational constant ($9.8\ m/s^2$), and t is in seconds. In a practical situation, the capabilities of the Lyle gun are known; hence, it is possible to adjust the buoy's total initial velocity V_0 as well as its launch angle θ relative to the horizontal. These values can be used to find values for the x and y components of the launch velocity V_o:

$$V_{xo} = V_0 \cos \theta \tag{4}$$

and

$$V_{yo} = V_0 \sin \theta, \tag{5}$$

where V_{xo} and V_{yo} at $t = 0$ are related to V_o by the equation:

$$V_0{}^2 = V_{xo}{}^2 + V_{yo}{}^2 \tag{6}$$

With this information, it's possible to fully analyze the buoy's trajectory and predict its landing point. The launch speed V_0 and the launch angle θ of the buoy are set by the user of the Lyle gun by adjusting the amount of explosive charge and cannon inclination, respectively. As suggested by Figure 3, the user must first choose the target point (presumably a waiting recipient on the stricken ship), then adjust V_0 and θ so that the rescue buoy hits the desired target. Although this process involves making decisions (*For which target point shall I aim?*) and setting parameters (*Which V_0 and θ shall I choose?*), and although the problem has more than one possible solution, it requires analysis only and involves no design.

In contrast, determining *how to build* the buoy catapult system and the Lyle gun most certainly involves design. Such a system can be built in more than one way, and the designer must decide which method is best. Should the carriage of the cannon be made

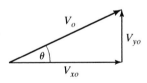

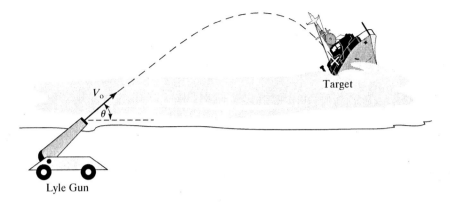

Figure 3.   A Lyle gun sends a projectile along a trajectory toward a target. Computing the parameters needed to hit the target is an example of analysis. Determining how to best build the device is an example of design.

from wood or metal? The former will be lighter and easier for the rescue brigade to bring to the closest shore, but the latter will be stronger and less likely to fail. Wood can rot, but steel can rust. Should the support for the breeching cable be H-shaped or X-shaped? How large should these devices be? Should the cannon rest on wheels or skids? Answering these questions requires experimentation, analysis, testing, evaluation, revision—and of course, creativity—all of which are elements of the design process.

The preceding example illustrates the difference between design and analysis. Specifically, design involves the creation of a device or product to meet a need or set of specifications, while analysis refers to the process of applying mathematics and other tools to find the answer to a problem. In contrast, the word *replication* refers to the process of re-creating something that has already been designed. Replication may involve an exact reproduction, or it may involve minor revisions whose consequences have already been determined. For instance, assembling the digital music player of Figure 4 from pre-made, constituent components—a circuit board, disk drive, memory module, and sound card—may involve some choices, but the bulk of the design work has been previously performed by other engineers. The task is principally a form of replication. Similarly, building a garden shed from a set of purchased plans involves replication, but no design. Replication is an important part of engineering and lies at the core of manufacturing, but it does not require the same set of skills and tools as does true design.

EXAMPLE 1: USING MATLAB TO PERFORM TRAJECTORY ANALYSIS

Equations (2) and (3) form a set of formulas that describe the motion of the buoy projectile after its initial launch event. Given an initial velocity V_0 and launch angle θ, these equations can be solved for the buoy's position coordinates $x(t)$ and $y(t)$ as functions of time. The techniques for obtaining an analytical solution to the problem involve the use of differential equations wherein the projectile coordinates $x(t)$ and $y(t)$ are expressed by the derivatives

$$\frac{dx}{dt} = v_x(t) \tag{7}$$

and

$$\frac{dy}{dt} = v_y(t) \tag{8}$$

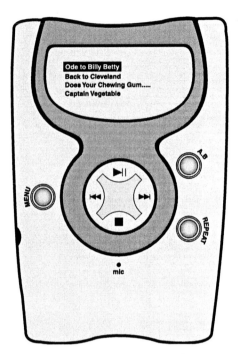

Figure 4.   Engineered devices, such as this digital music player, are mass produced using the process of replication.

Differential equations are covered in the math courses taken by most students of engineering; however, many first-year students do not yet have the math skills needed to solve differential equations. Hence, the solutions for $x(t)$ and $y(t)$ are simply stated here:

$$x(t) = V_{xo}\, t \tag{9}$$

and

$$y(t) = V_{yo}\, t - \tfrac{1}{2}gt^2 \tag{10}$$

Another method by which solutions for the projectile coordinates $x(t)$ and $y(t)$ can be found without differential calculus is to solve for them iteratively by computer. This second method is illustrated in this example. The flowchart of Figure 5 illustrates the basic roadmap for writing such a program.

The following code listing implements the program described by the flowchart of Figure 5 using the programming language MATLAB™. Although numerous programming languages can be used, MATLAB is chosen here because of its widespread use in the engineering community and the generic nature of its commands and functions. MATLAB code is case sensitive. The percent signs (%) denote comment lines, and the asterisks (*) denote multiplication. A semicolon (;) at the end of a line simply tells the program not to display the result of that particular calculation to the computer monitor. A plot of the x versus y trajectory for the initial conditions $V_0 = 15$ m/s and $\theta = 60°$ is shown in Figure 6.

```
%%% MATLAB PROGRAM CODE %%%

%THIS PROGRAM CALCULATES and PLOTS the TRAJECTORY of a BUOY PROJECTILE

%Prompt user for initial conditions:
Vo = input('Enter value of projectile launch velocity in m/s ')
```

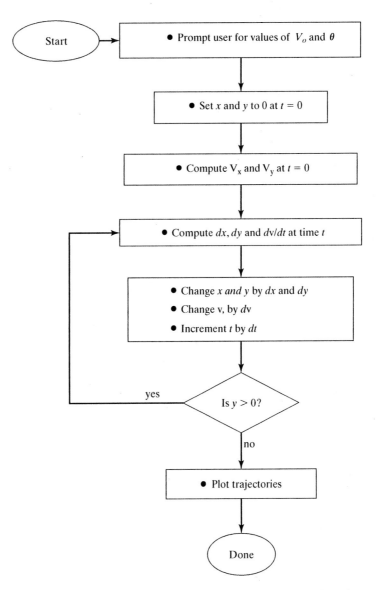

Figure 5. Flowchart for the iterative solutions of Equations (6) and (7). The solution requires that the initial velocity V_0 and launch angle θ be known ahead of time.

```
theta = input('Enter value of launch angle in degrees from horizontal ')

%Convert launch angle from degrees to radians:
theta = (theta/180)*pi;
%set x and y to zero at t=0:

x=0; y=0; t=0;
%set value of time increment dt to 10 milliseconds:
dt=1e-2;
%set gravitational constant in meters/sec^2 (MKS units):
g=9.8;
%Compute x- and y-components of launch velocity at t=0:
vx = Vo*cos(theta);
vy = Vo*sin(theta);
```

```
%Declare initially empty vectors X, Y, and T
%(A construct in MATLAB for storing calculated plots for later plotting)
X=[ ]; Y=[ ]; T=[ ];

%THE LOOP BEGINS HERE: Iterate around the flowchart loop
%while y is greater than zero
while y >0

    %compute incremental changes to x, y, and vy at time t
    dx = vx*dt;
    dy = vy*dt;
    dvy = -g*dt;      %downward acceleration due to gravity

    %update values of x, y,vy, and t:
    x = x + dx;
    y = y + dy;
    vy = vy + dvy;
    t = t + dt;

    %save updated values for plotting when iteration is finished
    X = [X x];
    Y = [Y y];
    T = [T t];

end  %THE LOOP ITERATES HERE (exit if y is not greater than zero)

%When calculations are finished, plot the results:
axis([0 100 0 100]); axis manual; hold on; %Set graph axes to fixed values
plot(X,Y);  %plot trajectory of projectile (x and y values)
title('PLOT OF BUOY TRAJECTORY')
xlabel('DISTANCE FROM LAUNCH POINT (meters)')
ylabel('HEIGHT ABOVE GROUND (meters)')
```

PRACTICE!

For Exercises 1 to 25, determine whether the indicated task involves analysis, design, or replication.

1. Find the best travel route between New York and Los Angeles.
2. Find the shape of soda bottle that will be able to withstand the highest pressure from carbonation.
3. Find a way to prevent people from burning their hands while removing a bagel from a toaster oven.
4. Find the best dimensions of a 16-ounce soup can so that a packing box for 24 cans has the smallest volume.
5. Find a way to mount a cell phone on a bicycle to permit safe, hands-free operation.
6. Find a way to produce individualized, bar-coded badges that can be distributed to the attendees of a technical conference.
7. Find a way to produce 1200 origami (folded paper) nut containers for a large alumni dinner.
8. Find a way to use a global positioning system (GPS) receiver to automatically navigate a lawn mower around a non-rectangular yard.
9. Find a way to store the information for a building directory so that it can be easily retrieved from a touch screen located in the lobby.

10. Find a foolproof method for counting and tallying votes in a national election.
11. Find a way to distribute meals on a transcontinental airplane (the method should not involve rolling carts).
12. Find a way to automate the oil-changing operation at a drive-in car-service facility.
13. Find a way to automatically label blood samples taken from a hospital patient wearing an identification wrist band.
14. Find a way to monitor the temperature of an unoccupied vacation home via telephone.
15. Develop a children's toy based on a TV cartoon character.
16. Develop a system that can make customized shirts for individual customers based on a database of previously acquired body measurements.
17. Develop a system for loading folded newspapers into protective plastic bags for daily home delivery.
18. Find a way to determine the amount of grass seed needed for an area of lawn.
19. Develop a system for downloading and updating the contact list in a cell phone from a wireless laptop.
20. Find a way to produce artistic glass globes via a process that requires multiple layers of liquefied, then solidified, colored glass.
21. Develop a system for identifying, distributing, and tracking paper telephone directories to households that do not have Internet service.
22. Find a way to assess the condition of the shingles or tiles on a pitched roof without requiring that a person climb on the roof.
23. Develop a system for fulfilling orders at a fast food establishment.
24. Find a way to determine the height of trees in need of trimming without requiring that the trees be scaled.

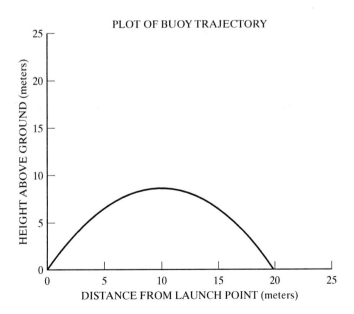

Figure 6. Result of the computation of Figure 5 for the case $V_0 = 15$ m/s and $\theta = 60°$.

25. Find a way to produce custom-printed books that allow a customer to select various available chapters for an individualized text.

26. *Challenge Exercise:* Show by direct solution that Equations (2) and (3) yield a parabolic trajectory.

27. Why does the mass of the projectile not affect the parabolic trajectory of Figure 6?

28. *Challenge Exercise:* For a given initial velocity V_0, find the launch angle θ that will yield the furthest target distance x.

29. *Challenge Exercise:* A projectile-buoy target lies 100 m away. Determine at least one possible set of values for V_0 and θ in Figure 3 such that a 5-kg projectile hits the target. How much energy must the Lyle gun impart to the projectile in order to meet this objective? (Hint: When the buoy first leaves the muzzle, its kinetic energy is $mV_0^2/2$.)

30. Modify the MATLAB program of Example 1 so that it plots a) the height of the projectile as a function of time, and b) the angle of the total projectile velocity relative to the horizontal as a function of time. A copy of the code can be found at *http://people.bu.edu/mnh/design*.

3   GOOD DESIGN VERSUS BAD DESIGN

Anyone who has taken a car in for repair recognizes the difference between a good mechanic and a bad mechanic. A good mechanic diagnoses the problem in a timely manner and makes repairs that last. A bad mechanic fails to find the real problem and masks the symptoms with expensive, unnecessary repairs. Engineers are a bit like auto mechanics in this respect. The world is full of both good engineers and bad engineers. Just because an engineer has produced something does not mean it has been designed well. Just because the product works initially doesn't mean that it will last over time. Although the criteria by which a product is judged varies with the nature of the product, the success of most design efforts can be judged by the characteristics summarized in Table 1.

The contrast between good and bad design is readily illustrated by the previously discussed buoy launcher example. Suppose that the Apex Rescue Catapult Corporation (ARCC) has been asked to produce this device for a shoreline rescue brigade. The buyers will judge the worthiness of the apparatus based on the considerations of good and bad design, as illustrated by the following discussion.

1. Does the product meet technical requirements?   It might seem simple to decide whether a buoy launcher meets its technical requirements. Either the tethered buoy hits its target, or it does not. But success can be judged in many ways. A launcher that is well designed will accommodate a wide range of buoy weights, sizes, and shapes. It will require the efforts of only one or two people to operate, and will repeatedly hit its target, even in strong wind or rain. A poorly designed launching system may work under ideal conditions but may accommodate buoys of only a single weight or shape. It may fail in strong winds, or it may not produce repeatable trajectories. The launcher might work fine for the first few practice launches, only to fail during a true emergency.

2. Does the product work?   During the development stage, the product cannot be expected to work flawlessly the very first time it is tested. However, it *must* work perfectly before it can be delivered to the customer. It must be durable, and it must not fail

TABLE 1   Characteristics of Good Design versus Bad Design

Good design	Bad design
1. Meets all technical requirements	1. Meets only some technical requirements
2. Works all the time	2. Works initially, but stops working after a short time
3. Meets cost requirements	3. Costs more than it should
4. Requires little or no maintenance	4. Requires frequent maintenance
5. Is safe	5. Poses a hazard to users
6. Creates no ethical dilemma	6. Raises ethical questions

in the field. The buoy launcher example provides an excellent illustration of this second principle. Even a bad designer could produce a launcher capable of meeting its specifications upon initial delivery. The Apex Company could make the Lyle gun from inexpensive aluminum and construct a simple carriage from wood and nails. A bad designer would build the launcher in an ad hoc fashion, adding new features on top of old ones without examining how each feature interacts with those before it. The launcher would likely pass inspection upon delivery and be able to launch projectiles during practice, only to fray a line, crack a cannon barrel, or break its trigger mechanism during an actual rescue. After a short period of use, the ill-designed frame might weaken, causing the device to fail during a particularly difficult rescue. Such shortcomings could prove disastrous to a ship's crew awaiting rescue.

A good designer would develop a robust launcher capable of many long hours of service even under the most adverse weather conditions. This conscientious engineer would test different building materials, carriage configurations, trigger mechanisms, and launch devices before choosing materials and design strategies. The good engineer would design the launcher as a whole, carefully considering how its various parts interact. The resulting product might require stronger and more expensive materials, but it would prove more reliable and allow the user to hit the target repeatedly under the stress of the most severe rescue operations.

3. Does the product meet cost requirements?
Some design problems can be approached without regard to cost, but in most cases, cost is a major factor that affects design decisions. Often a tradeoff exists between adding features and adding cost. A Lyle gun carriage made from cheap iron will be much less expensive than one made from stronger stainless steel. Will the consumer be willing to pay the higher price? Durable titanium will last even longer and be much lighter in weight, but the monetary cost might be extraordinary. Will the consumer absorb the cost of the more durable material? Painting the launcher might make it visually more attractive and longer lasting, but will not enhance performance. Will the customer want an attractive piece of machinery at a higher price? Will an attractive appearance make the rescue brigade feel more professional? An engineer must face questions such as these as part of the design process.

4. Will the product need extensive maintenance?
A durable product will provide many years of flawless service. Durability is something that must be considered as part of the design process, even when the cost of the final product is important. At each step, the designer must decide whether cutting corners to save money will lead to component failure in the future. A good designer will eliminate as many latent weaknesses as possible. A bad designer will ignore them as long as the product can pass its initial inspection tests. If the ARCC wishes to make a long-lasting rescue device worthy of its company's name, it must design durability into its product from the very start.

5. Is the product safe?   Safety is a quality measured in relative terms. No product can be made completely hazard free, so a "safe" product simply has a significantly smaller probability of causing injury than does an "unsafe" product. Assigning a safety value to a product is one of the harder aspects of engineering design, because adding safety features usually requires adding cost. Also, accidents are subject to chance, and it can be difficult to identify a potential hazard until an accident occurs. An unsafe product may never cause harm to any single user, but statistically, it's likely to cause injury to some fraction of a large group of users. The Lyle gun system provides an example of the tradeoff between safety versus cost. Can a launcher be designed to facilitate rescue without endangering people? When a buoy is launched at a stricken vessel, there is a small probability that it will hit a person instead. Perhaps designing a buoy that disperses its mass during flight will reduce the potential for human injury, but that may add to the cost of designing and producing a more complex projectile. Features also could be added to the Lyle gun to protect its primary users. Guards, safety shields, and interlocks would prevent accidental misfirings, but they would increase the cost and inconvenience of the finished product.

6. Does the product create an ethical dilemma?   Designing a device that can save lives seems like an unquestionably altruistic goal. Yet even such a task raises ethical questions. Although one of its primary goals is to help people, ARCC must ultimately make money if it is to stay in business. Imagine yourself as an employee of this company. If your boss asked you to use cheaper materials but not tell the customer, would you comply with these instructions or defy your employer? If you discovered a serious safety flaw in the system that might lead to human injury, would you insist on costly revisions that would reduce the profitability of the product? Or would you say nothing and hope for the best? Even the very use of the product raises questions of societal ethics. Some communities might be better able to afford a rescue system than would others. Will you advocate more expensive pricing to service affluent communities, or keep the price low so that everyone can afford it? These questions are never simple, but engineers face similar questions all the time. As part of your training as an engineer, you must learn to apply your own ethical standards to problems that you encounter on the job. This aspect of design will be one of the hardest to learn, but is it one that you must master if you wish to be an engineer.

PROFESSIONAL SUCCESS: CHOOSE A GOOD ENGINEER TO BE YOUR MENTOR

Will you become a good engineer or a bad engineer? Practicing engineers of both types can be found in the profession, and you must learn to distinguish between the two. As you make the transition from student to professional engineer, you are likely to seek a mentor at some point in your career. Be certain that the individual you choose practices good engineering. Seek an engineer who has an intrinsic feeling for why and how things work. Find someone who adheres to ethical standards that are consistent with your own. Avoid "formula pluggers" who memorize equations and blindly plug in numbers to arrive at design decisions but have little feeling for what the formulas actually mean. Avoid engineers who lack vision and perspective. Likewise, shun engineers who take irresponsible shortcuts, ignore safety concerns, or choose design solutions without thorough testing. In contrast, emulate engineers who are well respected, experienced, and practiced in the art of design.

4   THE DESIGN CYCLE

Design is an iterative process. Seldom does a finished product emerge from the design process without undergoing changes along the way. Sometimes, an entire design approach must be abandoned, and the product must be redesigned from the ground up. The sequence of events leading from idea to finished product is called the *design cycle*. Although the specific steps of the design cycle may vary with the product and field of engineering, as well as with the instructor of any given undergraduate design course, most cycles resemble the sequence depicted in Figure 7. The following section explores this diagram in more detail.

4.1   Define the Overall Objectives

A design team should begin any new project by defining its design objectives. This step may seem like a nuisance to the student eager to build and test, but it is one of the most important steps in the process. Only by viewing the requirements from a broad perspective can an engineer determine all factors relevant to the design effort. Good design involves more than just making technical choices. Consider, for example, a marine engineer who must design a new sailboat. In addition to technical constraints, the designer must consider the aesthetic, safety, and cost factors that go into a successful design. The engineer must thus ask the following questions: Who will use the product? Will it be a seasoned mariner or a first-time boater? What are the needs of the end user? Will it be used, for example, for business or recreation? What are the cost factors? Which features are critical, and which are only desirable? For example, should the boat have power winches, GPS navigation and a stereo sound system, or are these needless, expensive frivolities? What are the manufacturing constraints? Must the boat be made of fiberglass, or are other materials acceptable? What are the safety factors? How much risk is acceptable? Answering these questions at the outset will help at each subsequent stage of the design process.

4.2   Gather Information

In the early stages of a new project, a large amount of time should be devoted to gathering information. Learn as much as possible about the relevant technology. Identify off-the-shelf components, systems, or software elements that can be incorporated directly into your design, so that you don't have to "reinvent the wheel." Look for product descriptions, data sheets, and application notes on the Web. Keep this information in a file folder (either as a hard copy or on a computer), where you'll be able find it easily. Also look for reports or project descriptions in the same general area as your own project. Detailed specifications about most component parts and devices are available on company websites. Such electronic databases have largely supplanted printed catalogs as the primary source of information for design engineers.

Perusing advertisements in trade magazines and journals can be a good way to learn about commercial products that might be relevant to your project. Each field of engineering has many such publications, but the list in Table 2 provides a representative set. A more comprehensive directory of technical magazines can be found at *www.techexpo.com*.

4.3   Choose a Design Strategy

When working with the design cycle, the next step is to select a strategy for meeting your design objectives. At this stage, the design team (or sometimes an individual engineer) might decide whether the design technologies (e.g., electrical, mechanical, structural, systems, or software) will be incorporated into the product and whether the product will be designed from the ground up or synthesized from off-the-shelf components. If the system is complex, it should be divided into smaller pieces that can be designed by subdivisions of the team and later combined to form the complete product. These subsections, or modules, should be designed so that they can be tested individually before the entire system is assembled. Dividing a large job into several more manageable tasks simplifies

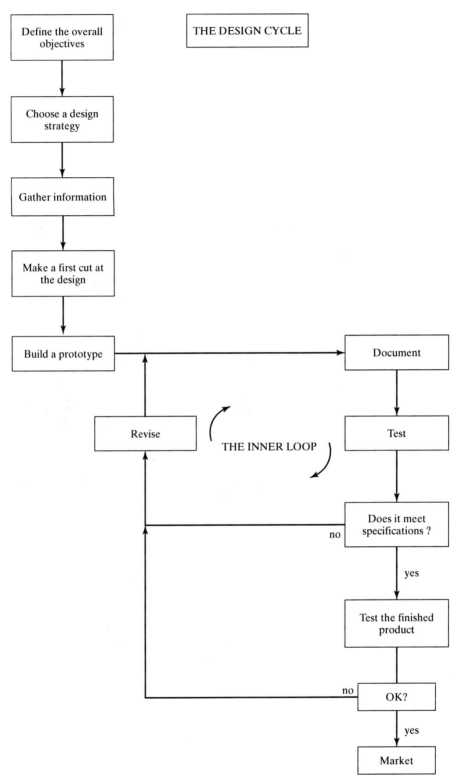

Figure 7.   One version of the design cycle. Successful design often requires many cycles around the inner loop. Sometimes, the iteration must be revisited when the finished product does not meet design goals.

TABLE 2   Some Engineering Trade Publications

Bioscience Technology	*Hydraulics and Pneumatics*
Compliance Engineering	*MFG (Industrial Product Bulletin)*
Computer Technology Review	*Machine Design,*
Design News	*Medical Design Technology*
EDN (Electronic Design News)	*OEM Technology News°*
Electronic Design	*Plastics Technology*

°OEM stands for "original equipment manufacturer"

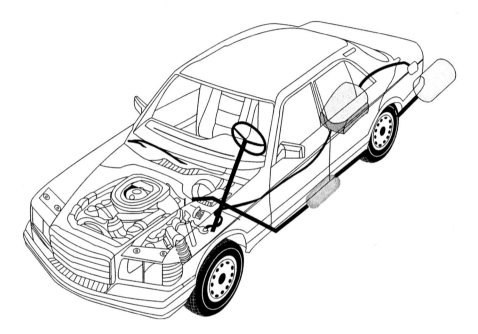

Figure 8.   Component systems of a typical automobile are designed as interacting modules.

synthesis, testing, and evaluation. In a team design effort, the modular approach is essential. For example, the various components of the automobile in Figure 8—the engine, cooling system, electrical system, suspension, braking system, chassis, and drive train—are each designed and tested individually before the entire automobile is assembled. Constant communication between individuals is vital to ensuring that the automobile's constituent components work together in harmony. This same modular strategy applies to large software systems, where each section should be designed as an independently testable module. In either case, the final integrated product will be more than the sum of its individual parts.

The design strategy should also consider similar efforts that may have been attempted in the past. Does a new technology exist that will improve upon an existing design? Perhaps a partial solution is already available in commercial form. For example, suppose that your design for a talking clock includes the amplification of voice or music. Should you design your own sound amplifier? Many inexpensive off-the-shelf kits (like the one shown in Figure 9) exist for constructing board-level amplifiers, hence designing your own amplifier would be an unnecessary duplication of effort. The wise engineer

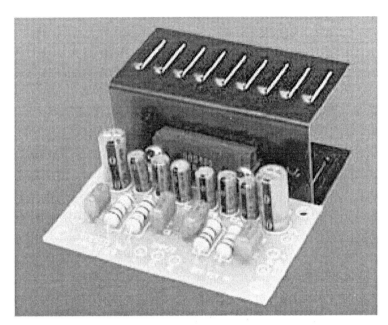

Figure 9. One of several modular amplifier kits available online from an electronic parts vendor.

uses existing products and components to simplify the design task. There is no shame in using off-the-shelf ingredients if they can help you achieve your design objectives more quickly and inexpensively. Typically, labor is the most expensive part of any development effort, so it's often cheaper (and sometimes more reliable) to buy something ready made and previously debugged than it is to design it from scratch. Imagine how needlessly complex it would be to design a house without using prefabricated windows, doors, electrical panels, radiators, and air conditioners that are available from other vendors. Be certain, however, that using another company's product does not create patent infringement problems if your product is destined for commercial sale.

4.4   Make a First Cut at the Design

Once a design strategy has been identified, it's time to make a "first cut" (initial attempt) at the design. This step typically involves rough approximations and estimates. If the product is to be a physical entity, tentative choices are made for dimensions, weight, user controls, construction materials, part numbers, and component values—whatever parameters might be relevant. If the objective is a software product, its outer shell, modular pathways, and user interface are laid out as part of the first-cut attempt. If the design involves a system—for example, a manufacturing procedure—then the overall flowchart might be specified at this time.

4.5   Model and Analyze

This step goes hand in hand with making the first design cut. In some design situations, it could even precede the latter step. In the modeling phase of the cycle, a combination of mathematics and/or software modeling tools is used to fine-tune design parameters to shorten the path to the finished product. Modeling and analysis is usually much less expensive (in terms of person-hours of labor) than building an actual prototype for testing.

During the modeling phase of design, commercially available computer simulation tools (such as Mathematica, MATLAB, AutoCAD, ProENGINEER, Solidworks, Orcad, or Simulink) can save time and expense by allowing the designer to predict performance before the actual construction of the prototype. These software packages can help identify hidden flaws before the product is built and provide some indication as to the success of the design approach. Whenever practical, however, computer simulations should never be used as a substitute for actual physical testing unless the product is very similar to one that you have previously designed. "Glitches," "bugs," and other anomalies caused by physical effects not modeled by the simulator have a nasty habit of appearing when a new product undergoes actual testing. Despite the usefulness of computer-aided design tools and simulators, there is simply no substitute for testing a real physical prototype. The use of scale models—for example, an aircraft model made one-tenth of actual size inside a wind tunnel—can be useful for testing large products.

4.6   Build, Document, and Test

After the design team has reached a consensus on a first cut, its next goal is to build a working prototype. In some situations, the cost of fabrication is so high that an initial prototype may not be practical. The design of an oil platform or space station, for example, would fall into this category. In such cases, modeling and analysis can help close the loop between the design concept and the final product.

The typical first prototype is destined to be revised many times before the design cycle has been completed. This first prototype should be functional, but it does not need to be visually attractive. Its primary purpose is to provide a starting point for evaluation and testing. If the product is software, for example, the prototype might consist of the main calculation sections without the fancy graphical interfaces that the user will expect in the final version. If the product is mechanical, it can be built as a mock-up from easy-to-modify materials, such as wood or pre-punched metal strapping. For instance, a prototype for a new self-standing ATM machine might be built inside an open wooden box made from framing lumber and hinged plywood. Such a structure would permit easy access to the inner machinery during testing, but obviously would never be used in a commercial installation. If the product is electrical, its prototype might be wired on a temporary circuit breadboard, such as the one shown in Figure 10.

Note that documentation is part of the inner loop of the design cycle of Figure 7. The typical engineer faces considerable temptation to leave documentation to the very end of the design process. Pressed with deadlines and project milestones, many inexperienced engineers think of documentation as an annoying intrusion rather than an integral part of the design process. After working diligently on a design project, the unseasoned engineer may panic at the reality of documentation. ("*Now I have to write all this up?*") Documentation added as an afterthought is often incomplete or substandard, because most of the relevant facts and steps have been forgotten by the time the writing takes place. Haphazard, after-the-fact documentation is the province of the bad design engineer. Many a product, developed at great cost but delivered with grossly inadequate documentation, has found its way to the trash heap of engineering failures because no one could figure out how to use or repair the product. Poor documentation also leads to a duplication of effort and reinvention of the wheel, because no one can remember the results of previous work.

A good engineer recognizes that documentation is absolutely critical to every step of the design process. The good engineer will plan for documentation from the very beginning, keeping careful records of everything from initial feasibility studies to final manufacturing specifications. As the design progresses, it's a good idea to write everything down, even if it seems unimportant at the time. Information should be written in such a

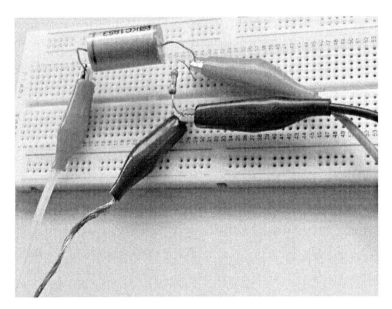

Figure 10. Temporary circuit breadboard for electronic prototyping.

way that another engineer with the same technical background could continue your work at any time by simply reading your documentation. Careful documentation will also aid in writing product literature and technical manuals should the product be destined for commercial sale. Good documentation provides the engineer with a running record of the design history and the answers to key questions that were addressed as part of the design process. It provides vital background information for patent applications, product revisions, and redesign efforts, and it serves as insurance in cases of product liability. Above all, documentation is part of an engineer's professional responsibility. Its importance to engineering design cannot be overemphasized.

4.7   Revise and Revise Again

One of the characteristics that distinguishes design from replication is that the finished product may be totally different from what was envisioned at the beginning of the design cycle. Elements of the system may fail during testing, forcing the engineer to rethink the design strategy. The design process may lead the engineer down an unexpected path or into new territory. A good engineer will review the status of a product many times, proceeding through numerous revisions until the product meets its specifications. In truth, this revision process constitutes the principal work of the engineer. An experienced engineer recognizes it as a normal part of the design process and does not become discouraged when some aspect of the product fails on the first or second try. The revision cycle may require many iterations before success is achieved.

4.8   Test the Product Thoroughly

As the design process converges on a probable solution, the product should be thoroughly tested and retested. Performance should be assessed from many points of view; the design should be modified, then tested again, whenever problems are identified. If, at any stage, the product does not meet design requirements, the designer should reenter the iterative loop once again.

   If the product is a physical entity, the effects of temperature, humidity, loading, and other environmental factors, as well as the effects of repeated and prolonged use,

Figure 11. Mass-produced electronic instruments for sale undergo a "burn-in" period prior to final shipment.

may hinder product performance. A physical product, such as one of the instruments in Figure 11, should be subjected to a "burn-in" (extended use) period to help identify latent defects that might cause the product to fail in the field. The human response to the product should also be assessed, because no two people are exactly alike. Exposing the product to many different individuals will help identify problems that may not have been apparent during the development phase, when the product was examined only by the design team. Only after a comprehensive test period is the product ready to be put into actual service. Nothing will discourage consumers faster than a new product that malfunctions in the field.

Like their physical counterparts, software products should also be tested by a variety of different users who can discover hidden bugs. Different individuals will exercise a software product in very different ways; hence, extensive testing by a multitude of users is essential if all software bugs are to be discovered. One way to discover hidden bugs is to release the software program to a control group of customers before widespread distribution. This control group understands that bugs may exist in the preliminary version, and the group is usually given incentives (e.g., a reduced cost or a jump on competitors) to serve as real-world testers. This type of trial is sometimes called a *beta test*.

PROFESSIONAL SUCCESS: HOW TO TELL A GOOD ENGINEER FROM A BAD ENGINEER

If you pursue engineering as a career, you will encounter many colleagues along the way. Some will be good engineers, and others will be bad engineers. In your quest to identify and emulate only good engineers, you should learn the differences between the two. The following list highlights the traits of both types of engineers:

A Good Engineer

- Listens to new ideas with an open mind.

A Bad Engineer

- Seldom listens to the ideas of others.

- Considers a variety of solution methodologies before choosing a design approach.
- Does not consider a project complete at the first sign of success, but insists on testing and retesting.
- Is never content to arrive at a set of design parameters solely by trial and error.
- Uses phrases such as "I need to understand why" and "Let's consider several possibilities."

- Has tunnel vision and only pursues the first design approach that comes to mind.
- Ships the product without thorough testing.
- Uses phrases such as "Good enough" and "I don't understand why it won't work. So-and-so did it this way."
- Equates pure trial and error with engineering design.

PRACTICE!

1. Consider the questions posed under "Define the Overall Objectives" in Section 4.1. Answer these questions in the context of designing a recreational sailboat.

2. Consider the questions posed under "Define the Overall Objectives" in Section 4.1. Answer these questions in the context of designing a high-performance bicycle.

3. Suppose that you are asked to build a recumbent bicycle (a low-profile bicycle in which the pedals are in front of the seat.) Make a list of the various ways in which you might gather information as part of the design cycle.

4. Draw a modified design cycle, similar to Figure 7, that includes feedback from a test group of individual users.

5. Define the design strategy that might have been used to invent the first personal computer. Imagine yourself before the days of hard disk drives, graphical user interfaces, color monitors, compact disks, USB ports, and inexpensive memory chips. (In the early days of computers, random-access memory chips were one of the most expensive components of the PC.)

6. Describe the various stages of the design cycle for the development of the ballpoint pen.

7. Write a chronology of the design cycle for a paper clip.

8. Specify the steps in Figure 7 as they might apply to the design of a microwave oven.

9. Discuss the elements of the design cycle that might apply to a heart rate monitor to be used as part of a medical diagnostic system.

10. Imagine that you were the American engineer who first invented the pinball machine. Write a short essay on your experience, trials, and errors in developing this widely used entertainment device.

11. In-flight refueling is a technique that makes most military air operations possible. Prepare a chronological table that shows how the design cycle may have proceeded when the technique was developed. Label each event in your table with the corresponding step in Figure 7.

12. The automobile airbag has become an indispensable safety device, but its history is rather short compared with the evolution of the automobile. Describe what you imagine to have been the first airbag prototype, and then document each of the changes that led to today's airbag design.

13. Imagine that your design team has developed a personal human rocket transportation device. List the design changes that helped you converge on a successful product.

14. Research the history of invention; identify one product that did not require design revisions before becoming successful. (Hint: Some inventions that *did* undergo extensive, iterative revisions during the design process include the airplane, the automobile, the sewing machine, and the ballpoint pen.)

15. Write a short essay that describes the evolution of the sewing machine. This product underwent numerous design changes from its inception to the first commercially viable machine.

16. Research the history of the modern dishwasher; draw a detailed design cycle that chronicles the development of this device by its inventor, Josephine Cochran.

17. How do the design steps for a production process differ from those of a physical product? List several examples.

18. Compare the design cycle of a commercial aircraft with the design cycle of a radio-controlled model airplane. How might the various elements differ?

19. The design of a large-scale solvent ore extraction plant will differ markedly from the design of a similar system that classifies ores on a laboratory scale. List several ways in which the design process will differ for these two products.

20. What differences might exist between the design of a reading lamp and the design of a light tower for a football stadium?

5   GENERATING IDEAS

The element of creativity is one of the more salient characteristics that distinguishes design from analysis. Creativity is quintessential to the human experience, particularly for engineers. Without it, the various versions of the design cycle could not take place.

When engineers gather to solve design problems, they can arrive at ideas through a variety of methods. One of these techniques is *brainstorming*. Brainstorming helps engineers channel their creative energies by requiring a spontaneous mode of thinking that frees the mind from traditional boundaries. All too often, we limit our problem-solving approach to obvious solutions that have worked in the past. Responsible engineering sometimes requires the consideration of other design alternatives. A good engineer will never settle on a solution just because it's the first one to come to mind. In the early stages of the design process, creativity should proceed spontaneously, unfettered by concerns that an idea is "way out," "ridiculous," or otherwise impractical. When the constraints of traditional paradigms are removed, new solutions often emerge. Hearing the ideas of others can tap ideas in the subconscious mind. Promising, but different, ideas can eventually be discarded as unfeasible, but only after study, analysis, and comparison with competing ideas. Brainstorming allows engineers to consider as many options as possible before choosing a design path.

Brainstorming follows many forms. It can be done informally, or it can follow one of several time-tested formal methods. The latter are appropriate for large group settings where organization is needed to avoid chaos. Less formal brainstorming methods are reserved for groups of, say, one to four people who wish to generate ideas. Although they differ in execution, formal and informal brainstorming methods share the same set of core principles. The primary goal is to foster the uninhibited free exchange of ideas by creating a friendly, nonjudgmental environment. Brainstorming is an art. It requires practice, but any team members who have open minds and imagination can learn this important skill.

5.1   Ground Rules for Brainstorming

The ground rules for brainstorming are designed to create a friendly, nonthreatening environment that encourages the free flow of ideas. Although the specific rules depend on the version of brainstorming, the following list can serve as a guideline:

1.   No holding back. Any idea may be brought to the floor at any time.
2.   No boundaries. An idea is never too outrageous or "way out" to mention.
3.   No criticizing. An idea may not be criticized until the final discussion phase.
4.   No dismissing. An idea may not be discounted until after group discussion.
5.   No limit. Another idea is never one too many.
6.   No restrictions. Participants may generate ideas from any field of expertise.
7.   No shame. A team participant should never be embarrassed by contributing an idea.

5.2   Formal Brainstorming Method

When a large group gets together to brainstorm, formal structure can be helpful. Without such structure, a flood of competing ideas, all brought to the floor simultaneously, can create chaos. Instead of thinking creatively, participants can become confrontational as they strive to gain a voice in the conversation. With so many randomly competing opinions, each person's creative process is inhibited, and the brainstorming session becomes unproductive. This effect is sometimes called *idea chaos*. Adding formal structure to a brainstorming session restricts the flow of ideas to a manageable rate without restricting the number of ideas generated. In fact, adding formal structure to large group settings can enhance the brain's creative process by preventing aggressive individuals from dominating the conversation and by providing time for people to think.

When a brainstorming session is in progress, one person should act as the facilitator, and another should record everyone's ideas. It's also possible to use video or audio tape in lieu of a human secretary.

Many formal brainstorming techniques exist, but the *idea trigger* method has been well tested and acknowledged to be an effective way to generate ideas in large groups. The idea trigger method enhances the brain's creativity via a process of alternating tension and relaxation to tap the brain's inner resources. By listening to other people's ideas and being forced to respond with counter ideas, a participant's behavioral patterns, personality constraints, and narrow modes of thinking can be broken momentarily. This allows ideas hidden in the recesses of the brain to come to the foreground. A shy participant who is reluctant to offer seemingly silly ideas, for example, may be more willing to speak under the alternating tension and relaxation of the purge-trigger sequence.

The idea trigger method requires a leader, at least four participants, and a printed form such as the one shown in Figure 12. The procedure has three phases, as follows:

Phase 1: Idea Generation Phase

The problem or design issue is summarized by the leader. Each person is given a blank copy of the form shown in Figure 12. Without talking, each participant rapidly writes as many ideas or solutions as possible. These entries are placed under Column 1. Key words suffice; whole sentences are not necessary. During the idea-generation phase, participants open their minds, consider many alternatives, and do not worry if ideas seem too trivial or ridiculous. "Pie in the sky," radical, or impossible ideas should definitely be included. In short, participants write down any relevant ideas that come to mind. Since the ideas are written down silently, the element of intimidation is removed from the idea generation process.

IDEA TRIGGER SESSION

COLUMN 1	COLUMN 2	COLUMN 3	COLUMN 4
120 SECONDS			
60 SECONDS			

CONTRIBUTOR:

Figure 12.　Blank form for the idea trigger session.

After the first 2 minutes of the session, the group takes a break and then attempts to write additional ideas under Column 1 for another 60 seconds. This *tension and relaxation* sequence has been shown to enhance creativity. It helps to extract all ideas from the brain's subconscious memory, much like squeezing and releasing a sponge several times to extract all the water.

Phase 2: Idea Trigger Phase

After the idea generation phase, participants take turns reading their entries from Column 1. As people recite their Column 1 entries, others silently cross out the duplicates on their own lists. Hearing other ideas will trigger new ideas, which should be immediately written under Column 2. This process is called *idea triggering*. Listening to others causes hidden thoughts stored in the subconscious to surface. The purpose of the idea trigger phase is not to discount the ideas from Column 1, but rather to amplify them, modify them, and add to them.

After all members have read their Column 1 entries and have completed their Column 2 entries, the idea trigger process is repeated. This time, entries from Column 2 are read, and any new ideas are entered under Column 3. The process is repeated, with entries added to Columns 4, 5, etc., until all ideas are exhausted. Complex problems may require as many as five rounds of the idea trigger phase.

The entries that appear under the second and third columns (and the fourth and fifth columns if the problem is complex) are usually the most creative. Such richness results from several factors. Often participants are secretly angry because their ideas were stolen by others. This simple competitive pressure can propel a person toward new, unexplored territory. Conversely, when ideas have not been duplicated by others, participants can receive positive reinforcement, which helps them create even better ideas. Some individuals may respond to their own unduplicated entries with a desire to produce more as a way of hoarding the good ideas. Yet others may subconsciously think that augmenting previously discussed ideas fosters group cooperation.

Phase 3: Compilation Phase

When the idea trigger phase has been completed, the leader compiles everyone's sheets and makes one master list of all the ideas that have been generated. The group then proceeds to discuss all ideas, discarding the ones that probably will not work, and deciding which of the remaining ideas are appropriate for further consideration and development.

EXAMPLE 2: A FORMAL BRAINSTORM- ING SESSION

Let's illustrate the formal idea trigger method with an example. Four engineers, Morris, Lawrence, Carly, and Shempathia are designing an entry for a college design competition. The overall objective is to design a self-propelled vehicle that can climb one side of a trapezoidal ramp, stop at the top, and prevail over an opposing vehicle that is climbing up the ramp from the other side. The basic elements of the challenge are as follows:

1. The vehicle must be self-contained. No wires or tethers are permitted.
2. The vehicle must fit inside a 25-cm cubical space.
3. The vehicle can be powered in only one of the following ways: a single 9-V battery, any number of rubber bands, or a mousetrap that measures 3 cm × 6 cm or less.
4. The vehicle's weight may not exceed 2 kg.

The specifications of the competition's ramp are shown in Figure 13.

The four students recently held a brainstorming session using the idea trigger method. They addressed all elements of the car design, including the issues of propulsion, offensive and defensive strategies, and a stopping mechanism. The following discussion chronicles their brainstorming session. Moe acted as the leader and timed the first 2 minutes, the break, and the subsequent 60-second idea generation phase. At the end of the phase, Larry's page showed the following ideas:

LARRY	IDEA GENERATION PHASE COLUMN 1 (2 MINUTES)
	Support structure = wood (easy to make)
	Use angle irons from Mechano™
	Plastic body for lighter weight
	Zinc air batteries (lightweight)
	Wheels taken from my radio-controlled car
	Rubber band for chain drive
	Small car will be harder for opponent to deflect

1 MINUTE
Ramming device
Wedge-shaped body

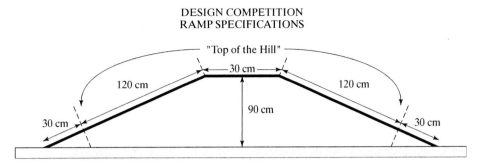

DESIGN COMPETITION
RAMP SPECIFICATIONS

Figure 13. Ramp specifications for the vehicle design competition.

Larry read his entries. As Carly listened, she crossed out her own duplicate entries. When Larry was finished, Carly's first column, including crossouts, showed the following ideas:

CARLY	IDEA GENERATION PHASE COLUMN 1 (2 MINUTES)
	~~No heavy batteries (use zinc air)~~
	Larger wheels for slower turning speed
	Gear box
	Higher torque (harder for opponent to push backwards)
	~~Use plastic for body~~
	Electronic timer for stopping mechanism
	Rechargeable batteries
	~~Wedge-shaped design~~

1 MINUTE
~~Buy wheels from hobby shop for radio-controlled car~~
Sense speed, determine distance traveled
Aluminum frame

Next Shemp read her entries that had not been duplicated by Larry. As Carly listened, an idea flashed into her head: *We can make the drive shaft from a threaded rod.* Carly reasoned that the threaded rod could screw a sliding nut toward a cut-off switch. The method would not be foolproof, because slipping wheels could ruin the system's ability to track distance. It seemed worth discussing, though, so she wrote "threaded rod" under her Column 2 entries.

When Shemp heard Larry read his "ramming device" entry, it made her think about using an ejected object as part of an offensive strategy. She wrote the words "ejected device" under her Column 2 entries. Moe reacted similarly to Larry's idea and wrote the words, "lob something on the track ahead of opposing car" under his Column 2 entries. The spoken trigger phase made its way around the group. When everyone had finished, Moe, acting as leader, started the process again. This time, everyone read their Column 2 entries and wrote new ideas under Column 3. As Shemp read her entry about ejected devices from Column 2, Moe had a fleeting image from the Herman Melville novel *Moby Dick*: He imagined a flying spear with a barbed tip shot ahead of the vehicle over the top of the hill. *After hitting the carpet in front of the opposing vehicle,* he thought, *the barbed tip will dig into the carpet, blocking the other car. This spear will be very difficult to dislodge.* Moe wrote "harpoon" under his Column 3 entries.

The second idea trigger round progressed, and Moe started a third. After about 45 minutes, the entire Phase 2 session was finished. Moe suggested a break so that he could compile everyone's lists of ideas. His combined list of entries from everyone's three columns showed the following ideas:

SHAPE

Small car = harder for opponent to deflect
Wedge-shaped vehicle having same width as track
Rolling can design
Snow-plow-shaped wedge

STRUCTURE

Support structure = wood (easy to make)
Aluminum frame
Plastic body for light weight
Use angle irons
Hot-melt glue balsa wood

POWER

Zinc air batteries (lightweight)
Rechargeable batteries
Change batteries after every run
Electronic timer for stopping mechanism
Microprocessor-controlled car with onboard sensors
Microprocessor speed determines distance traveled

PROPULSION

Wheels from radio-controlled car purchased at hobby shop
Large wheels
Rubber band for chain drive
Plastic-linked chain from junked radio-controlled car chassis
Single large mousetrap with mechanical links
Wind up large rubber band

STRATEGIES

Ramming device
Flying barbed harpoon
Pickup arm
Throw jacks in front of oncoming opponent
Roll over opponent with large roller

After the break, Moe reconvened the team to discuss the list of ideas. They weeded out the ones that did not seem feasible and compared ideas that looked promising. Finally, they combined multiple ideas and converged on a slow-moving, wedge-shaped vehicle concept for the prototype stage. They also decided to try Moe's flying harpoon strategy, where the harpoon is designed to dig into the carpet and block the path of the opposing vehicle.

5.3   Informal Brainstorming

As discussed in the previous section, the formal brainstorming method requires organization and planning. In contrast, informal brainstorming can be done anywhere. As a technique for engineering design, informal brainstorming in a round table format is appropriate for small groups of people. Ideas can be contributed in random order by any participant. The flow of ideas need not be logical, and new proposals can be offered whenever they come to mind. The ground rules introduced in Section 5.1 should still be enforced during an informal brainstorming session.

EXAMPLE 3: INFORMAL BRAINSTORM- ING	The following example of an informal brainstorming session describes a hypothetical conversation between two structural engineers who were asked to design a cross beam for a renovated building. As shown in Figure 14, the renovation involves gutting the building interior and tearing out existing internal walls. However, after the initial demolition, the designers discover a support column in the middle of a large room. The architectural plans require that the vertical column be removed. This column holds up the mid-span of a wooden cross beam that had previously been hidden inside the ceiling. The engineers must find some new way to support the cross beam and the upper floor it sustains, so that the column can be removed permanently. In its present form, the wooden cross beam is too weak to be supported only at its two ends. If left unsupported in the middle of its span, it will surely break and cause the floor above it to fall. The engineers, Robert and Ernest, discuss the problem using the informal brainstorming method. Note the ebb and flow of ideas between the two engineers. They do not immediately fixate on the first idea that comes to mind; instead, they allow the flow of ideas to lead them to the most feasible solution.

Bert: "Let's just install a new steel I-beam under the upper floor, running it side-by-side next to the existing wooden one. A steel beam is much stronger than a wooden beam, so we could remove the supporting column without worry."

Ernie: "OK, we could." *He thought for a while.* "But we'll have to enclose the existing beam in a box casing when we finish the ceiling. Adding another beam side-by-side will make this box *very* wide." *He drew the sketch shown in Figure 15.* "This wider-than-expected box will compromise the artistic interior design of the building and will also interfere with the planned layout of the hanging light fixtures.

"What if we *take out* the existing wooden beam and replace it with a steel I-beam? Thus, we can minimize the impact of the box casing."

Bert: "That might work, but we would need to make a temporary beam to support the upper floor while we remove the old beam; that would require a temporary column as well. We'd need to build a false wall in the basement to support the temporary column. It would take lots of time and lots of money. It may not be worth it." *Bert showed Ernie the sketch in Figure 16.*

Ernie: "Yeah, it would cost a lot. But the client will understand that we have no choice."

Bert: "But she would not be very happy about it. We need a better solution." *Bert thought for a while.* "I've got it. We can drill holes through the existing beam, and then create thin steel plates with holes in the same places. Then we can bolt the plates on either side of the wooden beam with these huge bolts." *He made a sizing gesture with his hands.* "The composite beam would be strong enough to support the upper floor without the column." *Bert drew the sketch of Figure 17 to illustrate his idea.*

Ernie: "I have a better idea. Let's have the plates made up first with the holes. We'll clamp the plates in place, and *then* drill the holes in the wooden beam, using the steel-plate sandwich as a template."

Bert: "Yeah! Good idea. The beam sandwich will be nice and strong and only a little bit wider than the wooden beam alone." *He thought a moment more.* "But we should

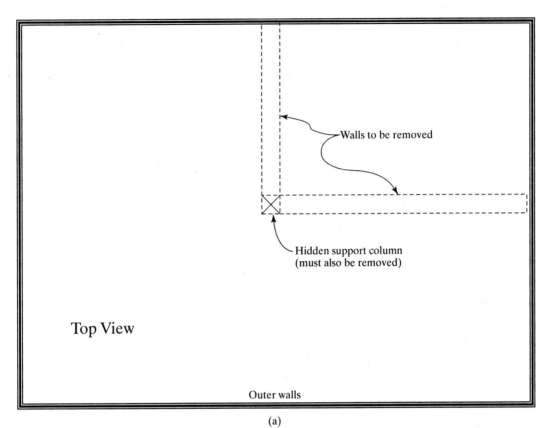

(a)

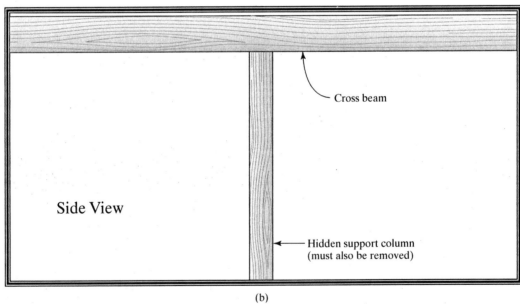

(b)

Figure 14. Demolition plan showing a previously hidden vertical support column and cross beam: (a) top view; (b) side view.

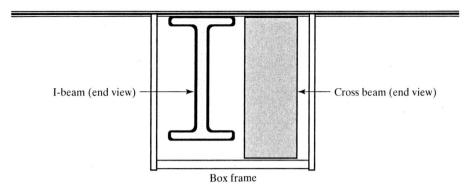

Figure 15. I-beam and wooden cross beam side by side. The box encasing the two beams is very wide and ugly.

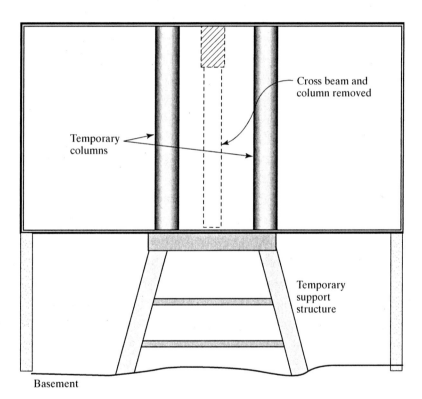

Figure 16. Replacing the existing wooden beam requires building a temporary structure in the basement so that the upper floor can be supported while the column and beam are removed.

do some analysis to be sure that the reinforced beam will be strong enough. I'll do some rough calculations to figure out how thin the plates can be, and then do some more precise computer modeling."

Ernie: "Good. In the long run, it will be cheaper to do it this way. I like this idea much better than the first two. It's a good compromise. "

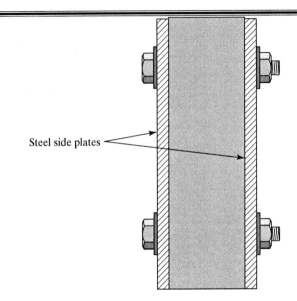

Figure 17.   Bert's idea for two side plates to strengthen the existing wooden beam.

Suppose that you are the leader of a brainstorming session, and one member of your team dominates the conversation. That person may criticize participants, dismiss unconventional ideas, cut off speakers, or otherwise break the rules. When this situation occurs, it's your responsibility to keep the offender in line. You might say to the group, "Hey, we need to stick to the formal rules of brainstorming. Let's institute a don't-speak-until-called-upon rule." This approach will tactfully short-circuit the behavior of the dominant person and maintain harmony among team members.

5.4   Idea Diagrams

The *idea diagram* is a concept that traditionally has been used in writing classes to teach students the art of structured writing. As we shall see shortly, the concept also has value in the context of engineering design. In writing classes, the main purpose of the idea diagram is to assist the student before an essay is actually written. A well-structured idea diagram makes it easier to write, especially for long documents. While the precise form of the diagram may vary, depending on the writing instructor, the road map to success can be summarized by the following steps:

1.   *Think carefully about the writing assignment.* What question will you answer in your essay? How can you best answer this question?

2.   *Open your notebook.* Write some possible answers to your questions.

3.   *Collect facts that relate to your essay topic.*

4. *Find the main idea of your essay.* Choose the most important point that you are going to present.

5. *Organize your facts and thoughts in a way that develops your main idea.*

You can easily create a basic form that illustrates the pathways described in steps 1 through 5. This form is easily made into a graphical chart. As a student, you may find such a chart useful when you are asked to commit ideas to paper.

The idea diagram can be easily morphed into a *design diagram*. Like the idea diagram, the design diagram provides yet another structured way in which to organize ideas and the design paths they imply. The five steps for writing success similarly transform into the following:

1. *Think carefully about your design assignment.* What need will you meet when your design is completed? How can you best meet this need?

2. *Open your logbook.* Write down some possible ways to solve the design problem.

3. *Collect facts that relate to your possible design approaches.*

4. *Converge on the best solution to the problem.* Using an iterative process, find the most feasible design solution.

5. *Organize your facts, tests, and concepts into an initial working prototype.*

PRACTICE!

1. Examine the final list of ideas compiled by Morris et al. during their idea trigger session. Conduct a one-person "mini-brainstorming session" and add as many ideas as you can. Allow yourself 4 minutes to compile your ideas.

2. A non-engineering friend complains about a pair of ear-bud headphones that keep falling out. Give yourself 5 minutes of brainstorming time, and compile a large list of ideas to solve your friend's problem. After the 5 minutes are over, take a short break, then sort your list, categorizing each idea with a "feasibility" rating of 1 to 5, with 5 being the most feasible.

3. In 2 minutes, write down as many ways as you can for safely confining a dog to a yard. Then rate your ideas in rank order, from least costly to most costly.

4. Write down as many ideas as you can for designing a hands-free water faucet.

5. To save energy, you'd like to devise a method for reminding people to turn off lights. Devise as many methods as you can to achieve this objective. Allow yourself 2 minutes of brainstorming time.

6. Can brainstorming be used to solve math problems? Why or why not?

7. Develop as many concepts as you can for a system that will automatically feed pellets to a pet hamster. Allow yourself 3 minutes of brainstorming time. If possible, work with a group of up to four people.

8. Get together with a teammate to conduct an informal brainstorming session. Take turns contributing a single new idea, one after the other, until one of you has run out of ideas. Then the other should declare all remaining ideas. Each of you should write down ideas as soon as they come to mind. Use this method to develop a concept for designing an automatic bagel-slicing machine.

9. Imagine that you are part of design team that is developing a method to synchronize a personal digital assistant (e.g., Palm Pilot™) with a companion program on a desktop computer. Compose the idea trigger session sheets that four

teammates might contribute to such a session. These sheets should have the form shown in Figure 12. Also, compile a composite sheet that summarizes the session.

10. Think of as many ways as possible to determine the depth and breadth of a newly discovered underground oil deposit.

11. The following exercise involves a futuristic problem. Meet with one or more classmates for a brainstorming session (either formal or informal). Write multiple ways to transfer information from a human into a computer without a keyboard or mouse. Provide details of each possible method.

12. You are given a barometer, a stopwatch, and a tape measure. In how many different ways can you determine the height of the Eiffel Tower in Paris, France?

13. You are given a barometer, a stopwatch, and a tape measure. How might you determine the height of Mt. Rainier in Washington State?

14. Design a sensing mechanism that can measure the speed of a bicycle.

15. You are given an egg, some tape, and several plastic drinking straws. Using only these materials, design a system that will prevent the egg from breaking when dropped from a height of 6 ft (2 m).

16. Devise as many different methods as you can for using your desktop computer as a stop watch to time a road race.

17. Think about a large aquarium (the kind the public visits to see large sea creatures). Design a system for washing the inside surfaces of the windows from the outside.

18. Design a system to help a quadriplegic turn the pages of a book.

19. Devise a system for automatically raising and lowering the flag at dawn and dusk each day.

20. Design a system that will automatically turn on a car's windshield wipers when needed.

21. Develop a device that can alert a blind person when a pot of water has boiled.

22. Devise a system to line up screws on an assembly-line conveyor belt. All screws must point in the same direction.

23. Develop a method for detecting pinhole leaks in latex surgical gloves during the manufacturing process.

24. Devise a method for deriving an electrical signal from a magnetic compass. The compass must interface with a computer running navigational software.

25. Given a coil of rope and eight poles, devise a method to build a temporary emergency shelter in the wilderness.

26. Devise an alarm system to prevent a thief from stealing memory chips from inside a personal computer.

27. Imagine custodial workers who are in the habit of yanking on the electrical cords of vacuum cleaners to unplug them from the wall. Devise a system or device to prevent damage to the plugs on the ends of the cords.

28. Develop a system for automatically dispensing medication to an elderly person who has difficulty keeping track of schedules.

29. Devise a system that will agitate and circulate the water in an outdoor swimming pool so that a chlorine additive will be evenly distributed. Assume that a ground-fault protected (GFCI) electrical outlet is available at the pool site.

30. Devise a system that will allow truck drivers to check their tires' air pressure without getting out of the vehicle.

6   DESIGN EXAMPLES

In this section, the principles of engineering design are illustrated by three specific examples. The approach in each case emulates the key elements of the design process.

6.1   Model Vehicle Design Competition

Imagine that you've entered a vehicle design competition in which the sponsor, your engineering college alumni association, offers textbook gift certificates to the college bookstore to the winners. Given the high cost of textbooks, you're eager to win.

The goal of the competition, as previously shown in Figure 13, is to design and construct a vehicle that can climb a ramp under its own power, stop at the top of the ramp, and sustain its position against an opposing vehicle coming up the other side of the ramp. The vehicle deemed "on top of the hill" is the one closest to the centerline after a 15-second time interval. Multiple runs against different pairs of competitors will determine the final winner.

The rules state that the vehicle can be powered by just one of the following energy sources:

- A battery of up to 9 volts
- A rubber band (4 mm $\times$ 10 cm maximum size in its unstretched state)
- A mousetrap (3 cm $\times$ 6 cm maximum spring size).

Imagine that you have entered this design competition and wish to design a competitive vehicle. Let's examine the problem using the design cycle of Figure 7. Remember that the problem can be addressed in many different ways. The solution presented here is but one of many.

1. Choose a Design Strategy   Many different design strategies will lead to a vehicle capable of competing. Building a *winning* design, however, requires careful consideration of several key issues. How can you know ahead of time what the right choices will be? In truth, you can't, especially if you've never built such a vehicle before. You can only start by making educated guesses based on your experience and intuition; then you can rely on the iterative nature of the design process to help you converge on a workable solution. The following list defines some possible design strategies that you might adopt:

1. *Design for speed.* The fastest vehicle will not necessarily be the winner, but one strategy could be to race to the top as fast as possible, then defend against a slower opponent by blocking access to the top of the ramp using a proper defensive strategy.

2. *Design for strength.* Alternatively, you could design a strong, steady, slower-moving vehicle capable of pushing away the opposing car as it "bulldozes" its way to the center of the ramp.

3. *Design for easy changes.* The rules state that modifications to the vehicle are permitted between runs. Adopting an easy-to-change construction strategy will facilitate "on-the-fly" changes to your vehicle.

4. *Design for durability.* During the competition, your vehicle must endure many trips up the contest ramp. Opposing vehicles and accidents can damage a fragile design. You must weigh the issue of durability against your desire to produce a vehicle that's flexible and easy to modify.

Note that strategies (3) and (4) are not independent of one another. For example, designing for easy changes may conflict with building a durable vehicle. Engineers typically face such tradeoffs when making design decisions. Deciding which pathway to take requires experience and practice, but making any decision at all means that you've begun the design process.

The rules of this particular competition provide for many alternatives in vehicle design. Regardless of the details, however, all vehicles will require the same basic components: an *energy source*, a *propulsion mechanism*, a *stopping method*, and a *starting device*. After some discussion with your teammate, you develop the *choice map* shown in Figure 18.

Although the choice map does not provide an exhaustive list, it serves as an excellent starting point for your design effort. The following paragraphs outline some of the thought processes that might accompany your design choices.

Energy Source

Batteries are attractive as an energy source because they require no winding or preparation. They will need frequent replacement, however, and will thus be more expensive than the mechanical alternatives. Rubber bands will require much less frequent replacement, but will store the smallest amount of energy among the three choices. Like a rubber band, a mousetrap does not need frequent replacing. It stores more energy than a rubber band, but because of its physical form, it offers the fewest options for harnessing its stored energy.

Propulsion Mechanism

Your choice of the propulsion device, or *energy converter*, will depend on your choice of an energy source. If you decide to use batteries, an electric motor will be the obvious choice for turning the vehicle's wheels. Rubber bands can be stretched to provide linear

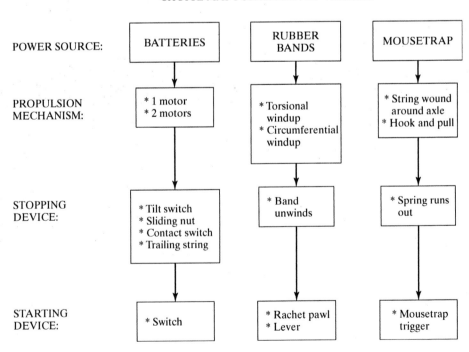

Figure 18. Choice map that outlines the decision tree for the first phase of the design process in the vehicle design competition.

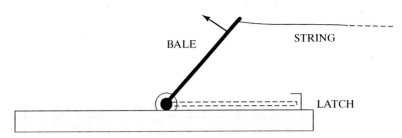

Figure 19. Harnessing the stored mechanical energy of a mousetrap. The bale retracts in an arc when the mousetrap is released.

motion or twisted for torsional energy storage to turn an axle or power shaft. Alternatively, a rubber band can be stretched around a shaft or spool like a fishing reel and used to propel the vehicle's wheels. A mousetrap can provide only one kind of motion. When released, its bale will retract in an arc, as depicted in Figure 19. In principle, this motion can be harnessed and used to propel the vehicle.

Stopping Method

According to the competition rules, your vehicle must stop when it arrives at the top of the ramp. This requirement can be met by interrupting propulsion power precisely at the right moment and relying on a combination of gravity and friction to stop the vehicle. A braking device to augment these forces might also be considered. If the vehicle is powered by batteries, there are many ways to interrupt power flow to the vehicle. A simple tilt switch can disconnect the battery when the vehicle is level, but connect the battery when the vehicle is on a slope. A metal ball that rolls inside a small cage and makes contact with two electrodes, as illustrated in Figure 20, might serve as a suitable tilt switch. Other choices include a spring-loaded contact switch, such as the one shown in Figure 21, or a system that cuts off power to the wheels after the car has traveled a preset distance as measured by wheel rotations. This latter scheme will work well only if the wheels do not lose traction and slip on the track.

One interesting alternative to a mechanical switch would be to use an electronic timer circuit that shuts off power from the battery after a precise time interval. Through trial and error, you could set the elapsed time so that the vehicle stops precisely at the top of the ramp. One problem inherent to this open-loop timing system is that the vehicle does not actually sense its own arrival at the top of the ramp, but rather infers it by interval timing. Because the speed of the vehicle may decrease with each successive run as battery energy is depleted, this timing scheme might cause problems. The method

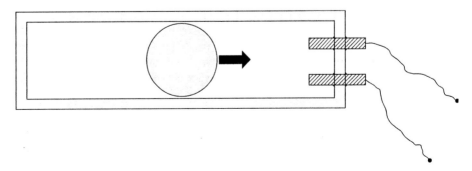

Figure 20. Tilt switch made from a small enclosure, a metal ball bearing, and two contact points.

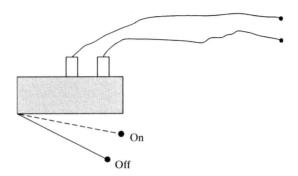

Figure 21. Spring-loaded contact switch.

will also fail if the wheels slip on the track. On the other hand, it is likely to be more reliable than solutions that involve mechanical parts.

If a rubber band or mousetrap is chosen as the power source, then stopping the vehicle will require something other than an electrical switch. One way of stopping a vehicle propelled by mechanical energy storage is simply to allow the primary energy source to run out (e.g., allow the rubber band to completely unwind). While this method is crude, it is reliable, because power input to the vehicle will *always* cease when the source of stored energy has been depleted.

Starting Device

If the vehicle is powered by a battery, then an electrical switch becomes the most feasible starting device. You could, however, design the vehicle so that the motor is brought up to speed prior to the start, then mechanically engaged at the starting time. This latter approach might enable a strategy involving rapid ascent up the ramp. A rubber-band power source will require a mechanical device such as a trip lever to initiate power flow to the wheels. A mousetrap can use its built-in trigger mechanism or any other starting mechanism that you might devise.

2. Make a First Cut at the Design   The first design iteration begins with rough estimations of the dimensions, parameters, and components of the vehicle to make sure that the design is technically feasible. After discussing the long list of design choices, you and your teammate decide to use a battery-powered vehicle. This decision allows many choices for a stopping device. You feel that the flexibility inherent to this design choice far outweighs the advantages of mechanical propulsion schemes. You decide upon a defensive strategy and agree to build a slower-moving, wedge-shaped vehicle powered by a small electric motor. The advantage of this design approach is that the motor can be connected to the wheels using a large gear ratio, thereby providing higher torque at the wheels and a mechanical advantage that would be unavailable to a very fast vehicle. Because your vehicle will be slower than the others, it may not reach the top of the ramp first, but its wedge-shaped design will help to dislodge any opposing vehicle that does arrive first at the top of the ramp. On the other hand, if your vehicle arrives first, its defensive wedge shape will cause your opponent's car to ride over your car's body, allowing you to maintain your position at the top.

A rough preliminary sketch of your car is shown in Figure 22. You've entered this sketch into a notebook that contains all information relevant to the project, including design calculations, parts lists, and sketches of various pieces of the car. Shown in Fig 22 are the car's wedge-shaped design; a single drive shaft driven by a motor, belt, and pulleys; and a single switch to turn off the motor when the vehicle arrives at the top of the ramp.

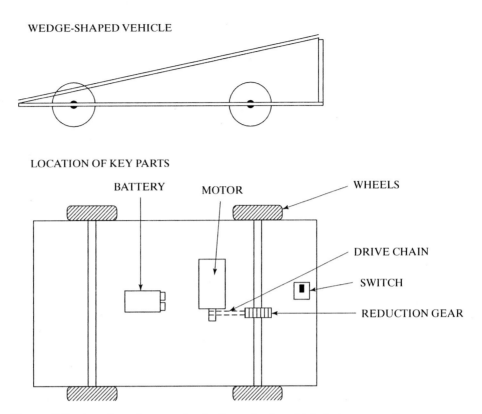

Figure 22. Rough, preliminary sketch of a car for the vehicle design competition.

3. Build, Document, Test, and Revise The sketch of Figure 22 represents a beginning, but it is not the finished product. You still have many hurdles to overcome and tests to run before your vehicle will be ready to compete. The next step in the design process should probably be the building and testing of a "first-cut" prototype. To help you in this phase of the design process, you've built a test ramp that mimics one side of the official test ramp. You begin by constructing a chassis shell in the form of a wedge, but without a motor drive or stopping mechanism.

You run your wedge-shaped vehicle up the ramp slope by hand. You soon discover that the bottom of the vehicle hits the ramp at the top of the hill, as depicted in Figure 23(a). The change in the angle of the ramp is large, and all four wheels do not always maintain contact with the track surface. You discuss several solutions to this problem with your teammate. One solution would be to increase the diameter of the wheels, as shown in Figure 23(b). This change would decrease the mechanical advantage between the motor and the wheels, requiring you to recalculate the torque required from the motor. Another solution would be to make the vehicle shorter, as in Figure 23(c), but you realize that this solution would lead to a more acute angle of your wedge shape and reduce its effectiveness as a defensive strategy. (The thinner the wedge, the more capable the car of wedging itself under opposing vehicles. However, the rear of the wedge must be the same thickness to leave space for the motor and gear box.)

4. Revise Again Your teammate suggests keeping the wheels and shape of the wedge the same and moving the rear wheels forward, as depicted in Figure 24. You rebuild the vehicle by moving the rear shaft mount forward, and you test your vehicle again. The redesigned vehicle no longer bottoms out on the track, and you claim success. Your

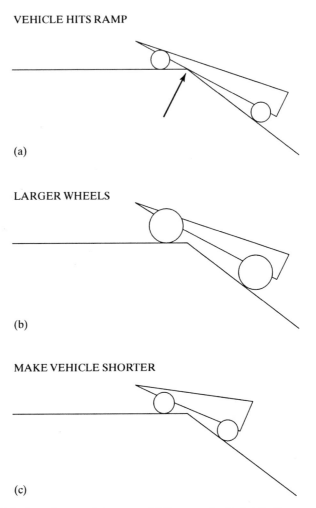

VEHICLE HITS RAMP

(a)

LARGER WHEELS

(b)

MAKE VEHICLE SHORTER

(c)

Figure 23.   Vehicle at the top of the ramp. (a) Bottom of vehicle hits the ramp; (b) vehicle with larger wheels; (c) a shorter vehicle.

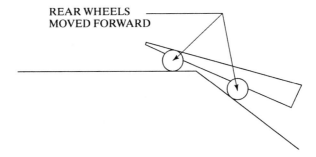

REAR WHEELS
MOVED FORWARD

Figure 24.   Moving the rear wheels forward.

professor sees your design changes and suggests that you test your vehicle under more realistic conditions. For example, what will happen when another vehicle rides over the top of your wedge-shaped body? You proceed to simulate such an event by placing a weight at various positions on the top of the car. The results of these additional tests suggest that

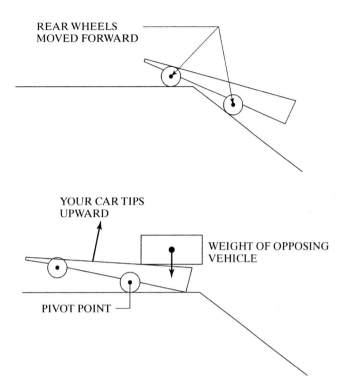

Figure 25. Weight of opposing vehicle on top of rear end causes car to topple backwards.

moving the wheel locations may not be the best solution to your problem. When you move the rear wheels forward, you change the base of support for the car's center of gravity. You discover that if an opposing vehicle rides over the top of your car, the net center of gravity moves toward the rear, eventually causing your car to topple backwards, as depicted in Figure 25.

5. Reality Check   This latest discovery may seem like a setback, but it's a normal part of the iterative design process. Some things work the first time, while others do not. By observing and learning from failure and by building, testing, revising, and retesting, you will be able to converge on the best solution to the problem.

6. More Revisions   After some thought, you decide that increasing the diameter of the wheels may be the best option after all. Your teammate points out that you can simply change the ratio of the gear box to preserve the net mechanical advantage between the motor and the wheels. This change will allow you to accommodate larger wheels. You buy some new wheels and try them with success. With the rear axle moved to its original location and the larger wheels in place, your car no longer bottoms out on the ramp.

PRACTICE!

1. Make a two-column list that outlines the advantages of the various power sources for traveling up the ramp of Figure 13 in the vehicle design competition.
2. Make a list of additional propulsion mechanisms that could be used to drive a design competition vehicle.
3. Make a two-column list that outlines the advantages of using gravity and friction versus an applied brake as a stopping mechanism for a design competition vehicle.

4. Determine the minimum energy needed to drive a 2-kg vehicle from the bottom of a ramp to the top, a net vertical distance of 1 meter.

5. How much electrical energy (in joules) is needed to exert one newton of force over a distance of 1 meter (m)?

6. How much electrical power (in watts) is needed to exert one newton of force on a body over a distance of 1 m for 10 seconds?

7. Determine the number of turns per centimeter (cm) of wheel diameter that will be required to move a vehicle from the bottom to the top of a 1-m ramp in a vehicle design competition.

8. For a 1-m design competition ramp, determine the wheel diameter needed to move a vehicle from the bottom of the ramp to the top with 50 turns of the drive axle.

PROFESSIONAL SUCCESS: PARALLEL PATHS TO DIFFERENT DESIGN SOLUTIONS

One of the interesting features of the design process is that more than one perfectly acceptable solution may exist to the same engineering problem. The endpoint of your design efforts may be affected more by arbitrary design decisions than by the intrinsic worth of one solution over another. This scenario is not unlike that found in any of several science fiction stories involving time travel, in which parallel time travel paths, each originating at the same point event, lead to drastically different outcomes. In the popular movie *Back to the Future*, for example, Marty McFly (played by Michael J. Fox) inadvertently travels back in time to his parents' 1955 high school. With the help of his scientist companion, Dr. Emmett Brown (played by Christopher Lloyd), he repeatedly travels back to the present, each time returning to a different reality based on small changes he made in his parents' past. The parallel time pathways depicted in the story all lead to valid, believable, but very different outcomes.

This same scenario exists in the world of engineering design. Small changes in a design approach can lead to very different, but equally valid, design solutions. If you find yourself in such a situation, know that the decision may be left to your whim and fancy—provided that each outcome will truly meet design objectives. In any given situation, take heed that the latter is really true. Sometimes, hidden factors (such as the availability of raw materials, public reaction to a particular style, or the ability to market one design over another) may, in fact, make the choice far from arbitrary.

6.2   DVD Production Facility

In this example, we'll examine the design cycle for the case where the product is a manufacturing process, rather than a tangible physical entity. Although the means of execution of the various stages of the cycle may differ, the basic principles will be identical to those used in the previous example.

The case involves a software interface that must be written for a company that makes digital video disks (DVDs). The disks are sold online by several vendors, including Amonia.com, BestVids.com, CircuitTown.com, and WebFlix.com. Each of these vendors wishes to minimize its physical inventory while maximizing its ability to fulfill orders quickly. A machine that can mass produce plastic DVDs from etched metal master disks is very expensive—on the order of a few million dollars—and none of the DVD vendors alone can afford that sort of capital investment. They each would like a subcontractor who can manufacture DVDs on demand as they are ordered from each vendor's individual website. In recognition of this need, your company, Disk Stamper Inc., has raised money from venture capitalists, purchased a stamping machine, and has contracted with each of

the four vendors separately to fulfill their orders on demand. The job of your design team is to determine a manufacturing system that can accomplish this task. Let's discuss this design problem in the context of the design cycle of Figure 7.

1. Define the Overall Objectives The overall objectives of this design problem are clear. First, you desire to keep your clients happy. You must stamp and ship their DVD orders as quickly as possible and strive for 100% accuracy. You must provide for contingencies should your machine (or machines) be out of service for repairs, and you must regularly back up data. In addition, you need to fulfill your prime directive as a small company: you must make money. This last objective is neither whimsical nor callous. If your company does not make money, you will not be able to sustain your operations, and you and your employees will be out of jobs.

2. Gather Information Your first step should be to interview your clients to determine their requirements. If you're lucky, their needs will coincide, and your design task will be simplified. In practice, however, their needs are apt to differ somewhat. One element of your information-gathering goal will be to seek common threads among your customers' aggregate needs. Perhaps it will be possible to persuade them to alter their stated requirements so that you can converge on a workable solution.

You should also investigate the operations of other companies involved in the order fulfillment business. You'll find that some, like you, actually manufacture the products they ship, while others simply act as wholesale distributors for other manufacturers—in essence, they act as the interface between the manufacturing company and online sales vendor. Some online bookstores, for example, work in this latter way, sending their orders to central distributors, called *fulfillment* companies, who in turn order the books from publishers and ship them.

3. Choose a Design Strategy At this stage of the design cycle, you outline one or more approaches to the overall problem. In one plan, you would allot a daily manufacturing time slot to each DVD seller. During each vendor's allocated time slot (6 hours total, for around-the-clock operations), its accumulated online orders would be fulfilled, and DVDs of the same title would be processed together. This approach, illustrated graphically in Fig. 26, would require that you change the master stamping disk several times during the vendor's time window, but it would enable you to group together each vendor's orders for shipment. An alternative strategy, shown in Fig. 27, would collect DVD orders by title regardless of vendor and then stamp all the DVDs of the same

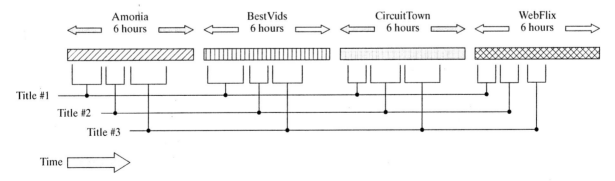

Figure 26. One possible implementation of the DVD order fulfillment process. Each of the four vendors is allocated one six-hour time slot, and individual orders for the same DVD title are processed as a batch within each vendor's time slot.

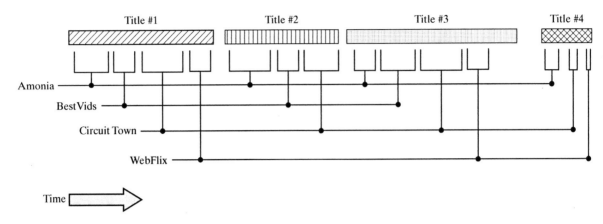

Figure 27. Another possible implementation of the DVD order fulfillment process. In this scheme, DVD titles are processed in batches independent of vendor.

title together, as a single batch. This approach would reduce the need to change stamp masters frequently, but it would require that you sort orders by seller at periodic intervals. After some discussion, you decide to investigate the latter approach: You will collect orders for all the vendors, sort them by DVD title, and then stamp single titles as a batch, changing masters only when it's time to change the DVD title. There is some motivation for this approach, because it's faster and will reduce labor costs. Once your business becomes operational, you'll need to pay machine operators by the hour. Given the low profit margin for DVDs (most of the profit in the movie industry goes to the movie production company), reducing labor costs seems like a good idea.

4. Make a First Cut at the Design   A block diagram of your proposed system is shown in Figure 28. At the present time, the only definite piece of hardware is the actual stamping machine; all other components will ultimately have to be designed and integrated into the system. Incoming data from the vendors is stored in an "orders" database, and the master disks are stored in a digitally controlled carousel. When the stamping machine becomes free for stamping, the controller retrieves a packet of orders from the input queue, then sends a signal to the carousel to load the correct master into the stamping machine. As each fabricated DVD exits the machine, it is labeled, then its carrier vessel is tagged with a bar code that links that specific disk to the shipping information stored in the orders database. Packaging occurs down the production line, where the shipping information is printed on the outside of the package.

5. Model and Analyze   In order to ensure that the system will work as expected, some engineering analysis is appropriate. Each physical transition of a disk from one station to another will require some time delay. If the system is to operate efficiently and provide the fastest overall throughput, proper coordination of events is necessary. Thus, several questions arise. For example, is it better to wait until the disk has been tagged with a bar code before loading the next blank disk in the stamping machine? Or should the blank disk be loaded immediately after its predecessor has left the machine, without regard for the tagging operation? Similarly, what steps must be taken to ensure that incoming orders do not arrive simultaneously, thereby confusing the system? Alternatively, if they do, what techniques can be incorporated into the system to deal with the conflict? A systems-level analysis, in which the dynamics of the queuing process are examined in detail, will help to optimize the system. Answering questions of this sort falls in the domain of *systems engineering*, usually included under the umbrella of *manufacturing* or *industrial engineering* in most college curricula.

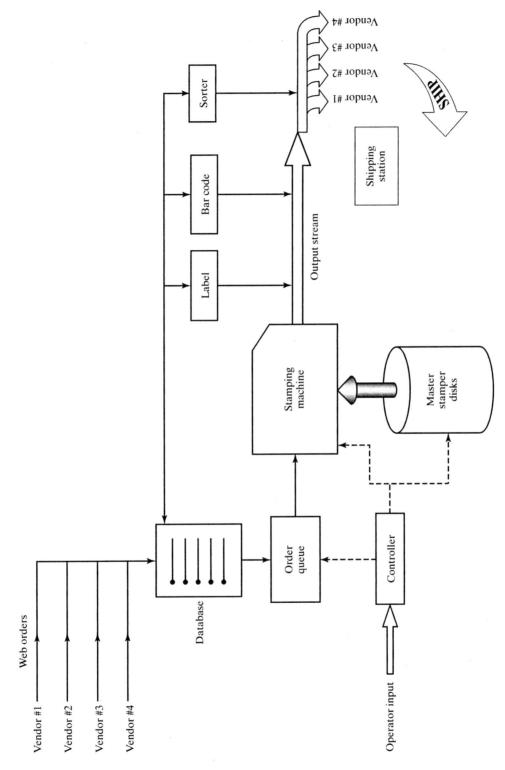

Figure 28. Block diagram of a system that can implement the production scheme of Figure 27.

6. Build, Document, and Test   Full-scale construction of your proposed system will be costly; hence, you decide (wisely) to attempt the build-and-document phase of the design cycle using simulation. Specifically, you choose to model the entire system using a commercial systems-analysis software package. Several excellent sources of such programs exist; you decide upon Simulink,™ a toolbox in the MATLAB software suite.

Your simulation and testing reveal no debilitating problems, but a major bottleneck develops at the packaging stage. Your vendors have specified different shipping methods (e.g., United Parcel Service, FedEx Ground, and the U.S. Postal Service). These different shipping methods require that you change shipping labels from order to order. Given that you have decided to process orders by DVD title, rather than by vendor, changing labels must occur often, possibly causing unneeded delays.

7. Revise and Revise Again   You solve the labeling problem by adding a package sorting station to the system downstream of the stamping operation. This feature will identify each packaged DVD by its bar code, then divert it to one of three shipping stations (one for each method of shipping). This addition to the system will increase capital costs—you will need to purchase and install the components of the additional sorting station—but the overall improvement in efficiency will more than pay for the added startup cost. Your systems-level analysis estimates the payback period for the additional feature to be about 4 months at a 100% production level. Your team decides to adopt this design revision.

8. Thoroughly Test the Finished Product   After extensive testing of your simulated system, you will then build the actual devices and connect them together on the factory floor. You will be able to approach this high-cost portion of the project with some confidence, having analyzed and revised the system prior to construction. Full-scale testing using a simulated order queue will be the next step before you open your company for business. Limited trials of actual orders will be next, followed by ramp up to full-scale production. Even in this final phase of implementation, you should expect to uncover previously hidden problems and be prepared to return to the design cycle for revisions and further tests.

6.3   Motorized Wheelchair Safety Flag

This example illustrates the analysis and testing that often accompany the design cycle of Figure 7. Suppose that you work for a company that makes motorized wheelchairs, and you've been assigned the task of choosing the proper drive motors for the left and right wheels. The wheelchair is powered by a large, 12-V lead-acid battery (the kind found under the hood of an automobile). How do you choose the correct motors? Motors of all sizes and voltage ratings are available, including some alternating current (*ac*) motors, as well as direct current (*dc*) motors.

Given that the wheelchair will be powered by its battery, a good choice would be a *dc* motor. This choice is not as obvious as it seems. In many high-powered operations, a *dc* power source is converted to variable frequency *ac* as a means to control the rotational speed of an ac motor. This approach, for example, is used in some public transit trains powered by electricity.

If you do decide to use a *dc* motor, what voltage specification should you choose? What power rating will be best? Must you consider torque? Several vendor catalogs list motors rated for 3, 6, 12, and 24 volts. You learn that the rating of a motor specifies its operating voltage for continuous use. If a motor is powered by a lower-than-specified voltage, the motor will not heat up significantly, but the maximum torque available from the motor will be reduced. Conversely, if the motor is connected to a higher-than-specified voltage, the available torque will increase, but the excess current will heat the windings inside the motor and possibly damage it. During wheelchair use, the motor is likely to be energized for long periods of time if the occupant travels long distances, and maximum available power will be required. Hence, a motor actually rated at 12 volts seems suitable for use with a standard, 12-V lead-acid car battery.

Your design team decides to purchase several different motors rated at 12 volts and validate each one for torque and current flow by connecting it to a variable voltage supply. You plan to measure the current flow at several values of applied voltage. The electrical power flow can be computed by multiplying the applied voltage by the current that actually flows into the motor. (Electrical power equals voltage times current.) You devise the apparatus shown in Figure 29 to measure the mechanical power delivered by the motor. The frictional rubbing of the weighted loop of string applies a mechanical load to the motor. Your contraption is a simple version of the industry-standard Prony brake used to measure motor torque.[1]

You plan to power each of your motors at a constant voltage and add weights until the motor stalls. The motor with the highest torque will be the one that sustains the largest weight before stalling. You record your mechanical loading and electrical power measurements in your logbook and use your data to determine which motor gives you the most mechanical torque when energized by a 12-volt power source.

Figure 30 depicts how a page from your logbook might appear. You've recorded a list of the motors tested plus the results of the mechanical loading tests. You've also included a sketch of the loading apparatus of Figure 29 in your notebook. It's important to record the characteristics of the motors that you *don't* use for the wheelchair, just in case you need to reconsider one of the rejected motors during a subsequent design revision.

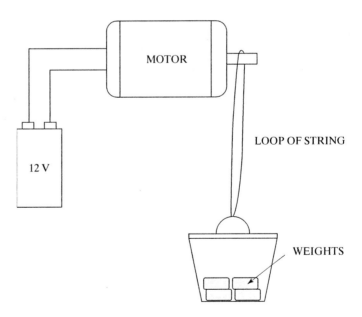

Figure 29.   Simple apparatus to measure motor torque.

---

[1]The Prony brake was invented in 1821 by Gaspard de Prony, a professor and examiner at the Ecole Polytechnique in France, as a way to measure the performance of machines and engines.

MOTOR A: TC-254			MOTOR B: RS-257-234		
# weights	V(volts)	I (amps)	# weights	V(volts)	I (amps)
0	9.0	0.02	0	9.0	0.05
1	8.9	0.05	1	8.8	0.1
2	8.9	0.07	2	8.7	0.17
3	8.8	0.1	3	8.5	0.23
4	8.7	0.2	4	8.0	0.3
5	8.0	0.5	5	7.6	0.7

MOTOR C: BOD-37A			MOTOR D: TOSH-7954		
# weights	V(volts)	I (amps)	# weights	V(volts)	I (amps)
0	9.0	0.01	0	9.0	0.01
1	8.9	0.04	1	8.9	0.11
2	8.9	0.05	2	8.9	0.21
3	8.8	0.1	3	8.8	0.31
4	8.7	0.25	4	8.7	0.41
5	8.0	0.52	5	8.7	0.51

Figure 30. Page from an engineer's logbook that documents mechanical loading tests on various motors.

Later, as your work proceeds, you record all calculations, specifications, and sketches pertinent to the drive train. Your objective is to have complete records available should they be required at any phase of the design cycle.

SUMMARY

In this chapter, the essential elements of the design process have been outlined at a very basic level. As an engineering endeavor, design differs from analysis and replication because it involves multiple paths to solution, plus decision making, evaluation, revision, testing, and retesting. The *design cycle* is an important part of engineering problem solving, as are knowledge, experience, and intuition. *Documentation* is critical to the success of a product and should be an integral part of the design cycle.

KEY TERMS

Analysis	Design cycle	Replication
Decision making	Evaluation	Revision
Design	Iteration	Testing

Problems

The following problem statements can be used to practice problem-solving skills and idea generation. Some of them involve paper designs, while others are suitable for actual fabrication and testing.

1. Develop a design concept for a mechanical device that will allow hands-free operation of a standard, wired telephone. Outline its basic form, key features, proposed

method of construction, and prototyping plan. Consider size, weight, shape, safety factors, and ease of use.

2. Develop a concept for a device that will allow hands-free use of a cellular telephone without the addition of accessories such as an earphone or remote microphone. Your design should be based solely on a mechanical solution.

3. Design a device for recording ideas that you develop while riding your bicycle. Your contraption should enable the rider to record notes while holding onto the handlebars with both hands.

4. Design a device for securing a coffee cup near the driver's seat of an automobile. The device should prevent the cup from spilling and should not interfere with proper operation of the car. It should be universally adaptable to a wide variety of vehicles. Address safety and liability issues as part of your design.

5. Develop at least three design concepts for a non-lethal mousetrap. Is your device cost-effective compared with an ordinary, spring-bale mousetrap? Is your trap more humane, and is it worth any added cost?

6. Devise a concept for a powered device that can dig holes in the ground for the installation of fence posts. Sketch a prototype and outline a test plan for your design concept.

7. Design a device that will allow the inside and outside surfaces of windows to be cleaned from the inside only. Compare the projected cost with that of a simple, handheld, squeegee-type window cleaner.

8. Design a system for feeding a pet lizard automatically when the owner is out of town.

9. Develop a design concept for a spill-free coffee cup that requires no detachable lid. Your cup should be easy to fill and clean.

10. Develop a design concept for a warning system that monitors the inside temperature of a food storage locker.

11. Design a device for conveying bricks to the top of a house for chimney repair. (The alternative is to carry them up a ladder by hand.)

12. Design at least three different methods for measuring the height of a tall building.

13. Design a system that will enable a self-propelled, unattended lawn mower to cut the grass in a yard.

14. Design a system for minimizing the number of red lights encountered by cars traveling east and west through a major city. The system should not unduly impede north–south traffic flow.

15. Devise a method for managing the flow of two-way railroad traffic on a one-track system. The track may have parallel spur tracks at regular intervals. These parallel sections of track allow one train to wait as another passes in the opposite direction. Note, however, that each parallel section adds cost to the system.

16. Develop a concept for a public transportation system in which every traveler can ride a private vehicle on demand from any one station to any other.

17. Design a transportation system based on locating free-use bicycles at strategic points around a large city.

18. Design a transportation system based on keeping fee-for-use, electric automobiles at strategic points around a large city.

19. Most large airports provide carts for travelers to transport luggage from baggage claim areas to taxi stands, transit stations, and parking lots. Develop a system for locating and reclaiming carts from various places around the airport for return to the baggage claim area.

20. Develop a design concept for a system to measure the speed of a passing train.

21. Design a system that will assist flight attendants in feeding passengers on an average-sized airplane without blocking the single central aisle with food and beverage carts.

22. Design a system for automatically turning off a small electric baking oven when a cake is done.

23. Design a system that will help a person locate misplaced eyeglasses.

24. Develop a concept that will assist individuals in finding keys that have been misplaced around the house.

25. Design an electric switch that will turn off lights if the room is vacated, but not sooner than some user-specified time interval.

26. Design a device that will enable a quadriplegic to change the channels on a television set.

27. Devise a system for turning on security lights at dusk and turning them off at dawn. These lights are to be installed throughout a large factory. Your system should have a single master override for all lights.

28. Design a remote warning system for your home freezer that will alert you at work to abrupt changes in temperature.

29. Design a method or concept for dispensing transparent adhesive tape in small, precut lengths.

30. Design a system that will automatically water houseplants when they are in need of moisture.

31. Design a system that will selectively water sections of a garden based on the moisture content of the soil at the location of each plant.

32. Design an irrigation system that will bring water from a nearby pond to your vegetable garden.

33. Develop a design concept for a system that will automatically pick apples from the trees of a commercial apple orchard.

34. Design a system that can aerate the pond in a city park so that algae growth will not overtake other forms of wildlife.

35. Design a device that will allow a one-armed individual to properly use dental floss.

36. Design a system that will prevent the user of a battery charger from inserting the batteries the wrong way. The unit charges four AAA batteries simultaneously, but each battery must be inserted with its positive (+) end in the correct direction.

37. Design a method for counting the number of people who attend a football game. The stadium has a maximum capacity of 40,000 fans and eight entry gates.

38. A big problem in nursing homes for the elderly is the misplacement of false teeth. Some dentures are inevitably discarded with dining room debris. Devise a system that will enable kitchen staff to detect dentures that appear in the waste stream.

39. Design a system for automatically steering a hot-air balloon along a desired compass heading.

40. Design a weatherproof mail slot for a house that will keep cold air out but permit the insertion of mail from outside.

41. Most small sailboats have a tiller (steering stick) in lieu of a steering wheel. Design a system for automatically steering a tiller-controlled sailboat on a course that lies along a user-specified compass direction. Design for a simple boat that has no onboard electricity.

42. Specify the components of a system that will allow a group of six to listen to music from a single MP3 player or iPod. All listeners will use headphones.

43. *Challenge Problem:* One of the problems with recycling postconsumer waste is the sorting of materials; for example, the various plastics and metal containers placed into curbside recycling bins. Consumers and homeowners do not always sort correctly; yet only a small amount of erroneously sorted material can ruin a large batch of recycled material when it is melted to raw material. At the present time, most municipalities resort to manual labor to sort recyclable materials. Devise a concept that will sort metal cans, plastic bottles, and plastic containers at a recycling plant. Develop a plan for modeling and testing your system.

44. Design a kitchen device that will crush aluminum and steel cans in preparation for recycling. Such a device would be helpful for households that practice recycling but have limited storage space.

45. Devise a system for painting car bodies automatically by robot. You must include a method for training the robot for each painting task.

46. Devise a plan for a campus-wide information system that allows any professor to access the grades of any student, while maintaining the privacy of the system to other users. Students also should be able to obtain their own grades, but not those of others.

47. Design an electric pencil sharpener that will turn itself off when the pencil has been properly sharpened.

48. Develop a design concept for a device that will automatically close a sun roof when rain falls. The sun roof should be closed partway when rainfall is light but should be closed completely when rainfall is moderate to heavy.

49. Design an apparatus that will keep a telescope pointed at a distant star despite the rotation of the Earth.

50. Design a system for keeping a satellite's solar panels pointed at the sun.

51.   Devise a system for transferring personnel in flight from one airplane to another.

52.   Devise a system for automatically collecting tolls from cars traversing a major interstate highway. Note that many such systems exist throughout the United States. (See, for example, *www.mtafastlane.com* or *www.ezpass.com.*) This problem asks you to imagine (or find out) the details of how these systems work.

53.   *Challenge Problem:* Laser communication, or "laser-com," is a system by which digital data is sent from one location to another via a modulated laser beam. Laser-com systems are used whenever hard connections via wires or fiber-optic cables are too expensive, not possible, or not desirable. It is much more difficult to eavesdrop on a laser-com link than on other forms of wireless communication; hence, such systems are of obvious interest to the military. One of the principal drawbacks of laser-com systems is the difficulty in maintaining beam alignment when the sender and receiver are moving. Design a system that will automatically direct the communication beams sent by two military vehicles to their respective receiving vehicles.

54.   *Challenge Problem:* Design a concept for a two-way communication system that works via a modulated laser beam. In this system, only a fixed ground station will emit a beam. The other participant in the link will be a moving person (e.g., a foot soldier) who will receive the beam and reflect a modified version back to the base station.

55.   *Challenge Problem:* Design a system consisting of several emergency buttons that will be installed at each of several workshop fabrication stations on a factory floor. Pressing any one of these buttons will activate a signal at a central control console and identify the location of the activated button. Voice communication over the system would also be a desirable feature. One matter to consider is whether a wired or a wireless system is preferable.

56.   *Challenge Problem:* An elementary school teacher needs a calendar-teaching system to help young students learn about dates, appointments, and scheduling events. Your professor has asked you to develop a design concept. The basic system should be a large pad over which a monthly calendar can be placed. The underlying pad should have touch-sensitive sensors that can detect a finger placed on each day block in the calendar. The entire unit should interface with a computer which will run a question-and-answer game or program. Typical questions might include "You have a dentist appointment two weeks from today. Point to the day on the calendar on which you should go to the dentist," or "Sara's birthday is on February 11. Point to that day on the calendar." An appropriate acknowledgement, either visual, auditory, or both, should be issued by the computer for correct answers. A non-intimidating signal should be issued for incorrect answers. Outline the key features of your system and devise a development plan.

57.   *Challenge Problem:* The rules of a particular design competition require an autonomous vehicle to be placed behind a starting line located 30 cm up the side of a 1.5-m inclined ramp. After the starting signal has been given, contestants may release their vehicles. Any vehicle that travels over the starting line prior to the "go" signal loses the race. Currently, the starting sequence is initiated orally by a judge and timed by stopwatch. This system leads to great variability among judges, as many use different starting signals (e.g., "on your mark, get set, go!" or "one, two, three, go!"), and any one judge may be lax in timing or checking for starting-line violations.

Design a system consisting of starting-line sensors, a start signal, and starting-line violation signals for each side of a double ramp. The judge should have a button that initiates the start sequence. A series of periodic beeps that mimic the rhythm of the words, "Ready, set, go!" should sound, with the final "go" being a loud and clearly distinguishable tone or buzzer. In addition, a green light or LED should illuminate when the "go" signal is sounded. The system should run for 15 seconds, then sound another tone or buzzer to indicate the end of the 15-second time interval signifying the end of the contest. If a vehicle crosses the starting line prior to the "go" signal, a red light should appear on the violating vehicle's side of the ramp, and a special "violation" signal should be sounded to alert the judge.

58. *Challenge Problem*: Teams in a model airplane design competition are called to the central runway when it is their turn to compete. After the initial call, each team has 3 minutes to arrive at its starting line. A team that does not arrive at the starting line after 3 minutes loses that run. Warnings are given 2 minutes and 1 minute before the deadline. Traditionally, the announcer has issued these warnings orally over a public address amplification system. There are several problems with this method, however. Acoustics are poor, three races run simultaneously, with different starting times, and only some teams require the full 3 minutes to arrive. Thus, the proper issuing of these cues has been lax. The judges need you to design an automated system that will inform a given team how much of its 3-minute sequence has elapsed. The system must send an appropriate signal (oral, auditory, or visual) only to the relevant team, and the timing sequence must be initiated from the judges' bench. As many as 80 teams may compete on a given day, and each is assigned one work table from a large array of 3 × 8-foot tables on the competition field. All too often, the team being called is delayed, because it is repairing or modifying its vehicle. One of the key design issues is whether a wireless or wired system is better, given the logistical constraints of the competition environment. Because the event operates on a strict budget, final cost also is an important factor.

59. The vehicles entering a student design competition must utilize batteries with a voltage no higher than a specified limit. Each vehicle is checked once with a voltmeter at the start of the day by the head judge. Having a standardized voltage-checking device would shorten the time for voltage checking. Design a unit that has a rotary (or other type of) switch that can select a predetermined battery voltage. If the measured battery falls within the acceptable range, a green light should appear. If the voltage falls below or above the range, yellow or red lights, respectively, should appear.

60. Outline the design of a general purpose software system for a track meet. Your system should enable judges to automatically pair up runners for matches, randomly at first, but by demonstrated ability thereafter (best runners against best runners; worst runners against worst runners). The program should display match sets before each round of the competition, and allow the recording judge to enter the result of each match after its winner has been determined. Assume a competition of up to 140 runners and six sets of matches between contenders.

61. Design a system for projecting matches on a display board so that audiences watching a tennis tournament can keep track of who is matched against whom, and monitor the results of each match. Assume a competition of 20 players with six sets of matches between contenders.

62. Design a system for detecting start-line violations for a horse race.

63. Design a system for determining the winner of each match in a road rally that requires the winning vehicle to be closest to a marker pole from any direction. Note that "nearest" can be an entirely subjective term; hence, your system for determining the winner must precisely define what "nearest" means.

64. Design a software system that will assist in registration for a fund-raising walk. Registration information includes the name, address, and age of the participants. Registrants must pay a small fee, sign photograph permission and liability waiver forms, and receive an event T-shirt and assigned walker number. Several volunteers will work simultaneously at the event to register participants as quickly as possible so that the event can begin on time, but a common, stored database is needed.

65. A local company employs several workers who sort and package small (1 to 2 cm) parts in the 10 to 100-gram range. A typical operation might consist of putting 10 small parts in a polyethylene bag for subsequent shipment. You've been asked to design a mechanical sorting apparatus for dispensing these parts one at a time so that the employees do not have to pick them out by hand. Develop an outline for how such a system might work, and draw a sketch of your proposed apparatus.

66. *Challenge Problem:* Ace Cleaning Services employees perform a variety of cleaning tasks at major office buildings in a downtown area. A crew from Ace has been assigned to a 22-story building with over 500,000 square feet of office space. Approximately 30 employees service this building between 5:00 P.M. and 9:00 P.M. with a staffing pattern of nine people. Workers are dispersed throughout the building to perform daily cleaning routines. Supervisors are responsible for training and for checking that the work has been performed to acceptable standards. A communication system is needed to provide on-the-job cues to the cleaning staff. One system is needed for individuals who are fluent in English and another for individuals who are not. Your task is to devise a system for providing recorded cues to Ace's employees. Develop a concept for the system, draw a sketch of one implementation, and outline how such a system might work.

67. *Challenge Problem:* A teacher wants a clock system that can help young students learn the relationship between time displayed by digital clocks and time displayed by analog clocks. The system should have a console that contains a large analog clock face, as well as a digital clock display with large digits. In operation, the teacher will set either clock, then ask the student to set the other clock to the same time. If the student sets the time correctly, the unit should signal the student appropriately. If the student fails to set the time correctly, the unit should also issue an appropriate response. Outline the salient mechanical and electrical features of such a system.

68. Your school has been asked by a wheelchair-bound individual to build a small motorized flagpole that can be raised and lowered by pressing buttons. The person needs a bright orange flag to provide visibility outdoors while navigating busy city streets and sidewalks. The flag must be lowered when the individual enters buildings so that the pole does not interfere with doorways and low ceilings. Here is a copy of the letter received by your school:

East Crescent Residence Facility
Eleven Hastings Drive
West Walworth, MA 02100

Prof. Hugo Gomez
College of Engineering
Correll University
44 Hartford St.
Canton, MA 02215

May 18, 2005

RE: Retractable flag for wheelchair

Dear Professor Gomez,

I am the supervisor of a residence facility that services adults with special needs. One of our residents is confined to a wheelchair and spends a great deal of time traveling throughout the community, often on busy streets, in a motorized wheelchair. Although a flag on a long pole would increase her safety, she is reluctant to install one on her wheelchair, because it becomes a problem in restaurants, crowded stores, and on public buses. I was wondering if you might have some students who could design an electrically retractable flag, possibly with visual enhancement (e.g., a flashing light) that could be raised or lowered by the individual on demand. The flag deployment mechanism could operate from either the wheelchair's existing automobile-type storage battery or its own self-contained battery. If such a device is possible, could you give me a call? I would appreciate any assistance that you might be able to offer.

Sincerely yours,

Liz DeWalt
Director

Professor Gomez has asked you to try to build such a device for Ms. DeWalt. How would you approach such a task? Such a seemingly simple device actually can be more complicated to design than you might think. Draw a sketch of the wheelchair device, then devise a design plan for building and testing several designs. Include a list of possible safety hazards to bystanders and the user. How can you include the user in the design process, and why is it advisable to do so? Also, write a report of your preliminary findings for Prof. Gomez. Your design strategy should begin with a conceptual drawing of the device that you can send to Ms. DeWalt for comments. Generate a specification list and general drawing of the apparatus as well as a cover letter to Ms. DeWalt.

Design Considerations: One goal of your design might be to make a flag device that can be mounted on any wheelchair, not just on that of Ms. DeWalt's client. Because many wheelchairs are custom designed for the user, your device must be easily adaptable for mounting on different wheelchair styles. Not all wheelchairs are motorized, hence your device must operate from its own batteries to accommodate hand-pushed wheelchairs. Another consideration in favor of separate battery power is that motorized wheelchair manufacturers usually specify that no other electrical or electronic equipment be connected to the primary motor battery for safety, reliability, and power integrity.

One last consideration concerns the placement of the switch needed to activate the flag. Like the flag itself, the activation switch must easily attach to structural features of the wheelchair and must be within easy reach of the user. At the same time, it must not distract the user and must not hurt anyone.

69. *Challenge Problem:* Develop a design concept for a computer-interfaced electronic display board that can be placed in the lobby of an office building to display messages of the day, announce upcoming seminars, or indicate the location of special events. The objective of the problem is to use a matrix of addressable light-emitting diodes (LEDs) rather than a video display. The system should accept messages by wire from a remote site. One approach might be to design your display board system so that it is capable of independently connecting to a local-area computer network. Alternatively, you could build a separate remote device that could be connected to a desktop computer and then brought down to the display board to load in the data. A wireless solution might also be possible. These examples are suggestions only. In general, any means for getting data to the board is acceptable, but a separate computer (PC) cannot become a dedicated part of the finished display.

70. *Challenge Problem:* An engineer is interested in measuring the small-valued *ac* magnetic fields generated by power lines and appliances. You have been asked to design a battery-powered, handheld instrument capable of measuring the magnitude of *ac* magnetic fields in the range 0.1 to 10 μT (microtesla) at frequencies of 50–60 Hz. Magnetic fields of this magnitude are very small and are difficult to measure accurately. For comparison, the earth's *dc* magnetic field is on the order of 50 μT, and the magnetic field inside a typical electric motor is on the order of 1 T.

Using your knowledge of physics, summarize the important features that such a device should have. Outline a design plan for its development and construction. You have several options for the primary sensor. For example, it may consist of a flat coil of wire of appropriate diameter and number of turns, or, alternatively, you might consider using a commercially available semiconductor sensor. Note that *dc* fields, such as those produced by the Earth or any nearby permanent magnets, are not of interest. Hence, any signal produced by *dc* fields in your instrument should be filtered out. Ideally, your unit should have a digital or analog display device and should accommodate a remote probe if possible.

71. Design a handheld medicine dispenser for dispensing pills at specific times of the day. The unit is to be carried by an individual and must have sufficient capacity to hold medication for at least 1 day. The unit should open a compartment and should emit an audible or visual signal when it dispenses medication. The unit must be easy to load and should be easy to program.

72. *Challenge Problem:* One perennial problem with radio-controlled model airplanes concerns the lack of knowledge about the flight direction and orientation of the airplane when it is far from the ground-based operator. When the airplane is too far away to be seen clearly, the operator loses the ability to correctly control its motion. Develop a design concept for a roll-, pitch-, and compass-heading indicator system that can be mounted on the model airplane and used to radio the information to the operator's control console. Your system should sense the pitch and roll of the airplane over the range +90 degrees to −90 degrees and be able to withstand a full 360-degree roll or "loop-de-loop."

73. *Challenge Problem:* Design a remote readout system for a vacation home to be interrogated by a remote computer over a modem and telephone line or cellular telephone. The unit in the vacation home should answer the phone after 10 rings, provide means for an entry password, and then provide the following information: inside and outside temperatures, presence of any running water in the house, presence of any loud noises or unusual motion, and status of alarm switches installed on doors and windows. Discuss the design specifications for such a unit and develop a block diagram for its design and implementation.

74. *Challenge Problem:* Design a system for identifying the basement circuit breaker associated with a given electrical outlet.

75. *Challenge Problem:* Design a system for personalized airport baggage handling. Luggage is to be directed to each waiting individual, or at least to small clusters of people waiting at specified stations.

76. Design a can opener that performs two tasks: a) It must not allow metal slivers to fall into the can, and b) it must catch and hold the cut lid for subsequent hands-free disposal.

77. Design a system for measuring and reporting accumulated snowfall at a remote monitoring station.

78. Design an ice tray that allows the user to easily extract a single cube at a time.

79. Design a system that can help a one-armed person tie a necktie.

80. Design a snow shovel for a one-armed individual.

81. Develop a design concept for trimming tall trees using a remote-controlled robot.

82. Design a method for automatically walking a dog in a safe and reliable manner. The system should require no human intervention other than setup.

83. Develop a concept for a scuba diving mask that is self-clearing. "Clearing" refers to the act of expelling water from inside the mask without surfacing.

84. Develop a system that can be worn by a downhill ski racer and can send the skier's traveling speed to an observing coach.

85. The earliest "self-winding" watches used the motion of the wearer to wind the mechanical spring of the timepiece. Develop a similar concept to be used as a backup source of power for portable electronic devices such as cell phones and MP3 players.

8

The Skills of the Engineer

"My work on the [Boeing] 777 posed some interesting engineering challenges," says Clay Hess. Hess managed a team that designed the installation of the hydraulic systems for the superjet, the first aircraft designed entirely with computers. "Our job was to route all the hydraulic plumbing, if you will, throughout the entire airplane—roughly 1,100 individual hydraulic hoses," says Hess. "We had to route the hoses down the main landing gear in such a way that it would not be damaged by foreign objects or material from the runway. We also had to make sure that the hoses would clear all the mechanisms that pull up as the gear comes down from the airplane. We had to go through quite a list of engineering questions to determine exactly what the best routing was."

After a year and a half, the team came up with a design they felt was adequate. The next step was to work with a group called Airplane Integration, whose job was to verify that every piece of the aircraft fit together properly. Hess says that's when a design problem was discovered: "In the initial design, we had eliminated the kinematics because it takes so much computer effort and time. So we basically tested the design in the 'gear-down' and 'gear-up' positions. We verified all our clearances from those two positions. But

SECTIONS

- 1   Engineering Skills
- 2   Mathematical and Analytical Skills
- 3   Problem-solving and Decision-making Skills
- 4   Communication Skills
- 5   Team Working Skills

OBJECTIVES

By reading this chapter, you will learn:

- The technical and nontechnical skills required for a successful engineering career.
- How mathematical and analytical skills might be applied in a typical engineering project.
- How problem-solving and decision-making skills might be applied in a typical engineering project.
- How communication skills might be applied in a typical engineering project.
- How team working skills might be applied in a typical engineering project.

when we started looking at the overall kinematic movement of the model, we found that as the gear moved from one position to the other, the hoses would hit the structure. That required a significant redesign of some of the hoses on the aft part of the gear."

Clay Hess believes that teamwork and communication skills are critical to the success of any engineering project. "There's an exceptional need to be able to communicate and work well with the other individuals on a team," he says. "When you are in a team environment, you are talking to groups of people all the time. On the 777 project, presentations occurred at least once a week, and more often when the initial design was being done.

"I think that it certainly would have been to my advantage to have gotten that team experience in college, as well as the communication experience," Hess adds. "I spent a lot of time in the mechanical engineering curriculum, taking courses above and beyond my degree requirements. The one mistake I made was that I didn't spend enough time taking classes that built communication and teamwork skills."

In this chapter, we discuss the necessary skills that are required by a successful engineer. As you read through this chapter, you will discover that strong technical skills are not the only requirements for success. Engineers also must have excellent communication skills and the ability to work effectively as members of a team.

1   ENGINEERING SKILLS

Over the course of your career as a practicing engineer, you likely will be required to identify and solve a wide variety of technically challenging problems. To do that, you will need a strong technical background that starts with a thorough knowledge of mathematics and science. Good engineers use mathematics and science as tools that allow them to best utilize their intelligence, problem-solving and decision-making abilities, and wisdom to investigate problems, evaluate what needs to be solved, determine the relevant parameters, simplify problems, and find solutions.

Although, there is nothing more important in engineering than mathematics—backed up by a healthy dose of creativity—practicing engineers must also have communication, organization, and interpersonal skills. A final necessary ingredient is a strong sense of ethical standards. Like knowledge in mathematics, science, and a chosen engineering discipline, these "people" skills are must be learned and practiced. Most of us are not natural speakers, writers, organizers, or leaders. And ethics, for most of us, is sometimes overlooked in the energy and excitement of a typical engineering project. Therefore, you must ensure that you receive training in these areas, as well as in the technical areas in which engineers have always received their training.

APPLICATIONS: THE PVTM PROJECT—THE PRODUCT

The Precision Vertical Turning Machine (PVTM) is a real-world project that developed an extremely high-precision metal-cutting lathe and the systems (equipment and building) required to support it.

Most *lathes*, also called *turning machines*, operate horizontally—that is, the cutting tool moves in a horizontal plane while the part being cut spins on a horizontal axis (e.g., a table leg carved on a woodcutting lathe). Horizontal lathes typically are used to cut relatively small, lightweight parts. Vertical lathes, on the other hand, are designed to cut large, disk-shaped parts on a rotating circular cutting table. The cutting tool moves in a vertical plane, up and down, from the center of the circular part to its edge. Such a lathe, sometimes called a *vertical boring mill*, is capable of holding and turning huge metal parts weighing many tons.

APPLICATIONS: THE PVTM PROJECT—THE PRODUCT

A vertical orientation is used because the parts that vertical lathes are designed to cut are so heavy that their shapes would distort significantly if they were hung on a horizontal lathe. A large, heavy part sags when mounted on a horizontal axis, becoming significantly thicker along its lower edge than along its upper edge. Under these conditions, the tolerances required of a high-precision lathe cannot be maintained.

The goal of the Precision Vertical Turning Machine (PVTM) project was to build a lathe that could cut parts to within a tolerance of one-millionth of one inch (1 microinch, or roughly the thickness of 100 atoms in solid aluminum). This would represent an advance in vertical lathe technology of at least one order of magnitude beyond existing precision-cutting capabilities. The lathe would cut metal parts up to 64 inches in diameter, 20 inches in height, and 3000 pounds in weight. The PVTM is shown in Figure 1. A part being cut sits on the cutting table shown in the figure. The cutting tool, mounted on the tool bar, moves in the plane of the X- and Z-axes.

To achieve the desired tolerance capability, project engineers would have to solve four particularly difficult problems:

1. Accurately controlling the position of the cutting tool;
2. Accurately measuring the position of the cutting tool;
3. Minimizing seismic motion that could cause undesirable movements in the lathe components and the part being cut;
4. Minimizing temperature variations that could cause changes in the size of the lathe components and the part being cut.

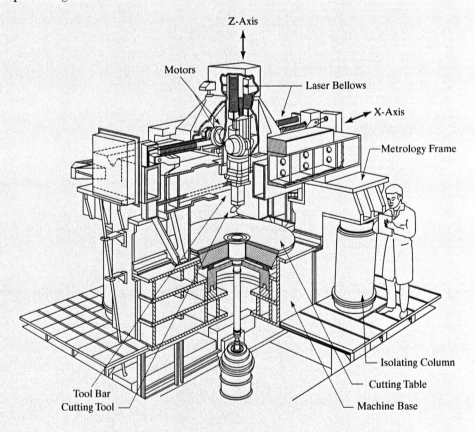

Figure 1.   The precision vertical turning machine (PVTM).

APPLICATIONS: THE PVTM PROJECT—THE PRODUCT

The PVTM project was conceived when an engineer at the company that developed it perceived an industry need. A large research grant from the federal government funded the project.

The company gave responsibility for managing the project to a project engineer with extensive experience in lathe design. He recruited three experienced engineers to lead the three subteams of mechanical, electrical, and civil engineers who would do the design work. The engineers were chosen primarily for their experience in designing lathe components and in computer modeling and simulation.

Including team leaders, the three subteams consisted of eight mechanical engineers (MEs); four electrical engineers (EEs), including one computer engineer; and four civil engineers (CEs). Also on the overall project team were three electronics technicians, four drafters, and four machinists. Including managers and secretaries, more than 30 people were involved in the four-year, $15 million project.

Every engineering project is conceived when a company perceives an industry need. Perhaps a large research grant from the federal government funded the project. The company gives responsibility for managing a project to a project engineer, usually one with extensive experience in that discipline. The project engineer then recruits subteams of mechanical, electrical, and civil engineers who will do the design work. The engineers are chosen primarily for their experience in design and in computer modeling and simulation.

Including team leaders, subteams can consist of mechanical engineers (MEs), electrical engineers (EEs), and civil engineers (CEs). The overall project team also can include electronics technicians, drafters, machinists, managers, and secretaries.

The ME team is responsible for the design and development of the product. The EE team is charged with designing and developing the systems and the computer interfaces and software. The CE team role is to design and direct the construction of the containment building in which the product would be produced or operated. The CEs would also be responsible for the installation of support systems, such as air conditioning equipment or security systems.

Once the team members have their assigned tasks, the project engineer meets with the team leaders and works out a budget and time schedule for the major parts (mechanical, electrical, and civil) of the project. The three team leaders then meet with each engineer on their teams and worked out a budget and a time schedule for each of their assigned tasks.

APPLICATIONS: THE PVTM PROJECT—THE TEAMS

The ME team was responsible for the design and development of the metrology frame, which acts as a reference for all cutting tool position measurements: the tool bar, the motors, the machine base, and the pneumatic isolators (see Figure 1). The team also worked on the design of the cooling system and the containment building.

The EE team was charged with designing and developing the cutting tool positioning systems, the cutting tool position measurement systems, and the computer interfaces and software.

The primary job of the CE team was to design and direct the construction of the containment building in which the lathe would operate. The CEs were also responsible for the installation of the lathe's support systems, such as the extensive air conditioning equipment and the coolant pumping system that would maintain a constant temperature environment for the lathe.

Once the team members had their assigned tasks, the project engineer met with the team leaders and worked out a budget and time schedule for the major parts (mechanical, electrical, and civil) of the project. The three team leaders then met with each engineer on their teams and worked out a budget and a time schedule for each of their assigned tasks.

2   MATHEMATICAL AND ANALYTICAL SKILLS

All projects begin with extensive mathematical analysis to determine exactly what will be required of the control and measurement systems. The ME team leader, with considerable experience in the design and a strong background in mathematics, performs most of the initial analysis.

APPLICATIONS: THE PVTM PROJECT—ANALYSIS AND TESTING

The PVTM project began with extensive mathematical analysis to determine exactly what would be required of the control and measurement systems. The ME team leader, with considerable experience in the design of vertical lathes and a strong background in mathematics, performed most of the initial analysis. Given the goal of 1 micro-inch tolerance and the size of the parts to be cut, she was able to determine the accuracy with which the cutting tool had to be controlled and its position measured. She also determined the maximum allowable expansion of the cut parts, establishing the extent of the measures that had to be taken to control part expansion.

The ME team leader also analyzed seismic data collected at the building site to determine the measures that would have to be taken to minimize lathe vibration. The team's zeal in eliminating external temperature and seismic effects was revealed during one of the early weekly team meetings when someone asked, "What about the moon? Will its gravitational effect distort the lathe or part so that it is pushed out of tolerance?" Good question. No one knew. The ME leader went to her calculator and books and came back within an hour. The answer, fortunately, was no.

Determining the electronic and computer control requirements was also a complex process. For example, the computer engineer determined, given the required accuracy of the cutting tool position measurements, that 64-bit electronics would be required of all position sensors and that 64-bit integer arithmetic would have to be used within the computer. Furthermore, 64-bit accuracy would be required when controlling the rotation of the motors that moved the tool bar on which the cutting tool was mounted.

Finally, simple mathematics showed that moving the cutting tool 1 microinch at a time over a typical 64-inch-diameter part would require 320,000,000 separate moves. The goal was to cut a part in three days, working around the clock. The computer engineer determined mathematically that moving the cutting tool 320,000,000 times in three days meant the PVTM computer had 1 millisecond to make each move. In other words, once each millisecond, the computer must

1.   Read the output of the cutting tool position sensors;
2.   Calculate the present position of the tool;
3.   Read the next required position of the tool from a database containing a description of the desired shape of the part; and
4.   Move the tool from its present position to the new position.

Engineers must always test the products, systems, and processes they design and analyze the test results to ensure that project specifications are met. As the PVTM engineers designed and constructed each component of the PVTM, they collected and analyzed test data to ensure that the components did the job they were intended to do. The position sensors were purchased as manufactured units but were tested for accuracy before being used. The ME team designed, built, and then tested the two motors that moved the tool bar along the X- and Z-axes (see Figure 1). The EEs designed, built, and tested the electronics that collected the position information from the sensors and sent positioning signals to the motors.

As the engineers interfaced the PVTM components to each other, they tested each resulting subsystem and analyzed the test results to ensure correct interaction between the components. Of course, once the engineers completed the project, they tested the entire lathe and all its support structures, including the containment building. The results of these tests were analyzed to ensure that project specifications were fully met.

As an engineer, your most important tool will be mathematics. Backed up by analytical skill and creativity, your mathematical skills will enable you to apply scientific principles to the solution of engineering problems.

One of the most important aspects of any engineering project is the initial design. One engineer recounts an important story of design and budget:

"Two of my most interesting clients are the largest and second largest carrot producers in the world. They have wonderfully automated carrot-handling equipment. One problem my firm solved for the carrot producers involved the great quantities of water used for carrot processing. They wanted to put a wastewater sump next to their building. The sump had to be concrete lined because the water must stay agitated so that dirt and heavy parts of the carrots can be separated and pumped out. It would be a small sump, but also a deep one.

"Our original idea was to construct a reinforced concrete tank that would be 12 to 15 feet deep. But according to federal regulations, when you dig a hole that deep, you have to take special precautions to ensure that the sides of the hole do not cave in and injure the people digging the hole. The requirement also meant that we would have to tear down part of the building next to the tank.

"We were weighing all the costs, and I said 'Why don't you put it in as a swimming pool?' So we dug the sump right next to the building. We did not have to tear down any part of the building, and we saved the client over $30,000 in concrete costs alone. Because the sump has curved walls, rather than the 90-degree corners we had originally planned, the system was much more efficient and stayed cleaner because there were no corners to trap debris. The project was so successful that we have now built several more of the tanks in the same way."

Joe Engel
Structural Engineer
Engel & Company Engineers

3   PROBLEM-SOLVING AND DECISION-MAKING SKILLS

In the course of any project, engineers must solve a series of problems and make many decisions, ranging from where to obtain materials to which design option to pursue. The quality of those individual solutions and decisions will determine, in large part, whether or not the team achieves its objectives.

The PVTM engineers had to solve four key problems: controlling the position of the cutting tool, measuring its position, minimizing seismic motion, and minimizing temperature variations.

CONTROLLING THE CUTTING TOOL POSITION

To achieve a tolerance of 1 microinch, clearly the PVTM engineers had to be able to control the position of the cutting tool and measure its position to an accuracy of better than 1 microinch. To develop a method by which the position of the cutting tool could be controlled to this accuracy, the MEs started with a fairly standard metrology frame, tool bar, and cutting tool (see Figure 1). The novelty for them was in the motors they designed to move the tool bar with the required accuracy. They designed two extremely low-speed motors that moved the tool bar in the X and Z directions, respectively. The motors were able to smoothly move the tool bar at a rate as low as 6.3 inches per year. At maximum speed the motors moved the cutting tool 1 milli-inch per second, or about 4 inches per hour. Again, the lathe computer used 64-bit electronics to control the positions of these motors.

MEASURING THE CUTTING TOOL POSITION

To meet the specification for measuring the cutting tool position, the MEs knew they would need very precise and accurate sensors. The initial concept design called for two laser interferometers, one each for measuring the X- and Z-axes positions of the tool bar. On the shaft that rotated the cutting table, they planned to mount a spindle encoder that measured the angular position of the table and the part sitting on it. However, some analysis of the data that these three devices would generate showed that it was not enough to allow the computer to determine the tool position with the specified accuracy.

The engineers generated several other potential design solutions and ultimately used 13 position-sensing devices to measure the position of the tool bar and therefore the cutting tool attached to it. Seven laser interferometers reflected laser beams at various places on the tool bar to determine the distance from the interferometers to the bar. The engineers mounted the interferometers on the metrology frame, which acted as a reference point. To increase the accuracy of the interferometers, the laser beams traveled in accordionlike evacuated laser bellows tubes that prevented air from slowing the beams of light (see Figure 1).

The MEs mounted five differential capacitance gauges around the perimeter of the cutting table to measure any tilting of the table from the horizontal. As stated earlier, once each millisecond, the computer sampled the output of the 13 position sensors, calculated the tool position from their data, and moved the tool to its next position. Tests showed that the final design easily met the specifications.

MINIMIZING SEISMIC MOTION

As previously stated, seismic measurements showed that vehicular traffic near the containment building could upset the lathe's accuracy. To isolate the vibration, the MEs designed and developed a pneumatic isolating column, 3 feet in diameter (see Figure 1). They mounted the lathe on four of these isolators. While apparently a simple solution, the result was a lathe that "floated" above its own foundation, contained in a building, but not a part of it.

MINIMIZING TEMPERATURE VARIATION

Perhaps the most serious issue in accomplishing the basic PVTM project goal of a 1-microinch tolerance was metal expansion and contraction due to temperature changes. To minimize temperature variations, the temperature of the lathe's metal parts was held to within 0.1 degree Fahrenheit by building passageways throughout the lathe and then pumping temperature-controlled coolant through the structure. The effect was similar to that of a car's radiator. To minimize the effects of the minor temperature variations that still occurred, the mechanical engineers specified special metal alloys for the metrology frame and other metal components of the PVTM. These alloys had very low coefficients of expansion.

A $5 million, seven-layer building was constructed to house the lathe. Each of the seven building layers, from the outdoors to the lathe, used increasingly accurate air conditioning units to maintain temperature control. The air in the small room in which the lathe operated was controlled to within 0.02 degree Fahrenheit. The actual temperature in the room was not so critical, but it was extremely critical that the temperature not vary. The engineers designed extensive soundproofing material into the building to prevent loud external sounds from reaching the lathe.

Three years into the project, while the MEs and EEs were testing their designs in a nearby building, the CEs had completed the PVTM containment building and were supervising the installation of the coolant pumping system. This system pumped water through the lathe and the extensive air conditioning equipment that cooled the seven layers of the building in order to minimize any expansion or contraction of the part being cut due to temperature variations.

The three PVTM teams had to make several important decisions to achieve their goals, including decisions about materials and equipment. Some of the decisions involved tradeoffs between cost and quality. For example, the MEs specified a metal for the metrology frame that was very expensive compared with alternative metals, but the team concluded that the expense was necessary to meet the project specifications. Similarly, the EE team decided to purchase an expensive minicomputer after the computer engineer on the team determined it was the only machine that could meet the required 1-millisecond turnaround time to measure the cutting tool position and move it to a new position. The civil engineers spent hundreds of thousands of dollars on the required air conditioning systems.

Engineers must decide not only how much to spend to accomplish a goal, but also from whom to purchase needed supplies, parts, and products. Engineers who attempt to save money by using a less expensive source might find themselves waiting for parts while a project falls behind schedule.

Often the major obstacle an engineer faces during the decision-making process is weighing the trade-offs among conflicting objectives. Can the project schedule slip a few days if it will save $5000? Is staying on schedule important enough to justify hiring an outside consultant at considerable expense? Which of the potential design solutions is best and should be adopted? Do these test results really indicate we have met our specifications? Who should design the interface between two system components—engineer A, who is immediately available, or engineer B, who is better at such tasks, but is already overloaded with work?

In addition to the many financial, technical, and personnel decisions engineers make are the ethical decisions. Should I cut the cost of this project as my client insists, even if it could result in an unsafe product? Should I "overdesign" this product to be absolutely sure it meets specifications, even if that means overcharging the customer? Should I use confidential information that I picked up while working for a previous employer?

Nearly all engineers function as a part of a team. In that context many decisions are made as a group after extensive discussions. All decisions, whether made individually or collectively, must be consistent with project objectives and customer needs. This will make some decisions unpopular with one or more engineers, and perhaps even with you. Engineers, however, must always hold the objectives of the project above their own interests.

How do successful engineers approach the problem-solving process? One engineer shares her insights.

"Before you put down the first solution you think of, or decide there is no good solution, you go back to the drawing board 10 or 12 times. And then, all of a sudden, you find a really elegant, really simple solution. That part of my work is a lot of fun."

Sharon Britton
Principal Hardware Engineer
Digital Equipment Corporation

4   COMMUNICATION SKILLS

In order for an engineering project to become a success, team members must be able to communicate effectively with one another and with all those who have a stake in the project. The larger the project, the greater the need for excellent verbal and written communication skills. For this reason, many engineering schools have incorporated communications in certain engineering courses, and some schools require students to take a separate communications course. Typical communications courses for engineers include those with an emphasis on both verbal and written communications. Note also that English is *the* language of engineering all over the world. In fact, many engineering schools in other countries train their students in English to better prepare them for work with international companies.

How do successful engineers approach proper communications? Three engineers share their insights.

"I think there is a greater need for communication skills than most people who come out of college with a technical degree realize. If you look around at the more successful engineers, you will see people who write very well and are able to communicate well orally. As an engineer, you often make presentations. You have to explain how you reached a certain decision, and you have to convince managers that the decision you're making is sound. You must be able to express yourself well."

Sharon Britton
Principal Hardware Engineer
Digital Equipment Corporation

"The most interesting part of my road simulator project was selling it to the vice president. Scientists have a tendency to explain theories, but a vice president wants to know the bottom line: "What is this really going to do for me?""

"I practiced for at least a month for this $25 million presentation. My boss went over it, took all the scientific items out of my slides, and put in more dollars and cents. But what I think really sold the vice president was when I told him the Japanese, who were our major competitors, had 20 of these simulators. I explained that there are no proving grounds in Japan because they don't have the real estate."

Ashland Brown
Dean of Engineering
University of the Pacific

"Our engineers generally have to give a written progress report every week, just a brief one-page summary of 'what we accomplished and what we're planning to do.' We require these reports partly because our clients generally want to see them. But it also helps us as managers to understand exactly where the engineers are on a project, what are their problems and concerns, and what they need from others."

Paul Olstad
Project Manager
Fluor Daniel

4.1   Verbal Communication

During the course of a project, engineering team members often are required to give oral presentations, usually at project milestones (Figure 2). Engineers usually give their first oral presentation when they have chosen a concept design for the problem at hand. This initial presentation gives engineers the opportunity to present their ideas and possibly to gain new ideas from those who attend the presentation. Managers and other engineers usually attend this presentation to ask important technical and economic questions about the approach.

Having to defend their ideas and answer questions during oral presentations helps engineers to clarify and better understand their work. It might even cause them to abandon an approach or design before much time and money have been invested in it. The audience at the presentation might then suggest alternative approaches.

Figure 2.   Verbal, and written communication are very important to engineers.

APPLICATIONS: THE PVTM PROJECT—VERBAL COMMUNICATION

The Precision Vertical Turning Machine team worked closely together in a single building. All of the parts of the lathe and its support systems had to work together in such an intimate way that the communication among the engineers was nearly continuous. As a result, the team leaders did not require much in the way of formal communication.

The entire PVTM project team, however, did meet weekly to review the overall progress of the project and to discuss any problems. Each meeting generally lasted one to two hours, with the project engineer and team leaders leading the discussion and making notes and drawings on a white board. It was important that all team members attend these meetings. All were expected to listen and learn, and to voice their problems and concerns.

It was particularly important that the machinists and technicians attend these presentations. Since it was their job to create the engineers' designs, it was vitally important that they understood, and were able to implement, those designs.

When an engineer finished the design of a major component of the PVTM project, the team leader required that individual to give an oral defense of the design. Such oral presentations lasted from 20 to 60 minutes, depending on the number of questions asked by the team members who attended. The speaker used transparencies, often depicting machine part blueprints, system diagrams, or schematics, to illustrate a design. Sometimes the speaker used a workstation to present and/or simulate a computer model.

4.2   Written Communication

Engineers must be able to communicate their ideas clearly in writing so that other team members and those outside the group can understand and act on them. One type of document engineers are required to write is the weekly or monthly progress report.

APPLICATIONS: THE PVTM PROJECT—WRITTEN COMMUNICATION

All members of the PVTM project teams were required to write monthly progress reports. The reports let the team managers know what their design team accomplished during the past month so they could report that information to their managers. The progress reports kept everyone involved in the project up-to-date and helped keep the project on schedule and within budget.

Most managers prefer concise progress reports, usually one to two pages in length. Managers do not have the time to read lengthy progress reports. As an engineer, you must learn to say much with few words. Each manager is different, however, and you will have to match the style and size of your reports to that desired by your manager. An example progress report is shown in Figure 3.

Another required document for any engineering project is the engineer's final project report. This document details every aspect of the engineer's work on the project. The key purpose of the project report is to enable an engineer in the future to modify

To: Gary Henderson

From: Julie Ackerman

Subject: July PVTM Laser Interferometer System Design Progress Report

A. Introduction

Work on the laser interferometer system progressed well during July. However, I discovered that my originally specified interface chips are out of stock, forcing me to redesign the interface to accommodate available chips. Fortunately, testing has shown that the interferometers will fully meet our specifications.

B. Accomplishments

1. Ordered new interface chips ("guaranteed" to be here by next week).
2. Redesigned the interferometer system interface.
3. Completely tested the interferometers.
4. Documented the interferometer test results.
5. Oversaw the technician's wiring of the interferometer control and data paths.

C. Work Remaining

1. Construct the new interferometer system design.
2. Test the interferometer system.
3. Complete the interfacing of the interferometer system to the lathe computer.

D. Problems

1. Time. I'm a bit behind schedule due to unavailability of some parts.
2. Manpower. I could use another technician to assist in the wiring effort.

Figure 3. Sample progress report.

the product, process, or system that was developed during the present project. Because this document usually is much longer than a weekly or monthly progress report, creating it is a time-consuming process that many engineers would prefer to avoid. Nevertheless, the final project report is critically important.

As indicated by the example table of contents in Figure 4, a project report usually begins with an abstract (which briefly describes the project goals), a table of contents, and a list of illustrations. The body of the report consists of a specifications list, a brief description of the concept design, and a detailed description of the design. Block

Hardened Data Recorder

Table of Contents

Figure 4.   Sample report table of contents.

diagrams, drawings, schematics, tables, and other figures are often included. The body of the report ends with a summary of the conclusions reached by the engineer.

A set of appendices should follow the body of the project report. Appendices usually include test data, in tabular and graphic form, that verify that the project meets its specifications. They also often contain blueprints, CAD drawings, sketches, schematics, program listings, graphs, parts and materials specifications, and instructions on how to use or modify the design. The report should conclude with a list of reference materials, if appropriate.

Most engineering designs must be modified at some later date, and the project report is intended to ease this process. As you write the project report, consider its purpose. Two years from now, it might be you who has to modify the design it describes.

APPLICATIONS: THE PVTM PROJECT—COMPLETE PROJECT REPORT

At the end of the PVTM project, each engineer wrote a complete project report, detailing the specifics of his or her design work. These reports averaged about 50 pages in length. They explained, among many things, the reasons for the decisions made in the design and how to build, use, and modify the design. An important feature of these reports was the documentation of the extensive testing done to ensure each design met its specifications.

5   TEAM WORKING SKILLS

Perhaps the most important skill you will need to succeed as an engineer is the ability to function effectively as a member of a team. Being a team player requires solid interpersonal and interdisciplinary skills.

Working as a team member involves compromise. Engineers often are called upon to let go of what they consider great ideas. A manager might veto an idea, or the team as a group might decide an idea is not workable. Team members must be willing to acknowledge the experience and judgment of managers and fellow engineers. They must be committed to the team effort, even when, at times, their work load is increased or they feel a situation is unfair.

APPLICATIONS: THE PVTM PROJECT—TEAM WORKING SKILLS

The civil engineers on the PVTM project chose a location for the containment building that was near a road on which heavy trucks sometimes traveled. This created special problems for the MEs, who would have to design and implement pneumatic columns that would isolate the lathe from the seismic vibration caused by the trucks. However, they agreed to do so after the CEs convinced them that the location was ideal in every other way.

The MEs on the PVTM project wanted to use air bearings in the lathe because they would allow virtually drag-free movement of the tool bar. Eliminating friction would prevent the creation of heat that would cause metal parts to expand. However, the EEs wanted the MEs to use oil bearings, which have a small amount of drag. The drag, while producing heat, would make the system more stable, allowing more accurate tool position control and measurement. The MEs compromised and used oil bearings.

The computer engineer and one of the EEs had to compromise on the interface between the cutting tool position-sensing devices and the computer that controlled the position of the cutting tool. The computer could read only 32-bit numbers via a parallel port, yet the electronics associated with the position-sensing devices generated 64-bit numbers that reflected the position of the cutting tool. Because the EE seemed to be the busier of the two, the computer engineer designed the interface, which read and stored the 64-bit numbers and then passed them on to the computer in 32-bit blocks. She then wrote the necessary software for the computer to read the 32-bit numbers from the parallel port and reconstruct them as 64-bit numbers internally.

In addition to having the willingness to compromise, a team player must have a broad knowledge base that extends beyond simply an engineering major. To this end, engineering students often take engineering courses outside their majors, as well as courses in communications, foreign languages, and international studies.

Having a wide array of interdisciplinary skills will bring you several benefits as an engineer. Most importantly, as you understand and take into account the requirements of other engineers, your work will more likely integrate well into the overall project. Interdisciplinary knowledge will also help you empathize with other types of engineers and their problems. Having a good understanding of other disciplines will enable you to work on tasks outside your specialty, making you a more valuable team member.

APPLICATIONS: THE PVTM PROJECT—INTERDISCIPLINE KNOWLEDGE

The ME who designed the low-speed motors on the PVTM project had little experience in this area. He would have preferred to have the task given to someone else, but the team leader assigned it to him. He began by reading some books and journal articles about the topic. As he worked on the design, he occasionally asked advice from his team leader, who did have experience in this area. In another instance, when one of the EEs suddenly quit the project, the computer engineer had to study the EE's work, complete it, and write the required documentation. The EE had finished more than 90 percent of his task, but he had kept poor records of his efforts, so the computer engineer had a difficult job on her hands, sorting out the work of the EE.

Not all engineers on the PVTM project were required to do design work outside of their disciplines. But they all had to understand the work done by team members in other disciplines so that the designs of all three teams integrated well into the overall project. For example, the MEs had to understand the functioning of the air conditioning system the CEs built so they could design a cooling system that would function effectively within the system. The ME who designed the low-speed motors had to understand the work of the EE who designed the motor drivers, as well as the work of the computer engineer who wrote the software interfaces. For the project to come together in a seamless manner, each engineer had to understand how his or her work fit into the overall project scheme.

At the end of the four-year PVTM project, the National Institute of Standards and Technology, in Gaithersburg, Maryland, used the PVTM to cut a part and then attempted to find a flaw in the part. Their best equipment, the most accurate and precise in the world, could not measure any variation in the part from its specified shape. It was declared to be cut within a 1-microinch tolerance.

The PVTM project succeeded in large part because the engineers involved had a variety of skills that are crucial to the successful completion of any engineering project: strong mathematical and analytical skills; a well-developed capability for solving problems and making decisions; excellent communication skills; and perhaps most important of all, the ability to work effectively as members of a team.

PROFESSIONAL SUCCESS: TEAMWORK

A successful engineer shares his insights on teamwork:

"I believe there are two main challenges in having a group of people work together as a team. First, the work has to be broken down into small, manageable tasks so that you can delegate responsibility to the individual people working on the project. Second, there has to be a good technical match between the task and the person responsible for doing the task.

"In my bullet-tracking project everything worked out very well, since I knew how to break the complete system into smaller pieces, and I also knew the people and their technical backgrounds relatively well. This allowed me to predict fairly accurately how long it would take to complete the project pieces so that they all came together at the end."

Jose E. Hernandez
Electrical Engineer
Lawrence Livermore National Laboratory

KEY TERMS

communication skills	problem solving	verbal skills
decision making	progress reports	written skills
engineering skills	project report	
ethics	team working skills	

Problems

1. Describe the skills required of the PVTM team members during each of the five design stages. For each stage list the difficulties the team members could have encountered, including technical, financial, and interpersonal issues.

2. It has been said that if automotive engineers were keeping up with computer engineers, cars would cost $5 and get 1000 miles per gallon. What kinds of real-world constraints limit automotive engineers (as opposed to computer engineers) so that this is not actually the case?

3. Do a brief study of the traffic control system in your town or some part of your city. Write a report describing the deficiencies of the system and how it might be improved. Include ideas on traffic light design and placement, as well as law enforcement. Discuss costs and other problems related to the implementation of your ideas.

4. Assume you were assigned the task of solving the one problem with automobiles that bothers you the most. What would the problem be, and how would you solve it?

5. Describe your decision-making process when you were choosing an engineering school. What made the process difficult? On what basis did you ultimately make the decision?

6. Think of your instructor as your boss and yourself as an employee hired to attend classes and take notes. Write a one-page progress report of your work for the last two weeks. Use Figure 3 as a model.

7. Write a project report about a problem you solved. Describe in detail exactly how you solved it, using Figure 4 and the five-step design process as guides. Keep the report short—two to three pages, at most.

8. Interview a practicing engineer who works (or has worked) on teams. Ask about the rewards and challenges of teamwork. Write a one-page report about your findings.

9. Consider a major purchase you made that involved a financial commitment (a loan or gift) from someone else. What personal skills and objective evidence did you use to gain the aid of your benefactor?

10. Prepare a three-minute oral presentation in which you introduce yourself to a group of strangers. Prepare three overhead transparency masters or three Power-Point slides that convey relevant information about yourself. Practice this introduction alone or in front of friends. Time yourself. Does your introduction convey the professional image that you want to present?

9

Engineering Disciplines

1 INTRODUCTION

Earlier, you were given some advice: to discover engineering, put down this book and talk to an engineer. Similarly, to find out more about any particular engineering discipline, speak to an engineer engaged in that discipline. Only a practitioner can give you the depth, history, and potential future of a field. Only an engineer can impart the excitement, challenges, and occasional frustrations of working in a given area. Only a working engineer can tell you what he or she does every day on the job.

So why read the rest of this chapter? The remainder of the chapter is devoted to giving you a brief taste of each of the major engineering disciplines. Its purpose is to whet your appetite rather than answer all your questions about a field of particular interest to you. This chapter is intended to motivate you to seek out engineers in the fields that pique your interest.

There are dozens of specific fields, each with dozens of types of engineers. Section 2 discusses how the many types of engineers can be organized into a small number of primary disciplines and emerging fields.

The other sections in the chapter are devoted to a general description of each of the principal engineering disciplines. The primary *technical areas* will also be presented to shed light on the core of each discipline. These technical areas are the tools that define what makes a chemical, civil, electrical/computer, industrial, or mechanical engineer. The technical areas are combined into *applications*, which show the fields in which each type of engineer works and illustrate the diversity of the engineering discipline. Finally, unique elements of the *curriculum* leading to an engineering degree in each discipline will be discussed. Only the typical core coursework is presented. For further information,

OBJECTIVES

After reading this chapter, you will be able to:

- list the principal engineering disciplines;
- discuss the technical areas, applications, and curricula for chemical, civil, electrical and computer, industrial, and mechanical engineering;
- explain how new engineering disciplines emerge.

Key idea: To learn about a specific discipline, speak with an engineer working in that discipline.

investigate the Web page of the pertinent engineering department at any major university. It is important that you have a general knowledge of all engineering disciplines, since engineers of different backgrounds frequently work together to solve problems.

2   HOW MANY ENGINEERING DISCIPLINES EXIST?

To answer this question, consider a seemingly unrelated question: how long is the coastline from Portland, Maine, to Miami, Florida? To estimate the coastline length, you might start with a globe and measure the distance with a straight ruler. This would be a crude estimate of the distance. You could refine your measurement by using a road map of the eastern United States. Now your measurement would take into account more details, such as the fishhook of Cape Cod and the coastline of the Chesapeake Bay. As a result, your measurement would likely be larger than the estimate from the globe. If you used state or local road maps, your measurement would continue to be refined and continue to grow. If, in desperation, you crawled the entire trip, measuring around each grain of sand, you would come up with a different (and larger) value.°

Key idea: The five principal engineering disciplines are chemical, civil, electrical and computer, industrial, and mechanical engineering.

Counting engineering disciplines is like measuring the distance along a coastline: as the scale narrows, the number of disciplines increases. One of the broadest views on the number of disciplines looks at the number of accredited engineering programs in the United States. The number of accredited programs is shown in Figure 1. In this text, the top five engineering disciplines (chemical, civil, electrical and computer, industrial, and mechanical engineering) will be called the *principal engineering disciplines*.

The engineering profession defines an engineer as someone eligible for professional registration. The Fundamentals of Engineering Examination (FE Exam) is required for professional registration as a licensed professional engineer. The specialty portion of the FE Exam is offered in the five principal engineering disciplines plus environmental engineering.

Using professional registration as a guide, your list of engineering fields can be expanded by examining the areas in which it is possible to take the Principles and Practice

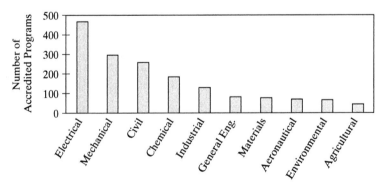

Figure 1.   Number of Accredited Engineering Programs in the United States by Discipline (*Electrical* includes electrical and computer engineering; other disciplines include related fields. Data obtained from www.abet.org.)

°An object that looks the same at every degree of magnification (or, formally, exhibits self-similarity across scales) is said to be *fractal*. Fractal analysis is used in signal processing to analyze anything from Internet traffic data to biomedical data.

Examination (PP Exam). The PP Exam is the last step in the professional registration process. The 17 different PP Exams are listed in Table 1.

Examining engineering disciplines on a smaller scale, you could make a list of relatively common engineering fields. A good list is shown in Table 2, with most fields listed under their closest principal engineering disciplines.

TABLE 1 Several Lists of Major Engineering Disciplines

Principal Disciplines	Fundamentals of Engineering Exam Areas	Principles and Practices Exam Areas
		Agricultural
		Architectural
Chemical	Chemical	Chemical
Civil	Civil	Civil
		Control Systems
Electrical/Computer	Electrical	Electrical and Computer
	Environmental	Environmental
		Fire Protection
Industrial	Industrial	Industrial
Mechanical	Mechanical	Mechanical
		Metallurgical
		Mining and Mineral
		Naval Architecture and Marine
		Nuclear
		Petroleum
		Structural (I and II)

Note: The manufacturing engineering FE Exam was discontinued after October 2003.

TABLE 2 Common Engineering Fields by Principal Discipline

Chemical	Civil	Electrical and Computer
Biological	Architectural	Control Systems
Biomedical	Construction	Electronics
Ceramic	Environmental	Signal Processing
Control Systems	Geotechnical	
Petroleum	Sanitary	
Plastics	Structural	
Polymer	Transportation	

Industrial	Mechanical	Other
Human Factors	Aeronautical	Agricultural
Operations Research	Aerospace	Fire
Production Systems	Automotive	Military
	Biomechanical	Mining
	Heating	Naval
	Manufacturing	Nuclear
	Materials	Ocean
	Metallurgical	Plant
	Robotics	Safety

Note: The "other" category contains unique or multidisciplinary fields.

A more complete list of engineering jobs has been developed by the Bureau of Labor Statistics (BLS). They list an unbelievable 431 engineering jobs, from absorption engineering to mud engineering to zoning engineering.*

So how can you make sense of all these disciplines, fields, subfields, and subsubfields? In this text, the five principal engineering disciplines will be discussed in Sections 3 through 7. The major subdisciplines will be explored in Section 8. The process of how new disciplines evolve will be discussed in Section 9.

3   CHEMICAL ENGINEERING

3.1   Technical Areas

Key idea: Chemical engineers work with the transformation of chemicals to form useful products or processes.

Chemical engineers work with the transformation of chemicals to form useful products or processes. The main technical areas are catalysis and reaction engineering, heat transfer and energy conversion, and separations. As you can see by these areas (and the name of the discipline), chemical engineers tend to have a strong interest in chemistry.

Reaction engineering and catalysis refers to the design and construction of engineered systems to bring about chemical change. In catalytic processes, materials are added to make the chemistry proceed more quickly. This can make the difference between an economically feasible and an economically infeasible process.

Chemical changes are driven by energy. Some chemical engineers specialize in *heat transfer*. Other chemical engineers focus on the conversion of energy from one form to another (especially in the presence of chemical transformations).

In the field of *separations*, chemical engineers assist in product purification. Examples of products benefiting from separation systems designed by chemical engineers range from perfume to gasoline to beer.

3.2   Applications

chemical process industry: any industry where chemicals are extracted, isolated, or combined (the primary application of chemical engineering)

Chemical engineers apply their technical skills to almost every industry. The primary application is in the **chemical process industries**—that is, any industry where chemicals are extracted, isolated, or combined. The main industries employing chemical engineers manufacture agricultural chemicals; food; industrial gases; petrochemicals and petroleum products; pharmaceuticals and personal care products; polymers (including plastics and rubber); pulp and paper; soaps and other fats; and synthetic fibers.

Other areas where chemical engineers work include biotechnology, environmental engineering, nuclear engineering, and advanced materials. Biotechnology is the synthesis of new products by using living organisms. Chemical engineers have teamed with scientists to develop new approaches to product development through biotechnology. From the development of artificial skin and blood to the biosynthesis of pharmaceuticals, chemical engineers are at the forefront of biotechnology. In fact, many chemical engineering departments have changed names from "chemical engineering" to "chemical and biological engineering."

pollution prevention: a contribution of chemical engineers, where industrial processes are modified to minimize pollution

Chemical engineers specializing in the environmental area often work with industry to make industrial processes cleaner (called **pollution prevention**). Chemical engineers also have contributed to nuclear engineering in its various forms (e.g., power generation, propulsion, and commercial uses). Chemical engineers have led the development of new materials with highly specialized properties for the aerospace, automotive, and photographic industries, as well as many others.

---

*To be fair, most of the BLS jobs are not engineering positions because they employ people who are not eligible for professional registration.

3.3   Curriculum

Chemical engineering students usually take engineering courses in thermodynamics; conservation and transport of mass, momentum, and energy; unit operations (i.e., industrial processes such as separations); and design. Science courses in organic chemistry and biochemistry frequently are required.

4   CIVIL ENGINEERING

4.1   Technical Areas

Key idea: Civil engineers are involved in the analysis, design, and construction of public works.

Civil engineering takes its name from Latin *civis*, meaning citizen. As with many technological fields, engineering once had a mainly military focus. As engineering applications broadened, engineering was divided into two areas: military engineering and civil (i.e., nonmilitary) engineering. The other four principal engineering disciplines eventually split off, leaving what we now know as civil engineering. As a result, civil engineering is one of the broadest engineering disciplines. In a nutshell, civil engineers are involved in the analysis, design, and construction of public works.

Although diverse, civil engineering shares the core technical area of engineering mechanics. This core is divided into three areas: solid mechanics, fluid mechanics, and soil mechanics. **Solid mechanics** refers to the behavior of solids at rest and in motion. It is the primary tool used to analyze the structural integrity of structures both large (such as buildings, roads, and bridges) and small (such as printed circuit boards). *Fluid mechanics* is used to understand the behavior of water and air in both natural systems (such as rivers and the atmosphere) and engineered systems (such as pipes and blowers). *Soil mechanics* studies the behavior of soils in response to stress. It is an important tool in the design of foundations and earthen structures (such as landfills).

solid mechanics: the behavior of solids at rest and in motion

4.2   Applications

The main applications of civil engineering are construction, environmental, geotechnical, structural, transportation, and water resources engineering. In the *construction engineering* area, civil engineers optimize the use of materials, money, and people in construction projects. *Environmental engineers* develop and design treatment processes for a variety of pollutants and follow the fate of pollutants in the environment (see Section 8.4). The **geotechnical** specialty in civil engineering is concerned with the design of foundations, embankments, retaining walls, and landfills. *Structural engineering* is one of the largest specialties in civil engineering. Structural engineers focus on the design of buildings, bridges, dams, and other systems. *Transportation engineers* study both traffic patterns and construction materials to maintain and improve transportation and other delivery systems. In the *water resources* area, civil engineers plan, manage, and design systems for the use and management of lakes, rivers, groundwater, storm water, and reservoirs. Examples include irrigation systems, dams, and storm water retention ponds.

geotechnical engineering: a specialty of civil engineering concerned with the design of foundations, embankments, retaining walls, and landfills

4.3   Curriculum

The civil engineering curriculum reflects both the core area of mechanics and the wide variety of applications. Civil engineering students generally take engineering courses in statics, mechanics (usually separate courses in solid mechanics, fluid mechanics, and soil mechanics), materials, structures, transportation, and environmental engineering. Often, courses in project management and foundation engineering are required.

5   ELECTRICAL AND COMPUTER ENGINEERING

5.1   Technical Areas

Key idea: Electrical engineers focus on the transmission and use of electrons and photons.

Electrical engineers focus on the transmission and use of *electrons* and *photons*. This simple statement does not do justice to the richness of electrical engineering. We use electric power through many different types of communication, computational, industrial, and consumer devices. Electrical engineering often includes the related field of *computer engineering*. In addition, electric energy is often transformed prior to use. Examples include alternating and direct current conversions, analog and digital transformations, and the interconversion of electricity and magnetism, sound, and light.

physical electronics: the study of solid-state electronic devices, such as transistors

electromagnetics: the study of the complex relationships between electricity and magnetism

The core technical areas of electrical engineering include circuits, physical electronics, signal processing, and electromagnetics. *Analog and digital circuits* are fundamental tools of the electrical engineer. The circuits area involves the analysis of networks, power delivery, specialized circuits (alternating current, radio frequency, and microwave circuits), and circuit design. **Physical electronics** includes the understanding of solid-state electronic devices, such as transistors. *Signal processing* (information engineering) involves the interpretation of time-dependent voltages and currents. **Electromagnetics**, the complex relationship between electricity and magnetism, is the theory that underlies much of modern-day electrical engineering.

5.2   Applications

To appreciate the far-reaching applications of electrical engineering, you only have to look around your home, office, or school. Electronic devices surround you. The diversity in the field is shown by the fact that the main professional society in electrical engineering (the Institute of Electrical and Electronics Engineers or IEEE) contains 38 technical societies and councils. To simplify this broad branch of engineering, consider four basic applications: communications, digital electronics, microelectronics and photonics, and power systems.

The *communications* area includes applications as varied as communications theory, telecommunications, and optical communications systems. Electrical engineers specializing in *digital electronics* focus on digital circuit design and instrumentation, control systems, image processing, and computationally efficient architectures. In the *microelectronics and photonics* area, electrical engineers develop microprocessor architecture, work with machine- and assembly-language programming, and develop systems with optical fibers using lasers and other light sources. The field of *power systems* includes the generation, transmission, and distribution of electrical power.

5.3   Curriculum

Electrical engineering students usually take courses in analog and digital circuit analysis and design, microprocessors, signal processing, electromagnetics, and programming. Common electives include power systems and communications.

6   INDUSTRIAL ENGINEERING

6.1   Technical Areas

Industrial engineers seek to analyze, design, model, and optimize complex systems. The traditional role of industrial engineers has been in the manufacturing sector. However, industrial engineering also is applied to areas as diverse as transportation, service industries (e.g., hospitals and banks), and supply and distribution problems.

The core technical areas in industrial engineering are simulation, statistics, and engineering economics. *Simulation* is important to the industrial engineer, because many improvements in manufacturing or other systems must be simulated (usually through

Key idea: Industrial engineers seek to analyze, design, model, and optimize complex systems.

computer models) before they are accepted and implemented. *Statistics* plays a large role because of the random nature of errors and disruptions in the work environment. More than the other engineering branches, industrial engineers address economic feasibility in their work with manufacturing and service industries.

6.2   Applications

ergonomics: relationships between people and the jobs they perform (now commonly called human factors engineering)

operations research: optimization of complex systems to meet one or more goals

The tools of industrial engineering are combined and applied in three basic areas: human factors engineering, operations research, and production systems engineering. *Human factors engineering* (or **ergonomics**, literally the management of work) concerns the relationship between people and the things they use or the jobs they perform. **Operations research** deals with the optimization of complex systems to meet one or more goals (called *objective functions*). In *production systems engineering*, the industrial engineer focuses on optimizing both the physical facilities (e.g., plant layout and materials handling) and production scheduling.

6.3   Curriculum

Industrial engineers typically take courses in probability and statistics; engineering economics; human factors; production systems and facilities planning; operations research; and simulation. Electives in economics, computer science, and psychology are common. Since knowledge of the manufacturing site is at the heart of industrial engineering, many industrial engineering programs offer cooperative experiences (co-ops) or internships in industry.

7   MECHANICAL ENGINEERING

7.1   Technical Areas

Mechanical engineering is synonymous with machinery. In fact, the words "mechanical" and "machine" both come from the Greek *mechos*, meaning expedient (because mechanized devices are often the most efficient way to carry out a task). Mechanical engineers develop, design, and manufacture machines.

Key idea: Mechanical engineers develop, design, and manufacture machines.

The primary technical areas in mechanical engineering are mechanics and thermodynamics. In mechanical engineering, the fields of *solid mechanics* and *fluid mechanics* are applied to machines rather than to structures (as they are in civil engineering). Since machines use, generate, or transmit power, mechanical engineers are interested in the use of energy and its loss as heat. Thus, *thermodynamics* is a primary tool of the mechanical engineer.

7.2   Applications

Mechanical engineers generally specialize in one or more of the following areas: applied mechanics, bioengineering, fluids engineering, heat transfer, tribology, and aeronautics. Using *applied mechanics*, engineers analyze and design machines. In *bioengineering*, mechanical engineers apply the principles of mechanics to solve problems with human anatomy (e.g., prosthetic and assistive devices) and physiology (e.g., devices to improve heart and lung function). *Fluids engineering* refers to the flow of fluids (e.g., air, ink, or blood) in mechanical systems. Mechanical engineers specializing in fluids engineering may perform complex calculations to predict fluid flow, a subspecialty called *computational fluid dynamics*. *Heat transfer* involves the study of heat transport by conduction, convection, and radiation. The study of heat transfer is critical, since all processes lose energy as heat. **Tribology** (from the Greek *tribein*, to rub) concerns friction, wear, and lubrication. Aeronautics and astronautics are major subdisciplines of mechanical engineering. (See Section 8.3.)

tribology: the study of friction, wear, and lubrication

Robotic arm on the Mars rover *Spirit* reaches out to a rock called Adirondack. Placing a rover on Mars required experts in nearly all fields of mechanical engineering (as well as other types of engineers). (Image credit: NASA/JPL.)

7.3   Curriculum

In accordance with the technical fields and primary applications, mechanical engineers usually take courses in machines, fluid mechanics, thermodynamics, instrumentation, materials, systems engineering, and design. Common technical electives include applied mathematics, aeronautics, and biomechanics.

8   MAJOR ENGINEERING SUBDISCIPLINES

Key idea: The major engineering subdisciplines are materials, aeronautical/aerospace, environmental, agricultural, and biomedical engineering.

8.1   Introduction

As shown in Figure 1, there are a number of accredited engineering programs in the United States outside of the principal engineering disciplines. The major subdisciplines—materials, aeronautical/aerospace, environmental, agricultural, and biomedical engineering—may exist as separate departments in universities, but more frequently are found within departments representing the five principal disciplines. Each major subdiscipline will be discussed in more detail in this section.

8.2   Materials Engineering

Materials engineers contribute to all aspects of materials used for engineering purposes, from the origin of a material (extraction or synthesis), through its transformations (processing, design, and manufacture), to its applications. Often called *material science and engineering*, the field emphasizes the science behind the properties of materials.

Materials engineering programs often are housed in mechanical engineering departments. However, the home department sometimes depends on the materials. For example, the materials engineering aspects of metals and their alloys often are taught in mechanical engineering departments (sometimes under the heading *metallurgical engineering*). *Polymers, ceramics,* and *biomaterials* may be the purview of chemical engineers. Civil engineers have been making more use of *composite materials*, while electrical engineers study and use *semiconductors*.

8.3   Aeronautical, Astronautical, and Aerospace Engineering

The fields of aeronautical and astronautical engineering are related subdisciplines of mechanical engineering. Aeronautics (from the Greek *aero*, air, + *nautes*, sailor) is the study of mechanized flight. Astronautical engineering, on the other hand, deals with mechanized flight beyond the Earth's atmosphere. (The term *aerospace*, first used in 1958, refers to both the atmosphere and outer space.)

One way to look at the diversity in aerospace engineering is to examine its largest professional society, the American Institute of Aeronautics and Astronautics (AIAA). The AIAA has over 60 technical committees, covering issues from lighter-than-air systems to modeling and simulation to space colonization.

8.4   Environmental Engineering

As stated in Section 4.2, environmental engineers both design treatment processes and model the fate of pollutants in the environment. Environmental engineering (previously called sanitary engineering) is traditionally part of civil engineering. However, some areas are associated with other principal engineering disciplines (e.g., pollution prevention with chemical engineering).

In the water treatment area, environmental engineers develop and design treatment facilities for drinking water, wastewater, and industrial wastes. Environmental engineers also work with treatment systems for air and contaminated soil. In the modeling area, environmental engineers track everything from global warming (caused, in part, by carbon dioxide emissions to the atmosphere) to leaking underground storage tanks at your neighborhood gas station.

8.5   Agricultural Engineering

Agricultural engineering (sometimes called food, biological, bioresource, or biosystems engineering) involves the solution of problems in the production and processing of food, fiber, timber, and renewable energy sources. Agricultural engineers seek to produce agricultural products from natural resources efficiently, while minimizing environmental impact. The major areas of agricultural engineering are food engineering, power systems and machinery design, and forest engineering.

8.6   Biomedical Engineering

Biomedical engineers use engineering and scientific principles to solve problems in medicine and biology. Two of the largest areas in this diverse field are biomaterials engineering and biomechanical engineering. In the biomaterials area, engineers (typically with training in chemical engineering) develop implants from both living tissue and artificial materials. Biomaterials engineers have contributed significantly to the development of artificial skin and artificial blood. In the biomechanical engineering area, engineers study fluid flow and materials properties in the human body. Biomechanical engineers have contributed greatly to the development of the artificial heart and artificial joint replacements. Electrical and computer engineers specializing in the biomedical engineering area have contributed to new imaging and surgical technologies, such as CAT (computer-aided tomography) scans and remote surgery.

9   HOW DO EMERGING ENGINEERING DISCIPLINES EVOLVE?

9.1   Introduction

Key idea: New engineering fields can be formed by the budding off of existing disciplines or by the creation of interdisciplinary fields.

A cursory glance at engineering curricula in the United States reveals that new types of engineering programs are constantly being developed. *Engineering disciplines evolve over time.* Why? If problems emerge that require more specialization, then new engineering fields will evolve to address the challenges. But how do new engineering disciplines form?

Engineering fields form in two ways. First, new engineering disciplines are created by *splitting off* from existing disciplines. Second, new engineering disciplines form when two or more fields *combine*.

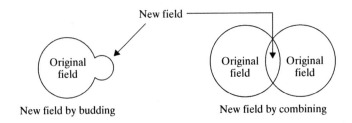

9.2   Creation of New Field by Budding

In some engineering fields, a subfield will mature and split off to form its own discipline like an amoeba reproducing. In fact, each of the five principal engineering disciplines formed in this way. The first split occurred when "engineering" (once used almost exclusively for warfare) divided into military engineering and "civilian" (civil) engineering. Subsequently, the other disciplines we know today budded off from civil engineering.

More recently, a number of engineering disciplines have been created by budding off of existing fields. From mechanical engineering, the field of robotic engineering has developed some independence. Photonic engineering is in the process of separating itself from electrical engineering. Photonic engineers use photons for useful purposes just as electrical engineers use electrons for useful purposes. Civil engineering has produced the developing discipline of renewal engineering. Renewal engineering is the study of the aging of engineered systems and the specification of repairs. Only time will tell if robotic, photonic, and renewal engineering will blossom into separate engineering disciplines or whether they will remain subfields of existing disciplines.

9.3   Creation of New Fields by Merging

Other new engineering disciplines are created as *interdisciplinary* fields. This occurs when skills from many different fields must be applied to a problem. In fact, *a great deal of the progress in science and engineering occurs where fields intersect*. Examples of emerging interdisciplinary engineering fields are bioengineering and nanoengineering. Nanoengineering is discussed in more detail in the *Focus on Emerging Disciplines: So You Want to Be a Nanoengineer?*

FOCUS ON EMERGING DISCIPLINES: SO YOU WANT TO BE A NANOENGINEER?

As stated in this chapter, engineering is a constantly evolving field. Advances in technology have opened up opportunities that would have been impossible to pursue even a few years ago. One of the most recent emerging fields is nanoengineering. The concept of nanoengineering was first described by Nobel laureate physicist Richard Feynmann in 1959. The prefix "nano-" (from the Greek *nanos*, dwarf) often refers to 10^{-9}. Thus, a nanometer is 10^{-9} m. How big is the nanometer scale? The hydrogen–oxygen bond length in water is about 0.1 nm. Thus, nanoengineering refers to building objects from the atomic level up.

To get an idea of the length scales possible with nanotechnology, the picture that follows shows URL of the National Nanotechnology Initiative in letters written with a carbon nanotube tip. The letters are about 7 to 8 nm thick and 20 nm tall. The diameter of a carbon atom is about 0.15 nm, so each letter is about 50 carbon atoms thick and 130 carbon atoms tall.

Nanolithography: writing on the nanometer scale

Working on the atomic or molecular scale changes the nature of engineering. For example, a biomedical engineer may look at the transport of red blood cells (about 2.5 μm or 2,500 nm in size), while a nanoengineer might consider the mechanical manipulation of DNA (about 2.5 nm in size). In addition, nano-sized systems often exhibit unique characteristics.

To illustrate the potential of nanoengineering, three existing product classes will be discussed: nanoparticles, nanostructured polymer films, and quantum dots. Nanoparticles are particles with diameters on the nanometer scale. Such particles have a great deal of surface area per gram of material. As a result, nanoparticles make very efficient catalysts. They are now being used in oil refining and to remove oxides of nitrogen in automobile exhaust.

Nanostructured polymer films are being used to make displays for a wide array of digital consumer devices (e.g., cell phones and digital cameras). The polymers are formed into organic light-emitting diodes (OLEDs) to produce brighter, lighter displays.

To illustrate the potential impact of nanoengineering, consider quantum dots. Quantum dots are nano-sized semiconductors that can trap a small number of electrons. These structures may someday be used to compute on a single-electron scale (called *quantum computing*). Quantum dots in the form of nanocrystals can be used to image biological processes. They can be designed to emit certain wavelengths based on their size. (For example, a 3-nm cadmium selenide particle

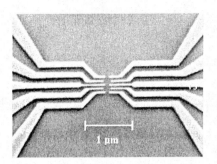

Quantum Dots. The small wires in this picture are 50 nm wide. They form two quantum dots (center of picture) that contain about 20–40 electrons. In the future, isolated electrons in the dots may be used for computers based on the behavior of single electrons. (Photo courtesy of Dave Umberger.)

emits at 520 nm—green light—while a 5.5-nm cadmium selenide particle emits at 630 nm—red light.) By using a variety of particle sizes, an array of biological processes can be imaged.

Engineers of your generation will certainly contribute to harvesting the potential of nanoengineering. Perhaps you will major in nanoengineering. (This is possible: the first undergraduate nanoengineering program was started by the University of Toronto in the fall of 2001.) Nanoengineering is an emerging, interdisciplinary engineering field with the potential to revolutionize the way we think about the world.

10   SUMMARY

This chapter focused on the five principal engineering disciplines: chemical, civil, electrical and computer, industrial, and mechanical engineering. For each branch, a general description of the discipline was presented, along with the major technical areas, applications, and curricula. Several major subdisciplines (materials, aeronautical/aerospace, environmental, agricultural, and biomedical engineering) were also explored.

Engineering is not static. New engineering fields evolve by splitting off of the major disciplines or by bringing together a variety of skills to address emerging challenges or to explore new opportunities.

This chapter ends with the same advice given in its beginning: to find out more about any particular engineering discipline, speak to an engineer engaged in that discipline.

SUMMARY OF
KEY IDEAS

- To learn about a specific discipline, speak with an engineer working in that discipline.
- The five principal engineering disciplines are chemical, civil, electrical and computer, industrial, and mechanical engineering.
- Chemical engineers work with the transformation of chemicals to form useful products or processes.
- Civil engineers are involved in the analysis, design, and construction of public works.
- Electrical engineers focus on the transmission and use of electrons and photons.
- Industrial engineers seek to analyze, design, model, and optimize complex systems.
- Mechanical engineers develop, design, and manufacture machines.
- The major engineering subdisciplines are materials, aeronautical/aerospace, environmental, agricultural, and biomedical engineering.
- New engineering fields can be formed by the budding off of existing disciplines or by the creation of interdisciplinary fields.

Problems

1. Describe your interest in two technical areas from two different engineering disciplines. Are there common elements in the two technical areas that interest you?

2. Discuss how *each* of the five principal engineering disciplines can contribute to the following applications:

   a. Development of a manned space station
   b. Design and production of an electric car
   c. Design of a new artificial heart valve
   d. Development of a motorized scooter aimed at the 16–25-year-old market

3. A company wishes to develop and sell a new ultracaffeinated beverage. Which principal engineering discipline(s) would be involved in the design of each of the following?

   a. Syrup formulation
   b. Syrup–water mixing apparatus
   c. Carbonation system
   d. Bottling line
   e. Bottling plant

4. Using the Internet, find two jobs performed by chemical engineers. Explain how the jobs use the technical areas listed in Section 3.

5. Using the Internet, find two jobs performed by civil engineers. Explain how the jobs use the technical areas listed in Section 4.

6.   Using the Internet, find two jobs performed by electrical and computer engineers. Explain how the jobs use the technical areas listed in Section 5.

7.   Using the Internet, find two jobs performed by industrial engineers. Explain how the jobs use the technical areas listed in Section 6.

8.   Using the Internet, find two jobs performed by mechanical engineers. Explain how the jobs use the technical areas listed in Section 7.

9.   Explain how new engineering disciplines form. Interview a professor to find how new fields are formed in his or her field of research. Summarize your findings in a short paragraph.

10.   Summarize the state of the field of robotic, photonic, or renewal engineering.

10

Professionalism and Codes of Ethics

Objectives

After reading this chapter, you will be able to

- Determine whether engineering is a profession
- Understand what codes of ethics are, and
- Examine some codes of ethics of professional engineering societies.

Late in 1994, reports began to appear in the news media that the latest generation of Pentium® microprocessors, the heart and soul of personal computers, was flawed. These reports appeared not only in trade journals and magazines aimed at computer specialists, but also in *The New York Times* and other daily newspapers. The stories reported that computers equipped with these chips were unable to correctly perform some relatively simple multiplication and division operations.

At first, Intel, the manufacturer of the Pentium microprocessor, denied that there was a problem. Later, it argued that although there was a problem, the error would be significant only in sophisticated applications, and most people wouldn't even notice that an error had occurred. It was also reported that Intel had been aware of the problem and already was working to fix it. As a result of this publicity, many people who had purchased Pentium-based computers asked to have the defective chip replaced. Until the public outcry had reached huge proportions, Intel refused to replace the chips. Finally, when it was clear that this situation was a public relations disaster for them, Intel agreed to replace the defective chips when customers requested it.

Did Intel do anything unethical? To answer this question, we will need to develop a framework for understanding ethical problems. One part of this framework will be the codes of ethics that have been established by professional engineering organizations. These codes help guide engineers in the course of their professional duties and give them insight into ethical problems such as the one just described. The engineering codes of ethics hold that engineers should not make false claims or represent a product to be something that it is not. In some ways, the Pentium case might seem to simply be a public-relations problem. But, looking at the problem with a code of ethics will indicate that there is more to this situation than simple PR, especially since the chip did not operate in the way that Intel claimed it did.

In this chapter, the nature of professions will be examined with the goal of determining whether engineering is a profession. Two representative engineering codes of ethics will be looked at in detail. At the end of this chapter,

From *Engineering Ethics*, Third Edition, Charles B. Fledderman. Copyright © 2008 by Pearson Education. Published by Prentice Hall, Inc. All rights reserved.

the Pentium case is presented in more detail along with two other cases, and codes of ethics are applied to analyze what the engineers in these cases should have done.

1 INTRODUCTION

When confronted by an ethical problem, what resources are available to an engineer to help find a solution? One of the hallmarks of modern professions are codes of ethics promulgated by various professional societies. These codes serve to guide practitioners of the profession in making decisions about how to conduct themselves and how to resolve ethical issues that might confront them. Are codes of ethics applicable to engineering? To answer this question, we must first consider what professions are and how they function and then decide if this definition applies to engineering. Then we will examine codes of ethics in general and look specifically at some of the codes of engineering professional societies.

2 IS ENGINEERING A PROFESSION?

In order to determine whether engineering is a profession, the nature of professions must first be examined. As a starting point, it will be valuable to distinguish the word "profession" from other words that are sometimes used synonymously with "profession": "job" and " occupation." Any work for hire can be considered a job, regardless of the skill level involved and the responsibility granted. Engineering is certainly a job—engineers are paid for their services—but the skills and responsibilities involved in engineering make it more than just a job.

Similarly, the word "occupation" implies employment through which someone makes a living. Engineering, then, is also an occupation. How do the words "job" and "occupation" differ from "profession?"

The words "profession" and "professional" have many uses in modern society that go beyond the definition of a job or occupation. One often hears about "professional athletes" or someone referring to himself as a "professional carpenter," for example. In the first case, the word "professional" is being used to distinguish the practitioner from an unpaid amateur. In the second case, it is used to indicate some degree of skill acquired through many years of experience, with an implication that this practitioner will provide quality services.

Neither of these senses of the word "professional" is applicable to engineers. There are no amateur engineers who perform engineering work without being paid while they train to become professional, paid engineers. Likewise, the length of time one works at an engineering-related job, such as an engineering aide or engineering technician, does not confer professional status no matter how skilled a technician one might become. To see what is meant by the term "professional engineer," we will first examine the nature of professions.

2.1 What Is a Profession?

What are the attributes of a profession? There have been many studies of this question, and some consensus as to the nature of *professions* has been achieved. Attributes of a profession include

1. Work that requires sophisticated skills, the use of judgment, and the exercise of discretion. Also, the work is not routine and is not capable of being mechanized;
2. Membership in the profession requires extensive formal education, not simply practical training or apprenticeship;

3. The public allows special societies or organizations that are controlled by members of the profession to set standards for admission to the profession, to set standards of conduct for members, and to enforce these standards; and,

4. Significant public good results from the practice of the profession [Martin and Schinzinger, 2000].

The terms "judgment" and "discretion" used in the first part of this definition require a little amplification. Many occupations require judgment every day. A secretary must decide what work to tackle first. An auto mechanic must decide if a part is sufficiently worn to require complete replacement, or if rebuilding will do. This is not the type of judgment implied in this definition. In a profession, "judgment" refers to making significant decisions based on formal training and experience. In general, the decisions will have serious impacts on people's lives and will often have important implications regarding the spending of large amounts of money.

"Discretion" can have two different meanings. The first definition involves being discrete in the performance of one's duties by keeping information about customers, clients, and patients confidential. This confidentiality is essential for engendering a trusting relationship and is a hallmark of professions. While many jobs might involve some discretion, this definition implies a high level of significance to the information that must be kept private by a professional. The other definition of discretion involves the ability to make decisions autonomously. When making a decision, one is often told, "Use your discretion." This definition is similar in many ways to that of the term "judgment" described previously. Many people are allowed to use their discretion in making choices while performing their jobs. However, the significance of the decision marks the difference between a job and a profession.

One thing not mentioned in the definition of a profession is the compensation received by a professional for his services. Although most professionals tend to be relatively well compensated, high pay is not a sufficient condition for professional status. Entertainers and athletes are among the most highly paid members of our society, and yet few would describe them as professionals in the sense described previously. Although professional status often helps one to get better pay and better working conditions, these are more often determined by economic forces.

Earlier, reference was made to "professional" athletes and carpenters. Let's examine these occupations in light of the foregoing definition of professions and see if athletics and carpentry qualify as professions. An athlete who is paid for her appearances is referred to as a professional athlete. Clearly, being a paid athlete does involve sophisticated skills that most people do not possess, and these skills are not capable of mechanization. However, substantial judgment and discretion are not called for on the part of athletes in their "professional" lives, so athletics fails the first part of the definition of "professional." Interestingly, though, professional athletes are frequently viewed as role models and are often disciplined for a lack of discretion in their personal lives.

Athletics requires extensive training, not of a formal nature, but more of a practical nature acquired through practice and coaching. No special societies (as opposed to unions, which will be discussed in more detail later) are required by athletes, and athletics does not meet an important public need; although entertainment is a public need, it certainly doesn't rank highly compared to the needs met by professions such as medicine. So, although they are highly trained and very well compensated, athletes are not professionals.

Similarly, carpenters require special skills to perform their jobs, but many aspects of their work can be mechanized, and little judgment or discretion is required. Training in carpentry is not formal, but rather is practical by way of apprenticeships. No organizations or societies are required. However, carpentry certainly does meet an aspect of the public good—providing shelter is fundamental to society—although perhaps not to the same extent as do professions such as medicine. So, carpentry also doesn't meet the basic requirements to be a profession. We can see, then, that many jobs or occupations whose practitioners might be referred to as professionals don't really meet the basic definition of a profession. Although they may be highly paid or important jobs, they are not professions.

Before continuing with an examination of whether engineering is a profession, let's look at two occupations that are definitely regarded by society as professions: medicine and law. Medicine certainly fits the definition of a profession given previously. It requires very sophisticated skills that can't be mechanized, it requires judgment as to appropriate treatment plans for individual patients, and it requires discretion. (Physicians have even been granted physician–patient privilege, the duty not to divulge information given in confidence by the patient to the physician.) Although medicine requires extensive practical training learned through an apprenticeship called a residency, it also requires much formal training (four years of undergraduate school, three to four years of medical school, and extensive hands-on practice in patient care). Medicine has a special society, the American Medical Association (AMA), to which a large fraction of practicing physicians belong and that participates in the regulation of medical schools, sets standards for practice of the profession, and enforces codes of ethical behavior for its members. Finally, healing the sick and helping to prevent disease clearly involve the public good. By the definition presented previously, medicine clearly qualifies as a profession.

Similarly, law is a profession. It involves sophisticated skills acquired through extensive formal training; has a professional society, the American Bar Association (ABA); and serves an important aspect of the public good. (Although this last point is increasingly becoming a point of debate within American society!) The difference between athletics and carpentry on one hand and law and medicine on the other is clear. The first two really cannot be considered professions, and the latter two most certainly are.

2.2 Engineering as a Profession

Using medicine and law as our examples of professions, it is now time to consider whether engineering is a profession. Certainly, engineering requires extensive and sophisticated skills. Otherwise, why spend four years in college just to get a start in engineering? The essence of engineering design is judgment: how to use the available materials, components and devices, to reach a specified objective. Discretion is required in engineering: Engineers are required to keep their employers' or clients' intellectual-property and business information confidential. Also, a primary concern of any engineer is the safety of the public that will use the products and devices he designs. There is always a trade-off between safety and other engineering issues in a design, requiring discretion on the part of the engineer to ensure that the design serves its purpose and fills its market niche safely.

The point about mechanization needs to be addressed a little more carefully with respect to engineering. Certainly, once a design has been performed, it can easily be replicated without the intervention of an engineer. However, each new situation that requires a new design or a modification of an existing design requires an engineer. Industry commonly uses many computer-based tools for generating designs, such as computer-aided design (CAD) software. This shouldn't be mistaken for mechanization of engineering. CAD is simply a tool used by engineers, not a replacement for the skills of an actual engineer. A wrench can't fix an automobile without a mechanic. Likewise, a computer with CAD software can't design an antilock braking system for an automobile without an engineer.

Engineering requires extensive formal training. Four years of undergraduate training leading to a bachelor's degree in an engineering program is essential, followed by work under the supervision of an experienced engineer. Many engineering jobs even require advanced degrees beyond the bachelor's degree. The work of engineers serves the public good by providing communication systems, transportation, energy resources, and medical diagnostic and treatment equipment, to name only a few.

Before passing final judgment on the professional status of engineering, the nature of engineering societies requires a little consideration. Each discipline within engineering has a professional society, such as the Institute of Electrical and Electronics Engineers (IEEE) for electrical engineers and the American Society of Mechanical Engineers (ASME) for mechanical engineers. These societies serve to set professional standards and frequently work with schools of engineering to set standards for admission and curricula. However, these societies differ significantly from the AMA and the ABA. Unlike law and medicine, each specialty of engineering has its own society. There is no overall engineering society that most engineers identify with, although the National Society of Professional Engineers (NSPE) tries to function in this way. In addition, relatively few practicing engineers belong to their professional societies. Thus, the engineering societies are weak compared to the AMA and the ABA.

It is clear that engineering meets all of the definitions of a profession. In addition, it is clear that engineering practice has much in common with medicine and law. Interestingly, although they are professionals, engineers do not yet hold the same status within society that physicians and lawyers do.

2.3 Differences between Engineering and Other Professions

Although we have determined that engineering is a profession, it should be noted that there are significant differences between how engineering is practiced and how law and medicine are practiced. Lawyers are typically self-employed in private practice, essentially an independent business, or in larger group practices with other lawyers. Relatively few are employed by large organizations such as corporations. Until recently, this was also the case for most physicians, although with the accelerating trend toward managed care and HMOs in the past decade, many more physicians work for large corporations rather than in private practice. However, even physicians who are employed by large HMOs are members of organizations in which they retain much of the decision-making power—often, the head of an HMO is a physician—and make up a substantial fraction of the total number of employees.

In contrast, engineers generally practice their profession very differently from physicians and lawyers. Most engineers are not self-employed, but more often are a small part of larger companies involving many different occupations, including accountants, marketing specialists, and extensive numbers of less skilled manufacturing employees. The exception to this rule is civil engineers, who generally practice as independent consultants either on their own or in engineering firms similar in many ways to law firms. When employed by large corporations, engineers are rarely in significant managerial positions, except with regard to managing other engineers. Although engineers are paid well compared to the rest of society, they are generally less well compensated than physicians and lawyers.

Training for engineers is different than for physicians and lawyers. One can be employed as an engineer after four years of undergraduate education, unlike law and medicine, for which training in the profession doesn't begin until after the undergraduate program has been completed. As mentioned previously, the engineering societies are not as powerful as the AMA and the ABA, perhaps because of the number of different professional engineering societies. Also, both law and medicine require licenses granted by the state in order to practice. Many engineers, especially those employed by large industrial companies, do not have engineering licenses. It can be debated whether someone who is unlicensed is truly an engineer or whether he is practicing engineering illegally, but the reality is that many of those who are employed as engineers are not licensed. Finally, engineering doesn't have the social stature that law and medicine have (a fact that is reflected in the lower pay that engineers receive as compared to that of lawyers and doctors). Despite these differences, on balance, engineering is still clearly a profession, albeit one that is not as mature as medicine and law. However, it should be striving to emulate some of the aspects of these professions.

2.4 Other Aspects of Professional Societies

We should briefly note that professional societies also serve other, perhaps less noble, purposes than those mentioned previously. Sociologists who study the nature of professional societies describe two different models of professions, sometimes referred to as the social-contract and the business models. The social-contract model views professional societies as being set up primarily to further the public good, as described in the definition of a profession given previously. There is an implicit social contract involved with professions, according to this model. Society grants the professions' perks such as high pay, a high status in society, and the ability to self-regulate. In return for these perks, society gets the services provided by the profession.

A perhaps more cynical view of professions is provided by the business model. According to this model, professions function as a means for furthering the economic advantage of the members. Put another way, professional organizations are labor unions for the elite, strictly limiting the number of practitioners of the profession, controlling the working conditions for professionals, and artificially inflating the salaries of its members. An analysis of both models in terms of law and medicine would show that there are ways in which these professions exhibit aspects of both of these models.

Where does engineering fit into this picture? Engineering is certainly a service-oriented profession and thus fits into the social-contract model quite nicely. Although some engineers might wish to see engineering professional societies function more according to the business model, they currently don't function that way. The engineering societies have virtually no clout with major engineering employers to set wages and working conditions or to help engineers resolve ethical disputes with their employers.

Moreover, there is very little prospect that the engineering societies will function this way in the near future.

2.5 If Engineering Were Practiced More Like Medicine

It is perhaps instructive to speculate a little on how engineering might change in the future if our model of the engineering profession were closer to that of law or medicine. One major change would be in the way engineers are educated. Rather than the current system, in which students study engineering as undergraduates and then pursue advanced degrees as appropriate, prospective engineers would probably get a four-year "preengineering" degree in mathematics, physics, chemistry, computer science, or some combination of these fields. After the four-year undergraduate program, students would enter a three- or four-year engineering professional program culminating in a "doctor of engineering" degree (or other appropriately named degree). This program would include extensive study of engineering fundamentals, specialization in a field of study, and perhaps "clinical" training under a practicing engineer.

How would such engineers be employed? The pattern of employment would certainly be different. Engineers in all fields might work for engineering firms similar to the way in which civil engineers work now, consulting on projects for government agencies or large corporations. The corporate employers who now have numerous engineers on their staff would probably have far fewer engineers on the payroll, opting instead for a few professional engineers who would supervise the work of several less highly trained "engineering technicians." Adoption of this model would probably reduce the number of engineers in the work force, leading to higher earnings for those who remain. Those relegated to the ranks of engineering technicians would probably earn less than those currently employed as engineers.

3 CODES OF ETHICS

An aspect of professional societies that has not been mentioned yet is the codes of ethics that engineering societies have adopted. These codes express the rights, duties, and obligations of the members of the profession. In this section, we will examine the codes of ethics of professional engineering societies.

It should be noted that although most of the discussion thus far has focused on professionalism and professional societies, codes of ethics are not limited to professional organizations. They can also be found, for example, in corporations and universities as well. We start with some general ideas about what codes of ethics are and what purpose they serve and then examine two professional engineering codes in more detail.

3.1 What Is a Code of Ethics?

Primarily, a code of ethics provides a framework for ethical judgment for a professional. The key word here is "framework." No code can be totally comprehensive and cover all possible ethical situations that a professional engineer is likely to encounter. Rather, codes serve as a starting point for ethical decision making. A code can also express the commitment to ethical conduct shared by members of a profession. It is important to note that ethical codes do not establish new ethical principles. They simply reiterate principles and standards that are already accepted as responsible engineering practice. A code expresses these principles in a coherent, comprehensive, and accessible manner. Finally, a code defines the roles and responsibilities of professionals [Harris, Pritchard, and Rabins, 2000].

It is important also to look at what a code of ethics is not. It is not a recipe for ethical behavior; as previously stated, it is only a framework for arriving at good ethical choices. A code of ethics is never a substitute for sound judgment. A code of ethics is not a legal document. One can't be arrested for violating its provisions, although expulsion from the professional society might result from code violations. As mentioned in the previous section, with the current state of engineering societies, expulsion from an engineering society generally will not result in an inability to practice engineering, so there are not necessarily any direct consequences of violating engineering ethical codes. Finally, a code of ethics doesn't create new moral or ethical principles. As described in the previous chapter, these principles are well established in society, and foundations of our ethical and moral principles go back many centuries. Rather, a code of ethics spells out the ways in which moral and ethical principles apply to professional practice. Put another way, a code helps the engineer to apply moral principles to the unique situations encountered in professional practice.

How does a code of ethics achieve these goals? First, a code of ethics helps create an environment within a profession where ethical behavior is the norm. It also serves as a guide or reminder of how to act in specific situations. A code of ethics can also be used to bolster an individual's position with regard to a certain activity: The code provides a little backup for an individual who is being pressured by a superior to behave unethically. A code of ethics can also bolster the individual's position by indicating that there is a collective sense of correct behavior; there is strength in numbers. Finally, a code of ethics can indicate to others that the profession is seriously concerned about responsible, professional conduct [Harris, Pritchard, and Rabins, 2000]. A code of ethics, however, should not be used as "window dressing," an attempt by an organization to appear to be committed to ethical behavior when it really is not.

3.2 Objections to Codes

Although codes of ethics are widely used by many organizations, including engineering societies, there are many objections to codes of ethics, specifically as they apply to engineering practice. First, as mentioned previously, relatively few practicing engineers are members of professional societies and so don't necessarily feel compelled to abide by their codes. Many engineers who are members of professional societies are not aware of the existence of the society's code, or if they are aware of it, they have never read it. Even among engineers who know about their society's code, consultation of the code is rare. There are also objections that the engineering codes often have internal conflicts, but don't give a method for resolving the conflict. Finally, codes can be coercive: They foster ethical behavior with a stick rather than with a carrot [Harris, Pritchard, and Rabins, 2000]. Despite these objections, codes are in very widespread use today and are generally thought to serve a useful function.

3.3 Codes of the Engineering Societies

Before examining professional codes in more detail, it might be instructive to look briefly at the history of the engineering codes of ethics. Professional engineering societies in the United States began to be organized in the late 19th century, with new societies created as new engineering fields have developed in this century. As these societies matured, many of them created codes of ethics to guide practicing engineers.

Early in the current century, these codes were mostly concerned with issues of how to conduct business. For example, many early codes had clauses forbidding advertising of services or prohibiting competitive bidding by engineers for design projects. Codes also spelled out the duties that engineers had toward their employers. Relatively less emphasis than today was given to issues of service to the public and safety. This imbalance has changed greatly in recent decades as public perceptions and concerns about the safety of engineered products and devices have changed. Now, most codes emphasize commitments to safety, public health, and even environmental protection as the most important duties of the engineer.

3.4 A Closer Look at Two Codes of Ethics

Having looked at some ideas about what codes of ethics are and how they function, let's look more closely at two codes of ethics: the codes of the IEEE and the NSPE. Although these codes have some common content, the structures of the codes are very different.

The IEEE code is short and deals in generalities, whereas the NSPE code is much longer and more detailed. An explanation of these differences is rooted in the philosophy of the authors of these codes. A short code that is lacking in detail is more likely to be read by members of the society than is a longer code. A short code is also more understandable. It articulates general principles and truly functions as a framework for ethical decision making, as described previously.

A longer code, such as the NSPE code, has the advantage of being more explicit and is thus able to cover more ground. It leaves less to the imagination of the individual and therefore is more useful for application to specific cases. The length of the code, however, makes it less likely to be read and thoroughly understood by most engineers.

There are some specifics of these two codes that are worth noting here. The IEEE code doesn't mention a duty to one's employer. However, the IEEE code does mention a duty to protect the environment, a clause added relatively recently, which is somewhat unique among engineering codes. The NSPE code has a preamble that succinctly presents the duties of the engineer before going on to the more explicit discussions of the rest of the code. Like most codes of ethics, the NSPE code does mention the engineer's duty to his or her employer in Section I.4, where it states that engineers shall "[a]ct … for each employer … as faithful agents or trustees."

3.5 Resolving Internal Conflicts in Codes

One objection to codes of ethics is the internal conflicts that can exist within them, with no instructions on how to resolve these conflicts. An example of this problem would be a situation in which an employer asks or even orders an engineer to implement a design that the engineer feels will be unsafe. It is made clear that the engineer's job is at stake if he doesn't do as instructed. What does the NSPE code tell us about this situation?

In clause I.4, the NSPE code indicates that engineers have a duty to their employers, which implies that the engineer should go ahead with the unsafe design favored by his employer. However, clause I.1 and the preamble make it clear that the safety of the public is also an important concern of an engineer. In fact, it says that the safety of the public is paramount. How can this conflict be resolved?

There is no implication in this or any other code that all clauses are equally important. Rather, there is a hierarchy within the code. Some clauses take precedence over others, although there is generally no explicit indication in the code of what the hierarchy is. The preceding dilemma is easily resolved within the context of this hierarchy. The duty to protect the safety of the public is paramount and takes precedence over the duty to the employer. In this case, the code provides very clear support to the engineer, who must convince his supervisor that the product can't be designed as requested. Unfortunately, not all internal conflicts in codes of ethics are so easily resolved.

3.6 Can Codes and Professional Societies Protect Employees?

One important area where professional societies can and should function is as protectors of the rights of employees who are being pressured by their employer to do something unethical or who are accusing their employers or the government of unethical conduct. The codes of the professional societies are of some use in this since they can be used by employees as ammunition against an employer who is sanctioning them for pointing out unethical behavior or who are being asked to engage in unethical acts.

An example of this situation is the action of the IEEE on behalf of three electrical engineers who were fired from their jobs at the Bay Area Rapid Transit (BART) organization when they pointed out deficiencies in the way the control systems for the BART trains were being designed and tested. After being fired, the engineers sued BART, citing the IEEE code of ethics which impelled them to hold as their primary concern the safety of the public who would be using the BART system. The IEEE intervened on their behalf in court, although ultimately the engineers lost the case.

If the codes of ethics of professional societies are to have any meaning, this type of intervention is essential when ethical violations are pointed out. However, since not all engineers are members of professional societies and the engineering societies are relatively weak, the pressure that can be exerted by these organizations is limited.

3.7 Other Types of Codes of Ethics

Professional societies aren't the only organizations that have codified their ethical standards. Many other organizations have also developed codes of ethics for various purposes similar to those of the professional engineering organizations. For example, codes for the ethical use of computers have been developed, and student organizations in universities have framed student codes of ethics. In this section, we will examine how codes of ethics function in corporations.

Many of the important ethical questions faced by engineers come up in the context of their work for corporations. Since most practicing engineers are not members of professional organizations, it seems that for many engineers, there is little ethical guidance in the course of their daily work. This problem has led to the adoption of codes of ethics by many corporations.

Even if the professional codes were widely adopted and recognized by practicing engineers, there would still be some value to the corporate codes, since a corporation can tailor its code to the individual circumstances and unique mission of the company. As such, these codes tend to be relatively long and very detailed, incorporating many rules specific to the practices of the company. For example, corporate codes frequently spell out in detail the company policies on business practices, relationships with suppliers, relationships with government agencies, compliance with government regulations, health and safety issues, issues related to environmental protection, equal employment opportunity and affirmative action, sexual harassment, and diversity and racial/ethnic tolerance. Since corporate codes are coercive in nature—your continued employment by the company depends on your compliance with the company code—these codes tend to be longer and more detailed in order to provide very clear and specific guidelines to the employees.

Codes of professional societies, by their nature, can't be this explicit, since there is no means for a professional society to reasonably enforce its code. Due to the typically long lengths of these codes, no example of a corporate *code of ethics* can be included here. However, codes for companies can sometimes be found via the Internet at corporate websites.

Some of the heightened awareness of ethics in corporations stems from the increasing public scrutiny that has accompanied well-publicized disasters, such as the cases presented in this book, as well as from cases of fraud and cost overruns, particularly in the defense industry, that have been exposed in the media. Many large corporations have developed corporate codes of ethics in response to these problems, to help heighten employee's awareness of ethical issues, and to help establish a strong corporate ethics culture. These codes give employees ready access to guidelines and policies of the corporations. But, as with professional codes, it is important to remember that these codes cannot cover all possible situations that an employee might encounter; there is no substitute for good judgment. A code also doesn't substitute for good lines of communications between employees and upper management and for workable methods for fixing ethical problems when they occur.

APPLICATION

Cases

Codes of ethics can be used as a tool for analyzing cases and for gaining some insight into the proper course of action. Before reading these cases, it would be helpful to read a couple of the codes in Appendix A, especially the code most closely related to your field of study, to become familiar with the types of issues that codes deal with. Then, put yourself in the position of an engineer working for these companies—Intel, Paradyne computers, and 3Bs construction—to see what you would have done in each case.

The Intel Pentium® Chip

In late 1994, the media began to report that there was a flaw in the new Pentium microprocessor produced by Intel. The microprocessor is the heart of a personal computer and controls all of the operations and calculations that take place. A flaw in the Pentium was especially significant, since it was the microprocessor used in 80% of the personal computers produced in the world at that time.

Apparently, flaws in a complicated integrated circuit such as the Pentium, which at the time contained over one million transistors, are common. However, most of the flaws are undetectable by the user and don't affect the operation of the computer. Many of these flaws are easily compensated for through software. The flaw that came to light in 1994 was different: It was detectable by the user. This particular flaw was in the floating-point unit (FPU) and caused a wrong answer when double-precision arithmetic, a very common operation, was performed.

A standard test was widely published to determine whether a user's microprocessor was flawed. Using spreadsheet software, the user was to take the number 4,195,835, multiply it by 3,145,727, and then divide that result by 3,145,727. As we all know from elementary math, when a number is multiplied and then divided by the same number, the result should be the original number. In this example, the result should be 4,195,835. However, with the flawed FPU, the result of this calculation was 4,195,579 [Infoworld, 1994]. Depending on the application, this six-thousandths-of-a-percent error might be very significant.

At first, Intel's response to these reports was to deny that there was any problem with the chip. When it became clear that this assertion was not accurate, Intel switched its policy and stated that although there was indeed a defect in the chip, it was insignificant and the vast majority of users would never even notice it. The chip would be replaced for free only for users who could demonstrate that they needed an unflawed version of the chip [Infoworld, 1994]. There is some logic to this policy from Intel's point of view, since over two million computers had already been sold with the defective chip.

Of course, this approach didn't satisfy most Pentium owners. After all, how can you predict whether you might have a future application where this flaw might be significant? IBM, a major Pentium user, canceled the sales of all IBM computers containing the flawed chip. Finally, after much negative publicity in the popular personal computer literature and an outcry from Pentium users, Intel agreed to replace the flawed chip with an unflawed version for any customer who asked to have it replaced.

It should be noted that long before news of the flaw surfaced in the popular press, Intel was aware of the problem and had already corrected it on subsequent versions. It did, however, continue to sell the flawed version and, based on its early insistence that the flaw did not present a significant problem to users, seemingly planned to do so until the new version was available and the stocks of the flawed one were exhausted. Eventually, the damage caused by this case was fixed as the media reports of the problem died down and as customers were able to get un-flawed chips into their computers. Ultimately, Intel had a write-off of 475 million dollars to solve this problem.

What did Intel learn from this experience? The early designs for new chips continue to have flaws, and sometimes these flaws are not detected until the product is already in use by consumers. However, Intel's approach to these problems has changed. It now seems to feel that problems need to be fixed immediately. In addition, the decision is now based on the consumer's perception of the significance of the flaw, rather than on Intel's opinion of its significance.

Indeed, similar flaws were found in 1997 in the early versions of the Pentium II and Pentium Pro processors. This time, Intel immediately confirmed that the flaw existed and offered customers software that would correct it. Other companies also seem to have benefited from Intel's experience. For example, Intuit, a leading man-ufacturer of tax preparation and financial software, called a news conference in March of 1995 to apologize for flaws in its TurboTax software that had become ap-parent earlier in that year. In addition to the apology, they offered consumers re-placements for the defective software.

Runway Concrete at the Denver International Airport

In the early 1990s, the city of Denver, Colorado, embarked on one of the largest public works projects in history: the construction of a new airport to replace the aging Stapleton International Airport. The new Denver International Airport (DIA) would be the first new airport constructed in the United States since the Dallas–Fort Worth Airport was completed in the early 1970s. Of course, the size and complexity of this type of project lends itself to many problems, including cost over-runs, worker safety and health issues, and controversies over the need for the pro-ject. The construction of DIA was no exception.

Perhaps the most widely known problem with the airport was the malfunc-tioning of a new computer-controlled high-tech baggage handling system, which in preliminary tests consistently mangled and misrouted baggage and frequently jammed, leading to the shutdown of the entire system. Problems with the baggage handling system delayed the opening of the airport for over a year and cost the city millions of dollars in expenses for replacement of the system and lost revenues while the airport was unable to open. In addition, the baggage system made the air-port the butt of many jokes, especially on late-night television.

More interesting from the perspective of engineering ethics are problems dur-ing the construction of DIA involving the concrete used for the runways, taxiways, and aprons at the airport. The story of concrete problems at DIA was first reported by the *Denver Post* in early August of 1993 as the airport neared completion. Two subcontractors filed lawsuits against the runway paving contractor, California con-struction company Ball, Ball, & Brosamer (known as 3Bs), claiming that 3Bs owed them money. Parts of these suits were allegations that 3Bs had altered the recipe for the concrete used in the runway and apron construction, deliberately diluting the concrete with more gravel, water, and sand (and thus less cement), thereby weakening it. 3Bs motivation for doing so would be to save money and thus to increase their profits. One of the subcontractors, CSI Trucking, whose job was to haul the sand and gravel used in the concrete, claimed that 3Bs hadn't paid them for materials that had been delivered. They claimed that these materials had been used to dilute the mixture, but hadn't been paid for, since the payment would leave a record of the improper recipe.

At first, Denver officials downplayed the reports of defective concrete, relying on the results of independent tests of the concrete. In addition, the city of Denver ordered core samples to be taken from the runways. Tests on these cores showed that the runway concrete had the correct strength. The subcontractors claimed that the improperly mixed concrete could have the proper test strength, but would lead to a severely shortened runway lifetime. The FBI also became involved in investigating this case, since federal transportation grants were used by Denver to help finance the construction of the runways.

The controversy seemed to settle down for a while, but a year later, in August of 1994, the Denver district attorney's office announced that it was investigating allegations that inspection reports on the runways were falsified during the construction. This announcement was followed on November 13, 1994 by a lengthy story in the *Denver Post* detailing a large number of allegations of illegal activities and unethical practices with regard to the runway construction.

The November 13 story revolved around an admission by a Fort Collins, Colorado, company, Empire Laboratories, that test reports on the concrete had been falsified to hide results which showed that some of the concrete did not meet the specifications. Attorneys for Empire said that this falsification had happened five or six times in the course of this work, but four employees of Empire claimed that the altering of test data was standard operating procedure at Empire.

The nature of the test modifications and the rationale behind them illustrate many of the important problems we will discuss in this book, including the need for objectivity and honesty in reporting results of tests and experiments. One Empire employee said that if a test result was inconsistent with other tests, then the results would be changed to mask the difference. This practice was justified by Empire as being "based upon engineering judgment" [*Denver Post,* Nov. 13, 1994]. The concrete was tested by pouring test samples when the actual runways were poured. These samples were subjected to flexural tests, which consist of subjecting the concrete to an increasing force until it fails. The tests were performed at 7 days after pouring and also at 28 days. Many of the test results showed that the concrete was weaker at 28 days than at 7 days. However, the results should have been the opposite, since concrete normally increases in strength as it cures. Empire employees indicated that this apparent anomaly was because many of the 7-day tests had been altered to make the concrete seem stronger than it was.

Other problems with the concrete also surfaced. Some of the concrete used in the runways contained clay balls up to 10 inches in diameter. While not uncommon in concrete batching, the presence of this clay can lead to runways that are significantly weaker than planned.

Questions about the short cement content in 3Bs concrete mixture also resurfaced in the November *Denver Post* article. The main question was "given that the concrete batching operation was routinely monitored, how did 3Bs get away with shorting the cement content of the concrete?" One of the batch plant operators for

3Bs explained that they were tipped off about upcoming inspections. When an inspector was due, they used the correct recipe so that concrete would appear to be correctly formulated. The shorting of the concrete mixture could also be detected by looking at the records of materials delivered to the batch plants. However, DIA administrators found that this documentation was missing, and it was unclear whether it had ever existed.

A batch plant operator also gave a sworn statement that he had been directed to fool the computer that operated the batch plant. The computer was fooled by tampering with the scale used to weigh materials and by inputting false numbers for the moisture content of the sand. In some cases, the water content of the sand that was input into the computer was a negative number! This tampering forced the computer to alter the mixture to use less cement, but the records printed by the computer would show that the mix was properly constituted. In his statement, the batch plant operator also swore that this practice was known to some of the highest officials in 3Bs.

Despite the problems with the batching of the concrete used in the runways, DIA officials insisted that the runways built by 3Bs met the specifications. This assertion was based on the test results, which showed that although some parts of the runway were below standard, all of the runways met FAA specifications. 3Bs was paid for those areas that were below standard at a lower rate than for the stronger parts of the runway. Further investigations about misdeeds in the construction of DIA were performed by several groups, including a Denver grand jury, a federal grand jury, the FBI, and committees of Congress.

On October 19, 1995, the *Denver Post* reported the results of a lawsuit brought by 3Bs against the city of Denver. 3Bs contended that the city still owed them $2.3 million (in addition to the $193 million that 3Bs had already been paid) for the work they did. The city claimed that this money was not owed. The reduction was a penalty due to low test results on some of the concrete. 3Bs claimed that those tests were flawed and that the concrete was fine. A hearing officer sided with the city, deciding that Denver didn't owe 3Bs any more money. 3Bs said that they would take their suit to the next higher level.

As of the summer of 2003, DIA has been in operation for many years and no problems have surfaced regarding the strength of the runways. Unfortunately, problems with runway durability might not surface until after several more years of use. In the meantime, there is still plenty of litigation and investigation of this and other unethical acts surrounding the construction of this airport.

Competitive Bidding and the Paradyne Case

Although competitive bidding is a well-established practice in purchasing, it can lead to many ethical problems associated with deception on the part of the vendor or with unfairness on the part of the buyer in choosing a vendor. The idea behind competitive bidding is that the buyer can get a product at the best price by setting up competition between the various suppliers. Especially with large contracts, the temptation to cheat on the bidding is great. Newspapers frequently report stories of deliberate underbidding to win contracts, followed by cost overruns that are unavoidable; theft of information on others' bids in order to be able to underbid them, etc. Problems also exist with buyers who make purchase decisions based on elements other than the advertised bid criteria, who leak information to a preferred bidder, or who give advance notice or detailed knowledge of evaluation procedures to preferred bidders. The Paradyne computer case is useful in illustrating some of the hazards associated with competitive bidding.

The Paradyne case began on June 10, 1980, when the Social Security Administration (SSA) published a request for proposals (RFP) for computer systems to replace the older equipment in its field offices. Its requirement was for computers that provide access to a central database. This database was used by field offices in the processing of benefit claims and in issuing new social security numbers. SSA intended to purchase an off-the-shelf system already in the vendor's product line, rather than a customized system. This requirement was intended to minimize the field testing and bugs associated with customized systems. In March of 1981, SSA let a contract for $115 million for 1,800 computer systems to Paradyne.

Problems occurred immediately upon award of the contract, when the Paradyne computers failed the acceptance testing. The requirements were finally relaxed so that the computers would pass. After delivery, many SSA field offices reported frequent malfunctions, sometimes multiple times per day, requiring manual rebooting of the system. One of the contract requirements was that the computers function 98% of the time. This requirement wasn't met until after 21 months of operation. After nearly two years of headaches and much wasted time and money, the system finally worked as planned [Davis, 1988].

Subsequent investigation by SSA indicated that the product supplied by Paradyne was not an off-the-shelf system, but rather was a system that incorporated new technology that had yet to be built and was still under development. Paradyne had proposed selling SSA their P8400 model with the PIOS operating system. The bid was written as if this system currently existed. However, at the time that the bid was prepared, the 8400 system did not exist and had not been developed, prototyped, or manufactured [Head, 1986].

There were other problems associated with Paradyne's performance during the bidding. The RFP stated that there was to be a preaward demonstration of the product, not a demonstration of a prototype. Paradyne demonstrated to SSA a different computer, a modified PDP 11/23 computer manufactured by Digital Equipment Corporation (DEC) placed in a cabinet that was labeled P8400. Apparently, many of the DEC labels on the equipment that was demonstrated to SSA had Paradyne labels pasted over them. Paradyne disingenuously claimed that since the DEC equipment was based on a 16-bit processor, as was the P8400 they proposed, it was irrelevant whether the machine demonstrated was the DEC or the actual P8400. Of course, computer users recognize that this statement is nonsense. Even modern "PC-compatible" computers with the same microprocessor chip and operating system can have widely different operating characteristics in terms of speed and the software that can be run.

There were also questions about the operating system. Apparently, at the time of Paradyne's bid, the PIOS system was under development as well and hadn't been tested on a prototype of the proposed system. Even a functioning hardware system will not operate correctly without the correct operating system. No software has ever worked correctly the first time, but rather requires extensive debugging to make it operate properly with a new system. Significantly, the DEC system with the P8400 label that was actually tested by SSA was not running with the proposed PIOS system.

Some of the blame for this fiasco can also be laid at the feet of the SSA. There were six bidders for this contract. Each of the bidders was to have an on-site visit from SSA inspectors to determine whether it was capable of doing the work that it included in its bid. Paradyne's capabilities were not assessed using an on-site visit. Moreover, Paradyne was judged based on its ability to manufacture modems, which was then its main business. Apparently, its ability to produce complete computer systems wasn't assessed. As part of its attempt to gain this contract, Paradyne hired a former SSA official who, while still working for SSA, had participated in preparing the RFP and had helped with setting up the team that would evaluate the bids. Paradyne had notified SSA of the hiring of this person, and SSA decided that there were no ethical problems with this. However, when the Paradyne machine failed the initial acceptance test, this Paradyne official was directly involved in negotiating the relaxed standards with his former boss at SSA.

This situation was resolved when the Paradyne computers were finally brought to the point of functioning as required. However, as a result of these problems, there were many investigations by government agencies, including the Securities and Exchange Commission, the General Accounting Office, the House of Representatives' Government Operations Committee, the Health and Human Services Department (of which SSA is part), and the Justice Department.

KEY TERMS

Code of ethics   Professions   Professional societies

REFERENCES

Charles E. Harris, Jr., Michael S. Pritchard, and Michael J. Rabins, *Engineering Ethics, Concepts and Cases,* Wadsworth Publishing Company, Belmont CA., 2000.
Roland Schinzinger and Mike W. Martin, *Introduction to Engineering Ethics,* McGraw-Hill, New York, 2000.

Intel Pentium Chip Case
"When the Chips Are Down," *Time,* Dec. 26–Jan. 2 1995, p. 126.
"The Fallout from Intel's Pentium Bug," *Fortune,* Jan. 16, 1995, p. 15.
"Pentium Woes Continue," *Infoworld,* Nov. 18, 1994, vol. 16, issue 48, p. 1.
"Flawed Chips Still Shipping," *Infoworld,* Dec. 5, 1994, vol. 16, issue 49, p. 1.
Numerous other accounts from late 1994 and early 1995 in The *Wall Street Journal, The New York Times,* etc.

DIA Runaway Concrete
Lou Kilzer, Robert Kowalski, and Steven Wilmsen, "Concrete Tests Faked at Airport," *Denver Post,* Nov. 13, 1994, Section A, p. 1.

Paradyne Computers
J. Steve Davis, "Ethical Problems in Competitive Bidding: The Paradyne Case," *Business and Professional Ethics Journal,* vol. 7, 1988, p. 3.
Robert V. Head, "Paradyne Dispute: A Matter of Using a Proper Tense," *Government Computer News,* February 14, 1986, p. 23.

PROBLEMS

1 What changes would have to be made for engineering to be a profession more like medicine or law?

2 In which ways do law, medicine, and engineering fit the social-contract and the business models of a profession?

3 The first part of the definition of a profession presented previously said that professions involve the use of sophisticated skills. Do you think that these skills are primarily physical or intellectual skills? Give examples from professions such as law, medicine, and engineering, as well as from nonprofessions.

4   Read about the space shuttle *Challenger* accident in 1986. (You can find information on this in magazines, newspapers, or on the internet.) Apply an engineering code of ethics to this case. What guidance might one of the engineering society codes of ethics have given the Thiokol engineers when faced with a decision to launch? Which specific parts of the code are applicable to this situation? Does a manager who is trained as an engineer still have to adhere to an engineering code of ethics?

5   Write a code of ethics for students in your college or department. Start by deciding what type of code you want: short, long, detailed, etc. Then, list the important ethical issues you think students face. Finally, organize these ideas into a coherent structure.

6   Imagine that you are the president of a small high-technology firm. Your company has grown over the last few years to the point where you feel that it is important that your employees have some guidelines regarding ethics. Define the type of company you are running; then develop an appropriate code of ethics. As in Question 2, start by deciding what type of code is appropriate for your company. Then, list specific points that are important—for example, relationships with vendors, treatment of fellow employees, etc. Finally, write a code that incorporates these features.

Intel Pentium Chip

7   Was this case simply a customer-relations and PR problem, or are there ethical issues to be considered as well?

8   Use an engineering code of ethics to analyze this case. Especially, pay attention to issues of accurate representation of engineered products and to safety issues.

9   When a product is sold, is there an implication that it will work as advertised?

10   Should you reveal defects in a product to a consumer? Is the answer to this question different if the defect is a safety issue rather than simply a flaw? (It might be useful to note in this discussion that although there is no apparent safety concern for someone using a computer with this flaw, PCs are often used to control a variety of instruments, such as medical equipment. For such equipment, a flaw might have a very real safety implication.) Is the answer to this question different if the customer is a bank that uses the computer to calculate interest paid, loan payments, etc., for customers?

11   Should you replace defective products even if customers won't recognize the defect?

12   How thorough should testing be? Is it ever possible to say that no defect exists in a product or structure?

13   Do flaws that Intel found previously in the 386 and 486 chips have any bearing on these questions? In other words, if Intel got away with selling flawed chips before without informing consumers, does that fact have any bearing on this case?

14   G. Richard Thoman, an IBM senior vice president, was quoted as saying, "Nobody should have to worry about the integrity of data calculated on an IBM machine." How does this statement by a major Intel customer change the answers to the previous questions?

15   Just prior to when this problem surfaced, Intel had begun a major advertising campaign to make Intel a household name. They had gotten computer manufacturers to place "Intel Inside" labels on their computers and had spent money on television advertising seeking to increase the public demand for computers with Intel processors, with the unstated message that Intel chips

were of significantly higher quality than other manufacturers' chips. How might this campaign have affected what happened in this case?

16   What responsibilities did the engineers who were aware of the flaw have before the chip was sold? After the chips began to be sold? After the flaw became apparent?

DIA Runaway Concrete

17   Using a code of ethics, analyze the actions of the batch plant operators and Empire Laboratories.

18   Is altering data a proper use of "engineering judgment"? What alternative might have existed to altering the test data on the concrete?

19   Who is responsible for ensuring that the materials used in a project meet the specifications, the supplier or the purchaser?

Paradyne Computers

20   Choose an engineering code of ethics and use it to analyze this case. Were the engineers and managers of Paradyne operating ethically?

21   In preparing their bid, Paradyne wrote in the present tense, as if the computer they proposed currently existed, rather than in the future tense, which would have indicated that the product was still under development. Paradyne claimed that the use of the present tense in its bid (which led SSA to believe that the P8400 actually existed) was acceptable, since it is common business practice to advertise products under development this way. Was this a new product announcement with a specified availability date? Is there a distinction between a response to a bid and company advertising? Is it acceptable to respond to a bid with a planned system if there is no indication when that system is expected to be available?

22   Paradyne also claimed that it was acting as a system integrator (which was allowed by the RFP), using components from other manufacturers to form the Paradyne system. These other components were mostly off the shelf, but they had never been integrated into a system before. Does this meet the SSA requirement for an existing system?

23   Once the Paradyne machine failed the initial test, should the requirements have been relaxed to help the machine qualify? If the requirements were going to be modified, should the bidding process have been reopened to the other bidders and others who might now be able to bid? Should bidding be reopened even if it causes a delay in delivery, increased work for the SSA, etc.?

24   Was it acceptable for Paradyne to submit another manufacturer's system for testing with a Paradyne label on it?

25   Was it acceptable to represent a proposed system as existing, if indeed that is what Paradyne did?

26   Is it ethical for a former SSA employee to take a job negotiating contracts with the SSA for a private company? Did this relationship give Paradyne an unfair advantage over its competition?

Codes of Ethics of Professional Engineering Societies

THE INSTITUTE OF ELECTRICAL AND ELECTRONICS ENGINEERS, INC.* (IEEE)

We, the members of the IEEE, in recognition of the importance of our technologies affecting the quality of life throughout the world, and in accepting a personal obligation to our profession, its members and the communities we serve, do hereby commit ourselves to the highest ethical and professional conduct and agree:

1. to accept responsibility in making decisions consistent with the safety, health and welfare of the public, and to disclose promptly factors that might endanger the public or the environment;
2. to avoid real or perceived conflicts of interest whenever possible, and to disclose them to affected parties when they do exist;
3. to be honest and realistic in stating claims or estimates based on available data;
4. to reject bribery in all its forms;
5. to improve the understanding of technology, its appropriate application, and potential consequences;
6. to maintain and improve our technical competence and to undertake technological tasks for others only if qualified by training or experience, or after full disclosure of pertinent limitations;
7. to seek, accept, and offer honest criticism of technical work, to acknowledge and correct errors, and to credit properly the contributions of others;
8. to treat fairly all persons regardless of such factors as race, religion, gender, disability, age, or national origin;
9. to avoid injuring others, their property, reputation, or employment by false or malicious action;
10. to assist colleagues and co-workers in their professional development and to support them in following this code of ethics.

Approved by the IEEE Board of Directors, February 2006

*Code of Ethics (© 2006 IEEE. Reprinted with permission.)

NATIONAL SOCIETY OF PROFESSIONAL ENGINEERS (NSPE) CODE OF ETHICS FOR ENGINEERS

Preamble

Engineering is an important and learned profession. As members of this profession, engineers are expected to exhibit the highest standards of honesty and integrity. Engineering has a direct and vital impact on the quality of life for all people. Accordingly, the services provided by engineers require honesty, impartiality, fairness and equity, and must be dedicated to the protection of the public health, safety, and welfare. Engineers must perform under a standard of professional behavior that requires adherence to the highest principles of ethical conduct.

I. Fundamental Canons

Engineers, in the fulfillment of their professional duties, shall:

1. Hold paramount the safety, health, and welfare of the public.
2. Perform services only in areas of their competence.
3. Issue public statements only in an objective and truthful manner.
4. Act for each employer or client as faithful agents or trustees.
5. Avoid deceptive acts.
6. Conduct themselves honorably, responsibly, ethically, and lawfully so as to enhance the honor, reputation, and usefulness of the profession.

II. Rules of Practice

1. Engineers shall hold paramount the safety, health, and welfare of the public.

   a. If engineers' judgment is overruled under circumstances that endanger life or property, they shall notify their employer or client and such other authority as may be appropriate.

   b. Engineers shall approve only those engineering documents that are in conformity with applicable standards.

   c. Engineers shall not reveal facts, data or information without the prior consent of the client or employer except as authorized or required by law or this Code.

   d. Engineers shall not permit the use of their name or associate in business ventures with any person or firm that they believe are engaged in fraudulent or dishonest enterprise.

   e. Engineers having knowledge of any alleged violation of this Code shall report thereon to appropriate professional bodies and, when relevant, also to public authorities, and cooperate with the proper authorities in furnishing such information or assistance as may be required.

2. Engineers shall perform services only in the areas of their competence.

   a. Engineers shall undertake assignments only when qualified by education or experience in the specific technical fields involved.

   b. Engineers shall not affix their signatures to any plans or documents dealing with subject matter in which they lack competence, nor to any plan or document not prepared under their direction and control.

   c. Engineers may accept assignments and assume responsibility for coordination of an entire project and sign and seal the engineering documents for the entire project, provided that each technical segment is signed and sealed only by the qualified engineers who prepared the segment.

3. Engineers shall issue public statements only in an objective and truthful manner.

   a. Engineers shall be objective and truthful in professional reports, statements, or testimony. They shall include all relevant and pertinent information in such reports, statements, or testimony, which should bear the date indicating when it was current.

   b. Engineers may express publicly technical opinions that are founded upon knowledge of the facts and competence in the subject matter.

   c. Engineers shall issue no statements, criticisms, or arguments on technical matters that are inspired or paid for by interested parties, unless they have prefaced their comments by explicitly identifying the interested parties on whose behalf they are speaking, and by revealing the existence of any interest the engineers may have in the matters.

4. Engineers shall act for each employer or client as faithful agents or trustees.

   a. Engineers shall disclose all known or potential conflicts of interest that could influence or appear to influence their judgment or the quality of their services.

   b. Engineers shall not accept compensation, financial or otherwise, from more than one party for services on the same project, or for services pertaining to the same project, unless the circumstances are fully disclosed and agreed to by all interested parties.

   c. Engineers shall not solicit or accept financial or other valuable consideration, directly or indirectly, from outside agents in connection with the work for which they are responsible.

   d. Engineers in public service as members, advisors, or employees of a governmental or quasi-governmental body or department shall not participate in decisions with respect to services solicited or provided by them or their organizations in private or public engineering practice.

   e. Engineers shall not solicit or accept a contract from a governmental body on which a principal or officer of their organization serves as a member.

5. Engineers shall avoid deceptive acts.

   a. Engineers shall not falsify their qualifications or permit misrepresentation of their or their associates' qualifications. They shall not misrepresent or exaggerate their responsibility in or for the subject matter of prior assignments. Brochures or other presentations incident to the solicitation of employment shall not misrepresent pertinent facts concerning employers, employees, associates, joint venturers, or past accomplishments.

   b. Engineers shall not offer, give, solicit or receive, either directly or indirectly, any contribution to influence the award of a contract by public authority, or which may be reasonably construed by the public as having the effect of intent to influencing the awarding of a contract. They shall not offer any gift or other valuable consideration in order to secure work. They shall not pay a commission, percentage, or brokerage fee in order to secure work, except to a bona fide employee or bona fide established commercial or marketing agencies retained by them.

III. Professional Obligations

1. Engineers shall be guided in all their relations by the highest standards of honesty and integrity.

   a. Engineers shall acknowledge their errors and shall not distort or alter the facts.

   b. Engineers shall advise their clients or employers when they believe a project will not be successful.

   c. Engineers shall not accept outside employment to the detriment of their regular work or interest. Before accepting any outside engineering employment they will notify their employers.

   d. Engineers shall not attempt to attract an engineer from another employer by false or misleading pretenses.

   e. Engineers shall not actively participate in strikes, picket lines, or other collective coercive action.

   f. Engineers shall not promote their own interest at the expense of the dignity and integrity of the profession.

2. Engineers shall at all times strive to serve the public interest.

   a. Engineers shall seek opportunities to participate in civic affairs; career guidance for youths; and work for the advancement of the safety, health and well-being of their community.

   b. Engineers shall not complete, sign, or seal plans and/or specifications that are not in conformity with applicable engineering standards. If the client or employer insists on such unprofessional conduct, they shall notify the proper authorities and withdraw from further service on the project.

   c. Engineers shall endeavor to extend public knowledge and appreciation of engineering and its achievements.

3. Engineers shall avoid all conduct or practice that deceives the public.

   a. Engineers shall avoid the use of statements containing a material misrepresentation of fact or omitting a material fact.

   b. Consistent with the foregoing, Engineers may advertise for recruitment of personnel.

   c. Consistent with the foregoing, Engineers may prepare articles for the lay or technical press, but such articles shall not imply credit to the author for work performed by others.

4. Engineers shall not disclose, without consent, confidential information concerning the business affairs or technical processes of any present or former client or employer, or public body on which they serve.

   a. Engineers shall not, without the consent of all interested parties, promote or arrange for new employment or practice in connection with a specific project for which the Engineer has gained particular and specialized knowledge.

   b. Engineers shall not, without the consent of all interested parties, participate in or represent an adversary interest in connection with a specific project or proceeding in which the Engineer has gained particular specialized knowledge on behalf of a former client or employer.

5. Engineers shall not be influenced in their professional duties by conflicting interests.

   a. Engineers shall not accept financial or other considerations, including free engineering designs, from material or equipment suppliers for specifying their product.
   b. Engineers shall not accept commissions or allowances, directly or indirectly, from contractors or other parties dealing with clients or employers of the Engineer in connection with work for which the Engineer is responsible.

6. Engineers shall not attempt to obtain employment or advancement or professional engagements by untruthfully criticizing other engineers, or by other improper or questionable methods.

   a. Engineers shall not request, propose, or accept a commission on a contingent basis under circumstances in which their judgment may be compromised.
   b. Engineers in salaried positions shall accept part-time engineering work only to the extent consistent with policies of the employer and in accordance with ethical considerations.
   c. Engineers shall not, without consent, use equipment, supplies, laboratory, or office facilities of an employer to carry on outside private practice.

7. Engineers shall not attempt to injure, maliciously or falsely, directly or indirectly, the professional reputation, prospects, practice, or employment of other engineers. Engineers who believe others are guilty of unethical or illegal practice shall present such information to the proper authority for action.

   a. Engineers in private practice shall not review the work of another engineer for the same client, except with the knowledge of such engineer, or unless the connection of such engineer with the work has been terminated.
   b. Engineers in governmental, industrial, or educational employ are entitled to review and evaluate the work of other engineers when so required by their employment duties.
   c. Engineers in sales or industrial employ are entitled to make engineering comparisons of represented products with products of other suppliers.

8. Engineers shall accept personal responsibility for their professional activities provided, however, that Engineers may seek indemnification for services arising out of their practice for other than gross negligence, where the Engineer's interests cannot otherwise be protected.

   a. Engineers shall conform with state registration laws in the practice of engineering.
   b. Engineers shall not use association with a nonengineer, a corporation, or partnership as a "cloak" for unethical acts.

9. Engineers shall give credit for engineering work to those to whom credit is due, and will recognize the proprietary interests of others.

   a. Engineers shall, whenever possible, name the person or persons who may be individually responsible for designs, inventions, writings, or other accomplishments.

b. Engineers using designs supplied by a client recognize that the designs remain the property of the client and may not be duplicated by the Engineer for others without express permission.

c. Engineers, before undertaking work for others in connection with which the Engineer may make improvements, plans, designs, inventions, or other records that may justify copyrights or patents, should enter into a positive agreement regarding ownership.

d. Engineers' designs, data, records, and notes referring exclusively to an employer's work are the employer's property. Employer should indemnify the Engineer for use of the information for any purpose other than the original purpose.

As Revised July 1996

"By order of the United States District Court for the District of Columbia, former Section 11(c) of the NSPE Code of Ethics prohibiting competitive bidding, and all policy statements, opinions, rulings or other guidelines interpreting its scope, have been rescinded as unlawfully interfering with the legal right of engineers, protected under the antitrust laws, to provide price information to prospective clients; accordingly, nothing contained in the NSPE Code of Ethics, policy statements, opinions, rulings or other guidelines prohibits the submission of price quotations or competitive bids for engineering services at any time or in any amount."

Statement by NSPE Executive Committee

In order to correct misunderstandings which have been indicated in some instances since the issuance of the Supreme Court decision and the entry of the Final Judgment, it is noted that in its decision of April 25, 1978, the Supreme Court of the United States declared: "The Sherman Act does not require competitive bidding."

It is further noted that as made clear in the Supreme Court decision:

1. Engineers and firms may individually refuse to bid for engineering services.
2. Clients are not required to seek bids for engineering services.
3. Federal, state, and local laws governing procedures to procure engineering services are not affected, and remain in full force and effect.
4. State societies and local chapters are free to actively and aggressively seek legislation for professional selection and negotiation procedures by public agencies.
5. State registration board rules of professional conduct, including rules prohibiting competitive bidding for engineering services, are not affected and remain in full force and effect. State registration boards with authority to adopt rules of professional conduct may adopt rules governing procedures to obtain engineering services.
6. As noted by the Supreme Court, "nothing in the judgment prevents NSPE and its members from attempting to influence governmental action ... "

NOTE: In regard to the question of application of the Code to corporations vis-à-vis real persons, business form or type should not negate nor influence conformance of individuals to the Code. The Code deals with professional services, which services must be performed by real persons. Real persons in turn establish and implement policies within business structures. The Code is clearly written to apply to the Engineer and items incumbent on members of NSPE to endeavor to live up to its provisions. This applies to all pertinent sections of the Code.

NOTE: There is also the NSPE Ethics Reference Guide, which fleshes out some of this information.

AMERICAN SOCIETY OF MECHANICAL ENGINEERS (ASME)

Ethics

ASME requires ethical practice by each of its members and has adopted the following Code of Ethics of Engineers as referenced in the ASME Constitution, Article C2.1.1.

Code of Ethics of Engineers

The Fundamental Principles

Engineers uphold and advance the integrity, honor and dignity of the engineering profession by:

I. Using their knowledge and skill for the enhancement of human welfare;
II. Being honest and impartial, and serving with fidelity the public, their employers and clients; and
III. Striving to increase the competence and prestige of the engineering profession.

The Fundamental Canons

1. Engineers shall hold paramount the safety, health, and welfare of the public in the performance of their professional duties.
2. Engineers shall perform services only in the areas of their competence.
3. Engineers shall continue their professional development throughout their careers and shall provide opportunities for the professional and ethical development of those engineers under their supervision.
4. Engineers shall act in professional matters for each employer or client as faithful agents or trustees, and shall avoid conflicts of interest or the appearance of conflicts of interest.
5. Engineers shall build their professional reputation on the merit of their services and shall not compete unfairly with others.
6. Engineers shall associate only with reputable persons or organizations.
7. Engineers shall issue public statements only in an objective and truthful manner.
8. Engineers shall consider environmental impact in the performance of their professional duties.
9. Engineers shall consider sustainable development in the performance of their professional duties.

    Adopted: March 7, 1976
    Revised: December 9, 1976
               December 7, 1979
               November 19, 1982
               June 15, 1984
               (editorial changes 7/84)
               June 16, 1988
               September 12, 1991
               September 11, 1994

June 10, 1998
September 21, 2002
September 13, 2003
(editorial changes 6/1/05)

The ASME Criteria for Interpretation of the Canons

The ASME criteria for interpretation of the Canons are guidelines and represent the objectives toward which members of the engineering profession should strive. They are principles which an engineer can reference in specific situations. In addition, they provide interpretive guidance to the ASME Board on Professional Practice and Ethics on the Code of Ethics of Engineers.

1. Engineers shall hold paramount the safety, health, and welfare of the public in the performance of their professional duties.

   a. Engineers shall recognize that the lives, safety, health, and welfare of the general public are dependent upon engineering judgments, decisions and practices incorporated into structures, machines, products, processes and devices.

   b. Engineers shall not approve or seal plans and/or specifications that are not of a design safe to the public health and welfare and in conformity with accepted engineering standards.

   c. Whenever the Engineers' professional judgments are overruled under circumstances where the safety, health, and welfare of the public are endangered, the Engineers shall inform their clients and/or employers of the possible consequences.

      (1) Engineers shall endeavor to provide data such as published standards, test codes, and quality control procedures that will enable the users to understand safe use during life expectancy associated with the designs, products, or systems for which they are responsible.

      (2) Engineers shall conduct reviews of the safety and reliability of the designs, products, or systems for which they are responsible before giving their approval to the plans for the design.

      (3) Whenever Engineers observe conditions, directly related to their employment, which they believe will endanger public safety or health, they shall inform the proper authority of the situation.

   d. If engineers have knowledge of or reason to believe that another person or firm may be in violation of any of the provisions of these Canons, they shall present such information to the proper authority in writing and shall cooperate with the proper authority in furnishing such further information or assistance as may be required.

2. Engineers shall perform services only in areas of their competence.

   a. Engineers shall undertake to perform engineering assignments only when qualified by education and/or experience in the specific technical field of engineering involved.

   b. Engineers may accept an assignment requiring education and/or experience outside of their own fields of competence, but their services shall be restricted to other phases of the project in which they are qualified. All other phases of such project shall be performed by qualified associates, consultants, or employees.

3. Engineers shall continue their professional development throughout their careers, and should provide opportunities for the professional and ethical development of those engineers under their supervision.

4. Engineers shall act in professional matters for each employer or client as faithful agents or trustees, and shall avoid conflicts of interest or the appearance of conflicts of interest.

   a. Engineers shall avoid all known conflicts of interest with their employers or clients and shall promptly inform their employers or clients of any business association, interests, or circumstances which could influence their judgment or the quality of their services.

   b. Engineers shall not undertake any assignments which would knowingly create a potential conflict of interest between themselves and their clients or their employers.

   c. Engineers shall not accept compensation, financial or otherwise, from more than one party for services on the same project, or for services pertaining to the same project, unless the circumstances are fully disclosed to, and agreed to, by all interested parties.

   d. Engineers shall not solicit or accept financial or other valuable considerations, for specifying products or material or equipment suppliers, without disclosure to their clients or employers.

   e. Engineers shall not solicit or accept gratuities, directly or indirectly, from contractors, their agents, or other parties dealing with their clients or employers in connection with work for which they are responsible. Where official public policy or employers' policies tolerate acceptance of modest gratuities or gifts, engineers shall avoid a conflict of interest by complying with appropriate policies and shall avoid the appearance of a conflict of interest.

   f. When in public service as members, advisors, or employees of a governmental body or department, Engineers shall not participate in considerations or actions with respect to services provided by them or their organization(s) in private or product engineering practice.

   g. Engineers shall not solicit an engineering contract from a governmental body or other entity on which a principal, officer, or employee of their organization serves as a member without disclosing their relationship and removing themselves from any activity of the body which concerns their organization.

   h. Engineers working on codes, standards, or governmental sanctioned rules and specifications shall exercise careful judgment in their determinations to ensure a balanced viewpoint, and avoid a conflict of interest.

   i. When, as a result of their studies, Engineers believe a project(s) will not be successful, they shall so advise their employer or client.

   j. Engineers shall treat information coming to them in the course of their assignments as confidential, and shall not use such information as a means of making personal profit if such action is adverse to the interests of their clients, their employers, or the public.

(1) They will not disclose confidential information concerning the business affairs or technical processes of any present or former employer or client or bidder under evaluation, without his consent, unless required by law or court order.

(2) They shall not reveal confidential information or finding of any commission or board of which they are members unless required by law or court order.

(3) Designs supplied to Engineers by clients shall not be duplicated by the Engineers for others without the express permission of the client(s).

k. Engineers shall act with fairness and justice to all parties when administering a construction (or other) contract.

l. Before undertaking work for others in which Engineers may make improvements, plans, designs, inventions, or other records which may justify seeking copyrights, patents, or proprietary rights, Engineers shall enter into positive agreements regarding the rights of respective parties.

m. Engineers shall admit their own errors when proven wrong and refrain from distorting or altering the facts to justify their mistakes or decisions.

n. Engineers shall not accept professional employment or assignments outside of their regular work without the knowledge of their employers.

o. Engineers shall not attempt to attract an employee from other employers or from the marketplace by false or misleading representations.

5. Engineers shall build their professional reputation on the merit of their services and shall not compete unfairly with others.

a. Engineers shall negotiate contracts for professional services on the basis of demonstrated competence and qualifications for the type of professional service required.

b. Engineers shall not request, propose, or accept professional commissions on a contingent basis if, under the circumstances, their professional judgments may be compromised.

c. Engineers shall not falsify or permit misrepresentation of their, or their associates', academic or professional qualification. They shall not misrepresent or exaggerate their degrees of responsibility in or for the subject matter of prior assignments. Brochures or other presentations used to solicit personal employment shall not misrepresent pertinent facts concerning employers, employees, associates, joint venturers, or their accomplishments.

d. Engineers shall prepare articles for the lay or technical press which are only factual. Technical Communications for publication (theses, articles, papers, reports, etc.), which are based on research involving more than one individual (including students and supervising faculty, industrial supervisor/researcher, or other co-workers) must recognize all significant contributors. Plagiarism, the act of substantially using another's ideas or written materials without due credit, is unethical. (See Appendix.)

e. Engineers shall not maliciously or falsely, directly or indirectly, injure the professional reputation, prospects, practice or employment of another engineer, nor shall they indiscriminately criticize another's work.

f. Engineers shall not use equipment, supplies, laboratory, or office facilities of their employers to carry on outside private practice without consent.

6. Engineers shall associate only with reputable persons or organizations.

   a. Engineers shall not knowingly associate with or permit the use of their names or firm names in business ventures by any person or firm which they know, or have reason to believe, are engaging in business or professional practices of a fraudulent or dishonest nature.

   b. Engineers shall not use association with nonengineers, corporations, or partnerships to disguise unethical acts.

7. Engineers shall issue public statements only in an objective and truthful manner.

   a. Engineers shall endeavor to extend public knowledge, and to prevent misunderstandings of the achievements of engineering.

   b. Engineers shall be completely objective and truthful in all professional reports, statements, or testimony. They shall include all relevant and pertinent information in such reports, statements, or testimony.

   c. Engineers, when serving as expert or technical witnesses before any court, commission, or other tribunal, shall express an engineering opinion only when it is founded on their adequate knowledge of the facts in issue, their background of technical competence in the subject matter, and their belief in the accuracy and propriety of their testimony.

   d. Engineers shall issue no statements, criticisms, or arguments on engineering matters which are inspired or paid for by an interested party, or parties, unless they preface their comments by identifying themselves, by disclosing the identities of the party or parties on whose behalf they are speaking, and by revealing the existence of any financial interest they may have in matters under discussion.

   e. Engineers shall be truthful in explaining their work and merit, and shall avoid any act tending to promote their own interest at the expense of the integrity and honor of the profession or another individual.

8. Engineers shall consider environmental impact in the performance of their professional duties.

   a. Engineers shall concern themselves with the impact of their plans and designs on the environment. When the impact is a clear threat to health or safety of the public, then the guidelines for this Canon revert to those of Canon 1.

9. Engineers shall consider sustainable development in the performance of their professional duties.

   a. Engineers shall consider development that meets the needs of the present without compromising the ability of future generations to meet their own needs. When the impact of the trade-off between economic, ecological, and social issues forms a clear threat to health or safety of the public, then the guidelines for this Canon revert to those of Canon 1.

10. Engineers accepting membership in The American Society of Mechanical Engineers by this action agree to abide by this Society Policy on Ethics and procedures for its implementation.

July 25, 2005

AMERICAN SOCIETY OF CIVIL ENGINEERS* (ASCE)

The Engineering Code of Ethics

Fundamental Principles

Engineers uphold and advance the integrity, honor, and dignity of the engineering profession by:
using their knowledge and skill for the enhancement of human welfare;
being honest and impartial and serving with fidelity the public, their employers, and clients;
striving to increase the competence and prestige of the engineering profession;
and supporting the professional and technical societies of their disciplines.

Fundamental Canons

Engineers shall hold paramount the safety, health, and welfare of the public in the performance of their professional duties.
Engineers shall perform services only in areas of their competence.
Engineers shall issue public statements only in an objective and truthful manner.
Engineers shall act in professional matters for each employer or client as faithful agents or trustees, and shall avoid conflicts of interest.
Engineers shall build their professional reputation on the merit of their services and shall not compete unfairly with others.
Engineers shall act in such a manner as to uphold and enhance the honor, integrity, and dignity of the engineering profession.
Engineers shall continue their professional development throughout their careers, and shall provide opportunities for the professional development of those engineers under their supervision.

AMERICAN INSTITUTE OF CHEMICAL ENGINEERS (AICHE)

AIChE Code of Ethics

American Institute of Chemical Engineers

Members of the American Institute of Chemical Engineers shall uphold and advance the integrity, honor, and dignity of the engineering profession by: being honest and impartial and serving with fidelity their employers, their clients, and the public; striving to increase the competence and prestige of the engineering profession; and using their knowledge and skill for the enhancement of human welfare. To achieve these goals, members shall:

- Hold paramount the safety, health, and welfare of the public and protect the environment in performance of their professional duties.
- Formally advise their employers or clients (and consider further disclosure, if warranted) if they perceive that a consequence of their duties will adversely affect the present or future health or safety of their colleagues or the public.
- Accept responsibility for their actions, seek and heed critical review of their work, and offer objective criticism of the work of others.

*Courtesy of ASCE

- Issue statements or present information only in an objective and truthful manner.
- Act in professional matters for each employer or client as faithful agents or trustees, avoiding conflicts of interest and never breaching confidentiality.
- Treat fairly and respectfully all colleagues and co-workers, recognizing their unique contributions and capabilities.
- Perform professional services only in areas of their competence.
- Build their professional reputations on the merits of their services.
- Continue their professional development throughout their careers, and provide opportunities for the professional development of those under their supervision.
- Never tolerate harassment.
- Conduct themselves in a fair, honorable, and respectful manner.

(Revised January 17, 2003)

12

Introduction to Technical Communications

1   INTRODUCTION

Some people think the term *technical communications* is a contradiction in terms. Technical information, they say, is just numbers. They may snicker that engineers are not always natural after-dinner speakers. Why spend your time on the presentation side of things when some engineers are more comfortable grinding out the numbers?

People with these attitudes are sadly misinformed. Engineering often results in complex answers that need to be communicated simply and effectively. The truth is that *engineering work has no impact unless the message is delivered successfully.*

Technical presentations also must "tell a story." The conclusions of the story, of course, must be supported by data and solid reasoning. In evaluating your own technical writing or technical presentations, it is always important to ask yourself, Has the audience understood my story?

The purpose of this chapter is to introduce you to the importance of technical communications (Sections 2 and 3) and present ground rules common to all technical communication (Sections 4 through 9). In Section 4, the important questions you should answer before you start writing your report or technical talk will be discussed. Some techniques for organizing the presentation material will be presented in Section 5. In Sections 6, 7, and 8, you will learn in detail the ways that data are presented, including the design and construction of tables and figures. Section 9 discusses creativity in technical presentations.

You will notice some new terminology in this chapter. The recipients of the presentation will be referred to simply as the "audience," since the recipients could be either *readers* of your technical document or *listeners* of your technical talk. The word "presentation" will include both written documents and technical talks.

SECTIONS

OBJECTIVES

After reading this chapter, you will be able to:

- explain why technical communication skills are important to engineers;
- list common misconceptions about technical communication;
- discuss how the presentation goals, the target audience, and the constraints shape technical communication;
- devise an outline for a technical presentation;
- use tables and figures to communicate technical information effectively.

2   ROLE OF TECHNICAL COMMUNICATION IN ENGINEERING

2.1   Technical Communication as a Professional Skill

Your interest in engineering may have been fueled by the important role of engineers in society and the challenges that engineers face every day. Take a moment to make a mental list of what engineers do.

PONDER THIS

What activities do engineers perform?

Key idea: Technical presentations must tell a story; always ask yourself whether the audience understood your story.

Your list may include activities such as designing, modeling, testing, building, and optimizing. While most engineers do at least one of these activities *some* of the time, all engineers communicate *all* the time. In a real sense, engineering is not engineering until you, the engineer, successfully communicate the results to someone else. Technical communication is not effective unless the audience understands the message you wish to deliver.

2.2   Technical Communication and Employment

Key idea: Strong technical presentation skills aid in obtaining a job and in advancing a career.

If you remain unconvinced of the importance of technical communication, consider a more practical reason to improve your communication skills. Engineering faculty frequently receive telephone calls requesting information about students (or former students) applying for jobs. Nearly every potential employer asks two questions: Can the person *write* effectively? Can he or she *speak* well? Potential employers ask these questions because they know that engineers spend a great deal of their time communicating. The result of a survey of graduates from the University at Buffalo's School of Engineering and Applied Sciences showed that respondents spent an average of *64% of their working hours* on written communication, oral presentations, and other oral discussions. To compete for employment opportunities, engineers must develop strong technical communication skills. Technical excellence is necessary (but not sufficient) to secure a good job in today's employment market.

Technical communication skills affect not only your ability to get a job, but also your ability to progress in your profession. In a survey cited by Paradis and Zimmerman (1997), over half of the research and development engineers and scientists polled (and 71% of the managers) knew of cases where technical communication skills had a serious impact on a person's career. Respondents to the University at Buffalo survey indicated that good technical communication skills can make the difference between receiving a raise and not receiving a raise. Good technical communication skills are prerequisites for success in your career.

3   MISCONCEPTIONS ABOUT TECHNICAL COMMUNICATIONS

Few areas of the engineering profession are more poorly understood or more underappreciated than technical communication. Common misconceptions are discussed in the next several sections.

3.1   Misconception #1: Technical Communication Is Inherently Boring

Key idea: Technical communication is a creative process.

Some people feel that engineers excel in dry facts and even drier numbers. How can an engineer possibly communicate creatively? The truth is that designing effective communication strategies is one of the most creative activities in engineering. Technical communication does not mean linking dull facts to form a sleep-inducing document or boring oral presentation. Today, engineers have many tools at their disposal for communicating ideas: everything from sketches on the back of a napkin to 3-D visualization techniques to Internet-based teleconferencing. Effectively communicating technical work is a challenging part of the optimization process that lies at the heart of engineering. Creativity in technical communication is discussed in more detail in Section 9.

Technical talks are *not* inherently boring.

3.2   Misconception #2: Engineering Communication Is Passive

Key idea: Technical communication is usually meant to be persuasive.

Many people think of technical communication as flat and one-sided. In this view, technical speakers and writers lay out a smorgasbord of facts that the audience records passively (as in a poorly designed lecture). In truth, much technical communication is both interactive and *persuasive*. Engineers often try to convince others of their point of view. Facts and figures rarely speak for themselves. They require thoughtful presentation to convince people of their worth.

3.3   Misconception #3: Technical Communication Is Best Left to Nonengineering Specialists

Key idea: Engineers can benefit from communication specialists, but the engineer must take responsibility for making sure the correct message is delivered.

In your career, you will benefit from working with many other professionals. Engineers often work collaboratively with communication specialists, such as technical writers and graphic designers. However, *you as the engineer are always responsible for making sure that the technical information is communicated clearly and concisely to the intended audience.* Remember, all your work (whether in a homework assignment or the design of a multimillion-dollar facility) is for naught if the intended audience does not understand your message. Taking control of the message is as important as taking control of the design calculations.

3.4   Misconception #4: Good Technical Communicators Are Born, Not Made

Key idea: All engineers can improve their technical communication skills.

It is true that not all of us will mesmerize° our audiences each time we stand before them or each time we put pen to paper. However, each of us can improve our speaking and writing skills *every time* we set out to communicate with our peers and others. Specific steps for honing your technical communication skills will be presented in Sections 4 through 9. Whatever level of comfort you have now with public speaking and technical writing, *know that you can improve your communication skills throughout this semester, throughout your university days, and throughout your career.*

°The word "mesmerize" comes from the Austrian-born physician Friedrich Anton Mesmer (1734–1815), who popularized the idea that doctors could induce a hypnotic state by manipulating a force he called "animal magnetism."

4 CRITICAL FIRST STEPS

Before you write a single word of a technical presentation, three elements must be identified clearly: the goals of the presentation, the target audience, and the constraints on the presentation. Each of these elements will be discussed in more detail in this section.

4.1 Presentation Goals

Key idea: Before preparing a technical presentation, write down the goals of the presentation.

One of the most important activities in the design of any technical talk or document is the identification of the *presentation goals*. It is absolutely critical to know what you are trying to accomplish in a presentation. The presentation will fail unless its goals are identified. Why? First, you cannot decide what information should be presented (or how to present it) unless you have described the objectives thoughtfully. Second, you need to know the goals to evaluate whether or not you have communicated the ideas successfully. In fact, *every* engineering project requires objectives so that the success of the project can be determined at its conclusion.

You should write out the presentation goals. For example, you might write, "The goal of the lab write-up is to tell the professor about the experimental methods employed, the results obtained, and the answers to the three discussion questions." This goal allows you to decide what should go in the lab write-up and how the material should be prioritized. Also, you now have a tool to judge whether your write-up was successful. You could compare the completed lab report with the goal to see if you met the goal. Remember, *a goal not written down is just a dream.*

4.2 Target Audience

target audience: the intended recipients of the information to be presented

The presentation goal should identify the ***target audience***. The target audience consists of the intended recipients of the information you are presenting.

PONDER THIS

What is the target audience of this text?

Although professors order the text and professionals may read it, the target audience of this text is freshman engineering students.

As with presentation goals, identification of the target audience is critical to the success of your presentation. In your career, you will give oral and written presentations to many audiences, including colleagues (i.e., fellow engineers), managers, elected officials, students, and the general public. You must keep the background and technical sophistication of the target audience in mind when developing your presentation material. For example, you would not use the same approaches to communicate a bridge design to a city council as you would to communicate the same ideas to a professional engineering society.

Key idea: Identify the target audience (and their technical sophistication, interests, and backgrounds) before preparing a technical presentation.

The interests and backgrounds of the audience are as important as their technical sophistication. Each audience member will interpret the presentation through his or her own point of view. To engage the audience fully, you must know the backgrounds of its members. As an example, consider the choices available to an engineer presenting an idea for a new computer design. For an audience of managers and corporate executives, she may wish to emphasize the low cost and high profit margin of the new personal computer. For fellow engineers, she would likely focus on the technical specifications and performance data. Subtle changes often can make the presentation match the interests and background of the audience more closely.

4.3 Constraints

Identification of *constraints* on the presentation also is important. Engineering, like life, is a constrained optimization problem. Similarly, technical presentations almost always are

Know your audience

Key idea: Before preparing a technical presentation, quantify the constraints on the presentation (i.e., length limits, your time, and other resource limitations).

constrained. Common constraints are *presentation length* (page limits for written documents or time limits on oral presentations) and *resource limitations* (e.g., your time or money for photographs or specialized graphics). It is very important to heed the presentation length constraints. In oral presentations, going well over or under the allotted time limit is rude and unprofessional. With technical documents, many engineering proposals (and term papers) have gone unread because they exceeded the imposed page limit.

The resources required for technical presentations cannot be ignored. As a student, you know you must allocate time for *writing* a term paper as well as time for reading about the term paper topic. Similarly, practicing engineers learn to budget time for report preparation. Other resources required to produce a high-quality technical document (or oral presentation) include money for personnel, graphics creation, printing, reproduction, and distribution.

Common constraints on technical communication: time and money

5   ORGANIZATION

Once you have identified the goals, target audience, and constraints, you can begin to write the presentation. Technical documents and talks can be made or broken on their degree of organization. In a well-organized presentation, the audience always knows where in the presentation they are and where they are going. There are two keys to creating an effectively organized presentation: *structuring the material* and *showing your structure* to the audience.

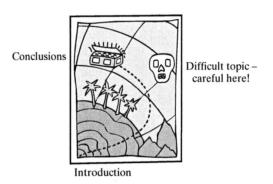

Organization is the map that guides your audience through the presentation.

5.1   Outlines

outline: a list of the major headings and subheadings in the presentation, showing the order of the main ideas and showing the secondary topics supporting the main ideas

The primary tool used to structure a presentation is the *outline*. An outline is a structured (or hierarchical) list showing the skeleton of the presentation. An example is shown in Example 1.

The purpose of the outline is to divide the presentation into manageable pieces. An outline shows three elements of the presentation:

- The main ideas (listed in the outline as major headings)
- The order of the main ideas
- The secondary topics (subheadings) that support and flesh out the main ideas

The main ideas, of course, depend on the goal of the presentation and the audience.

EXAMPLE 1 OUTLINE

Write an outline for a technical presentation on computer-aided manufacturing (CAM) in the production of aircraft.

SOLUTION

An example outline, with the parts of the outline labeled, is as follows:

Computer-Aided Manufacturing (CAM) in Aircraft Production

    I.   Introduction [major heading]
    II.   Background
          A.   History [subheading]
          B.   Contemporary examples
          C.   Current problems

III.   Use of CAM in Aircraft Production

    A.   CAM principles

    B.   Applications

        1.   potential barriers [subheading]

        2.   examples

    C.   Future trends

IV.   Conclusions

Key idea: To organize a presentation, structure the material using an outline and show the structure to your audience.

The outline is a wonderful tool for organizing a presentation. It shows at a glance the relationships between parts of the document or talk. The outline helps you to see if the presentation is balanced; that is, whether the level of detail in a certain part of the presentation corresponds to the importance of that part in achieving your goals. The outline also helps determine the needs for more data or more presentation tools (i.e., more tables and figures). An outline can be changed easily as the presentation evolves. In fact, as the outline is annotated (that is, as more levels of subheadings are added), the document or oral presentation will nearly write itself.

signposting: indicators used to show the audience where they are in the presentation

5.2   Signposting

Organizing a presentation is only half the battle. You also must *let the audience know* that you are well organized. Showing the audience that you are organized is called **signposting**. An example of signposting is the headings used in this text. The consistency of the headings tells you where you are in the text:

Chapter title: 32 point Futura font, with the initial letters capitalized

Example: # Introduction to...

Section titles: 11-point Copperplate30ab font, all caps

Example: **5   ORGANIZATION**

Subsection titles: 11-point Futura Book font, initial letters capitalized

Example: **5.2   Signposting**

6   USING TABLES AND FIGURES TO PRESENT DATA

Nearly every technical presentation you develop will contain data. The number of ways of presenting quantitative information is limited only by your imagination. However, some data presentation tools are more appropriate in a given situation than others.

6.1   Use of Tables and Figures

The two main ways to present numbers are *tables* and *figures*. Tables are used when the *actual values are important*. For example, a table would be an excellent way to show the estimated construction, operation, and maintenance costs for three polymer extruder designs. In this case, the exact costs are important and the audience wants to see the numbers.

Key idea: Use tables when actual values are important; use figures to show trends in the data.

On the other hand, figures are used to *show trends in the data*: that is, to show the relationships between variables. For example, suppose you collect data on the movement of an artificial limb in response to stimuli of varying voltage. A figure would be an appropriate way to show the trend in the dependent variable (here, the limb movement) as a function of the independent variable (here, the applied voltage).

6.2   Common Characteristics of Tables and Figures

While tables and figures are very different, they share several features. First, every table and figure in a technical document must have a number. Many numbering schemes are possible (e.g., "Table 1" or "Figure 4.2" or "Table II" or "Figure C"), but table and figure numbers are essential in technical writing. Why number your tables and figures? A number allows the figure or table to be *referred to* from the text. For example, in the text, you may write

> In Figure 2.3, the average wait time at the stoplight is plotted against the daily pedestrian traffic.

> Remember, *do not include a table or figure in a technical document that is not referred to by number in the text.*

Second, every table and figure in a technical document must have a title. Titles are needed to give the audience a short description of the content of the table or figure. Titles should be concise and descriptive. They need not be complete sentences. Examples of table and figure titles are listed in Table 1. The numbers and titles appear together either at the top or bottom of the table or figure. Commonly (but not universally), table titles are placed at the *top* of tables and figure titles are placed at the *bottom* of figures. (Note that Table 1 has a number and title located together at the top of the table. Also, Table 1 was referred to in the text, so you knew when to look at it.)*

Third, tables and figures must be *interpreted*. This means that you should discuss the table or figure in the text. To continue the example at the beginning of Section 6.2, you may write

> In Figure 2.3, the average wait time at the stoplight is plotted against the daily pedestrian traffic. Note that the average wait time increases from baseline only when the pedestrian traffic exceeds 150 people per day.

Many inexperienced technical writers make the mistake of simply throwing the data at the audience rather than *presenting* the data. They write

> The data from the first study are shown in Figure 2.3. A second study was conducted in May 2005.

You included the table or figure for a reason. To satisfy that reason (and help you achieve your presentation goals), you need to guide the audience through the interpretation of the data in your tables and figures.

Fourth, units must be listed for all data in tables and figures. In tables, units usually accompany the column or row headings. In figures, the axes must be labeled with units shown. You may want to take a moment and look through this text for examples of tables and figures with units in the headings or axis labels.

TABLE 1   Examples of Poor and Improved Table and Figure Titles

Poor Title	Problems with Poor Title	Improved Title
Table 2: Experimental Data	too vague: what data will the table contain?	Table 2: Ergonomic Data for Three Automobile Seat Designs
Figure 4.2: Problems with Acid Rain	insufficient detail: figure titles usually list the dependent and independent variables	Figure 4.2: Effects of pH on the Survivorship of Brown Trout in Lakes Receiving Acid Rain
Figure A.32: Current vs Voltage	insufficient detail: lists *only* the dependent and independent variables without putting the information in context	Figure A.32: Current–Voltage Curves for Four Electrode Configurations

*The astute reader will notice that some pictures in this text have no title and are not referred to in the text. An example is the cartoon labeled "Know your audience" in Section 4. The use of such pictures for illustrative purposes is common in textbooks and reflects the fact that the target audience of the text is students.

7 TABLES

Key idea: In tables, list the independent variables in the leftmost columns.

As stated previously, tables are used to present data when the actual values are important. Tables should be limited to the minimum number of columns needed to show the relevant data. In general, independent variables are listed in the first or leftmost columns, with dependent variables listed in the columns to the right.

With today's software, it is easy to create tables with myriad types of lines, shadings, colors, and font styles. However, these devices should be used sparingly and consistently. Each table has a goal; "bells and whistles" should be used only to make your point clearer.

An example table is given in Table 2.

PONDER THIS

Critique Table 2.

Table 2 is well constructed. Note that it is numbered and has a descriptive title. The independent variable (reinforcing bar type) is listed first. Units are given for all data (i.e., for every column). Lines are used minimally and mainly serve to separate the table from the surrounding text.

To demonstrate the importance of the order of the columns, examine Table 3. Table 3 contains the same data as Table 2, but the column order has been changed. Note how difficult it is to interpret Table 3. Even though the most important information probably is the weight, placing a dependent variable first does not communicate the information very effectively.

Table 4 demonstrates the potential for distractions in table design. The use of many fonts, lines, and types of shading adds little to the message and can be distracting.

TABLE 2 Characteristics of Standard Steel Reinforcing Bars

[*Caution:* Table may contain errors! See text for discussion.]

Type	Diameter (in)	Weight (lb/ft)
#2	0.250	0.167
#3	0.375	0.376
#4	0.500	0.668
#5	0.625	1.043
#6	0.750	1.502

TABLE 3 Characteristics of Standard Steel Reinforcing Bars

[*Caution:* Table may contain errors! See text for discussion.]

Weight (lb/ft)	Type	Diameter (in)
0.167	#2	0.250
0.376	#3	0.375
0.668	#4	0.500
1.043	#5	0.625
1.502	#6	0.750

TABLE 4 Characteristics of Standard Steel Reinforcing Bars

[*Caution*: Table may contain errors! See text for discussion.]

Type	Diameter (in.)	Weight (lb/ft)
#2	0.250	0.167
#3	0.375	0.376
#4	0.500	0.668
#5	0.625	1.043
#6	0.750	1.502

8   FIGURES

Key idea: Use scatter (*x–y*) plots when the independent variable is continuous.

scatter (x–y) plot: a type of plot using symbols or lines that is employed when the independent variable is continuous

Key idea: In general, use symbols for data and lines for calculated values (i.e., model output).

Recall that figures are used when the relationships between variables are important. There are three common types of figures used in technical presentations: scatter (or *x–y*) plots, bar charts, and pie charts.

8.1   Scatter Plots

The **scatter plot** (or **x–y plot**) is the most common type of graph in technical work. It is used when the *independent variable is continuous*; that is, when the independent variable could take any value. Examples of continuous variables are time, flow, and voltage. In the scatter plot, the independent variable is plotted on the *x*-axis (also called the *abscissa*) and the dependent variable is plotted on the *y*-axis (also called the *ordinate*). In general, symbols are used for data and lines are used for calculated values (i.e., for model fits or model predictions). An example of a scatter plot is shown in Figure 1.

PONDER THIS

Critique Figure 1.

In Figure 1, the independent variable (vapor pressure) is continuous. Thus, a scatter plot is appropriate. Note the important elements: figure title (here, at the bottom of the figure), axis titles with units, tick marks (small lines) near axis labels, and symbols that represent data. If more than one dependent variable were plotted, a legend would

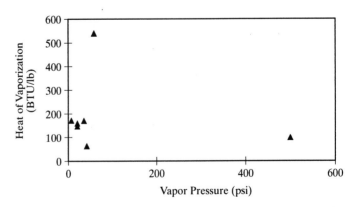

Figure 1.   Heat of Vaporization of Some Common Refrigerants [*Caution*: Figure may contain errors! See text for discussion.]

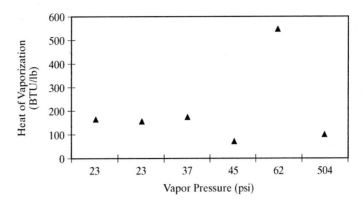

Figure 2.   Heat of Vaporization of Some Common Refrigerants [*Caution*: Figure may contain errors! See text for discussion.]

Key idea: Use the line chart type carefully in technical presentations (or, better yet, avoid it completely).

be necessary. Note that *a legend is not necessary if only one dependent variable is plotted*. (Legends are discussed with bar charts in Section 8.2.)

One final note on scatter plots. Most common graphing programs (including Microsoft Word, Microsoft Excel, Corel WordPerfect, and Corel QuattroPro) have a figure type (also called a *chart type*) called "line." With the line chart type, the *x* data points are spaced evenly, *regardless of their values*. The data in Figure 1 are replotted as a line chart in Figure 2. Notice that the relationship between heat of vaporization and vapor pressure appears to be distorted in the line chart. There are almost no cases where the line type is the *best* way to present technical data. It is recommended that *you avoid the line chart type completely*.

8.2   Bar Charts

bar chart: a type of plot using bars that is employed when the independent variable is not continuous

Key idea: Use bar charts when the independent variable is not continuous.

legend: a listing of the property represented by each symbol, bar, or line

Key idea: In figures, select the axis ranges to encompass all the data without distorting the relative values.

Bar charts are used when the independent variable is discrete (i.e., not continuous). Discontinuous independent variables are common in engineering. For example, you may wish to show how the properties of magnets vary with material type or how energy efficiency varies with industry category. The type of material or category of industry is a discrete variable and the use of a bar chart is appropriate.

An example of a bar chart° is given in Figure 3. Note the descriptive title, inclusion of units, and tick marks on the *y*-axis. Tick marks generally are not used on the *x*-axis in bar charts with vertical bars, since the tick marks would interfere with the bars. Note also in Figure 3 that two *y*-axes are used. Multiple *y*-axes are useful when the independent variables have different units or vastly different scales.

In Figure 3, two variables are plotted; therefore, a legend is required. A *legend* tells the audience the meaning of each symbol, bar, or line. In this case, the legend tells you that the white bar represents the resistivity and the black bar represents tensile strength.

In both scatter and bar charts, you must select the ranges of the axes carefully. Clearly, the ranges must be selected to encompass all data. In addition, it is generally a good idea to start the *y*-axis at zero.[†] Why? Starting at zero gives the audience a better view of the relative values of your data. In Figure 3, for example, it is obvious that the tensile strength of silver is about twice that of gold. If the data are replotted using smaller ranges for the *y*-axes, a skewed view of the relative resistivities and tensile strengths is created (see Figure 4). For example, the tensile strength of silver appears to be about five times that of gold in this figure.

°The common name for the plot in Figure 3 is a bar chart. Some software packages call it a *column chart* if the bars are vertical and a *bar chart* if the bars are horizontal.
[†]Do not, of course, start the *y*-axis at zero if you have negative *y* values. Also, avoid starting the *y*-axis at zero if the *y* values cluster around a large value.

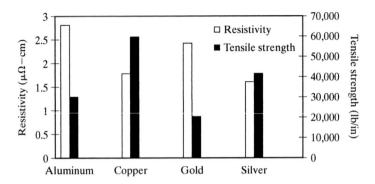

Figure 3. Physical Properties of Conductors

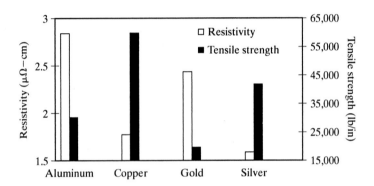

Figure 4.   Physical Properties of Conductors [*Caution*: Figure may contain errors! See text for discussion.]

Key idea: Do not accept the default table or figure produced by the software without questioning whether it meets your objectives.

This lesson can be extrapolated. In general, *do not let the software pick the look of your tables and figures.* Always look critically at the default table or figure produced by the software package. Use your judgment: edit tables and figures to best meet your presentation goals.

pie chart: a type of plot using pie slices that is employed to show the relative contributions of several factors to a whole

8.3   Pie Charts

Pie charts are used to show the relative contributions of several factors to a whole. In most cases, pie charts are used to show percentages. Thus, pie charts have no independent variable. Although pie charts are not used very frequently in engineering, they can show the relative importance of discrete factors very effectively.

Key idea: Use pie charts to show relative contributions.

An example of a 3-D pie chart is shown in Figure 5. The slices of the pie may be defined with a legend or labels.

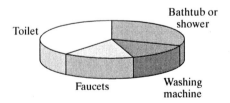

Figure 5.   Water Use in the Home

An example of how the design of a figure may influence engineering decision making is shown in the *Focus on Figures: Of Plots and Space Shuttles*.

The explosion of the Space Shuttle *Challenger* on the cold morning of January 28, 1986, rocked the world. Subsequent investigation into the disaster pointed to the likely cause: hot gases from fuel combustion bypassed two seals, leading to the destruction of the booster segment and the loss of the lives of all seven astronauts. The booster segments were sealed with O-rings made out of a rubber-like material called Viton®. The two O-rings (primary and secondary) protected the segments from the combustion gases. The primary O-ring was closest to the fuel.

The *Challenger* disaster is often discussed as an example of engineering ethics. Although some facts are in dispute, it is clear that some of the engineers involved vigorously argued that the launch should be aborted. Why? The temperature at launch was forecasted to be much lower than previously experienced. Like typical rubber, the flexibility of Viton (and thus its ability to seal against the enormous pressures at launch) is dependent on temperature.

It has been argued (Tufte, 1993) that the available data, if plotted in the most meaningful way, would have provided overwhelming evidence for aborting the launch. According to this argument, the engineers were remiss in not presenting the data in the most powerful way. In other words, technical communication problems may have contributed to the launch and loss of *Challenger*. This point of view has been strongly challenged by the engineers involved (Robison et al., 2002). The arguments and counterarguments are complex and cannot be summarized in this short section. The interested reader is urged to read the cited papers. The purpose here is to show how data presentation can lead and mislead the engineer.

To appreciate the importance of how the data were plotted, it is necessary to understand what data were available at the time. There are several indicators of O-ring damage. One indicator is soot marks made by blackened grease as it blows through the primary O-ring. Soot is a very bad sign, indicating that the primary O-ring has been breached and the shuttle health depends only on the remaining secondary O-ring. The size of the soot marks (for shuttle launches with measurable

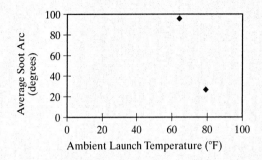

Figure 6. Influence of Temperature on Soot Including Only Data Where Soot Was Observed

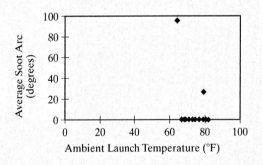

Figure 7. Influence of Temperature on Soot Including All Available Data

soot) are shown as a function of ambient temperature at launch in Figure 6. Based on these data, would you recommend launching at the launch temperature of 26°F on January 28, 1986?

Based on the data plotted in Figure 6, you *might* conclude that a launch at 26°F is inadvisable. Although there *appears* to be a trend that soot area increases with decreasing temperature, two data points are hardly enough to justify a quantitative relationship. The picture becomes even cloudier when all available data are included (Figure 7). Note that no soot was observed at many launch temperatures between the values shown in Figure 6. Does the trend appear weaker now?

Results of the testing of isolated rockets revealed no soot at O-ring temperatures between 47 and 50°F (see Figure 8). How would the rocket test data influence your decision to launch?

History proved that the advice not to launch was justified. It is impossible to know with certainty whether a plot such as Figure 7 or Figure 8 would have enhanced the argument of the engineers. Rather than a clear-cut lesson in technical communications, we are left with a tragedy.

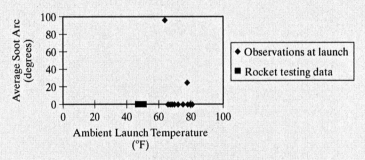

Figure 8.   Influence of Temperature on Soot Including All Available Data and Rocket Testing Results

9   CREATIVITY IN TECHNICAL PRESENTATIONS

This chapter has emphasized the need for structure in technical presentations and has introduced numerous rules. However, please do not forget that technical communication is a creative process. Much of the creativity in technical presentations is focused on two areas: conciseness and thinking visually.

9.1   Creative Conciseness

When in doubt, favor conciseness over verbosity in technical presentations. Simply filling the page or presentation time with words is always obvious and insulting to the audience. In addition, calculations, data, or analysis that are necessary, but secondary to the main points being made, can be very distracting. In a written document, they may be best placed in an appendix.

Finding the right degree of conciseness is not easy. Technical presentations, like homemade bread, are hard to digest if they are too dense. To use another food analogy: wine can be very pleasant. It can be distilled into a complex brandy. Overdistill and you end up with ethanol: harsh and undrinkable. Often a dense presentation can be made more palatable by building in repetition and explanatory text.

The idea of conciseness also applies to figures. Consider the three plots of the same data in Figure 9. The top panel is a typical figure produced by the built-in plotting software of a word processing program.

PONDER THIS   **What unnecessary elements do you see in the top panel of Figure 9?**

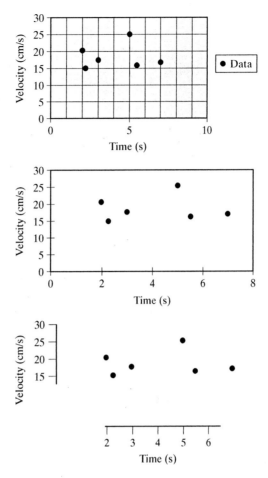

Figure 9.   Example of Conciseness in Figures [*Caution*: Figure may contain errors! See text for discussion.]

The extraneous graphical elements in the top panel of Figure 9 include background color, grid lines, and legend. (No legend is needed, since there is only one set of symbols.) A clearer presentation (middle panel of Figure 9) is produced by eliminating the extraneous elements. In the bottom panel of Figure 9, nearly all extraneous lines have been removed. For most engineers, the bottom panel is on the verge of being too abstract: perhaps too much information has been removed. Figure 9 shows that some redundancy is needed to best communicate the information.

9.2   Thinking Visually

Another important creative element in technical presentations is the ability to *think visually*. The layout of the page or the slides can help make your points or distract the audience from your goal.

For more details (and fascinating examples), peruse the books by Edward Tufte listed in the references (Tufte, 1983, 1990). These are truly amazing and beautiful books that will greatly influence your thinking about the design of figures and tables.

10   SUMMARY

Technical communication is important in turning engineering ideas into reality. In addition, good technical communication skills are essential for obtaining an engineering job and advancing in the engineering profession.

Engineers must take responsibility for communicating their ideas and their work to a large and varied audience. As an engineer, you should think about technical communications as a creative and persuasive engineering tool. You must take control of the message, ask yourself if your message is understood, and seek to improve your communication skills at every opportunity.

Several general aspects of technical presentations (i.e., technical writing and technical speaking) were discussed in this chapter. Before putting pen to paper, you should take several steps. First, always identify the goals of the presentation, the target audience, and the constraints of the presentation. Second, organize the material to be presented. This can be done by using an outline to structure the information. Be sure to show your structure to the audience. Third, use the proper technique to present data. Tables are used when the actual values are important, while figures are used to show trends in the data. Every table and every figure in a technical document must have a number and a descriptive title. In addition, every table and figure must be referred to from the text of a written document, and its main points must be summarized.

Be sure to use the most appropriate type of figure: scatter (x–y) plots when the independent variable is continuous, bar charts when the independent variable is not continuous, pie charts to show relative proportions, and line charts almost never. Look critically at the default table or figure produced by software and ask how it could be modified to best meet *your* presentation goals.

SUMMARY OF KEY IDEAS

- Technical presentations must tell a story; always ask yourself whether the audience understood your story.
- Strong technical presentation skills aid in obtaining a job and in advancing a career.
- Technical communication is a creative process.
- Technical communication is usually meant to be persuasive.
- Engineers can benefit from communication specialists, but the engineer must take responsibility for making sure the correct message is delivered.
- All engineers can improve their technical communication skills.
- Before preparing a technical presentation, write down the goals of the presentation.
- Identify the target audience (and their technical sophistication, interests, and backgrounds) before preparing a technical presentation.
- Before preparing a technical presentation, quantify the constraints on the presentation (i.e., length limits, your time, and other resource limitations).
- To organize a presentation, structure the material using an outline and show the structure to your audience.
- Use tables when actual values are important; use figures to show trends in the data.
- Tables and figures should have a number (by which they are referred to in the text) and a short, descriptive title.

- Tables and figures must be interpreted in the text.
- Include units in the row or column headings of tables and the axes of figures.
- In tables, list the independent variables in the leftmost columns.
- Use scatter (x–y) plots when the independent variable is continuous.
- In general, use symbols for data and lines for calculated values (i.e., model output).
- Use the line chart type carefully in technical presentations (or, better yet, avoid it completely).
- Use bar charts when the independent variable is not continuous.
- In figures, select the axis ranges to encompass all the data without distorting the relative values.
- Do not accept the default table or figure produced by the software without questioning whether it meets your objectives.
- Use pie charts to show relative contributions.

Problems

1. Identify the goals, target audience, and constraints for the following types of communication:
   a. Two roommates discussing how to divide the telephone bill
   b. A review article on the avian flu virus in a newsmagazine
   c. A NASA news briefing on the evidence of water on Mars

2. Write an outline for a research paper on career opportunities in the engineering field of your choice.

3. Discuss whether you would use a figure or a table to present the following data. If you choose a figure, state which type of figure you would use.
   a. The chemical composition (in percent by weight) of a concrete formulation
   b. Operation and maintenance costs of three pavement types
   c. Effect of fiber-optic cable length on the transmission of photons
   d. Percentage of zebra mussels killed under a specified treatment regime

4. Figure titles often are missing or incomplete in the popular press. Find two data figures in a newspaper or newsmagazine. Critique the figure titles and then write your own.

5. Find two data tables in a newspaper or newsmagazine. Critique and write your own table titles. Edit the table, if necessary, following the principles discussed in this chapter.

6. Some people refer to line charts as "bar charts with symbols." Explain this definition of line charts.

7. Write Newton's Second Law of Motion in a concise form for a technical audience and in a more expansive form for a general audience.

8. Pick a figure in this text, critique it, and improve upon its design. State why your design is an improvement.

9. Interview a practicing engineer and write a paragraph about the importance of technical communication in his or her professional life.

10. Explain the differences and similarities between technical communication and written or oral presentations you did in high school in nontechnical courses.

13

Written Technical Communications

1 INTRODUCTION

In this chapter, written technical communications will be discussed in much detail. Organization is the key to good technical communication. Thus, most of the chapter (Sections 2 and 3) is devoted to the organization of written documents. Grammar and spelling issues are reviewed in Section 4. Section 5 provides details on the types of engineering documents you will write, from formal reports to casual email.

2 OVERALL ORGANIZATION OF TECHNICAL DOCUMENTS

2.1 Introduction

The key to good written and oral presentations is organization. Technical documents must be organized on several levels. In this section, the general organization of technical documents will be discussed. Organization at the paragraph, sentence, and word levels is the subject of Section 3.

2.2 General Organization Schemes

Outlines should be used to develop organized presentations. What headings and subheadings should be employed? Clearly, the details of the outline will depend on the goal of the presentation and nature of the technical work. Although every technical report is different, several elements are common to many technical presentations. Important elements found in many technical presentations are given in Table 1. The common elements are as follows:

OBJECTIVES

After reading this chapter, you will be able to:

- list the elements of technical documents;
- organize a technical document;
- identify common grammatical and spelling errors in technical documents;
- proofread technical documents;
- write an effective technical document.

- Abstract
- Introduction/Background/Literature Review
- Methods/Modeling
- Results
- Discussion
- Conclusions/Recommendations
- References

Each of the common elements will be illustrated with a report on a laboratory exercise conducted to test the conservation of momentum.

2.3   Abstract

Technical documents typically begin with an *abstract*. The purpose of the abstract is to provide a brief summary of the remainder of the document. The abstract should include the important points from each element in the document. An extended abstract (often written for nontechnical audiences) is sometimes called an *executive summary*.

A properly written abstract should be a miniature version of the entire technical document. The word *abstract* comes from the Latin *abstractus*, meaning drawn off. In a true sense, think of the abstract as being *drawn off of the whole document*. Thus, an abstract should include the following sections:

- An introduction (with enough background material to show the importance of the work),
- A statement on the methods or models employed,
- A short summary of the results and their meaning, and
- Conclusions and recommendations.

For the lab report on the conservation of momentum, the abstract might read as follows:

Abstract

The purpose of this lab was to test the law of conservation of momentum. Experiments were conducted with disks designed to remain together after collision. The masses and velocities of the disks were measured before and after collision. On average, the total momentum of the system after the collision was 101% of the total momentum before the collision. The calculated momentums were interpreted to be consistent with the conservation of momentum law.

TABLE 1   Elements in a General Technical Document

Section Title	Purpose
Abstract or Executive Summary	Summarizes the entire report, including all other elements
Introduction or Background or Literature Review	Brings the reader to the topic of the report; may give project history and/or a review of the appropriate technical literature
Methods or Modeling	Describes study approach, methods used, and model development (if any)
Results	Presents the results, including "raw" data with trends indicated but little interpretation of the data
Discussion	Interprets of the results
Conclusions and Recommendations	Summarizes main points and gives suggestions for further work, often in a list format
References	Lists references cited (may be in an appendix)

Note that the abstract contains all the elements of the full report: introduction (first sentence), methods (second and third sentences), results (fourth sentence), and conclusion (last sentence).

2.4   Introduction

The next element is the *introduction*. In writing the introduction section, assume that the reader knows only the information in the title of the report. After reading the introduction, the reader should have a good idea of the *motivation* for the report (i.e., why the report was written).

Key idea: The introduction should take the reader from the report title to an understanding of why the report was written.

In some cases, the introduction section may be fairly long. It may include a discussion of the project history, a review of pertinent technical literature, and a presentation of the goals and objectives of the work. On other occasions, the introduction is short and the other material is placed in separate sections (i.e., a background or a literature review section or a goals/objectives section).

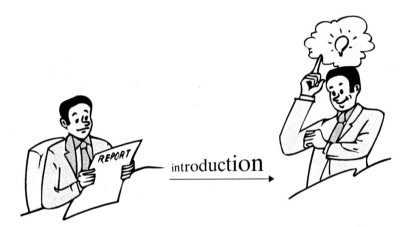

The introduction section takes the reader from the title to an appreciation of why the document was written.

For the lab report on the conservation of momentum, the introduction might read as follows:

Introduction

Science and engineering are founded on a number of conservation laws. One example is the conservation of momentum. Momentum is the product of the mass of an object and its velocity. The law of conservation of momentum states that the momentum of a closed system remains unchanged.

The conservation laws are impossible to prove experimentally because of error. However, the data collected in a well-planned experiment should be consistent with the conservation laws. In this lab, a comparison was made between the momentum calculations from laboratory data and the law of conservation of momentum.

Key idea: In the methods section, justify the study approach, present data collection techniques, and discuss data analysis methods.

2.5   Methods

The introduction is usually followed by a section on the *methods* employed in the study. The methods section should describe three elements of the work. First, the methods section should justify the *study approach*. In most engineering studies, there are many ways to achieve the study goals.

PONDER THIS   **How many ways can you think of to "test" the law of conservation of momentum?**

For example, you could explore the conservation of momentum law under controlled conditions with billiard balls or model cars or hockey pucks. You also could collect data in the real world. For example, a visit to a county fair would allow you to make measurements using bumper cars or the demolition derby. Even in this simple example, there are many ways to test the hypothesis of interest. As an engineer, you *choose* to follow a certain approach. It is important to justify your choice.

Second, the methods section should discuss the techniques involved in data collection. For experimental work, this means describing the measurement methods. For modeling studies, this means presenting the models developed specifically for your study.

Third, the methods section should discuss the approaches used to analyze the data. For example, suppose you measured temperature using a thermistor. A thermistor is a resistor that has resistance related to temperature in a known fashion. In a study using a thermistor, it may be necessary in the methods section to describe how the temperature was calculated from electrical measurements.

The three parts of the methods section can be summarized as follows:

- *Why* did you do the work? (study approach)
- *How* did you do the work? (experimental procedure)
- *What* did you do with the work? (data analysis)

Often, the information about experimental set-up can be communicated most effectively by drawings or photographs. It should be noted that in some technical fields, information on methods is placed in an appendix rather than in the body of a report.

Elements of a methods section

For the lab report on the conservation of momentum, the methods section might read as follows:

Methods

Data collection was performed in a laboratory setting to enhance reproducibility. Tests were conducted on an air table to minimize friction.

Six experiments were conducted. For each experiment, the masses of two plastic disks were recorded. The disks were 5 cm in diameter and 0.5 cm thick. The rims of the disks were covered with a strip of Velcro tape to allow the disks to stick together upon impact. The disks were positioned about 2 m apart. One disk was propelled by hand towards the other disk. Disk velocities were measured immediately before and after collision.

Masses were determined with a Model 501 balance. To measure disk velocities, a digital video camera (VideoCon Model 75) capable of recording images at 30 frames per second was positioned above the initially stationary disk. The sides of the air table were marked in 0.1 cm increments. Images were examined frame by frame, with the instantaneous velocity calculated as (distance traveled between frames) divided by (time between frames). The velocities of the disks were averaged over one second prior to and after collision.

The average momentum was calculated as $p = mv$, where m represents mass and v denotes velocity.

In this example, the study approach is presented and justified in the first paragraph. The second paragraph gives the overall experimental procedure, with the measurement details in the third paragraph. The fourth paragraph outlines the data analysis approach.

2.6   Results and Discussion

Key idea: In the results section, present the results and note the general trends.

Key idea: Interpret data in the discussion section.

The results section comes next. In this section of the typical engineering report, the results are *presented* but not *interpreted*. The general trends shown by the data in tables and figures should be highlighted as the data are presented.

In the results section, there is generally little interpretation of the data. Data interpretation comes in the *discussion* section. Here, elements of the results section are combined and interpreted to reach the main conclusions of the engineering study. Often, data are compared with predictions from models in the discussion section. In a design report, alternative designs may be compared and a final alternative selected in this section.

In a results section:

The measured force values are shown against mass in Figure 1. The measured force (in newtons) increased nearly linearly with the increase in mass (in kg).

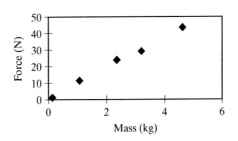

Figure 1: Dependency of Measured Force Values on Mass

In a discussion section:

Measured forces are compared with model predictions in Figure 2. The experimental results were consistent with the model, $F = ma$.

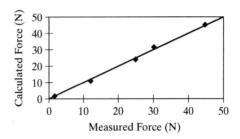

Figure 2: Comparison of Measured Forces and Model Results
(Line is calculated force = measured force)

The division between the results and discussion sections is not always clear cut. In fact, the results and discussion sections usually are combined in short reports. To illustrate the difference between the results and discussion sections, consider a large report on the effects of fatigue on the performance of assembly line workers. In the results section, the data on fatigue measures and performance measures might be reported. General trends (for example, that time to completion of critical tasks decreased as the level of fatigue increased) may be noted. More detailed interpretation of the data would be placed in the discussion section, where, for example, the predictions of a performance model might be compared with the data collected in the study.

For the conservation of momentum lab report, the results and discussion sections probably would be combined because the scope of the report is small. Example results and discussion sections are separated here for illustrative purposes.

Results

Measured masses and mean velocities from the six experiments are shown in Table 1. Note that the measured masses of the single disk (before collision) are similar, as expected. In addition, the measured masses of the coupled disks (after collision) are nearly double the masses of the single disk. By inspection of the data in Table 1, it appears that the velocity decreased by nearly a factor of two as the mass increased by about a factor of two.

TABLE 1   Measured Mass and Mean Velocity Data

	Before Collision		After Collision	
Experiment	**Mass (g)**	**Mean Velocity (cm/s)**	**Mass (g)**	**Mean Velocity (cm/s)**
1	2.5	99	5.0	51
2	2.5	102	5.1	48
3	2.4	96	4.9	48
4	2.5	93	5.0	45
5	2.6	102	5.1	51
6	2.5	105	5.1	54

Discussion

The calculated momentum values before and after collision are listed in Table 2. Note that the calculated momentum values before and after collision are nearly equal. As shown in the fourth column of Table 2, the momentum after collision averaged 101% of the momentum before the collision.

TABLE 2   Calculated Momentum Values (p) Before and After Collision

Expt.	p **Before Collision** (g-cm/s)	p **After Collision** (g-cm/s)	(**p After)/(p Before)** (%)
1	250	260	104
2	260	240	92
3	230	240	104
4	230	230	100
5	270	260	96
6	260	280	108
mean			101

The approach used in this lab was to compare two momentum values. Therefore, it is important to estimate the uncertainty in the mass and velocity measurements. The precision of the mass measurements can be estimated by the precision of the balance (given by the manufacturer as ±0.01 g). The instantaneous velocity was calculated as (distance traveled between frames) divided by (1/30 second per frame). The distance traveled was rounded to the nearest 0.1 cm, since the scale of the side of the table was marked in 0.1-cm increments. A difference of 0.1 cm over 1/30 s represents (0.1 cm)/(1/30 s) = 3 cm/s. The uncertainty in velocity (3 cm/s) represents about 1.2% of the average velocity of 250 cm/s. Thus, the difference of 1% between momentum values before and after collision is not unreasonable. Given the uncertainty, the data collected are consistent with conservation of momentum during the collision of two disks.

2.7   Conclusions and Recommendations

Key idea: Conclusions and recommendations are often in list form and should be written very carefully.

The last main section of a typical engineering report is the *conclusions and recommendations* section. The conclusions and recommendations must be among the most carefully worded sections of an engineering report, since many readers may turn here first. Conclusions and recommendations often appear in a list format. The conclusions should stem directly from the discussion. In other words, no *new* information should be presented in the conclusions.

The recommendations section is a critical part of an engineering report. Why? Recall that engineers often select intelligently from among alternatives. The preferred alternative often is highlighted in the recommendations section.

An example of a conclusions section is given next.

Conclusions

An experimental study was conducted to explore the conservation of momentum law as applied to a collision of two discs on an air table. The momentum after the collision averaged 101% of the momentum before the collision. The experimental results were consistent with the conservation of momentum.

2.8   References

Key idea: Although many reference formats are acceptable, the references must be complete and consistent.

The last section of a technical report (often found in an appendix) is a list of references. There are many acceptable formats for listing references in technical material. The guiding rules are that the references should be *complete* (so that the reader can find the referenced material easily) and *consistent* (i.e., use the same format for all books or journals cited). Following are some examples of reference formats:

For books:

Author's last name, author's initials (for second authors, initials followed by name), book title in bold, publisher's name, publisher's location, publication date.

Example: Keller, H. **The Story of My Life**. Doubleday, Page & Co., New York, NY, 1903.

For journal articles:

Author's last name, author's initials (for second authors, initials followed by name), article title, journal name in bold italic, volume number, issue number in parentheses, page range, date.

Example: Dallard, P., A. J. Fitzpatrick, and A. Flint. The London Millennium Footbridge. ***Structural Engineer***, **79**(22), 17–35, 2001.

For Web pages:

Author's last name, author's initials (for second authors, initials followed by name), article title, URL, date visited in parentheses.

Example: Anon., Standard Contract Documents, http://www.nspe.org/ejcdc/home.asp (visited March 21, 2005).

bibliography: a list of useful sources of information, including sources not cited in the text (as contrasted with the references, in which only cited material is listed)

Be careful about the differences between a list of references and a ***bibliography***. A reference list consists only of the material cited in the text. A bibliography lists all useful sources of information, even if they are not specifically cited in the text. For examples, please see the References appendix of this text.

2.9   Signposting in Technical Writing

As discussed in Section 2.2, a good technical presentation is well organized and the organization is clear to the audience. The idea of showing the audience where you are in a technical presentation is called *signposting*. A common mistake in technical writing is to give the reader page after page of text with no guide to the content of the text.

Key idea: Use section headings or numbering schemes as signposts in technical documents.

In technical documents, signposting is usually accomplished in one of two ways. First, you may use *section headings* to show the readers where they are in the document. The divisions described in Section 2.1 (e.g., Introduction, Methods, Results, and so on) may be good section headings. Be sure to use a consistent theme to show the hierarchy of the headings. For example, major headings might be left aligned, while subheadings are indented. Or major headings might be all in capital letters, while subheadings are in initial caps.

Second, you can signpost with a *numbering scheme*. Numbers are an excellent way to show the hierarchy of headings. For example, a major section may be given a number (e.g., "3. Assessment of Alternatives"), with subheadings listed as sections under the number (e.g., "3.1 Soldered Joints Alternative"). Hierarchy can be shown by the numbering scheme (4, 4.1, 4.1.1, or I, I.A, I.A.1, or others), indentation, or use of boldface fonts.

Regardless of the system used, signposting *must be applied consistently*. If you use a bold font with initial caps with second-level subheadings, then use a bold font with initial caps with *all* second-level subheadings. Your readers will rely on your signals. Do not confuse the reader with inconsistent signposting.

3   ORGANIZING PARTS OF TECHNICAL DOCUMENTS

3.1   Paragraph Organization

Beyond organizing the overall presentation, each paragraph also should be structured. Each paragraph should tell a complete story and be structured by sentence. The paragraph should begin with a ***topic sentence***. The topic sentence states the purpose of the paragraph. Each following sentence should *support the topic sentence*. Paragraphs should end with a *concluding sentence*, which summarizes the main points of the paragraph. Thus, each sentence in the paragraph has a specific purpose.

topic sentence: the first sentence in a paragraph in which the purpose of the paragraph is stated

PONDER THIS

Reread the previous paragraph and evaluate whether it is structured correctly.

3.2   Sentence Organization

Key idea: Each sentence should express a single idea.

A sentence is a grammatical structure containing a subject and a verb. Sentences should express a *single idea*. There are two common problems with sentences in technical documents: overly long sentences (with more than one idea) and too short sentences (lacking a subject or verb). Avoid using conjunctions (e.g., *and, but, or, nor, for, so,* or *yet*) to combine disparate ideas into one sentence. Consider the following sentence:

> Design parameters were calculated by standard procedures and all results were rounded to three significant figures.

This sentence contains two ideas. It should be split into two sentences at the word *and*:

> Design parameters were calculated by standard procedures. All results were rounded to three significant figures.

sentence fragment: an incomplete sentence (usually lacking a subject or verb)

Sentences can be *too short* if they do not include both a subject and a verb. Incomplete sentences are called **sentence fragments**. A common sentence fragment in technical writing creeps in when stating trends. For example,

> The higher the temperature, the shorter the annealing time.

PONDER THIS

Why is the sentence fragment "The higher the temperature, the shorter the annealing time" *not* **a sentence?**

This fragment has no verb and thus is not a sentence. Try to avoid such constructions in your technical writing. Say instead: "Annealing time decreased as the temperature was increased."

3.3   Word Choice

Key idea: Choose words to make your writing concise, simple, and specific.

The lowest level of organization is the choice of words. In choosing words to form sentences, try to be as *concise, simple,* and *specific* as possible.

Concise writing means that you should use the minimum number of words to express the thought clearly. To write concisely, avoid long prepositional phrases. Examples of common wordy phrases and suggested substitutions are listed in Table 2.

TABLE 2   Examples of Long Prepositional Phrases to Be Avoided
(adapted from Smith and Vesiland, 1996)

Wordy Prepositional Phrase	Possible Substitute
due to the fact that . . .	because . . .
in order to . . .	to . . .
in terms of . . .	reword sentence and delete phrase[a]
in the event that . . .	if . . .
in the process of . . .	delete, or use "while" or "during"
it just so happens that . . .	because . . .
on the order of [b] . . .	about . . .

[a] *Example*: The sentence "In terms of energy use, Alternative 3 was lowest" could be rewritten as "Alternative 3 had the lowest energy use."

[b] This phrase sometimes is used to indicate an order of magnitude (i.e., a power of 10), as in the following sentence: "On the order of 10,000 bolts were employed in the construction project."

For example, instead of writing

In order to find the optimum temperature, we conducted experiments.

it is preferable to write

To find the optimum temperature, we conducted experiments.

Although the general public sometimes feels that technical writing is impenetrable, written technical communication should be *simple*. In other words, use simple words to express your ideas as clearly as possible. Avoid sentences such as

System failure mode was encountered on three sundry occasions.

Instead, write more clearly:

The system failed three times.

Key idea: Avoid making up new words or new uses of words in conventional technical writing.

A common and annoying device used to make writing sound more technical is the use of nouns as verbs. One way this is accomplished is by adding the suffix *-ize* to almost any noun (e.g., initialize, prioritize, customize, and the like). Writers are converting nouns into verbs with increasing frequency. For example, a nationwide company offering photocopying services used to advertise itself as "The new way to office." (What does "to office" mean?) In your writing, avoid making up new verbs from nouns.

The heart of technical writing is its *specificity*. Make your writing specific by avoiding general adjectives such as *many*, *several*, *much*, and *a few*. Quantify your statements when you can:

Engine temperatures were 5°C above normal.

not

Engine temperatures were several degrees above normal.

4   GRAMMAR AND SPELLING

Important ideas about spelling and grammar will be reviewed in this section. The purpose of this discussion is not to provide you with a comprehensive list of the rules of grammar, but rather to identify common trouble spots in technical writing.

There are no excuses for errors in grammar or spelling in technical writing. The most important rules are reviewed here. Problem words will be discussed at the end of this section. For more details, please examine any of the excellent books listed in the bibliography at the end of the text.

You should be aware that there is some disagreement on several grammatical rules. It is important to differentiate firm rules from one writer's opinion. It is frustrating to learn and use one approach from a mentor, only to have it totally dismantled by another mentor. When in doubt about the feedback you have received, always ask questions.

4.1   Subject–verb match

Key idea: Make sure that the subject and verb agree in number (i.e., they must be both singular or both plural).

The subject and verb must match in number. In other words, use plural forms of verbs with plural nouns and singular forms of verbs with singular nouns. For example, you should write

The contacts of the integrated circuit were corroded.

not

The contacts of the integrated circuit was corroded.

The subject of the sentence is plural ("contacts") and thus a plural verb ("were") is required.

In most cases, the "subject–verb match" rule is simple. However, some sticky situations arise. For example, is the noun "data" plural or singular? In most technical literature, the word *data* is considered to be a plural noun. (Formally, it is the plural of the noun *datum*.) A growing number of technical writers consider *data* to be singular when referring to a specified set of data. The safe bet is to treat *data* as a plural noun:

The data fall within two standard deviations of the mean.

not

The data falls within two standard deviations of the mean.

If you wish to use a singular noun, use *data set*:

The data set was larger last year.

4.2   Voice

In grammar, *voice* refers to the person (people) or things doing the action. There are two general voices: active and passive. In the active voice, the subject is identified. In the passive voice, the person performing the action is not identified (either directly or by category).

There is some difference of opinion about which voice is best for technical writing. In general, the active voice is preferred. Why? In engineering, you usually want to know who did the action. You should write

Field technicians backfilled the soil.

not

The soil was backfilled.

The passive voice is appropriate when the identity of the person doing the action is obvious or unimportant. Thus, you will find the passive voice used in many engineering reports where the subject already has been identified. For example, the passive voice was used in the conservation of momentum example in Section 3. Regardless of the voice used, be consistent and use the same voice throughout.

Although the active voice is preferred, you should always avoid the use of the first person in technical writing. For example, write

XYZ Engineering personnel developed an ergonomic design.

or

We developed an ergonomic design.

not

I developed an ergonomic design.

4.3   Tense

Tense refers to when the action occurred. In technical writing, use the present tense unless describing work done in the past. Thus, write

Values were calculated by a nonlinear optimization algorithm.

This is in the past tense, since the calculation took place in the past. On the other hand, you might write

The results indicate the importance of the new quality assurance procedures.

Use the present tense here, since the results and their interpretation exist now.

4.4   Pronouns

Pronouns are substitutes for nouns. Examples of pronouns include *he, she, it, they,* and *them.* An all-too-common problem with pronouns in technical (and nontechnical) writing is *gender bias.* In the older technical literature, scientists and engineers were identified as males. It used to be common to write

An engineer must trust his abilities. [*incorrect*]

This construction is **not** proper, as it implies that all engineers are men.

One approach to remedying this situation is the use of the pronouns *they* or *their* in place of *he* and *his.* This leads to the statement

An engineer must trust their abilities. [*incorrect*]

Unfortunately, the solution is grammatically incorrect.

What is wrong with the statement, "An engineer must trust their abilities"?

In this case, the subject ("an engineer") is singular and the pronoun ("their") is plural. A much better solution to gender-specific pronouns is to rework the sentence completely so that the subject and pronouns match in number:

Engineers must trust their abilities.

Key idea: Use *who* as a pronoun for human subjects, *that* for specific nonhuman subjects, and *which* for nonhuman subjects in clauses set off by commas.

Another common problem is the proper use of the pronouns *who*, *that*, and *which*. When in doubt, use *who* for human subjects and *that* or *which* for nonhuman subjects. The pronoun *that* is used in reference to a specific noun, while *which* adds information about a noun and usually is used in clauses set off by commas. Thus,

The engineer *who* was on site had the contract documents.

The human subject takes the pronoun *who*. On the other hand,

The bolt *that* ruptured was installed improperly.

Here, use *that* in referring to a specific bolt. (We are discussing a particular bolt: the bolt that ruptured.) Finally,

The submitted proposal, *which* was missing page three, was thrown in the garbage can.

In this case, use *which* to add information in a separate clause. Often, you can avoid *who*, *that*, and *which* problems by incorporating the information as an adjective. For the examples just presented, you could write

The on-site engineer had the contract documents.

The ruptured bolt was installed improperly.

The submitted proposal was missing page three. It was thrown in the garbage can.

4.5   Adjectives and Adverbs

Adjectives modify nouns and adverbs modify verbs. Avoid using long lists of adjectives, sometimes called ***adjective chains***. In adjective chains, it is often difficult to identify the noun. Consider the sentence:

adjective chain: a long list of modifiers to a noun (to be avoided)

High-grade precut stainless steel beams were specified.

The beam characteristics are clearer if the sentence is rewritten:

Precut beams made of high-grade stainless steel were specified.

split infinitive: insertion of a word between *to* and the verb (to be avoided)

Adjective and adverb *placement* also can be problematic. You should avoid placing an adverb between the word *to* and the verb. This construction is called a ***split infinitive***. For example, you should write

The gear ratio was designed to drive the system efficiently.

not

The gear ratio was designed to efficiently drive the system.

Key idea: With adjectives and adverbs, avoid adjective chains and make sure the adverb or adjective modifies only the verb or noun you intend to modify.

Having railed against them, it should be noted that split infinitives are a tricky construction. The rule against split infinitives appears to stem from Latin, where splitting an infinitive is impossible. Place an adverb between *to* and the verb only to emphasize the adverb or to produce a sentence that sounds better. For example, there is a split infinitive in the phrase

To boldly go where no one has gone before …

However, it sounds better (at least to many people) than

To go boldly where no one has gone before …

Adjectives should be located next to the nouns they modify. Consider the following two sentences:

They only constructed three prototypes.

They constructed only three prototypes.

In the first sentence, *only* modifies *constructed*: they only *constructed* the prototypes, they did not construct and test the prototypes. In the second sentence, *only* modifies *three* (which, in turn, modifies *prototypes*): they constructed only *three* prototypes, rather than four prototypes. Make sure that the adverb (or adjective) modifies only the verb (or noun) you intend to modify.

4.6   Capitalization and Punctuation

Many neophyte technical writers find it necessary to use nonstandard capitalization and abbreviations. Please do not give in to this temptation. Few words in technical writing are capitalized. As suggested by Smith and Vesiland (1996), you usually capitalize the names of organizations, firms, cities, counties, districts, agencies, and states. In general, do not capitalize general references to these entities. Thus, you can write

The City of Rochester contracted for engineering services.

Here, capitalize "city" because it is specific to Rochester, New York, but

The city council met for three hours.

or

The federal government will meet the deadline.

Do not capitalize "city" and "federal" because they are general adjectives here. In addition, the titles of engineering reports are capitalized, and official titles of people are capitalized when they precede the names of the people (but not when they follow the name).

Key idea: Avoid nonstandard capitalization and abbreviations.

Standard abbreviations for scientific and engineering units and parameters should be used. If in doubt, define an abbreviation *the first time it is used*. There is no need to capitalize the words as an abbreviation is defined. Thus, write

The standard operating procedure (SOP) was followed.

not

The Standard Operating Procedure (SOP) was followed.

and not

The SOP was followed.

The last construction is improper if using the abbreviation for the first time, but desirable if the abbreviation *SOP* already has been defined in the document.

Common nontechnical abbreviations include the following:

e.g. (*exempli gratia* = for example)

i.e. (*id est* = that is)

etc. (*et cetera* = and so forth), and

et al. (*et alia* = and others)

(*Note*: The last term is **not** abbreviated et. al or et. al.) These common abbreviations sometimes are italicized (e.g., *e.g.*) to indicate their non-English origins.

Commas should be used to define clauses and separate items in a list. Usually, a comma is used even before the last item in a list. For example,

Materials included wood, steel, and concrete.

If the items in a list are long (or the items include commas or conjunctions), use semicolons to separate them:

Materials included wood, natural materials, and fiber; steel and concrete; and thermoplastic resins.

4.7   Spelling

Key idea: Never assume a document is free of errors because it passes the spell checker.

There is no room for spelling errors in technical documents. One misspelled word could destroy an otherwise strong document. The fundamental rule of spelling is *Never, never, never trust your spell checker.* Spell-checking software is a good first start, but you must learn to proofread your writing very carefully. Spell checkers miss misspellings that result in another word (e.g., house/horse, dear/deer). A proofreading example is given in Section 4.10.

4.8   Citation

plagiarism: using someone else's words or ideas without proper credit

You are professionally and morally obligated to give credit when you use ideas from other people. Taking someone else's words or ideas without credit is called **plagiarism**. Plagiarism is defined in the University at Buffalo's University Standards and Administrative Regulations as

copying or receiving material from a source or sources and submitting this material as one's own without acknowledging the particular debts to the source (quotations, paraphrases, basic ideas), or otherwise representing the work of another as one's own.

Key idea: Make sure you give credit (by use of a citation) when presenting someone else's words or ideas.

Students who plagiarize are subject to disciplinary action. Engineers who plagiarize can lose their professional licenses.

Plagiarism is not just copying *words* from someone else. Plagiarism also means taking another person's *ideas* without giving them due credit. Always read your work carefully to make sure that you have not inadvertently included someone else's ideas "without acknowledging the particular debts to the source."

Credit is shown by *citing the work from which the material was taken.* There are many citation styles. One style (employed in this text) is to list the author's name and publication date in parentheses following the material cited, as in "Smith (2002)." Numbers, usually written as superscripts (e.g., Smith[2]), may be used with a numbered reference list.

paraphrase: to rewrite an idea in your own words

In nearly all cases, you **paraphrase** the material (i.e., rewrite it in your own words). On rare occasions (when the original words are required), it may be necessary to quote the words exactly. Quotation should be done sparingly and the citation always must be given. Indicate a direct quotation by the use of quotation marks or by doubly indenting the material. Examples of paraphrasing and quotation are shown in Example 1.

EXAMPLE 1 PARAPHRASING AND QUOTATION

Use the following material, from Paradis and Zimmerman (1997), in a paragraph, and cite it properly:

"Long sentences, often amounting to more than 30 words, are usually too complicated. Determine the main actions of the sentence. Then sort these into two or more shorter sentences."

SOLUTION

Here are several citation options:

1. Paraphrase with citation (preferred approach):

   Long sentences should be broken up into smaller sections according to their main actions (Paradis and Zimmerman, 1997).

2. Quotation using quotation marks with citation:

   Overly long sentences can be problematic. According to Paradis and Zimmerman (1997): "Long sentences, often amounting to more than 30 words, are usually too complicated. Determine the main actions of the sentence. Then sort these into two or more shorter sentences."

3. Quotation using indentation with citation:

   Overly long sentences are confusing to the reader. Several approaches have been developed to identify and eliminate run-on sentences. For example,

   > Long sentences, often amounting to more than 30 words, are usually too complicated. Determine the main actions of the sentence. Then sort these into two or more shorter sentences. (Paradis and Zimmerman, 1997).

The following approach is plagiarism because the work is paraphrased but no citation is given [*Warning*: **This material is not cited properly!**]

Long sentences—some can be up to 30 words long—should be subdivided. To do this, find its main actions and create a shorter sentence for each main action.

4.9   Other Problem Areas

In addition to the rules discussed previously, several other words and phrases cause problems in technical writing. Most of the words and phrases listed below were found in Strunk and White (1979) or Smith and Vesiland (1996):

affect/effect: These two words cause many difficulties in technical writing, but the rule regarding their use is simple. The word *affect* is almost always a *verb*. The word *effect* is almost always a *noun*. Thus, write "The effects of temperature were noted" (*effects* is a noun) and "Temperature affected the results" ("affected" is the verb).°

among/between: Use *between* when two people or things are involved and *among* when more than two or more people or things are involved. For example, write "The voltage was split between two capacitors," but "The work was divided among four engineers."

comprise: *Comprise* means *to consist of*: "The frame comprises four steel rods" (i.e., the frame *consists of* four steel rods) and "Four steel rods make up the frame" (*not* "Four steel rods comprise the frame").

Key idea: Avoid double negatives in formal writing.

double negatives: Avoid the **use** of two or more negatives (*not* or words starting with *un*) in the same sentence. Rewrite by canceling out pairs of negatives: "The project was like our previous work" (*not* "The project was not unlike our previous work.")

farther/further: *Farther* refers to distance, while *further* refers to time or quantity. Thus, "The ultrahigh-mileage vehicle went farther on a tank of gas," while "Further negotiations are necessary to seal the contract."

°While *affect* is usually a verb, it is used in psychology as a noun (for example, the Jones affect). The word *effect* almost always is a noun, but it is used *very rarely* as a verb, as in "Temperature effected a change in elasticity." (This means temperature *brought about* a change in elasticity.)

fewer/less: *Fewer* is used in reference to the *number* of things, while *less* refers to the *quantity* (or amount) of an object. For example, "Our model has fewer adjustable parameters" (i.e., fewer number of parameters), and "The high-efficiency engine used less gasoline" (i.e., a lesser amount of gasoline).

irregardless: *Irregardless* is an example of a double negative. The prefix *ir-* and the suffix *-less* both negate *regard*. Please write *regardless* anytime you are tempted to write *irregardless*.

its/it's: Here is a nagging exception to the rule that you add an apostrophe to indicate the possessive form. The word "its" is the possessive form: "Its color was red." The word *it's* is a contraction of *it is*: "It's hot today." In general, *avoid contractions in formal writing.*

Key idea: Avoid contractions in formal writing.

personification: Personification (also called anthropomorphism) is the assignment of human characteristics to nonhuman objects, as in "The day smiled on me." Personification should be avoided in technical writing. Some people dislike the assignment of any active verb to any inanimate objects. In this view, some say you should avoid statements such as "The data show . . . " or "The experiments demonstrate . . . ." Although there is a difference of opinion on this matter, it is best to avoid egregious examples of personification in your technical writing (such as "The data really grabbed me by the throat," which is too informal as well).

precede/proceed: *Precede* means *to come before*, while *proceed* means *to continue or move forward*. Thus, "The air-conditioning study preceded the heating study" (meaning that the air-conditioning study was conducted first) and "The work proceeded without interruption" (meaning that the work continued without interruption).

presently: *Presently* means both *soon* and *currently*. Strunk and White (1979) suggest that *presently* be used only in the sense of *soon*.

4.10   Proofreading

Key idea: Always proofread your work.

The secret to good proofreading is practice. You can check your proofreading skills by asking others to read your work and give you feedback. An example of proofreading is given in Example 3.

EXAMPLE 3: PROOF-READING

Read the following paragraph and list the errors you encounter. Allow 60 seconds for this exercise. Rewrite the paragraph to eliminate the errors. [**Warning:** The following text may contain errors!]

Abstract

Project personnel conducted a laboratory study to definitively determine the engineeering feasability of polychlorinated biphenyl (PCB) removal by granular activated carbon. The study used an expanded bed granular activated carbon reactor in the upflow mode. PCB concentrations in the column effluent was measured by standard techniques. Study data is consistent with surface diffusion as the rate-limiting step, although much scatter in the data is observed. Columns were sacrificed at the conclusion of the study and carbon analysis revealed PCB saturation is the first 50% of the bed. Future studies will be conducted on the affect of the recycle rate on column performance.

SOLUTION

A list of errors (with the corresponding section numbers in parentheses) is given in Table 3.

TABLE 3 Errors in Proofreading Example

Sentence	Error(s)
First sentence	"to definitively determine" is a split infinitive (4.5), "engineeering" (engineering) and "feasability" (feasibility) are misspelled (4.7)
Second sentence	" ... expanded bed granular activated carbon reactor ... " contains an adjective chain (4.5)
Third sentence	" ... concentrations ... was ... " is a subject/verb mismatch (4.1). The use of the passive voice (4.2) is discouraged, unless it is clear who analyzed the samples from other parts of the report.
Fourth sentence	" ... data is ... " is a subject/verb mismatch (4.1). *Note*: The sentence " ... much scatter in the data is ... " is fine, since the subject, "scatter," is singular.
Fifth sentence	This sentence is a long sentence (3.2). Also, the sentence should read, " ... saturation *in* the first ... " (rather than " ... saturation *is* the first ... ").
Sixth sentence	Use of passive voice is inconsistent with the active voice used elsewhere in the paragraph (4.2). Also, "affect" should be "effect" (4.9).

Here is an improved version of the abstract:

Abstract

Project personnel conducted a laboratory study to determine definitively the engineering feasibility of polychlorinated biphenyl (PCB) removal by granular activated carbon (GAC). The study used an expanded bed GAC reactor in the upflow mode. A contract laboratory measured PCB concentrations in the column effluent by standard techniques. Study data are consistent with surface diffusion as the rate-limiting step, although much scatter in the data is observed. Columns were sacrificed at the conclusion of the study. Carbon analysis revealed PCB saturation in the first 50% of the bed. We plan to conduct future studies on the effect of the recycle rate on column performance.

5   TYPES OF ENGINEERING DOCUMENTS

5.1   Introduction

Thus far in this chapter, you have been exposed to the organization of engineering reports. Reports are used to present the results of a study. A report may transmit the results of the entire project (called a *final* or *full report*), transmit the results of a portion of the project (called a *progress report*), or transmit a small piece of a report in a short form (often called a *letter report*).

In addition to reports, engineers write several other kinds of documents. Common document types include letters, memorandums, and email.

5.2   Reports

Key idea: Reports should include a cover page and a transmittal letter.

The general outline of an engineering report was discussed in Section 2. Two other elements of a report deserve mention. First, every report should have a cover page. A cover page includes the names of the authors (and their professional titles), the names of the recipients (and their professional titles), the report or project title, a project identifier, and the date. Many formats are possible, as long as this information is included. Locate the required information for a cover page in the example cover page in Figure 1.

Second, most reports have a *transmittal letter* (also called a *cover letter*). The transmittal letter is a short letter that accompanies the report. The format of letters is presented in Section 5.3.

**Pumping Options for Stormwater Management
in Rivertown, Ohio**

Draft Final Report for
Rivertown DPW Project #2005-5-1214

Submitted to:

Mary J. Bremer, PE
Director of Public Works
Rivertown Public Works Department
1120 Bank Road
Rivertown, Ohio

Submitted by:

John H. Seal, PE
Senior Associate Engineer
AZA Engineering
12 Cunningham Parkway, Suite 114
Warsaw, Ohio

February 7, 2007

Figure 1. An Example of a Cover Page

Key idea: Letters should have a heading (including the date, recipient's name, and title), closing (including your name, title, and signature), and structured paragraphs (the first paragraph should summarize previous correspondence and state the purpose of the letter, the next paragraphs should present supporting information, and the last paragraph should summarize the main point and state the required actions or follow-up communication).

memorandum: a short note used to document engineering work

Key idea: Memos should have a heading (including to whom the memo is written, who wrote the memo, the memo topic, the date, and the word *Memorandum*), and the same structured paragraphs as a letter.

5.3   Letters

Engineers use letters to document the transmission of ideas to the client or other agency. Letters must have structure. The heading of a letter includes the date and recipient's name and title. The first paragraph of a letter should summarize previous correspondence and state the purpose of the letter. In the next paragraph or paragraphs, supporting information should be presented. The last paragraph of the letter should summarize the main points and state the required actions or follow-up communication. In the closing information of a letter, include your name, title, and signature. An example letter is shown in Figure 2. Note the heading information; introductory, supporting, and concluding paragraphs; and closing information.

5.4   Memorandums

A **memorandum** (plural: memorandums or memoranda) is a short note. Similar to letters, memorandums are used for short documentation of engineering work. In fact, the word *memorandum* is a shortened form of the phrase *memorandum est*—Latin for "it is to be remembered." Memorandums are frequently used for messages inside an organization (called *internal memorandums*).

Memorandums (or memos) are structured similarly to letters (see Section 5.3), but without the heading and closing information of a letter. Heading information in a memo tells you to whom the memo is written, who wrote the memo, the memo topic, the date, and the word *Memorandum*.

AZA *Engineers*
Warsaw • Milton • Cleveland

March 10, 2006

Mary J. Bremer, PE
Director of Public Works
Rivertown Public Works Department
1120 Bank Road
Rivertown, Ohio

Dear Ms. Bremer,

As per our telephone conservation of March 9th, I am writing to summarize your comments on the draft stormwater report. Our responses to your comments also are included in this letter.

My notes indicate that your staff had three main comments on the draft report. First, the name of the Bilmore Pump Station was misspelled on page 6-2. Second, the flow calculations for the West Branch were based on 1980-2000 rainfall data, while all other system design calculations were based on 1970-2000 rainfall data. Third, your staff requested that the cradle design for Option 4 use a smaller factor of safety than the 2.5 safety factor in the report (p. 7-7).

We will correct the spelling error on page 6-2 and update the design calculations for the West Branch with rainfall data from 1970-2004. However, we feel best engineering practice requires the safety factor of 2.5 in the pump cradle design. Based on conversations with the pump manufacturer, lower safety factors will increase the chance of catastrophic failure. Therefore, we wish to retain the 2.5 safety factor in the design of Option 4.

To summarize, we plan to resubmit the report before March 31, 2006 with the spelling error corrected and with the design calculations for the West Branch updated to use rainfall data from 1970-2000. We will retain the safety factor of 2.5 in the pump cradle in Option 4.

Thank you for your thoughtful comments. I will call you next week to confirm the changes. We look forward to delivering you the final report on this project.

Sincerely,

J H Seal

John H. Seal, PE
Senior Associate Engineer

Figure 2. Example of a Technical Letter

MEMORANDUM

To: Yvonne Ringland
From: J.H. Seal, PE
Re: Comments on Rivertown stormwater report
Date: March 9, 2006

I spoke with Mary Bremer at the Rivertown DPW today about the draft stormwater report. She requested that we use the same rainfall data for the West Branch design calculations as we did for the rest of the report. We used 1970-2000 rainfall data for the majority of the report.

Please redo the West Branch design with 1970-2000 rainfall data. The final report is due by March 31st. Please have the revisions to me by March 25th so we can get the changes to the word processing staff.

If you have questions about the requested changes, please call me at extension 36.

Figure 3.   Example of a Memorandum

Memo paragraphs are similar to those of letters: previous correspondence and memo purpose should be summarized in the first paragraph, supporting information in the following paragraphs, and main points summarized in the last paragraph. An example of a memo is given in Figure 3. Note the heading information and purpose of each of the three paragraphs. A copy of this memo likely would be placed in the project file to document the internal communication of the consulting firm.

5.5   Email

Key idea: When writing business email, avoid contractions and emoticons, proofread carefully, double-check the recipient list, and do not include anything in an email that you would not include in other business documents.

Nearly every college student in the 21st century has used email, usually for informal conversation. Email also can be used in formal business correspondence, sometimes in place of a letter or memo.

Although email is less formal than other forms of written communication, it is easy to let an overly familiar style creep into your formal email correspondence. You use different words in speaking to clients and colleagues than you use to speak to friends at a party. Similarly, use more formal language in business email. Following are some rules for business email correspondence:

- Avoid email contractions (e.g., *RU* for *are you* and *°s°* for *smile*).

- Avoid *emoticons*—text characters used to express emotions (such as :-) for a smiley face).

- Proofread carefully before you hit "send." Look for language that may be offensive or inappropriate.

- Double-check the names on the "to" list before you send the email. "Replying to all" with the results of your recent medical check-up (when you intended to forward the results to your roommate) is a serious breach of business protocol.

- Emails are as much a part of the technical and legal record as are other documents. Do not include anything in an email that you would not include in other business documents.

An example of a business email message is shown in Figure 4.

Email is not the only kind of electronic written document in engineering today. For a look at the future of written technical communication, see the *Focus on Writing: Whither Paper Reports?*

To: Roger Yee (rty@azaengineers.com)
From: John H. Seal (jhs@azaengineers.com)
Subject: Pump cradle design for Rivertown Project
Cc: Cynthia Cronin (cronin@rgoldpumps.com)
Bcc:
Attached: Draft Rivertown report.doc

Roger -

Rivertown has questioned our use of a 2.5 safety factor for the cradle design in Option 4 of the stormwater project. Attached is the draft report.

Are we sure about this safety factor? If so, please help me to justify it. I am copying Cindy Cronin at Rheingold Pumps on this message. We are specifying Rheingold Pumps and Cindy might be able to help.

Please get back to me by the end of the day on this, Roger.

Thanks,

John H. Seal
Senior Associate Engineer
AZA Engineering

Figure 4.   Example of a Business Email

FOCUS ON WRITING: WHITHER PAPER REPORTS?

BACKGROUND

Probably since the first pyramid was built, engineers have been summarizing their work by writing reports. This chapter was devoted to helping you write better reports and other engineering documents. There are many cases in which the results of engineering work are better communicated by electronic documents. Many clients now are requesting electronic or on-line reports.

ELECTRONIC MANUALS

As an example of electronic reporting, many industries are replacing entire bookshelves of operation and maintenance (O&M) manuals with *on-line manuals*. The on-line O&M manuals typically are written in HTML, XML, or other programming languages used in Web page development. In addition, manuals and other electronic engineering documents commonly are written in Adobe's proprietary *portable document format* as PDF files.

Electronic manuals have a number of advantages over traditional documentation. First, they reduce the need for operations and maintenance training. Perez et al. (2001) estimated that the effectiveness of O&M training at a drinking-water treatment plant was increased four- to sixfold using on-line materials as compared with paper manuals. More effective training results in fewer errors and cost savings.

Second, electronic manuals are much easier to keep current. Engineers struggle to maintain current sets of plans about engineered systems. Facilities personnel need to know the actual conditions of the structure (as-built conditions), not the system as originally designed (design conditions). Electronic manuals allow engineers to update material very quickly and accurately. The underlying database of equipment and other system attributes can be updated centrally, allowing users to access up-to-date information from any location.

Third, electronic manuals are easier to access. Facility personnel sometimes dread the thought of flipping through literally thousands of pages of manuals in three-ring binders to find the information they need. Electronic manuals are written with *hyperlinks* (as on Web pages). This allows the user to find related information quickly. In fact, electronic manuals look like Web pages. As with the Web itself, e-manuals can be very graphically oriented, with liberal use of drawings, photographs, and videos. In addition, electronic manuals can be linked to manufacturer's Web pages. If, say, you need a new gasket for a pump, you can click on the manufacturer's link and find the part easily.

Fourth, electronic manuals are portable. Many electronic manuals are mounted on company intranets, allowing for secure access by facility personnel from any location. In other cases, the manuals are burned onto CD-ROMs. One CD-ROM can replace up to 1,540 pounds of paper manuals (Perez et al., 2001).

WILL YOU EVER SEE A PAPERLESS OFFICE?

For the foreseeable future, engineers probably will continue to produce reports on paper. The "paperless office" continues to be frustratingly just out of reach. However, the engineer's life is becoming increasingly "webcentric" (i.e., centered on the World Wide Web). As an engineer of the future (and as a person brought up to think of the Internet as an important resource), you should think creatively about how information needs in engineering can be addressed by electronic sources. Always ask whether electronic documents will add value to the information (by allowing linkage to other data sources or by providing real-time data or by using multimedia formats).

Perhaps in your lifetime, paper reports will become as quaint as slide rules and manual typewriters. Regardless of the delivery medium, engineering reports will still be based on the principles outlined in this text: organization, signposting, and clarity.

6   SUMMARY

The key to good written technical documents is *organization*. The typical structure of an engineering report includes several aspects: the abstract (or executive summary), introduction/background/literature review, methods, results, discussion, conclusions/recommendations, and references.

Technical documents also must be organized at the paragraph, sentence, and word levels. Choose words to make your writing concise, simple, and specific. In your technical writing, be aware of the rules of grammar and spelling. Strive to use the active voice and avoid gender-specific language. Always proofread your work before allowing it to leave your hands.

In addition to reports, engineers produce letters, memos, and emails almost daily in their working lives. Letters have a heading, a closing, and structured paragraphs. The first paragraph summarizes previous correspondence and states the purpose of the letter. The next paragraphs present supporting information. The last paragraph summarizes the main points and states the required actions or follow-up communication. Memos have the same paragraph structure, with a different heading and no closing. Business emails are part of the business record and should be created and sent in a professional manner.

SUMMARY OF KEY IDEAS

- Organize technical documents from the largest to smallest scale: outline level, paragraph level, sentence level, and word level.
- Common elements of technical documents include the abstract (or executive summary), introduction/background/literature review, methods, results, discussion, conclusions/recommendations, and references.
- The abstract should contain a summary of each element of the report.
- The introduction should take the reader from the report title to an understanding of why the report was written.
- In the methods section, justify the study approach, present data collection techniques, and discuss data analysis methods.
- In the results section, present the results and note the general trends.
- Interpret data in the discussion section.
- Conclusions and recommendations are often in list form and should be written very carefully.
- Although many reference formats are acceptable, the references must be complete and consistent.
- Use section headings or numbering schemes as signposts in technical documents.
- Each sentence should express a single idea.
- Choose words to make your writing concise, simple, and specific.
- Avoid making up new words or new uses of words in conventional technical writing.
- Make sure that the subject and verb agree in number (i.e., they must be both singular or both plural).
- Use a consistent voice, with preference for the active voice.
- Generally use the present tense, unless describing work done in the past.
- Avoid the use of gender-specific pronouns.
- Use *who* as a pronoun for human subjects, *that* for specific nonhuman subjects, and *which* for nonhuman subjects in clauses set off by commas.
- With adjectives and adverbs, avoid adjective chains and make sure the adverb or adjective modifies only the verb or noun you intend to modify.
- Avoid nonstandard capitalization and abbreviations.
- Never assume a document is free of errors because it passes the spell checker.
- Make sure you give credit (by use of a citation) when presenting someone else's words or ideas.
- Avoid double negatives in formal writing.
- Avoid contractions in formal writing.
- Always proofread your work.

- Reports should include a cover page and a transmittal letter.
- Letters should have a heading (including the date, recipient's name, and title), closing (including your name, title, and signature), and structured paragraphs (the first paragraph should summarize previous correspondence and state the purpose of the letter, the next paragraphs should present supporting information, and the last paragraph should summarize the main points and state the required actions or follow-up communication).
- Memos should have a heading (including to whom the memo is written, who wrote the memo, the memo topic, the date, and the word *Memorandum*) and the same structured paragraphs as a letter.
- When writing business email, avoid contractions and emoticons, proofread carefully, double-check the recipient list, and do not include anything in an email that you would not include in other business documents.

Problems

1. Pick two textbooks other than this one. What kinds of signposting are used in the texts? Describe the scheme used to show hierarchy in the signposting.

2. What are the characteristics of a good sentence?

3. What are the three aspects of good word choice in technical writing? Find good and poor examples of word choice in a newspaper or technical journal.

4. List whether the following nouns should take a singular or plural verb form: engineer, axes, phenomena, axis, datum, criterion, thermodynamics, phenomenon, Microsoft, and criteria. You may need to use a dictionary.

5. Find five examples of the use of passive voice in this text. Rewrite them in the active voice.

6. Repair the following paragraph, if necessary. [**Warning: The following material may contain errors!**]

   Plans and specifications who lack careful preparation may be faulty. The engineer must use all his skill to find and correct the problems. The engineer that refines her own design is more likely to find their own errors.

7. For each of the following, identify the problem or problems in the use of adjectives or adverbs, if any, and correct the errors. [**Warning: The following material may contain errors!**]

   a. "The mass-produced germanium junction transistor was a major advance."

   b. "The project manager attempted to slowly accelerate the production rate."

   c. "The contract only required plant construction, not the operation of the plant."

   d. "Alternating current power transmission first occurred at Niagara Falls in 1895."

8. Select any paragraph in this text. Paraphrase the idea without a direct quotation, and include a citation and a reference. Repeat with a paragraph from a technical journal of interest to you.

9. Write a letter to your professor asking for permission to take a make-up exam.

10. Write a memo to a classmate to organize a study session for one of your courses.

14

Oral Technical Communications

1 INTRODUCTION

Few activities intimidate new engineers more than public speaking. Technical oral presentations need not be painful. They can be tamed by focusing on three kinds of activities:

- What to do *before* the talk,
- What to do *during* the talk, and
- What to do *after* the talk.

Many people think that the *delivery* is the key to technical talks. While the delivery is important, the truth is that oral presentations are made or broken by the work put in *before* the talk is delivered. A good technical talk is well organized, with instructive visual aids. It is delivered with the help of useful but nonintrusive memory aids. The talk will be rehearsed, but not overly practiced. These critical activities—organization, visual aids design, memory aids design, and practice—take place well before the oral presentation is made to the audience. The details of talk organization and preparation will be presented in Sections 2 through 4.

What is your gut reaction to the thought of standing up before a handful or dozens or hundreds of people and delivering technical material? If your palms are sweating already, then Section 5 may help. In Section 5, your plan of action immediately before the talk (including how to deal with nervousness) will be reviewed. You will learn what to say and how to say it.

Finally, improvement in your technical speaking skills is made only by what you do after the talk. Section 6 will provide hints on obtaining feedback and implementing good speaking habits.

SECTIONS

OBJECTIVES

After reading this chapter, you will be able to:

- organize a technical oral presentation;
- design visual aids;
- design memory aids;
- deliver an effective technical oral presentation.

2   BEFORE THE TALK: ORGANIZATION

Key idea: Technical presentations can be improved by considering the activities before the talk, during the talk, and after the talk.

Key idea: Identify the presentation goals, target audience, and constraints on the presentation (especially time constraints).

visual aids: media used to accompany oral presentations (e.g., slides and overhead transparencies)

title slide: visual aid containing the presentation title and information about the authors

Recall that before writing a single word of the oral presentation, you must identify the goals of the presentation, the target audience, and the constraints on the presentation. The main constraint on oral presentations is the time allotted for the talk. In your career, almost every oral presentation you give will have time constraints. One key to good oral presentations is to respect your audience's time and use their time wisely.

Only after identifying goals, audience, and constraints can an outline be written. With an outline in place, the individual **visual aids** can be designed. Technical talks usually begin with a **title slide.**° The title slide contains the title of the talk and the names and affiliations of the authors. The title slide is the oral presentation equivalent of the cover page. Any example title slide is shown in Figure 1.

In many technical presentations, the second slide is an outline or overview of the talk. While an outline slide is optional, it serves as a good road map for the remainder of the talk. Audiences may feel more comfortable if they know where the presentation is going. The outline slide is the first opportunity for signposting in an oral technical presentation. An example outline slide is shown in Figure 2.

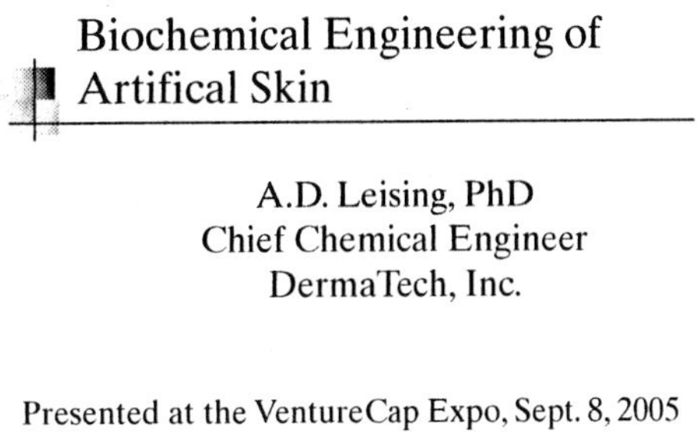

Biochemical Engineering of
Artifical Skin

A.D. Leising, PhD
Chief Chemical Engineer
DermaTech, Inc.

Presented at the VentureCap Expo, Sept. 8, 2005

Figure 1.   An Example of a Title Slide

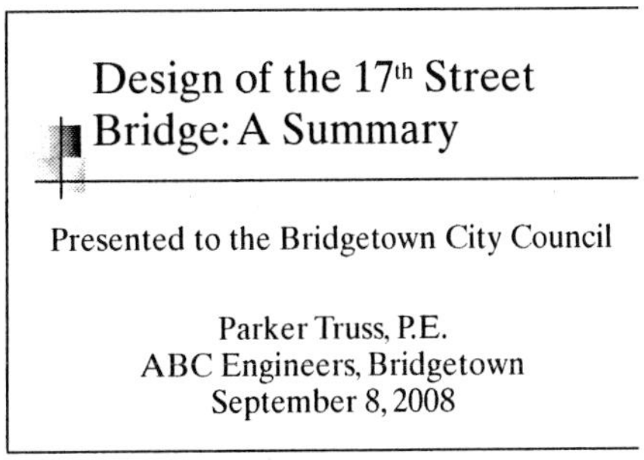

Design of the 17th Street
Bridge: A Summary

Presented to the Bridgetown City Council

Parker Truss, P.E.
ABC Engineers, Bridgetown
September 8, 2008

Figure 2.   An Example of an Outline Slide

°To simplify the language here, visual aids in general will be called "slides." Information of the types of visual aids may be found in Section 3.2.

Key idea: Use an outline to organize the talk and an outline slide to show your organization.

The remaining sections of a technical talk vary with the goals and target audience. A generic structure that includes an introduction/background, methods, results, discussion, conclusions, and recommendations is a good place to start. Technical talks rarely include an abstract, formal literature review, or list of references.

3   BEFORE THE TALK: DESIGNING VISUAL AIDS

Key idea: The number of visual aids should be about $^3/_4$ times the number of minutes allotted to the presentation.

Once the outline has been established, you can start to design the visual aids. A major difference between written and oral presentations is the reliance on visual aids in oral communication. You must select the number, type, and content of visual aids.

3.1   Number of Visual Aids

The number of visual aids depends most strongly on the length of the presentation. *To estimate the maximum number of visual aids, multiply the number of minutes in the presentation by 0.75.* For example, a 30-minute talk should have no more than 21 to 23 slides.

The natural tendency is to prepare too many visual aids. After all, if the number of slides is $^3/_4$ of the number of minutes, then the average time per slide is $^4/_3$ minutes = 80 seconds. Many first-time speakers reason that several of the slides in the presentation (e.g., the title and outline slides) will take much less than 80 seconds to present. They conclude that they can have *many more* slides than the number calculated from $^3/_4$ (number of minutes). *This logic almost always leads to very rushed and incoherent presentations.* Until you become very experienced in oral technical presentations, use the "$^3/_4$ times the number of minutes" value as a firm guide.

3.2   Types of Visual Aids

Several types of visual aids are available, including slides, overhead transparencies, poster boards and flip charts, blackboards and whiteboards, and computer displays and projectors. Physical models and material to be passed around the audience also are used as visual aids.

Hmm... 20 minute talk... 24 slides? 48 slides?

$3 \times 20/4 = 15$ slides!

Key idea: In selecting the type of visual aid, consider image quality, eye contact, and production cost and time. Then use only one type of visual aid in a talk.

In selecting a type of visual aid, three factors are important: image clarity, maintenance of eye contact, and production cost and time. The advantages and disadvantages of several types of visual aids are summarized in Table 1. In many professional presentations, image clarity may be paramount. It may be worth the money to produce the highest quality images available.

Eye contact is important for two reasons. First, it allows you to get feedback from the audience. Are they bored? Engaged? Having trouble hearing you? Second, eye contact allows the audience to be drawn into your words. Try listening to a movie or television program with your eyes shut. The magic is reduced when the eye contact is lost. Still not convinced? The next time you speak before a group of people, notice how much time the audience spends looking at your *eyes* rather than the screen.

Visual aids also can be expensive and time-consuming to produce. Always estimate the cost and time required to produce any visual aid before committing to a type of visual aid. If the turnaround time for producing visual aids is long, you may have to adjust your schedule to meet the presentation deadline.

Regardless of the type of visual aid selected, it is important to use only one type of visual aid. Switching back and forth between two types can be distracting to the audience, especially if the room lights are turned on and off repeatedly. For the vast majority of technical talks, stick to one type of visual aid. Each type of visual aid will be discussed in more detail.

Slides

Color photographic slides provide the sharpest images. Slides come with a major disadvantage: they require the room to be darkened. In a dark room, you risk losing eye contact with the audience. Slides also can be expensive and time-consuming to produce.

Overhead Transparencies

Overhead transparencies, also called *overheads*, provide a good trade-off between image clarity and eye contact. The images may be poorer than slides (although color laser printers are capable of producing very high quality overheads on special transparency film).

In presenting overheads, the room lights generally are on, but dimmed. Thus, eye contact is still possible. Unless you have an assistant, overheads require you to stand

TABLE 1   Types of Visual Aids and Their Characteristics

Type	Image Quality	Eye Contact	Cost and Time	Other
Slides	Very high	Moderate (room dark)	Moderate	Image very sharp
Overhead transparencies	High	Good	Small	Good compromise
Poster boards and flip charts	Very high	Excellent	Moderate to large	Good for smaller audiences
Whiteboards and blackboards	Low	Excellent	Very small	For informal work
Computers	Can be very high	Moderate (room dark)	Small	Watch compatibility problems

near the projector. Avoid blocking the audience's view of the projection screen with your body.

Poster Boards and Flip Charts

Poster boards and flip charts are large-format visual aids, displayed on an easel. They are used frequently by consulting engineers because they allow the lights to be on; thus, they maximize eye contact with the audience and increase audience participation. Poster boards and flip charts are not appropriate for large audiences.

Blackboards and Whiteboards

Blackboards and whiteboards are appropriate for informal technical presentations. Their use allows the audience to write notes at the same pace as the speaker/writer. They are a good choice when note taking is important or when audience participation is critical.

Computers

Computer-based presentations quickly are becoming the most common delivery mode for technical presentations. Computer-based presentations have a number of advantages over other media:

- They can be changed at the last moment.
- They can include Internet-based materials, videos, and animations.
- They avoid the expense and lead time required to make photographic slides.

Computer-based presentations have several disadvantages as well. Compatibility problems often arise between notebook computers and projection devices. It is important to make sure that your notebook computer interfaces properly with the intended projector. The ability to change computer-based presentations at the last minute may tempt you to throw together the talk at the last minute. As always, do not let the technology control the message.

Computer-based presentations offer their own challenges regarding the content of the slides. Information on content specific to computer-based presentations is presented in Section 3.5.

3.3   Content of Visual Aids: Word Slides

There are two types of visual aid content: word slides and data slides. Word slides typically contain only words, symbols, and/or equations. Data slides communicate data and may include tables or figures.

Key idea: Word slides should contain as few words as possible.

Word slides should contain as few words as possible to communicate the required information. *It is undesirable to fill a word slide with text*: the audience will read the words rather than look at you.° *You* want to take control of the material and present it to the audience yourself.

Sometimes, symbols or equations can be used in place of words. The choice of equations or words depends on the audience. For a technical audience, a word slide about Newton's Second Law of Motion might contain the equation $F = ma$. For a less technical audience, the gist of the Second Law may be more clearly made with words:

°You can prove this point to yourself with a simple experiment. Gather a group of 20 or so people. Prepare two overheads: one with a wordy message and one with an abbreviated form (e.g., "The rain in Spain falls mainly in the plains" and "Spain: Rains in plains"). Show the first overhead and present the message word for word. Show the second overhead and use the same word-for-word speech as the first overhead. You will notice that the audience's eyes are on the screen when you show the first overhead. Their eyes are more likely to be on you when you show the second overhead.

"Force is proportional to both acceleration and mass." For a nontechnical audience, perhaps a cartoon would best illustrate the point.

For a technical audience:
Newton's Second Law

$$F = ma.$$

For a less technical audience:
Newton's Second Law

Force is proportional to both acceleration and mass.

For a nontechnical audience:

Newton's Second Law

The force doubles when the mass doubles.

Word slides should take into account the shape of the visual aid. For example, overhead transparencies and computer-based presentation slides have a length-to-width ratio of $11:8.5 \approx 1.3:1$. Photographic slides usually have a ratio of about 0.7:1. It is pleasing to the eye to have the word shape match the visual aid shape.

Matching the word shape to the visual aid shape also means that the font size can be as large as possible. It is important in word slides to use a large font size. Typically, slides and overheads should have font sizes from about 28 to 44 point. Use consistent font sizes (i.e., major headings all in one size and minor headings all in another size). Presentation software (such as Microsoft PowerPoint or Corel Presentations) can help in maintaining a consistent presentation format. Two word slide examples may be found in Figures 3 and 4.

**History of Chemical
Engineering (ChE) Education**

- 1888: First ChE B.S. degree
- 1901: "Handbook of Chemical
  Engineering" (G.E. Davis)
- 1908: AIChE formed
- 1915: "Unit operations"
  (intro. by A.D. Little)
- 1925: First accredited degrees

Figure 3.   Word Slide Example 1 (dates from
http://www.cems.umn.edu/~aiche_ug/history/h_toc.html)

**A Short History of Education in
Chemical Engineering**

- 1888: First chemical engineering
  B.S. degree offered
- 1901: G.E. Davis published "Handbook
  of Chemical Engineering"
- 1908: American Institute of Chemical
  Engineering (AIChE) formed
- 1915: The concept of "unit operations"
  was first introduced by A.D. Little
- 1925: First accredited degrees offered

Figure 4.   Word Slide Example 2

PONDER THIS

**Critique the examples in Figures 3 and 4. Which would be more appropriate for
an oral presentation? How could both examples be improved?**

Note the use of abbreviations in Figure 3. Abbreviations allow for a larger font size
to be used. Small words (*the* and *of*) are eliminated to avoid having the audience read the
text rather than listen to the words. In both examples, the slide needs to be *presented*.
Figure 3 would make a better slide in an oral presentation. Figure 4 might be better in a
written document, where no additional words are used to explain the text.

3.4   Content of Visual Aids: Data Slides

Key idea: Create tables
specific to the point you wish
to make.

Data slides can be tables or figures. In oral presentations, it is critical that *tables contain
only the data required*. Speakers sometimes photocopy large tables onto overhead transparencies and present the tabular material as follows: "I know you can't read all the
numbers in this table, but note that the gear ratio of 20-to-1 was optimal." If you wish to
speak about a gear ratio of 20:1, design a data or word slide specific to that point.

Properties of Air

Temp. (°C)	Density (kg/m³)	Viscosity (N·s/m²)	Speed of Sound (m/s)
−40	1.514	1.57	306.2
−20	1.395	1.63	319.1
0	1.292	1.71	331.4
20	1.204	1.82	343.3
40	1.127	1.87	349.1
60	1.060	1.97	365.7

"I know you can't read all the tiny numbers, but the speed of sound in air is less than 350 m/s in the temperature range of 0 to 20°C."

"As you can see, the speed of sound in air is less than 350 m/s in the temperature range of 0 to 20°C."

Properties of Air

Temperature (°C)	Speed of Sound (m/s)
0	331.4
20	343.3

Make tables specific to the points you wish to emphasize.

3.5   Special Notes about Computer-Based Presentations

Today's software allows you to prepare amazing computer-based presentations, with vibrant colors, inspiring animations, and hundreds of fonts. While all those embellishments are possible, you must ask yourself if they are right for your presentation and your audience.

PONDER THIS

How can you decide if animations and other embellishments are appropriate?

Key idea: With computer-based presentations, watch the colors, number of fonts, and animations.

Use the same criteria that you applied to all other aspects of your presentation: Do the embellishments help you to deliver your message to the target audience?

You should keep a few thoughts in mind as you design computer-based presentations. First, *go easy on the color combinations*. Start with the prepackaged color combinations in the presentation software. Stick with two to four colors, using them consistently for signposting. If you have poor color vision or are unsure of your artistic skills, then you may wish to have a friend review your work prior to presentation.

Second, *use a small number of font families*. You can use font size and font weight (bold, italic, etc.) to create a style, but using many font families is distracting. For example, some textbooks are written with only two font families (Times New Roman and Arial), but over a dozen combinations of font size and weight. If you use nonstandard fonts, then you can run into font availability problems if you use a different computer for the presentation than you used to create the talk.

Third, *be very careful about animations* (e.g., flying text and swirling slide transitions). Some people find animations very annoying. Use them sparingly unless you know your audience well.

4   BEFORE THE TALK: PREPARING TO PRESENT

4.1   Practicing Oral Presentations

Several tricks can make your practice time more valuable. First, practice your talk for the first time *before* the visual aids are finalized. In this way, you can identify and edit

Key idea: Practice before
the visual aids are finalized.

any slides that do not make your points as cleanly as you want. Last-minute changes in visual aids can be expensive and stressful (although computer-based presentations are making last-minute changes easier).

Second, record the duration of *each section* of your talk during the first few practice rounds. This approach allows you to judge the *balance* of the talk. The meat of the talk (e.g., the results and discussion if you are presenting project results) should occupy at least half the time. Timing the talk also helps you to know where cuts or additions should take place if the first run-throughs show that the talk is too long or too short.

Key idea: When
practicing, time each section
as you practice alone and in
front of others.

Third, practice the talk both by yourself and in front of others. When practicing by yourself, always *speak aloud* so you can rehearse any troublesome phrases or transitions. In addition, try to practice in front of others to get feedback about the talk before the main presentation (see also Section 6).

How often should you practice the talk before the big day? This is a matter of personal preference. Some people require many practice runs before they feel comfortable with the material, while others become stale after just a few practice sessions. *Experiment with different degrees of practicing to determine what level of preparation suits your personality.*

memory aids: notes used
to help remember the main
points in the talk

4.2   Memory Aids

Memory aids are the notes or devices that help ensure a smooth talk. Memory aids should be designed to help you remember the main points in the talk. Always practice the talk with the same memory aids you intend to use in the final presentation. Common memory aids include

- An outline of the talk
- Note cards containing a list of the key points for each slide
- Speaker's notes in presentation software

An outline lets you see quickly where you are in the presentation. Note cards are useful for making sure that you cover the important points before you go to the next slide. Most computer-based presentation software allows you to put your speaker notes near a miniature version of the slide so you can remind yourself to make the main points you wish.

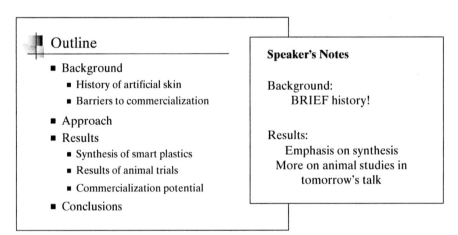

Speaker's notes in a computer-based presentation

It pays to take a few seconds to glance at your notes or outline before you change slides. Although a few seconds may feel like an eternity when you are in front of an audience, the slight pause will help you gain confidence that you are not forgetting anything important. Audiences generally appreciate the small respites as well.

Key idea: Avoid memorizing or reading oral presentations.

A final note about memory aids. Do not read the talk or memorize it completely. We all write differently than we talk. A read speech usually sounds "written." A memorized talk almost always sounds mechanical and forced. Read or memorized talks have another pitfall. If you lose your place or become flustered when reading or reciting by memory, general meltdown often occurs. If you use streamlined notes, it is much easier to get back on track.

5   DURING THE TALK

5.1   Pre-Talk Activities

Key idea: Learn about the facilities and coordinate introductions well before the talk.

Before walking to the podium or to the front of the conference room to give your talk, it is important to know what to expect. Examine the podium or speaking area well before the talk begins. Before you begin speaking, you want to know the answers to several questions:

- Is there a pointer?
- Is the projection equipment in working order?
- Who is responsible for changing computer or slide-projector slides? Are personnel available to help with your overhead transparencies?
- What type of microphone is in use?
- Is there a podium light to allow you to read your notes when the room lights go off? (Memory aids are useless if the room is in complete darkness, a fact you do not want to learn during your first technical presentation!)

It is also helpful to find and introduce yourself to the person who will introduce you. He or she may require some background information from you and may be able to help answer questions about the availability of pointers and the like. You should ask whether he or she will signal you when the allotted time has nearly expired.

5.2   Group Presentations

Key idea: Practice transitions between speakers in group presentations.

Group presentations raise their own set of challenges. It is critical to practice the transitions between the speakers. In general, it is better not to have too many speakers in a short period of time. Make sure the responsibilities of each speaker are understood, including whether one speaker will introduce the next speaker.

5.3   Nervousness

The main concern of most neophyte speakers is the control of nervousness. Being nervous means you care about the presentation. This is a positive attribute, as long as you can control the outward signs of nervousness.

Key idea: Do not worry about *being* nervous; learn to control or avoid the *signs* of nervousness.

The key to dealing with "the jitters" is to determine how nervousness affects you. If being nervous makes you speak more quickly, then focus on slowing your pace. If nervousness makes your hands shake, then avoid holding anything (such as notes or a pointer) during the talk. *It is natural to be a little apprehensive, but desirable to minimize the manifestations of nervousness.*

Remember also that for many talks you will give, the audience *wants* you to succeed. You are giving the talk for a reason. It is likely that the members of the audience desire the information you will share with them. Engineers face truly hostile audiences only rarely in their career.

5.4   What to Say

Key idea: Paraphrase information in word slides and point to each item in a list.

Technical presentations consist of two elements: presentation of word or data slides and making transitions between slides. When presenting word slides, it is often useful to paraphrase the material rather than reading it to the audience (see also Section 3.3). Again, you are trying to control the message. With lists, gesture to each item as you present it to remind the audience where you are in the slide.

Keep a mental checklist of the items to be covered during the presentation of figures. You should

Key idea: When presenting figures, tell what the figure is showing, identify the axes, communicate the meaning of each plot, and enumerate the main points to be made.

1. Tell the audience what the figure represents.
2. Identify the axes (with units).
3. Communicate the meaning of each plot (i.e., state the legend information).
4. Enumerate the main points to be made.

Figure 5 contains a sample figure and text showing how the figure would be presented orally. Look at the text in Figure 5 carefully and note the elements presented: a description of what the figure is showing ("removal of dye over time using the new technology"), identification of the axes with units ("time in minutes" and "dye concentration in milligrams per liter"), the meaning of each plot ("solid squares are the experimental data and the line is the first-order model fit"), and enumeration of the main points ("two points to notice in this figure. First, the technology ...").

Tell 'em Rule: the idea that you present information three times in a talk: you tell 'em what you will tell them, then tell 'em the information, and finally tell 'em what you just told them

Recall that it is necessary to remind the audience of your organization. This is crucial in oral presentations. If audience members feel lost, they will tune out completely. There is an old doctrine in public speaking called the **Tell 'em Rule**. According to the Tell 'em Rule, you present information three times in a talk: you tell 'em what

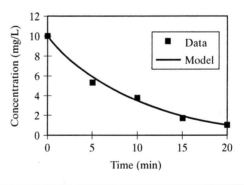

Sample Presentation Text:

Shown here is the removal of dye over time using the new technology. The x-axis is time in minutes and the y-axis is the dye concentration in milligrams per liter. The solid squares are the experimental data and the line is the first-order model fit. There are two points to notice in this figure. First, the technology could reduce the dye concentration to below two milligrams per liter in 20 minutes. Second, the exponential model fits the data reasonably well.

Figure 5.   Example of the Presentation of Data in a Figure

you will tell them, then tell 'em the information, and finally tell 'em what you just told them. Following this rule allows for smooth transitions (also called *segues*) between parts of the talk. For example, you may say,

> I wish to give you a little background information on rotary engines. Rotary engines were used first in the automotive industry in .... [text omitted for clarity]. Now that I've told you about the history of rotary engines, let's turn to the modern versions of this unique engine type.

Notice the three presentations of the information ("I wish to give you ...," "Rotary engines were used first ...," and "Now that I've told you about ..."). Also note the transition to the modern versions of the rotary engine ("... let's turn to the ...").

The process of telling the audience where you are during transitions between major portions of a talk is called *signposting*. The word *signposting* comes from the analogy with road signs: well-spaced markers tell the audience where you are in the talk. Most technical speakers do not signpost enough. Audiences are much more comfortable when they know they are in synch with the speaker. To assist in signposting, it is helpful to present an outline of the presentation near the beginning of the talk. By referring to the outline, you can keep the audience with you through the talk. Intermediate outlines can be placed in the middle of the talk for complicated sections. For example, you may wish to have an outline of the results to guide the audience through the results section.

5.5   How to Say It

The audience responds to two features of a speaker: the speaker's voice and body. The voice should vary in pitch and intensity: a monotone voice leads to a sleeping audience. Speak through each sentence to avoid swallowing words at the end of the sentence. Be aware of the *speed* and *volume* of your voice. It is useful to have a colleague in the audience signal you (discreetly, of course) if you are speaking too quickly or too softly. The volume of your speech depends on the room and amplification.

Key idea: Speak loudly and slowly. Use meaningful hand gestures and move your body without pacing.

Your body movements should be purposeful and strong. The main problem for most speakers concerns what to do with the hands. Use them to your advantage! Hand gestures are a great way to emphasize important points. For the most important messages, make your gestures higher. Avoid holding pens, pencils, or other mental crutches, and **never** leave your hands in your pockets.

Your legs can work for you as well. Avoid standing stock-still. Walk toward the audience and engage its members at critical points in the talk. While mechanical pacing should be avoided, small steps can make a speaker seem more human to the audience.

In spite of your best preparation, things sometimes go wrong in oral presentations. A few true stories are shared in the *Focus on Talks: Horror Stories*.

6   AFTER THE TALK

Key idea: Seek feedback and incorporate changes into your speaking style.

After a talk, seek out feedback from colleagues in the audience. Listen to their constructive criticism and think about modifications to your speaking style that will make communication more effective. Do not be afraid to identify weaknesses in your speaking style and practice ways to overcome them.

Finally, be an attentive listener. Listen critically to other speakers (such as colleagues, professional speakers, actors, and your professors) and note what you like and dislike about their speaking styles. Ask yourself why you like or dislike their speaking style. Why do good speakers engage you personally? Are they friendly, open, and confident? Incorporate the good aspects and avoid the bad in your next presentation.

FOCUS ON TALKS: HORROR STORIES

INTRODUCTION

Even after reading this chapter, you may still approach your first professional oral presentation with some trepidation. In this section, a few true stories of oral presentations gone awry are shared. Do not panic when you read these stories. They are offered in the spirit of comic relief and to show you that bad things sometimes happen to good presenters. (*Note*: Stories labeled "Lytle" come from the "Stress of Selling" articles compiled by Chris Lytle on the Monster.com Web site. Stories labeled "Hoff" come from Ron Hoff's (1992) very readable book on oral presentations. All other stories come from my experiences or the experiences of my colleagues.)

FROM THE "DRESS FOR SUCCESS" DEPARTMENT

Numerous speakers have walked back to their seat after an oral presentation, only to discover in horror that their pants or skirt zipper was in the down position. Perhaps "check your zipper" is as important as "check your slides." During a graduate course, I noticed my students giggling every time I turned to face them after writing on the blackboard. When I asked them what was going on, they gleefully informed me that I had a sticker of a lamb on my derrière (courtesy of my then-two-year-old daughter). I keep the sticker on my class notebook to this day to remind me to check my attire.

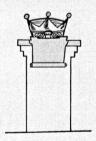

FROM THE "LOCATION, LOCATION, LOCATION" DEPARTMENT

A colleague of mine relates the tale of a presentation he gave for a job interview. He used a long wooden pointer to emphasize his points. But being a good speaker, he kept good eye contact with the audience. Part way through the talk, he realized that he was pointing *behind* the screen with the pointer.

Podiums also can be a source of frustration. Lytle collected the story of a presenter who stood on a stool behind the podium during a speech to 1,500 people. Shortly after the presentation started, the heel of her pump broke. She fell off the stool and crashed onto the concrete floor. Her sympathetic audience gave her the courage to complete the presentation.

Hoff reports that the Queen of England stepped up to a podium during a visit to the United States, only to find that the podium was higher than her head.

FROM THE "NEVER LET THEM SEE YOU SWEAT" DEPARTMENT

Obviously nervous presenters make the audience a little uncomfortable, so never draw attention to your nervousness. I witnessed a student presentation at a state conference where the speaker was using a laser pointer. The pointer danced all over the screen as the speaker's hand shook. Rather than letting it pass, he said, "Well, look at that—I must be really nervous!"

Hoff reports a company treasurer starting a speech with "I'm so nervous this morning. I hope you can't see how badly my knees are shaking." Guess where the audience's eyes were glued for the remainder of the speech. Of course, you should avoid bringing attention to overconfidence as well. Al Gore probably regrets the sighs picked up by microphones during the first presidential debate of 2000.

FROM THE "EQUIPMENT MALFUNCTION" DEPARTMENT

A colleague of mine gave a technical talk in another country, where a more powerful slide projector bulb was in use. She stared in shock as her first slide literally melted before her eyes. Needless to say, she completed the talk without slides.

Lytle reports a presenter panicking when the overhead projector did not turn on. Reaching down to plug in the power cord resulted in a loud ripping noise as the seam of his pants gave out.

FROM THE "WATCH YOUR LANGUAGE" DEPARTMENT

Word choice is important in oral presentations. Lytle relates a story from a salesman giving a presentation before a defense contractor with a product representative (rep). The product rep had a way of choosing the worst possible words to express himself. Quoting from the Web site: "Discussing the ease with which you can use the product, the other rep stated, 'You don't have to be a rocket scientist to use this.' Twenty rocket scientists [in the audience] sat back in their chairs and crossed their arms. After 20 minutes of weasel words to get their interest back … [the rep said], 'We just have to get your propeller heads to talk to our propeller heads to work it out.' With that, their propeller heads stood up and walked out." Phrases like *propeller head* or *gear head*—both derogatory terms for technical staff—are inappropriate in formal speech.

Written words on slides can bite you, too. A consulting engineer reports that she made up slides with the client's names based on a telephone call she made to the client. Unfortunately, several of the names were misspelled, leading to embarrassment and, not surprisingly, an unsuccessful bid for the project.

The moral of these stories? Be prepared, be relaxed, and go with the flow. While you never may face the discomfort of the speakers in these stories, remember that audiences often are pulling for you. If something unusual happens, finish with grace and hope for the best.

7   SUMMARY

Most of the work in an oral presentation occurs before the talk is presented. Before the talk, take the time to organize the material, construct the visual aids (which should number no more than $3/4$ times the number of minutes), and practice. Learn about the facilities in the room before you walk to the podium.

During the talk, do not worry about being nervous, but learn to control or avoid the signs of nervousness. Take your time in presenting data slides (especially figures). During transitions from one part of the talk to another, be sure to "tell 'em" three times: preview the material, present the material, and summarize the material. Modulate the speed and volume of your voice and use your hands effectively.

After the talk, seek feedback to become a better speaker. Remember, the best way to become an effective technical speaker is to take every opportunity to give technical talks.

SUMMARY OF KEY IDEAS

- Technical presentations can be improved by considering the activities before the talk, during the talk, and after the talk.
- Identify the presentation goals, target audience, and constraints on the presentation (especially time constraints).
- Use an outline to organize the talk and an outline slide to show your organization.
- The number of visual aids should be about $3/4$ times the number of minutes allotted to the presentation.
- In selecting the type of visual aid, consider image quality, eye contact, and production cost and time. Then use only one type of visual aid in a talk.
- Word slides should contain as few words as possible.
- Create tables specific to the point you wish to make.

- With computer-based presentations, watch the colors, number of fonts, and animations.
- Practice before the visual aids are finalized.
- When practicing, time each section as you practice alone and in front of others.
- Avoid memorizing or reading oral presentations.
- Learn about the facilities and coordinate introductions well before the talk.
- Practice transitions between speakers in group presentations.
- Do not worry about *being* nervous; learn to control or avoid the *signs* of nervousness.
- Paraphrase information in word slides and point to each item in a list.
- When presenting figures, tell what the figure is showing, identify the axes, communicate the meaning of each plot, and enumerate the main points to be made.
- Use signposting liberally in technical oral presentations.
- Speak loudly and slowly. Use meaningful hand gestures and move your body without pacing.
- Seek feedback and incorporate changes into your speaking style.

Problems

1. Pick an engineering topic of interest to you and identify a target audience. How will the target audience influence the visual aids you select and the material you present in your talk?

2. Write an outline for a 15-minute talk on the topic and target audience selected in Problem 1.

3. How would your outline change if you were asked to prepare a five-minute talk? A two-minute talk?

4. How many visual aids will you need for the talk?

5. Prepare visual aids for the talk using the principles presented in this chapter.

6. Practice the 15-minute talk. Prepare a table showing the percentage of time in the talk devoted to each of the major sections of the presentations. Refine the talk to better use the time allotted and summarize your refinements.

7. Before presenting the talk, what questions do you anticipate from the audience?

8. Present the talk to a group of people pretending to be your target audience. Did you predict (in Problem 7) the questions that were asked? What feedback did you receive from the audience?

9. Rewrite your talk using double the number of visual aids that you prepared in Problem 7. Present the revised talk to a group of people pretending to be your target audience. What feedback did you get about the number of visual aids?

10. Attend lectures delivered by three different public speakers. For each speaker, list and explain two aspects of his or her speaking style that appeal to you the most and two aspects that appeal to you the least.

Index